FUN WITH THE FAMILY™

in MICHIGAN

HUNDREDS OF IDEAS
FOR DAY TRIPS WITH THE KIDS
THIRD EDITION

By WILLIAM SEMION

The Globe Pequot Press

Guilford, Connecticut

Copyright © 1996, 1998, 2000 by The Globe Pequot Press

All rights reserved. No part of this book may be reproduced or transmitted in any form by any means, electronic or mechanical, including photocopying and recording, or by any information storage and retrieval system, except as may be expressly permitted by the 1976 Copyright Act or by the publisher. Requests for permission should be made in writing to The Globe Pequot Press, P.O. Box 480, Guilford, Connecticut 06437.

Fun with the Family is a trademark of The Globe Pequot Press.

Cover and text design by Nancy Freeborn
Cover photograph by Julie Bidwell
Maps by M. A. Dubé

Library of Congress Cataloging-in-Publication Data
Semion, William.
        Fun with the family in Michigan : hundreds of ideas for day trips with the
    kids / by William Semion. — 3rd ed.
        p. cm. — (Fun with the family series)
        Includes index.
        ISBN 0-7627-0808-5
        1. Michigan—Guidebooks. 2. Family recreation—Michigan—
    Guidebooks. I. Title. II. Series.
    F564.3.S46 2000
    917.7404'43—dc21   00-056175

Manufactured in the United States of America
Third Edition/Second Printing

Contents

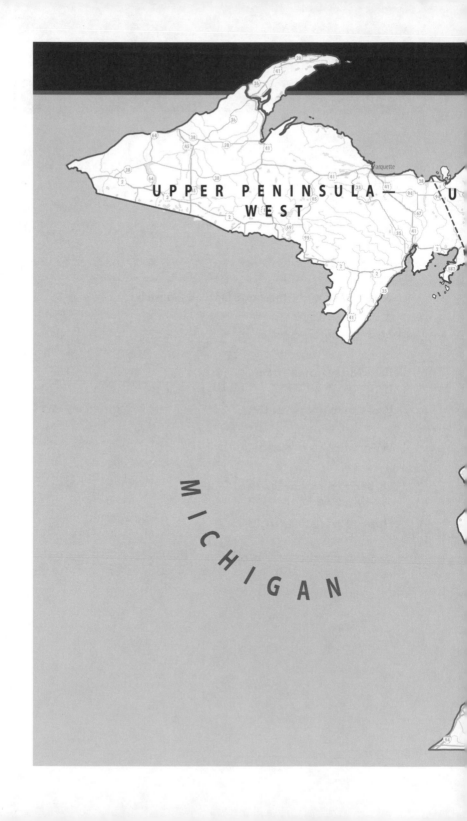

UPPER PENINSULA—
WEST

U

Marquette

MICHIGAN

Acknowledgments

I wouldn't have tried and couldn't have succeeded in this endeavor without the support, encouragement, and suggestions from lots of others. I am grateful for the unfailing support of Laura Bollman; to my research assistant, Scott Renas, for his resourcefulness; to Larry Keller; to my father, Alex, for his direction; to my daughter, Sonya, for checking phone numbers; and to my brother Al, my sister Sandra, and to Dixie, for their support. Thanks also to Robert Brodbeck. Thank you all.

Bill

Introduction

I have been fortunate, indeed. From the time I was old enough to remember, my parents loved to travel in Michigan. In fact, the Wolverine State was the only place they ever went. And I suspect that's true of a lot of us Michiganians. Try as we may, we just can't find a place to match the combination of attractions, both natural and otherwise, that our state offers.

I've seen Michigan in all of its seasons, from the tip of the Keweenaw Peninsula in the north, dipped in autumn brilliance and summer greenery, to the Lake Erie shoreline on its south, brimming with life both on and under the water; from Lake Michigan's white sand beaches on its west to the public fishing piers and quiet resort towns along Lake Huron on its east; from its huge expanses of state and national forests—which number among the nation's largest tracts of publicly held land—to its fun-loaded cities with excitement for the family that's found nowhere else. This is a place that stands up to the cliché "something for everyone."

One of my earliest memories is of crossing the Straits of Mackinac on one of the big ferryboats that took cars between the peninsulas as the Mackinac Bridge was being built. (Strange that the bridge, the island, the straits, and the county are spelled "Mackinac," but the city is "Mackinaw"—and that no one has been able to tell me why yet.) We spent a part of each summer along Lake Huron, frolicking on the beach and enjoying the lake's offerings, including perch fishing and driving its magnificent shoreline.

Michiganians take our Great Lakes for granted. When foreigners or even those from other parts of the nation catch their first eyeful of Huron, Michigan, or, especially, mighty Superior, they're awestruck. And they grow incredulous when they realize that no, you really can't see across them. Did you know, for example, that Lake Michigan is more than 80 miles across at its widest point and more than 900 feet deep at its deepest point? And that scientists now think of Lake Superior, more than 1,000 feet deep, as more of a freshwater ocean than a lake?

I am lucky to have a job that allowed me to continue my family's tradition of travel. Over the last twenty years, I've helped introduce my children to the wonders that are found in our state so they, too, will have an appreciation someday of what Michigan offers.

So many people rush outside their familiar surroundings to explore. They travel to Europe or the Caribbean. But it seems many never get around to discovering the delights in their own backyard. It's been estimated that fewer than half of all Michiganians have ever seen the span that connects the Upper and

Lower Peninsulas, and when asked, many think the Mackinac Bridge goes to Mackinac Island instead.

I hope this book enlightens you, whether you're a Michigan resident or a first-time visitor who doesn't know Saginaw from Manistee—at least not yet. Through this book I hope to convince you of the bounty of activities that my state has to offer the family. And in the next pages, I've touched on only a sampling of the thousands of attractions you'll find. There are plenty more adventures awaiting you and your family if you're willing to explore and open new doors to discovery. Try a Michigan adventure or two, no matter the season. You'll learn more about our beautiful state and perhaps about yourself in the process. And by introducing your family to travel, you'll be helping them learn to appreciate the wonder all around them.

See you on the road!

LODGING AND RESTAURANT RATES

Below is a key to the dollar sign designations found throughout this book in the sections "Where to Stay" and "Where to Eat."

Rates for Lodging		Rates for Restaurants	
$	up to $50	$	most entrees under $5
$$	$51 to $100	$$	entrees $5 to $10
$$$	$101 to $150	$$$	entrees $11 to $20
$$$$	$151 and up	$$$$	entrees over $20

If you do not find a restaurant or lodging listing for a particular area, please refer to the surrounding towns for information on the best family-friendly restaurants and lodging in the area.

> The prices and rates listed in this guidebook were confirmed at press time. We recommend, however, that you call establishments to obtain current information before traveling.

Attractions Key

The following is a key to the icons found throughout the text.

 Swimming

 Animal Viewing

 Boating / Boat Tour

 Food

 Historic Site

 Lodging

 Hiking / Walking

 Camping

 Fishing

 Museums

 Biking

 Performing Arts

 Amusement Park

 Sports/Athletic

 Horseback Riding

 Picnic

 Skiing

 Playground

 Park

 Shopping

Help Us Keep This Guide Up-to-Date

Every effort has been made by the author and editors to make this guide as accurate and useful as possible. However, many changes can occur after a guide is published—establishments close, phone numbers change, facilities come under new management, etc.

We would love to hear from you concerning your experiences with this guide and how you feel it could be improved and kept up-to-date. While we may not be able to respond to all comments and suggestions, we'll take them to heart, and we'll make certain to share them with the author. Please send your comments and suggestions to the following address:

The Globe Pequot Press
Reader Response/Editorial Department
P.O. Box 480
Guilford, CT 06437

Or you may e-mail us at: editorial@globe-pequot.com

Thanks for your input, and happy travels!

Detroit Southwest

Only a few minutes' drive south and west of downtown Detroit's skyscrapers, is one of the country's top universities nestled in a town that has attractions ranging from the offbeat to the educational. The region takes in Monroe, Washtenaw, and western Wayne Counties.

Bill's Favorite Events
in Detroit Southwest

- **Ann Arbor Folk Festival** (January), Ann Arbor, (734) 761–1451
- **Black History Month Blues Concert** (February), Monroe, (734) 241–5277
- **Flower and Garden Show** (March), Ann Arbor, (734) 998–7061
- **Antique Market** (April), Saline, (734) 662–9453
- **Orphan Car Show** (June), Ypsilanti, (734) 482–5200 or (734) 483–4444
- **Frog Island Jazz and Blues Festival** (June), Ypsilanti, (734) 761–1800 or (734) 763–8585
- **Celtic Fourth of July Festival** (July), Saline, (734) 429–4494
- **Canton Liberty Festival** (July), Canton Township, (734) 397–5110
- **Heritage Festival** (August), Ypsilanti, (734) 483–4444
- **Rod Custom Car Show** (August), Belleville, (734) 699–8921
- **Ann Arbor Blues and Jazz Festival** (September), Ann Arbor, (734) 995–7281
- **Ann Arbor Winter Art Fair** (October), Ann Arbor, (734) 995–7281
- **Monroe Holiday Parade** (November), Monroe, (734) 242–3366
- **New Year Jubilee** (December), Ypsilanti, (734) 483–4444

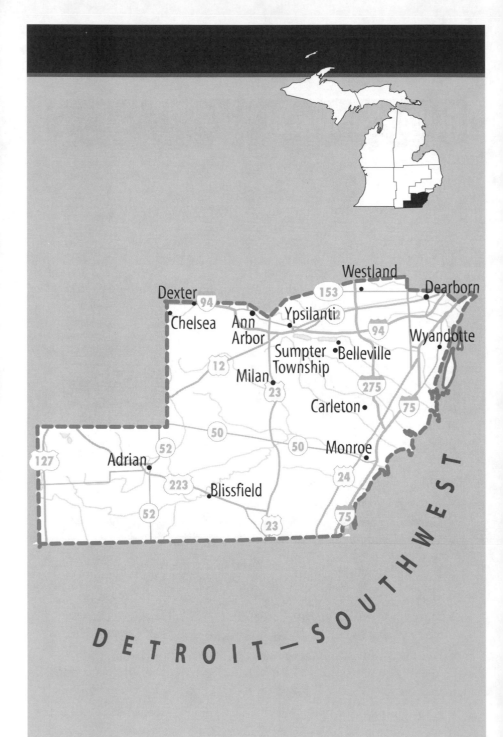

Dexter

Chelsea

Ann
Arbor

Ypsilanti

Westland

Dearborn

Sumpter
Township

Belleville

Wyandotte

Milan

Carleton

Adrian

Monroe

Blissfield

DETROIT – SOUTHWEST

Monroe

Monroe is one of the state's oldest cities, founded in 1780 by the French. The last major city in southeast Michigan before the Ohio border, Monroe is home to manufacturing (if you're reading this in a La-Z-Boy recliner, its headquarters is here) and recreation provided by nearby Lake Erie.

 ### JIM ULRICH'S TRADEWINDS CHARTERS (ages 6 and up)

Ulrich's boats are moored just off I–75 at exit 11 (La Plaisance Road, Monroe 49270), at the Erie Party shop and docks just south of Monroe. They make two trips into the lake's Michigan waters each day. For information call Tradewinds Charters at (734) 243–2319. The $60-per-person tab includes use of a fully rigged rod. Bait's included, too, and you can keep your catch in the boat's cooler until you get ashore. All that's needed for an angler older than age sixteen is a one-day or an annual Michigan fishing license, available at the dock for a small fee. Annual license fees range from $13.00 for residents to $26.00 for nonresidents. Daily fees are $7.00. Your money will be refunded in case of bad weather. Bring plenty of sunscreen and seasickness medication if you're prone; Erie is shallow and can kick up quickly.

It's party time on Lake Erie! Party-boat time, that is. No, we're not talking about dancing and rock-and-roll bands. If the kids—or you, for that matter—have never gone fishing before, this is the perfect way to get hooked.

Up to six persons per trip climb aboard one of Captain Jim Ulrich's three, stable, 30- to 32-foot craft and head out after walleye in the waters of Lake Erie near Monroe, which has been termed the nation's walleye capital. Ulrich and his captains scour the lake for schools of the voracious fish, and once they reach a "hot area" the engines are shut off, and you're ready to lower your bait.

Ulrich will know when he's found a hot spot by the football-shaped blips on his computerized fish-finder. Walleyes are usually found near the bottom, so look at the finder to spot 'em, and the captain will tell you how many seconds to let the bait sink. Two tips for best catches: (1) "jig" (raise and lower) your fishing rod often when slowly reeling in to attract fish, and (2) try to cast your line on the windward side of the boat; that way it will freely drift past your quarry, rather than being tugged under the vessel first. Reel steadily and tell your kids not to pull too hard, or the hook might pull out of the walleye's mouth. Ulrich will be there to net your catch and urge you on to take your limit of ten big ones.

3

RIVER RAISIN BATTLEFIELD VISITOR CENTER (ages 5–16)
At the corner of Detroit and Elm, Monroe 48162; (734) 243–7136 or 240–7780. Open 10:00 A.M. to 5:00 P.M. daily Memorial Day through Labor Day. **Free**, *but donations are accepted. Web site: www.geocities.com/Pentagon/Quarters/7550/index.html.*

The center recaps the story of the War of 1812 battle where the Americans suffered one of their worst defeats in one of the war's largest battles. Native Americans, helped by the British and led by warrior chief Tecumseh, killed more than 400 settlers. Small children may be bored, but it's interesting local history. There's a short presentation on the battle and its importance in the fight for who controlled the Great Lakes.

Where to Eat

Bob Evans, *I–75 at exit 15 (M–50, Monroe 48161); (734) 289–4225.* Good budget chain food for breakfast, lunch, dinner. Children's menu. $

Joe's French-Italian Inn, *2896 North Dixie Highway, Monroe 48162. Take I–75 exit 15, then head east two miles on M–50; (734) 289–2800. A landmark in the region for decades, specializing in seafood, steaks and (guess what?) Italian dishes. Children's menu available. Lunch and dinner served.* $$

Where to Stay

Cross Country Inn, *Monroe 48162. At I–75 exit 15; (734) 289–2330.* Motel features 120 rooms on two stories with an outdoor pool and **Free** coffee in the lobby. Restaurants nearby. $$

Holiday Inn Monroe, *Monroe 48162. At I–75 exit 15; (734) 242–6000.* Property has 160 rooms and new suites, heated indoor pool, and other typical Holiday Inn amenities. $$$

Hometown Inn, *Monroe 48162. At I–75 exit 15; (734) 289–1080.* Property has 89 rooms, including some with kitchens. $

Sterling State Park, *Monroe 48162. Exit off I–75 at M–50 (exit 15), and turn east on Elm to the park entrance; (734) 289–2715. State motor-vehicle permit is required for entry, $4.00 daily or $20.00 annually. Camping costs $14.00 a night.* The park is just north of the city, with a campground, but sites may be too close together for some. It's a marshy area, so bring plenty of bug repellent early in the year. There's a beach and a well-designed, protected boat launch.

Carleton

 CALDER DAIRY FARM (ages 2–12)

Take Telegraph Road to South Stony Creek Road. Head west about 5 miles to Finzel Road; then go south and watch for the signs; Carleton 48117. Call (734) 654–2622. Open 10:00 A.M. to 8:00 P.M. in summer; 10:00 A.M. to 7:00 P.M. in winter. Visits to the farm are Free.

Where does milk really come from? Do brown cows give chocolate milk? And how do cream, sugar, and a lot of hard work become all those luscious flavors of ice cream at the local store? Answer all your kids' questions and more with a visit to the Calder Dairy Farm near Carleton in Monroe County, south of Detroit. The maker of out-of-this-world chocolate milk and holiday eggnog so thick it's like liquid ice cream, milk that's still sold in glass bottles, and twenty-two flavors of ice cream has opened its farm for tours to show kids and others how the milk that's in your fridge gets there. They'll see up close that no, it doesn't just come from the back room of the supermarket.

Your family can stroll the 180-acre farm to see and pet the Holstein and Brown Swiss cows. A viewing room lets kids see the milking process from 4:00 to 5:00 P.M. daily. Elsewhere on the farm kids can see and pet more than a hundred other animals, such as waddling ducks and honking geese. They can hop aboard a real hay wagon hitched to huge, stately Belgian horses for a trip to see even more exotic species, like llamas, squawking peacocks, and fallow deer. They'll also learn that pigs aren't as dirty as they've read, and they can touch sheep's wool on the hoof to feel that it's actually a bit sticky from its rich lanolin.

Afterward, take your gang to the farm's small on-site store, where they can sink their teeth into a huge Calder ice-cream cone. You can also head to the main store in Lincoln Park, near Detroit, to buy everything from cottage cheese to old-fashioned buttermilk.

Where to Eat and Stay

See Monroe.

For More Information

Monroe County Convention and Tourism Bureau, *111 East First Street, Monroe 48161; (734) 457–1030 or (800) 252–3011. Information on the area includes a list of charter operators.*

Along northbound I-75, near the city at the 10-mile marker, a state-operated welcome center has more information on Michigan and the area.

Blissfield

Blissfield is along U.S. Highway 223, reached off U.S. Highway 23, north and west of Monroe. Take the family aboard the railroad and then introduce the kids to the way small-town life used to be—but with all the stores and other comforts of the present—in Blissfield and its next-door-neighbor, Adrian, in southeastern Michigan. Both have some surprising finds. They are part of the charm of small-town Michigan. Blissfield was settled about the same time as Adrian and remains Michigan's biggest village.

ADRIAN & BLISSFIELD RAILROAD (all ages)

Leaves from the Blissfield East in downtown Blissfield along U.S. Highway 223; (517) 486–5979 or (888) GO–RAIL–1. Themed trips take place Friday through Sunday. Dinner trains run Friday and Saturday and select Sundays and aren't recommended for small children not used to sitting still for long stretches. Kids are, however, encouraged on the other excursions. Dinner trips are $47.95, with the special murder mystery trip $69.95 Friday and Saturday and $61.95 Sunday. Other trips start at around $9.00 for adults, $8.00 seniors, and $6.00 for children ages three through twelve. Web site: www.hathawayhouse.com.

Step aboard the 1940s-era, air-conditioned-and-heated coaches of the Adrian & Blissfield Railroad. Your kids will be amazed as the diesel engine enters the station. Then they'll sit back and be treated to a ninety-minute trip through the countryside past manicured, tilled farm fields and over at least two old trestles that cross the Raisin River. If they're especially vigilant, they might even see a deer or two.

Themed rides take place throughout the year. During the winter holidays, Santa himself makes an appearance on every trip in December to take toy orders from the kids. A special "Ghost Train" appears during the two weeks before Halloween and features ghosts and goblins on board as well as ghoulish sights along the tracks.

The interactive dinner murder mystery trip is the most popular. The owner rates it PG-13, so young children shouldn't attend. Up to a hundred persons are served dinner on china and linen in two dining cars, with choice of prime rib, fresh salmon, or chicken with soup, salad, and dessert. All the food is catered by Blissfield's Hathaway House restaurant (see Where to Eat).

 OLD COUNTRY STORE

122 South Lane, Blissfield 49228; (517) 486–3621. Hours are 10:00 A.M. to 5:30 P.M. Monday through Saturday, noon to 5:30 P.M. Sunday.

After you ride the rails, stroll downtown Blissfield's main street, a browser's delight lined with shops that are especially festive during the holidays. In the Country Store you'll find country furnishings, accessories, and collectibles. Other downtown shops specialize in crafts, too. Kids can hunt for presents for Mom and Dad and then meet up with you for a treat at the old-fashioned soda fountain.

The entire area also is a hotbed for antiques hunters, with five year-round antiques malls hosting hundreds of dealers.

Where to Eat

Hathaway House (ages 8 and up). *424 West Adrian (U.S. 223), Blissfield 49228; (517) 486–2141 or (888) 937–4284. Reservations requested. Web site: www.hathawayhouse.com.* Besides catering meals for the train, this beautifully restored 1851 mansion serves up finely prepared meals including specialties like potato-crusted walleye and prime rib or rack of lamb. $$$

Main Street Stable and Tavern, *Blissfield 49228. Behind Hathaway House; (517) 486–2144.* If the kids are in tow and aren't in the mood to sit still, head for burgers in the former carriage house for lunch and dinner. $$

Where to Stay

Ellis Inn. *415 West Adrian (U.S. 223), Blissfield 49228; (517) 486–3155. Web site: www.cass.net/~ellisinn.* Kids and adults alike are welcome at this 1883 bed-and-breakfast furnished in period antiques. $$ It's one of several accommodations in the area. Contact the Lenawee Conference and Visitors Bureau (738 South Main, Adrian 49228; 517–263–7747 or 800–536–2933) for more information about other places to stay in the area.

Chelsea

Settled in 1820 and named after Chelsea, Massachusetts, the town was a farming center until Ann Arborites discovered it and it was developed into a suburb.

CHELSEA MILLING COMPANY (ages 6 and up)

Take I–94 west from Ann Arbor to the Chelsea exit and head north—you'll soon see the company's silos; (734) 475–1361. Chelsea Milling Company's Free *tours take place Monday through Friday between 8:30 A.M. and 1:30 P.M. Reservations are required. Web site: www.jiffymix.com.*

Such a deal! The kids will think you're taking them on another one of your educational tours. It's that, yes, but there's a special treat at the end that will make them eager to learn how grain is made into the flour that makes the brownies, cakes, and muffins at the Chelsea Milling Company, a landmark in this friendly rural town.

The Chelsea Milling Company began when "Grandma Mabel" Holmes came up with the idea of a flour that's ready to use for making pancakes, biscuits, and other goodies without having to mix all the ingredients first. Today as many as 14,000 visitors a year—split between children and adults—stroll through the plant where Jiffy All-Purpose Baking Flour and sixteen other products are produced.

Tours last up to two hours, depending on the size of the crowd. First you'll be treated to a slide show that starts with a history of the company and how Grandma Mabel's idea in 1930 launched the Jiffy line of mixes. The slide show over, tour guides then take you to the packaging operations, where you'll see boxes made and filled with what's being produced that day, everything from corn-muffin mix to pizza dough.

Last stop on the tour is a treat for both adults and kids. Grown-ups receive a Free package of muffin, cake, or frosting mix and a recipe booklet, while the kids can latch onto a box of brownie mix or pizza dough that they can take with them and bake at home.

PURPLE ROSE THEATER (ages 12 and up)

137 Park Street, downtown Chelsea 48118; (734) 475–7902. Ask about current productions and schedules. Occasional productions may be too intense for children under sixteen, so check before making reservations. Web site: www.home. earthlink.net/purplerose/.

Plan to take in a performance of mostly original plays at this newly restored theater. Who knows? You might even see Chelsea resident and Hollywood actor Jeff Daniels, who's starred in such varying roles as Harry in *Dumb and Dumber* and a Union hero in the movie epic *Gettysburg*. After all, he is part owner and writes some of the plays presented here. The theater is very popular, so call early for seat information.

CHELSEA COMMUNITY FAIR (all ages)

At the corner of Old U.S. 12 and Old Manchester Road (Chelsea 48118), 1 mile north of the I–94 Chelsea exit; (734) 475–8153. Admission: twelve and under Free, *$5.00 per day all others.*

This fair takes place during the last full week of August, starting on Tuesday and ending on Saturday. There's a midway, demolition derbies on the first two nights, and a rodeo the third night. Kids can also see and pet baby livestock.

WATERLOO RECREATION AREA (all ages)

16345 McClure Road; (734) 475–8307. Take I–94 west of Chelsea and watch for signs to the Eddy Geology center, or take exits 147, 150, 156, or 157. A state park motor-vehicle permit ($4.00 daily, $20.00 annually) is required for entry.

The lower peninsula's largest state park, Waterloo Recreation Area features more than 20,000 acres of camping from modern to primitive, including rustic cabins for rent, and a riding stable. More than 30 miles of biking trails, plus picnicking and swimming, are available. The recreation area contains a section of the longest hiking trail in southern Michigan. An adjacent Audubon Society preserve often hosts sandhill cranes.

Where to Eat

Common Grill. *112 South Main Street, Chelsea 48118; (734) 475–0470.* Lunch and dinner. Closed Monday. The city's best restaurant welcomes children, too. It features a casual atmosphere with an original pressed-tin ceiling, hardwood floors, and a zinc bar. Well-prepared meals feature a variety of seafood and meats, vegetarian items, children's menu, and Sunday brunch. $$$

Where to Stay

Lyndon Oaks. *17720 North Territorial Road, Chelsea 48118; (734) 475–7590.* Located in three acres of forest and surrounded by state land. Features two guest rooms and a common room with fireplace. Breads, cereals, fruit, plus hot items such as French toast and waffles for breakfast. $

South House Chelsea. *120 South Street, Chelsea 48118; (734) 475–9300.* An 1887 Victorian home behind the Common Grill and near the Purple Rose Theater. Four rooms with private baths and television; full breakfast. Rooms are traditionally decorated. $$

Dexter

Located just northwest of Ann Arbor. From I-94, exit at Baker Road and head north into town. Dexter, until it became a western suburb of Ann Arbor, started out as a small farm community.

DELHI METROPARK (all ages)

Located on the Huron River's banks on Huron River Drive (Ann Arbor 48103), which skirts the river a good way and is a beautiful drive in itself; (800) 477–3191. To reach the park from Dexter, head east on Huron River Drive. Entry fee per vehicle is $3.00 weekends, $2.00 weekdays; Wednesdays are Free. *Open 6:00 A.M. to 10:00 P.M. Web site: www.metroparks.com.*

Picnic facilities and canoe rentals are available here (see Huron River Canoeing), as well as fishing in the Huron River at this park, part of the Huron-Clinton Metroparks system, which rings metro Detroit.

DEXTER-HURON METROPARK (all ages)

Along Huron River Drive (Dexter 48130), downstream from Hudson Mills; (800) 47–PARKS. Entry fee per vehicle is $3.00 weekends, $2.00 weekdays; Wednesdays are Free. *Open 8:00 A.M. to 10:00 P.M. Web site: www.metroparks.com.*

A great 125-acre park along the Huron with picnic facilities and baseball diamonds. It's a favorite picnic spot for canoeists using the river as well as for motoring families seeking a quiet uncrowded park.

HUDSON MILLS METROPARK (all ages)

8801 North Territorial Road, Dexter 48130; (800) 47–PARKS. From Ann Arbor, take U.S. Highway 23 north to North Territorial Road, then head west. The park is open year-round 6:00 A.M. to 10:00 P.M. Entry fee per vehicle is $3.00 weekends, $2.00 weekdays; Wednesdays are Free. *Web site: www.metroparks.com.*

The largest of the three related parks, Hudson Mills, also along the Huron River, includes a golf course, bicycle and cross-country ski rentals, bike and ski trails, picnic areas, "frisbee golf," plus camping for groups and canoeists making overnight trips on the Huron.

 HURON RIVER CANOEING (ages 1 and up)
Headquartered at Delhi Metropark, Ann Arbor 48103; (734) 769–8686. Canoes are rented from mid-May through October. Cost is $24 for the three-hour trip to Delhi Metropark from Hudson Mills, and $14 for the approximately two-hour trip from Dexter-Huron Metropark to Delhi. All life jackets are provided. There are small, beginner-type rapids. Maximum number of people in canoe is two adults and two nonpaddling children.

This is a wonderful way to introduce the family to a taste of the outdoors only a few minutes outside the city. Starting from Delhi Metropark, the livery will drive you upriver to nearby Hudson Mills Metropark to begin your journey. Canoeists put in at the park and cruise the river for about three hours. In fall, a great stop is the **Dexter Cider Mill** in downtown Dexter, where you can enjoy a break and some cider and doughnuts, or you can stop for a picnic at Dexter-Huron Metropark, downstream.

Where to Eat

Choose from small local restaurants in towns described previously or head for more selections in nearby Ann Arbor.

Where to Stay

See listing of accommodations under Ann Arbor, which is a few miles east on I-94.

Saline

Settled in 1824 and named for its salty springs used by Native Americans, Saline sits on the upper River Raisin, a few miles south of Ann Arbor. It's known chiefly for its beautiful nineteenth-century homes and as an eastern gateway to the Irish Hills area described in chapter 4.

WELLER'S RESTAURANT

555 West Michigan Avenue (U.S. 12), Saline 48176, on the west side of town; (734) 429–2115.

Not only good food, but historical, too. It's located inside one of Henry Ford's community experiments, a mill he once used to process soybeans into oil for his auto plants and help bring employment to local farmers. $$$

Ann Arbor

Imagine about as eclectic city as you can, catering to all tastes with theaters and street performers, surprising restaurants, and a vibrant atmosphere unlike any other in the state, and you've just described Ann Arbor, the home of the University of Michigan. This is a great place for families to explore.

All University of Michigan museums are **Free** and are open to the public. To get to Ann Arbor's campus area, take the State Street exit north off I-94. Main Street shopping is a few blocks to the west. What's as tall as a house and has rows of huge, sharp teeth? What animal that's a cousin of the elephant once roamed Michigan and other parts of the United States? Ever see a real Egyptian mummy? At the museums you'll find the mummy's

Away for the Weekend My pick for a weekend jaunt with the kids in the region? Ann Arbor and its environs, of course. Headquarter at one of the city's hotels and explore the region, which is close enough to just about any of the activities mentioned in this chapter. Chelsea is only a few minutes west by I-94. The Irish Hills area (see chapter 4) is just to the south and west. There's fun from restaurants to live theater and inexpensive movies in Ann Arbor, which alone probably deserves a weekend to explore everything within the city limits. Detroit's downtown cultural attractions (see chapter 2) are a forty-five-minute drive away via I-94. There's all the vibrancy and excitement of a college town. It's simply *the* place to be in the region.

tomb (minus the curse), dinosaurs straight out of *Jurassic Park,* plus a lot more finds worthy of Indiana Jones himself.

Ann Arbor Art Fair (all ages) This popular attraction

draws hundreds of thousands of families to Ann Arbor each year and virtually closes the city's downtown to traffic. It may be crowded, noisy, and occasionally offbeat, but it's fun for the entire family. It's an annual gathering of more than a thousand artists who take over downtown for four days, usually in the third week of July. Although the event is collectively known as "the art fair," there are actually three simultaneous art festivals. While the three fairs may be separate, each flows into the other, which makes walking the entire area easy.

The **State Street Art Fair** runs the length of the State Street shopping district and has grown so large since its beginning in 1967 that it's spilled over into four surrounding streets. The **Summer Art Fair** is spread out along Main Street and adjoining avenues. While it's been known as more commercial in years past, it's come a long way in the past few summers. Artists' booths are set up down the middle of each street, with passages wide enough for wheelchairs and strollers despite the crowds. Only a few tents ask that children be carried, owing to cramped quarters. As you peruse the artwork, you'll find everything from original pottery and woven clothing to wildlife art and photography. If your teens are into beads, they'll find plenty, along with amulets for make-your-own necklaces.

At the **Ann Arbor Street Art Fair,** the oldest of the three—dating from 1959—face-paint experts deftly design flowers, flags, and hundreds of other forms on willing young faces, and youngsters can even try their own hand at the easel with watercolors. There's a Free family art activity center at the Summer Art Fair, too, with lots of chances for kids to create the next art craze.

Much of the entertainment isn't at the booths, however. At intersections between each fair and along the expanse of grass and diagonal sidewalks along State known as the "diag," magicians, jugglers, and other street buskers love to coax child "assistants" from the crowds, and the kids love it, too. They're trying to earn a living at it, and they often pass the hat at the end of each show. In addition, local merchants use the event as an excuse to offer discounts and sidewalk sales.

For more information contact the Ann Arbor Street Art Fair at (734) 994–5260 (Web site: www.artfair.org), the State Street Art Fair at (734) 663–6511, and the Summer Art Fair at (734) 662–2787.

EXHIBIT MUSEUM OF NATURAL HISTORY (all ages)
*Corner of Geddes Road and Washtenaw on the campus's east side; (734) 764–
0478. Open Monday through Saturday from 9:00 A.M. to 5:00 P.M., Sunday noon
to 5:00 P.M. Free. Web site: www.umich.edu.exhibits.lsa.*

Hundreds of families come here, especially on weekends, to entertain
and teach their children at the exhibits at two museums. First on the list
to visit should be this treasure storehouse of prehistoric Michigan and
other discoveries that will appeal especially to kids. What excites kids the
most is when they come face-to-face with the fossilized bones of a
snarling allosaurus standing over its "kill," a fossilized stegosaurus like
those that roamed the earth millions of years ago and were unearthed
near Cleveland, Utah. At another exhibit, they can stand next to a skeleton of a huge, elephant-like, 10,000-year-old mastodon that was found
in a Michigan farmer's field near Owosso.

When it opened, kids lined up into the street to view the long, deadly
claws of the museum's newest exhibit: a rapacious deinonychus, relative
of the velociraptors of *Jurassic Park* fame. Other exhibits on the third
floor are presented through dioramas that create a picture of what
Michigan was like at various times through prehistory and what you
might find in the region's forests and ponds today. There is also a planetarium that presents weekend shows.

A new permanent exhibit, said to be the largest of its kind in existence, focuses on the evolution of whales, with six skeletons of prehistoric cousins to the world's largest mammals that were unearthed in
China, Egypt, and Pakistan by university scientists. It includes a complete cast of a fifty-six-million-year-old ancestor.

At the well-stocked museum store, kids can take home smaller,
model versions or books that provide more details about what they saw
inside, or they can go home wearing a velociraptor T-shirt.

 KELSEY MUSEUM OF ARCHAEOLOGY (all ages)
*434 South State Street, Ann Arbor 48104; (734) 764–9304. Open from 9:00
A.M. to 4:00 P.M. Tuesday through Friday, 1:00 to 4:00 P.M. Saturday and Sunday. Closed Monday. Free. Web site: www.umich.edu/~kelseydb/.*

A few blocks west of the exhibit museum near the Michigan Union
Building on South State Street, this museum is one that wannabe
Indiana Joneses won't want to pass up. Part of the exhibit is the sar-
cophagus of Djheutymosc, a former priest who lived in southern Egypt
sometime between 685 B.C. and 525 B.C.

Museum visitors will see other artifacts unearthed during university digs, and there are other rotating exhibits, too.

HANDS-ON MUSEUM (toddlers and up)

220 East Ann, Ann Arbor 48104; (734) 995–5439. From U.S. Highway 23, take Main Street south to Huron and turn left. Hours are Tuesday through Saturday from 10:00 A.M. to 5:00 P.M. and Sunday from noon to 5:00 P.M.; closed Monday and holidays. Admission is $3.00 for seniors and children two to seventeen, under two **free***, and $6.00 for others. Web site: www.aaahom.org.*

This is a museum kids can't get enough of. And, recently they got a lot more of it. An extensive expansion quadrupled its size.

One of the state's oldest museums that caters to children of all ages, Hands-On is a place where, as one eleven-year-old noted, kids can learn and have fun at the same time. Where else could they have the opportunity to look inside a living beehive? Or peer into a mirror while riding a stationary bike and actually see a skeleton move?

Opened in 1982 in the city's renovated red Central Fire House—the new location includes the firehouse and neighboring buildings—the Hands-On Museum contains more than 250 exhibits. One colorful section is devoted to tots, who can develop their motor skills and at the same time start on the road to discovery about how things work.

Other parts of the museum are divided into subject areas. One area teaches kids about their bodies and how they work. Among other things, they can measure their own heart rate and try to beat the clock to measure their reaction time. In a special room a strobe light flashes, and kids are amazed as their own shadows are captured on the opposite wall.

In another area kids can learn about physics and nature, from building an arch and exploring fossils to seeing the aforementioned bees, busy as, well, bees, preparing their plastic-encased hive. (Kids can even follow the workers as they head outside and return via a clear plastic tube.) While exploring light and optics, they'll marvel at a hologram and see the tricks a strobe light can play on the eye, and they'll try out a computer or find out what really happens when they flush a toilet. Explanations are provided for everything, but they're mostly ignored by the kids, who often seem to flit from one exhibit to another, just having fun and not really knowing or caring that they're actually learning something.

The museum also draws kids in through unique programs such as overnight camp-ins, birthday party programs, and special workshops and weekend activities that range from maze making to exploring potential careers. One event teaches how rocks are formed by doing something every youngster likes: baking chocolate-chip cookies.

BURTON MEMORIAL TOWER (all ages)

In the middle of campus on South Thayer; (734) 764–2539. **Free**.
Just look for the multistory pinnacle of this University of Michigan landmark and follow the music during weekly concerts at 10:15 A.M. on Saturday during the school year. Lorie Tower on the North Campus also has concerts on Monday at 7:00 P.M. in June and July. Burton Tower is open to watch the fifty-five-bell Baird Carillon played weekdays from noon to 12:30 P.M. during the school year.

DOMINO'S FARMS (all ages)

Domino's Farms is easily reached by exiting U.S. Highway 23 at Ann Arbor–Plymouth Road, turning east, and following the signs. For dates of activities call (734) 930–5032. Farm admission: $3.00 for adults, under twelve $2.50, under two **Free**. *The Christmas display Web site: www.spiritofchristmas.org.*
Located next to the Frank Lloyd Wright–inspired headquarters in Ann Arbor, Domino's Farms is meant to depict a Michigan farm of the early 1900s, and it hosts a plethora of programs geared to youngsters of all ages.

Come Easter, for instance, there's an annual egg hunt for the wee ones, with up to 1,500 eager youngsters divided into four age groups and loosed to scour the grounds for plastic eggs that contain candy, stickers, or coupons redeemable for age-appropriate prizes such as mugs and beach towels. And of course there's a visit by the Easter Bunny, as well as face painting, hayrides, clowns, and other entertainment.

In summer kids can ride a hay wagon to view a herd of sixty buffalo in a fenced area. If your children are able to spot the sometimes shy animals, wait to see the look in their eyes when you tell them the woolly beasts can weigh as much as the family car and can run nearly as fast.

In the petting farm area, kids are encouraged to stroke the chickens, sheep, goats, peacocks, potbellied pigs, and horses, the latter ranging from an American miniature to one of the largest, a Belgian. Events appealing to the older set include arts-and-crafts shows and annual classic-car exhibitions.

During the holidays, Domino's is the site of one of the largest outdoor light shows in the state. Kids will marvel at webs of lights shaped like animals that climb up trees to create living statues and lights that arch over your car and spell out festive holiday messages as you travel the roads in the complex. There's also a major indoor display, and the Domino's Pizza store is open during the show to let viewers grab a bite to eat on the go. The festival runs from the weekend before Thanksgiving to December 31, from 6:00 to 10:00 P.M. The entry fee of about $5.00 per car helps pay the electricity bill, and what's left over goes to charity. So far, more than $500,000 has been raised by the show.

GALLUP PARK (all ages)

3000 Fuller Road, Ann Arbor 48105, on the city's near-north side; (734) 662–9319. Web site: www.ci.ann-arbor.mi.us.

From April through October, rent a paddleboat, a canoe, or a bike and enjoy one of the city's best parks along the banks of the Huron River. Sorry, no swimming. Rental prices are as follows: On weekdays canoes and kayaks can be rented for $10.00 for two hours (there is a $10.00 refundable deposit). Paddleboats are $5.00 for each half-hour, and bikes are $6.00 for singles, $7.00 for tandem. On weekends canoes and kayaks cost $13.00 for two hours; paddleboats cost $7.00 per half-hour, and bikes are $5.00 per hour.

Ann Arbor Pow Wow, Dance For Mother Earth

(all ages) The Ann Arbor Pow Wow takes place in mid-March, at Crisler Arena, 333 East Stadium Boulevard, just east of U–M stadium. Tickets cost about $8.00 for adults, $6.00 for students and seniors, $4.00 for ages four through twelve, and Free for children age three or younger. There also are weekend tickets available. Web site: www.umich.edu/~powwow. Call (734) 647–6999 or (734) 763–9044.

Each year, for the last twenty-seven years, as Mother Earth once again begins to shake off the pall of winter, more than 1,000 Native American dancers, drummers, and singers gather from Friday through Sunday under the arena dome to pay homage. There is competitive dancing and lots of handmade crafts. It's an exciting and authentic way to introduce children to Native American culture.

FOX VILLAGE THEATER (all ages)

In the Maple Village shopping center near Maple and Jackson Roads on the city's west side; (734) 994–8080.

If you're looking for a place to take the family for an inexpensive movie, this is it. All seats are $1.50, $2.00 on Friday and Saturday nights.

Where to Eat

Ann Arbor is eclectic when it comes to restaurants. From Indian and Korean to German, African, and American, there are hundreds of places to eat here. Here's a sample:

Argerio's. *300 Detroit on downtown Ann Arbor's north side; (734) 665–0444.* A small, family-run restaurant using family recipes for great Italian fare from sausage to eggplant for lunch and dinner. $$

Bill Knapp's. *Two area locations: off exit 37A on U.S. 23, Ann Arbor 48104, (734) 971–1610; and 2501 Jackson Road, off I–94 exit 172, Ann Arbor 48103, (734) 663–8579. Web site: www.billknapps.com.* Good selection of family fare. Good bets include the burgers and macaroni and cheese and side dishes including scalloped potatoes. Children's menu. $

Blue Nile. *221 East Washington in Ann Arbor, east of Main Street; (734) 998–4746.* It's a rare treat to try ethnic food like this. Ethiopian food is prepared using low-fat, low-cholesterol methods and is served either all vegetarian (spiced spinach, squash, and potatoes with carrots are among the items) or with spicy beef, chicken, and lamb on a bed of *injera,* a spongy, soft flat bread. Kids will get a kick out of eating here because there are no utensils. Everything's served family style, with an all-you-can-eat option, and begins and ends with hot towels to clean your hands. Try the spiced cinnamon tea. $$

Gratzi. *326 South Main Street, Ann Arbor 48104; (734) 663–5555. Sidewalk, first floor, even balcony seating.* Don't just expect spaghetti and meatballs at Gratzi. Lunch and dinner. $$$

Grizzly Peak Brewing Co. *129 West Washington, Ann Arbor 48104, just west of Main Street downtown; (734) 741–7325.* Eclectic menu with pizzas, pastas, ribs, and burgers. Watch as eight varieties of beer are made on premises. Freshly made root beer also available. Children's menu. $$–$$$$

Kana Korean Cuisine. *114 West Liberty (near Main Street), Ann Arbor 48104; (734) 662–9303.* Authentic Korean cuisine for lunch and dinner, including a lunch buffet. Try the bulgogi, marinated charcoal-grilled beef strips. Warning: The kim-chee, pickled cabbage, is an acquired taste. $$

Krazy Jim's Blimpy Burgers. *551 South Division at Packard, Ann Arbor 48105; (734) 663–4590.* A Michigan student with either too much time on his hands or who wanted a mathematical challenge once calculated you could order 1,245,760 variations of burgers here. Any way you do, they're great. It's the oldest burger outlet in the city, here since 1953, and was voted one of the nation's best by *USA Today.* $

Le Dog. *410 East Liberty Street, Ann Arbor 48104 and in the mall at 306 South Main Street, Ann Arbor 48104; (734) 665–2114.* The original Le Dog is an unpretentious red take-out stand with two ordering windows—an eatery that only wanted to be a hot dog stand when it started almost twenty years ago. It now has something for kids as well as for adults with a more educated palate. Owner-chef Jules VanDyck-Dobos now serves everything from lobster bisque and bouillabaisse to New Orleans–style jambalaya. Treat your kids to one of Le Dog's famous triple-chocolate shakes, or clear your palate with the newest offering, Italian ices. $

Seva Restaurant. *314 East Liberty downtown, Ann Arbor 48104; (734) 662–1111.* A vegetarian restaurant featuring imaginative breakfast, lunch, and dinner. $$

Stucchi's. *320 South State Street, Ann Arbor 48103; (734) 662–1700.* Great locally made ice cream.

Zingerman's Delicatessen. *422 Detroit on downtown Ann Arbor's near north side; (734) 663–3354.* You have to experience a Zingerman's sandwich at least once. This deli may look like it's been there forever, but it began in 1982. It has one of the largest selections of imported and local cheeses, meats, and breads you'll find in the area, although a mite expensive. A Saturday tradition for many Ann Arborites, so expect some lines, especially in the morning. Restaurant includes a "kids' room" with a special menu. $$

Where to Stay

Best Western Wolverine Inn. *3505 South State Street, Ann Arbor 48108, at I–94 exit 177; (734) 665–3500.* One hundred nineteen rooms with in-room movies. Near Briarwood Mall. $$

Hampton Inn South. *925 Victors Way, Ann Arbor 48108, just northeast of I–94 exit 177; (734) 665–5000. Web site: www.hamtpon-inn.com.* One of two in town, featuring 150 rooms with heated indoor pool, free continental breakfast and in-room movies. Near Briarwood Mall. Kids under age eighteen stay free. $$

Red Roof Inn. *3621 Plymouth Road, Ann Arbor 48105, at U.S. 23 and Plymouth*

Road; (734) 996–5800. Typical Red Roof budget-minded amenities. Restaurants nearby. $$

Weber's Inn. *505 Jackson Road, Ann Arbor 48103, off I–94 exit 172; (734) 769–2500 or (800) 443–0506. Web site: www.webersinn.com.* One hundred fifty-eight poolside or other rooms and suites. Indoor pool and recreation area with fitness and game centers and poolside cafe. Weber's restaurant is an Ann Arbor tradition that serves American cuisine. Great place for family getaways. Weekend packages available. $$$

For More Information

Ann Arbor Convention and Visitors Bureau, *120 West Huron, Ann Arbor 48104; (734) 995–7281 or (800) 888–9487. Web site: www.annarbor.org.*

Milan

This small farming community south of Ann Arbor along U.S. Highway 23 has two reasons to visit, neither one of them being the local federal prison.

MILAN DRAGWAY (ages 8 and up)

Located 4 miles east of U.S. Highway 23 exit 25, about 10 miles south of Ann Arbor, Milan 48160; (734) 439–7368. Open from April through late October. Bring earplugs for kids, as some of the dragsters can be very, very loud. Admission: Entry rates vary. Regular weekday entry is $8.00 for adults, $4.00 for kids ages seven through twelve, and **Free** *for ages six and under. On weekends, adult entry is $10.00, and rates for kids are the same as on weekdays. Admission prices may be higher for special events, so call the dragway and listen for the tape-recorded message. Web site: www.milandragway.com.*

Watch as the best of Michigan—and on special weekends, nationally ranked—drag racers burn up the ¼-mile track here. Special weekends salute devotees of Fords, Chevys, and Chrysler products. In late June, the biggest event of the season comes to town with the Michigan Top Fuel Invitational, bringing several "funny" car dragsters capable of hitting close to 300 mph. Local boy—and girl—racers who have driver's licenses can see how fast the family van can go every Wednesday and Friday, when the track is open to all for an entry fee, and at times, even kids compete in special miniature drag cars. Not only is the car watching fun, but the people watching is often just as entertaining.

HEATH BEACH (all ages)

Off U.S. 23 at exit 22. Follow the signs from the exit; (734) 439–1818. Admission: $6.00 on weekends, $5.00 on weekdays. Kids ages nine through twelve are $3.00; eight and under **Free** *all the time. Season passes available. Web site: www.heathbeach.com.*

A spot that started as a result of freeway construction is now a regional summer fun institution. When U.S. Highway 23, visible from the beach, was being poured, builders needed fill and got it by digging "borrow pits" close to the right-of-way. In 1962 Milan resident Charles Heath saw a gold mine in one six-and-a-half-acre hole in the ground that used to be his horse pasture. With encouragement from friends, Heath made improvements in his family swimming hole and then opened it to the public. Now Heath Beach bumper stickers are everywhere.

Where to Eat

Lighthouse Coffee Co. *9 West Main Street; (734) 439–3623.* Features Zingerman's breads (see Ann Arbor) for breakfast through dinner and gourmet coffees. Closed Sunday. $

Roy's Burgers-n-BBQ. *25 Wabash; (734) 439–1737.* Half-pound burgers and barbecue sandwiches are served in a diner setting. $

Where to Stay

See Ann Arbor and Ypsilanti entries for nearby accommodations.

Ypsilanti

Home of Eastern Michigan University and its landmark brick water tower, the city was one of the mainstays of what President Franklin Roosevelt called the Arsenal of Democracy during World War II.

The giant Willow Run bomber plant poured out B–24 "Liberator" bombers at the rate of about one an hour. Later the plant, which was the largest factory under one roof, was home to several auto companies. Today it is part of General Motors. Willow Run is still an active airport and home to one of the city's major attractions.

YANKEE AIR FORCE MUSEUM (all ages)

Just east of Ypsilanti, only a ten-minute drive east of Ann Arbor on the west side of Willow Run Airport, Belleville 48112; (734) 483–4030. To reach the museum from Interstate 94, exit at Belleville Road (exit 190) and go north to Tyler Road; then turn west, drive to Beck Road, and turn north. Go about ¾ mile and you'll spot a sign for the museum on the left. Guided tours are available for groups (two weeks' reservation notice is usually required). Call for information about admission fees and hours of operation. Web site: www.yankeeairmuseum.org.

What began in 1981 as a way to remember Michigan's role in World War II (1939–45) and in America's aviation history has grown into a major family attraction at the Yankee Air Force Museum. The museum features twenty-one restored military aircraft, many of them flyable. It's located in a wooden hangar that served as a school for mechanics when B–24 "Liberator" bombers were produced here.

21

Air buffs in your family can examine craft like a B-25D Mitchell, the only flying example in the United States. Outside, kids can see a giant B-52D jet bomber and by appointment can even climb inside. Other craft include Korean War–era jets, trainers, and the newest addition, a rare flyable B-17 bomber, named the *Yankee Lady*. The museum's "Women in Aviation" room details the contributions of Amelia Earhart and other female pioneers.

Every other spring, on Memorial Day weekend, the museum welcomes visitors to an open house including the Wayne County Air Show at the Willow Run Airport. The event fills two afternoons and always includes appearances by thrilling precision flight teams like the U.S. Navy's Blue Angels, flybys, wing walkers, aerobats, and other aviators. On the ground, displays and tours let junior pilots peer inside military and civilian aircraft. Call (734) 482-8888.

WIARD'S ORCHARDS (all ages)

5565 Merritt Road, Ypsilanti 48197; (734) 482–7744. Take Huron Street/ Whitaker Road, exit 183, off I–94 near Ypsilanti, and travel 2 miles south to the blinking light. Then follow Stony Creek Road south about 2 miles, turn right on Merritt, and follow the signs. The $7.00 admission charge includes rides and a trip through the daytime haunted barn. The "Ultimate Haunted Barn" is not recommended for children under twelve. Web site: www.wiards.com.

Each weekend in September and October, up to 15,000 persons head for Wiard's for its annual Country Fair Weekends. Kids are catered to farmwide, with goats and pigs to feed, ponies to ride, and eager helpers ready to paint young faces. Two "trains" (actually converted trucks) take families on orchard tours past trees heavy with fruit and fields of ripe pumpkins. Kids get a kick out of yanking apples right off the tree and picking out candidates for their Halloween jack-o'-lanterns. There's even a haunted October-evening hayride through the orchard that is perfect for youngsters, plus the "Ultimate Haunted Barn" for teens and adults who like their surprises scarier.

Crafts will tempt Mom and Dad, and they can even try out those new country dance steps in front of a live band after touring the orchards, where there are nine varieties of apples to pick. Next stop: glasses of fresh-squeezed cider. Then head for the bakery.

On certain weekends the farm features military themes, such as Civil War and Revolutionary War encampments, with participants living as soldiers of each era did and a steam and gas engine show the last weekend in September.

Where to Eat

Haab's. *18 West Michigan Avenue, Ypsi-lanti 48197, downtown; (734) 483–8200.* Lunch and dinner, including children's and senior's menu. At the location since 1934. Each year, the restaurant celebrates its anniversary, rolling back prices to 1934 levels for dishes including its trademark "chicken in the rough," half a chicken served in a basket with honey, a biscuit, and shoe-string potatoes. $$

Where to Stay

Ypsilanti Marriott. *I–94 and Whittaker Road, Ypsilanti 48197, south of exit 183; (734) 487–2000.* Upscale property has 242 rooms, indoor pool, and other amenities including a weight room and a restaurant. Also home of Eastern Michigan University's Eagle Crest university golf course. $$$

For More Information

Ypsilanti Convention and Visitor's Bureau, *106 West Michigan Avenue, Ypsilanti 48197; (734) 483–4444. Web site: www.ypsilanti.org.*

Belleville

Suburbia may be eating into the neighboring farmlands in this Detroit-area community, but Belleville still retains a small-town feel—and the festival that makes the area famous every Father's Day.

NATIONAL STRAWBERRY FESTIVAL (all ages)

From I–94 take the Belleville Road exit and turn south into town. There's Free *parking at the Wayne County Fairgrounds, with shuttle rides to the festival; for a festival information recording call (734) 697–3137. The farm is within only a few minutes of downtown. For picking information call Rowe's Strawberry Farm at (734) 482–8538 and Potter's at (734) 461–6348.*

Come Father's Day weekend, the farm fields around this part of southern lower Michigan blush bright red as one of the state's most lus-cious crops comes into its prime. It's strawberry-picking time. Two farms offer pick-your-own family fun. The Rowe Farm, with twenty-seven acres of berries, and Potter's, with two acres, offer row upon row of the luscious fruit over the picking season. Berries, best picked in the morning, are sold by the pound, now around 75 cents, and considering their size, it doesn't take long before you and your kids are lugging four or five pounds of the beautiful, ripe red treats up to the weigh-in center.

The picking, though, is just a prelude to the festival, which each year draws up to 100,000 berry lovers to Belleville over the weekend and closes downtown to traffic. Organizers pride themselves on making the entire festival a family affair, with lots of kids' events and even a family circus. At games designated especially for young children, players can win prizes by reaching for a plastic duck, blowing the biggest bubblegum bubble, or joining in a tug-of-war. There are pony rides and places where young hands can make arts-and-crafts items. Carnival rides at two locations include a special section just for the youngest. The big Saturday parade features more than 200 units. At Saint Anthony's Church you'll find an old-fashioned family circus under the big top, with jugglers, clowns, and other performers who delight in plunging into the audience and involving the children in the fun.

Even if the local crop isn't quite ready yet, there are strawberry treats everywhere you turn, from shortcake and pies to sundaes. Whatever they can put strawberries in, they do. Fresh strawberries also are sold by the quart or case, in case you got to the party too late to join the picking.

Where to Eat

Belleville Grille. *146 High Street, downtown Belleville; (734) 699–1777.* Exit I-94 at Belleville Road, turn south, and take the first right after the bridge over the lake. The restaurant features outdoor, lakeside dining with steaks, seafood, and pasta among the entrees. Step down to the wheelchair-accessible lower level, where the kids can enjoy ice cream and perhaps feed the ducks and fish. $–$$$$

For More Information

Belleville Area Chamber of Commerce, *397 Main Street, Belleville 48111; (734) 697–7151. E-mail: Belleville.ch@earthlink.net.*

Sumpter Township

Sumpter Township has a distinctive country atmosphere. It was named for the Revolutionary War hero Gen. Thomas Sumter, but a spelling error by a nineteenth-century clerk gave it its different name—and no one bothered to change it.

 CROSSWINDS MARSH WETLAND INTERPRETIVE PRESERVE (all ages)

Take I–275 south from I–94 to exit 8, Will Carelton Road. Head west 3³⁄₁₀ miles until it becomes Oakville-Waltz Road. Turn north on Haggerty, and the entrance is a ½-mile on the left; (734) 261–1990. **Free**. *Call for seasonal hours.*

Sometimes something good comes from "progress." Built to replace the wetlands scheduled to be destroyed to expand Detroit Metropolitan Airport, Crosswinds's 1,000 acres makes it one of the largest artificially created wetlands in the country. Any threatened plants and animals were moved from the construction zone to here, which ironically was farmland that originally was a wetland. There are five hiking loops, from ³⁄₁₀ mile to 5 miles, to take visitors over boardwalks, through marshland, and past two fishing docks. A 2-mile canoe trail that includes a stop at an island has interpretive markers for paddlers to follow and learn about what they're floating past. Canoe rental is $5.00 per hour. Rent binoculars for $1.00 to get a closer glimpse of more than 105 species of birds. There also are several miles of bridle paths, but no rentals at this point.

Westland

Ever heard of a city named after a shopping mall? This is one. What used to be called Nankin Township changed its name when the mall, one of the region's first enclosed shopping centers, was built at its center. It's now a typical Detroit suburb but has some interesting stop-offs for visitors, besides that mall, which expanded.

 WESTLAND MALL (all ages)

At the corner of Wayne and Warren Roads at 35000 Warren Road, Westland 48185; (734) 421–0877. Hours: 10:00 A.M. to 9:00 P.M. Monday through Saturday, 11:00 A.M. to 6:00 P.M. Sunday. Strollers may be rented for a small fee.

The mall features eighty-eight stores, plus an arcade to keep the teens busy while you shop. There are anchor stores including Hudson's, Sears, and J. C. Penney.

WAYNE COUNTY LIGHTFEST (all ages)

Between Westland and Dearborn Heights on 4½ miles of Hines Drive; (734) 261–1630. Runs between mid-November and January 1 (closed Christmas night). There's a $5.00 minimum donation per car to help keep the fest operating. Traffic is one-way after the roadway is closed from 7:00 to 10:00 P.M., following rush hour. Enter at Hines Drive and Merriman, 2½ miles south of the Merriman/I–96 exit.

Nearly one million lights grace the sweeping arcs and tree-lined straights of Hines Drive in what's billed as the Midwest's largest holiday light show. Drive past more than thirty-five displays that shine nightly, sponsored by regional businesses. At the end, a special shelter offers refreshments, gift shopping, and, after Thanksgiving, visits with Santa.

Dearborn

About a mile south and then east about 12 more miles from Canton is Dearborn, the city that Henry Ford's car built. Here two museums are dedicated to what Ford admired most: middle America. Lots of other activities draw tourists here, too.

 HENRY FORD MUSEUM AND GREENFIELD VILLAGE (all ages)
The village and museum are at 20900 Oakwood Boulevard, Dearborn 48124; (313) 271–1620. From Interstate 94, exit to the Southfield Freeway (Michigan 39) northbound and go 3 miles to northbound Oakwood, then continue about 2 more miles to the entrance. Admission is $12.50 for adults, $11.50 for seniors age sixty-two and older, $7.50 for kids ages five to twelve, and kids four and under are **Free**. *AAA member discounts. Call for details and dates for special events, like the antique auto muster, sheep shearing at Firestone Farm, and more. Web site: www.hfmgv.org.*

This complex, begun by Ford himself, today is much more than what he had envisioned when it opened in the 1930s. From the car in which President John F. Kennedy rode in Dallas on November 22, 1963, and the chair President Abraham Lincoln sat in at Ford's Theater on April 14, 1865, to the tiny clapboard bicycle shop in Ohio where two brothers taught the world how to fly, this gathering of more than a hundred historic buildings and one of the world's great museums makes the ninety-three-acre complex in Dearborn one of the state's top family tourist destinations.

At the entrance to the grounds stands the Henry Ford Museum, surrounded by the Ford Motor Company. Inside, be sure to take the youngsters, who may have possibly never seen a drive-in, to the miniature version showing old film clips. It's right next to the full-size old-fashioned service station. Peer inside a real New York diner and one of the first rooms of what then was a new motel chain, Holiday Inn. Walk past the museum's collection of more than a hundred antique and classic cars, including the only remaining 1896 Duryea, America's first production vehicle. And wait until the kids stand dwarfed next to the giant, 600-ton steam locomotive.

Greenfield Village is dedicated to the history of small-town America and American inventiveness. See where the Wright brothers designed their first airplane and where they lived. Then step into the laboratory where Thomas Edison invented the lightbulb. Edison's chair remains just as the inventor left it. That's because it was nailed to the floor by his friend Henry Ford when Edison visited to celebrate his most famous invention's fiftieth anniversary.

Recent additions have remembered the nation's African-American community, too. A log cabin is similar to the one in which scientist, inventor, and teacher George Washington Carver grew up; another exhibit depicts how African-Americans lived both before and after slavery. Take a carriage or steamboat ride aboard the *Suwanee* in summer, or if you visit in winter, ride in a horse-drawn sleigh when the snow cooperates. Walking tours are offered in fall.

AUTOMOTIVE HALL OF FAME (ages 8 and up)

Adjacent to the Henry Ford Museum at 21400 Oakwood Boulevard, Dearborn 48124; (313) 240–4000. Hours from Memorial Day through October 31 are 10:00 A.M. to 5:00 P.M. daily; from November to Memorial Day, 10:00 A.M. to 5:00 P.M. Tuesday through Sunday. Admission $6.00 for ages thirteen through sixty-one; $5.50 for ages 62 and older; $3.00 for ages five through twelve. The Hall of Fame and Henry Ford Museum offer a combination ticket allowing visits at a reduced price. Tickets for two consecutive days are $15.00 January through March, $27.00 April through December for adults, $8.75 and $16.00, respectively, for children ages five through twelve and $14.50 and $26.00, respectively, for seniors. Kids ages four and under get in Free. *Web site: www.automotivehalloffame.org.*

The Hall of Fame honors the greats in the auto industry, including some who've until now gone unsung. In mock-ups of the inventor's workshops, kids can push buttons and hear portrayals of industry greats. Through hands-on displays, kids can learn how pioneers like Chevrolet, Chrysler, Ford, Honda, Mack, and Benz lent their names to their vehicles. The hall is not dedicated just to those who created auto accessories, but also to the pioneers who led the fight for worker rights in the 1930s, including a depiction of the West Virginia kitchen where United Auto Works leader Walter Reuther grew up, and the workshop of Ransom Olds that became the birthplace of mass production.

A classic car display includes a Cord L-29, displayed in a mock-up of a 1930s Cord dealership, plus lots of murals and a moving sculpture visitors can operate. There's also a lobby gift shop and a cafe with light refreshments.

 FAIR LANE (ages 8 and up)

On the campus of the University of Michigan at Dearborn, off Evergreen Road north of Michigan Avenue, Dearborn 48126; (313) 593–5590. From the Southfield Freeway (M–39), head west on Michigan and north on Evergreen, then follow the signs. Tours of the grounds, powerhouse, and mansion are $8.00 for adults, $7.00 for seniors ages sixty-two and older, and $5.00 for children ages five to twelve. Children under five ꭍ𝐫𝐞𝐞. *Self-guided grounds maps are $2.00. Call to check on tours, as they vary by season. Web site: www.umd.umich.edu/fairlane.*

The mansion where Henry Ford entertained luminaries of his day from Lindbergh to President Hoover offers 30- or 60-minute tours. The tours include a look through the restored powerhouse, which once more produces enough electricity using the Rouge River to light the home, plus part of the university campus. Built in 1914, its cornerstone was laid by Thomas Edison, and the mansion has six levels.

The newest addition to the estate is the restoration of the Ford garage, featuring many of Henry Ford's personal vehicles, especially his Model T and the Model A he was riding in the day he died. Also there is the 1920s camper that Ford, Edison, and friends vacationed with in Michigan's Upper Peninsula and which many credit with starting the recreational vehicle industry. You'll also see a cutter sleigh that Henry and wife Clara used at the estate, a prototype electric car that he was to build with Edison, and an early Fordson tractor, the vehicle that helped modernize the American farm.

The estate's gardens have been totally restored and include the Ford Discovery Trail, a forty-five-minute walking tour with stops at the estate's oldest living object, a three-hundred-year-old burr oak, and at waterfalls and meadows designed by renowned landscape designer Jens Jensen.

 ## IMAX THEATER (ages 5 and up)

Located on the west side of Henry Ford Museum, 20900 Oakwood Boulevard, Dearborn 48124; (313) 271–1620. From the Southfield Freeway (Michigan 39), exit at Michigan Avenue. Turn south at Oakwood to the museum entrance, or if headed south on M–39, exit at Michigan and continue on the service drive. Turn west at the village entrance on Village Road. Theater entry fees vary by showing, but plan around $10.00 for adults, $8.00 for children and seniors. Admission is separate from the museum and village. Web site: www.hfmgv.org.

Located on the grounds of the same museum that pays homage to American inventions and in particular, the inventor of the motion picture, Thomas Edison, the new IMAX Theater is one of the additions that is breathing life into the museum that has been criticized in the past as being too static.

It's a huge addition, and so far, a huge hit. It was one of a handful of theaters in the country to introduce Disney's *Fantasia 2000,* the first full-length IMAX film ever created, and some say the wave of the future in movie-making. Usually, the theater will alternate showing other films across the panoramic 60- by 80-foot screen. The theater is capable of showing both two- and three-dimensional films, with seating for 400 persons and sound system that will impress even teenagers.

Outside the theater, there's also a great gift shop with museum and theater-related items. The theater is a great addition to an already great museum, the world's largest indoor-outdoor museum. You can't miss it.

 ## SPIRIT OF FORD (ages 5 and up)

At 1151 Village Road, Dearborn 48124; (313) 31–SPIRIT. Open 9:00 A.M. to 5:00 P.M. Monday through Sunday except major winter holidays. From the Southfield Freeway (Michigan 39), exit at Michigan Avenue. Turn south at Oakwood to the museum entrance, or if headed south on M–39, exit at Michigan and continue on the service drive. Turn west at the village entrance on Village Road. Theater entry fees vary by showing, but plan around $10.00 for adults, $8.00 for children and seniors. Admission is separate from the museum and village. Web site: www.spiritofford.com.

Many Michigan residents still fondly remember the Ford Rotunda, which sadly burned to the ground in the 1960s. Well, this is a twenty-first-century reincarnation of the same, with lots of pizzazz thrown in. In the huge oval reception hall, see the latest in Ford concept cars. Kids and adults can have fun challenging each other during a simulated pit stop on a real NASCAR racer. They can visit three theaters, including the best, a rock 'em, shake 'em simulated trip down a Ford assembly line, complete with the sounds and smells of paint, new upholstery, and the shakes of a trip on a Ford test track. Guests sit in computer-controlled seats that bounce, bend, and turn to the movie they're watching. It's great fun and one of the best parts of your visit. Youngsters can design their own cars on a computer, and there's also a gift shop.

Where to Eat

Big Fish. *700 Town Center Drive, on the south side of the Fairlane Town Center shopping mall complex, between Michigan Avenue and Hubbard Drive; (313) 336–6350.* A great place to treat the family to fresh seafood dinners, including seafood pastas and whole fish. $$$

Eagle Tavern. *Inside Greenfield Village, Dearborn 48124 (village admission required); (313) 271–1620.* If you want to show the kids what an 1850s stagecoach stop may have looked like, head here, where you can sample fare of the era and be greeted as if you are city slickers just off the stage, right down to the comments about those "strange city clothes" you're wearing. It's one of six restaurants in the complex. $$$

The Gate Room. *5101 Evergreen Road, Dearborn 48128. In the student center on the campus of Henry Ford Community College, just north of Fair Lane and U–M Dearborn on Evergreen Road between Ford Road and Michigan Avenue; (313) 845–9600. Serving lunch Tuesday and Thursday at 11:00 A.M. and 12:15 P.M. and dinner Wednesday at 6:00 and 7:15 P.M.* A unique experience featuring meals concocted by culinary arts students at the community college. It's a chance to enjoy great meals at a great price. $$

Kowloon. *22905 Michigan Avenue, Dearborn 48124, east of Outer Drive; (313) 565–4521.* Inexpensive Cantonese and some Szechwan Chinese dishes. Sweet and sour chicken, almond chicken, and spicy General Tsao's chicken are favorites. $$

La Pita. *22435 Michigan Avenue, Dearborn 48124, between Outer Drive and Military; (313) 565–7482.* Introduce your family to Middle Eastern food at this friendly restaurant in a small shopping center across from the city's Catholic church. Try the chicken *shawarma,* either lunch or dinner portion. It's roasted, shaved chicken with sauce and even a pickle slice wrapped in pita bread. Lots of other dishes, too, plus tasty, freshly made fruit drinks. Children's menu includes burgers and chicken.

The Pool. *At the Fair Lane estate, Dearborn 48124; (313) 436–9196.* Called The Pool because it's built over the former swimming pool used by the Fords. Lunch only. $

Richter's Chalet. *23920 Michigan Avenue, Dearborn 48124, just east of Telegraph Road; (313) 565–0484.* Serves great authentic German cuisine. When they're available, try the great bacon, applesauce, or sour cream potato pancakes. Park in rear. $$

Where to Stay

Dearborn Bed and Breakfast.
22331 Morley, Dearborn 48124; (313)
563–2200. From Michigan Avenue, turn
north on Military for 2 blocks, then head
west. A 1927 Victorian home with four
rooms. A great way to get a historical
feel of the city. Close to restaurants in
western Dearborn, including La Pita
and others. $$$

Dearborn Inn & Marriott Hotel.
20301 Oakwood Boulevard, Dearborn
48124, just south of Greenfield Village com-
plex; (313) 271–2700. Built by Henry
Ford to accommodate travelers using
his Ford Tri-Motor airplanes landing
across the street at the complex, which
is now a Ford test track, the inn has
222 rooms and serves breakfast, lunch,
and dinner in two restaurants. For a
treat, try staying in one of five cottages
built as replica homes of famous Amer-
icans. $$$

Hyatt Regency Dearborn. Fairlane
Town Center, at the northwest corner of
Michigan Avenue and Southfield Freeway
(M–39), Dearborn 48126; (313)
593–1234. A thirteen-story modern
hotel with 786 rooms, with open interior balconies for each floor. Dining
rooms, coffee shop, and deli for breakfast, lunch, and dinner. Also a pool,
hot tub, sauna, and fitness club. $$$

Red Roof Inn. 24130 Michigan Avenue,
Dearborn 48124, near the corner of Tele-
graph Road; (313) 278–9732. Inexpen-
sive lodging in 111 rooms with Red
Roof quality. Continental breakfast. $

Ritz Carlton–Dearborn. 300 Town
Center Drive, Dearborn 48126, at the
southwest corner of Hubbard Drive and
Southfield Freeway (M–39); (313)
441–2000. Going north, exit Southfield at
Michigan Avenue and continue north on the
access drive to Hubbard, then go west about
1 block. Going south, exit M–39 at Ford
Road and continue on the access road
to Hubbard, then head west about 1
block. Elegant rooms located within
walking distance of the Fairlane Town
Center shopping mall. The property has
308 rooms and dining rooms that serve
expensive breakfast, lunch, and dinner.
Head for other mall-area restaurants
off Town Center Drive and in the mall
if your budget doesn't allow eating at
the Ritz. $$$$

For More Information

Dearborn Chamber of Commerce,
15544 Michigan Avenue, Dearborn

48126–2996; (313) 584–6100. Web site:
www.dearbornchamber.org.

Wyandotte

This city that once was known only for its odiforous chemical plant and steel
mills has undergone a renaissance that has transformed it into a bustling
recreational community and close-knit Detroit suburb south of Dearborn.

Take the Southfield Freeway (eventually it becomes Southfield Road) to its end at the Detroit River at Jefferson Avenue. Turn right and parallel the river a few miles, and you're there.

Wyandotte Art Fair
Nearly as big as the one in Ann Arbor, Wyandotte's annual fair is another street celebration, with the lower Detroit River providing a beautiful watercolor background. Hundreds of artists set up stalls as streets close and the city parties. The fair takes place in downtown every mid-July. Call (734) 324–4500 for information.

FORD-MACNICHOL HOME AND WYANDOTTE MUSEUM (ages 5 and up)

2610 Biddle Avenue, Wyandotte 48192; (734) 324–7297. Hours: Monday through Friday, 9:00 A.M. to 5:00 P.M. The first Sunday of each month and selected weekends throughout the year, the museum is open 2:00 to 5:00 P.M.

The historic home is decorated in the style of the Victorian era. The basement museum chronicles the history of the city from the early 1800s, when it was a Native American village, to the 1900s, when it was a smoky chemical and steel-making center. It also has examples from the present, since it became a trendy, near-Detroit residential community.

Where to Eat

Porto Fino. *3445 Biddle, Wyandotte 48192, on the Detroit River; (734) 281–6700.* Specializing in Italian and seafood. Dine indoors or on the dock next to boats tying up at riverside. Great atmosphere. The dock tends to be a bit congested and noisy, especially on weekends, but the river views are worth the wait. $$$

Speedboat Bar. *749 Biddle, Wyandotte 48192; (734) 282–5750.* Look for the bow of a boat that seemingly has propelled itself onto the roof of this landmark neighborhood downriver eatery. Specialty is chili, which has won the Michigan Chili Cook-Off title at least once. Eat outside on the deck or indoors. $$

For More Information

Wyandotte City Community Relations Office, *3131 Biddle Avenue, Wyandotte 48192; (734) 324–4502. Web site: www.wyandotte.net.*

Detroit

I n World War II, when President Franklin D. Roosevelt referred to the "Arsenal of Democracy," he was talking about the Motor City. If you believe all you see on the nightly news, you'd think Detroit might have few things to offer the traveling family. If you look closer, however, you'll find the city that's been slammed so much is on the way back and actually has so many activities to offer families that it deserves its own chapter. There's something to do all year long in the city that still rightly claims its title as the world's automotive capital, from feeding deer while race cars compete nearby on the grounds of an urban park to visiting the world's largest museum devoted to the African-American experience. Leave your preconceived notions behind and see what the city offers. You'll be surprised.

Belle Isle

Located in the middle of the Detroit River; the island is reached by exiting I-75 at Jefferson Avenue and heading east. Turn right and cross onto the island by the Douglas MacArthur, or Belle Isle Bridge, from Jefferson Avenue.

Belle Isle is Detroit's downtown playground, home to its own herd of deer, within sight of the state's tallest buildings. On the 985-acre island in the middle of the Detroit River are so many family attractions, you couldn't do justice to them in an entire summer. There are about 8 miles of roads on the island, with top speed limits of 20 mph in most areas, including a 5½-mile drive circling the perimeter. You'll find plenty of picnic and other relaxing opportunities, including a beach on the calm, quiet side of the Detroit River. Many of the activities are within walking distance of one another. Just park your car along one of the tree-lined boulevards and enjoy.

University
Cultural
Center

Theater
District

Belle Isle

Tiger Stadium

DETROIT

BELLE ISLE ZOO (all ages)

Located on Central Avenue, Detroit 48208. Head right from the MacArthur bridge (also called the Belle Isle Bridge) and follow the signs; (313) 852–4083. Open May through October 31. Admission is $3.00 for ages thirteen and older, $2.00 for seniors, and $1.00 for ages two to twelve. Web site: www.detroitzoo.org.

Originally called the Children's Zoo, this island version of Detroit's zoo in Royal Oak was recently expanded from three to thirteen acres. With an African theme, it offers a rare opportunity for kids to get a look at wild animals from a ¾-mile-long elevated boardwalk over such creatures as Sumatran tigers, African lions, and wild turkeys among the twenty-one exhibits.

Young children aren't forgotten, as there are domestic farm animals to pet and a fascinating "World of Spiders" where kids can pit their squeamishness thresholds against one another.

Bill's Favorite Events in Detroit

- **North American International Auto Show** (mid-January), Cobo Center, (248) 643–0250; Web site: www.dada.com

- **Detroit Boat Show** (early February), Cobo Center, (248) 877–8240

- **Detroit Grand Prix** (mid-June), on Belle Isle, (313) 259–7749 or (800) 338–7648; Web site: www.grandprix.com

- **Freedom Festival Fireworks** (late June), downtown along the riverfront, (313) 923–7400

- **Spirit of Detroit Thunderfest** (early July), Detroit River off Belle Isle, (313) 331–7770; Web site: www.thunderfest.com

- **Michigan State Fair** (late August through Labor Day), at the fairgrounds, Woodward and Eight Mile Road, (313) 369–8250; Web site: www.mda.state.mi.us/statefair

- **Detroit International Jazz Festival** (Labor Day weekend), at Hart Plaza, (313) 963–7622

- **Thanksgiving Day Parade** (November), downtown along Woodward Avenue, (313) 923–8259

- **Noel Night** (December), Detroit Institute of Arts, (313) 577–5088

BELLE ISLE NATURE CENTER (all ages)
Near the zoo; just follow the signs; (313) 852–4056. Open Tuesday through Sunday from 10:00 A.M. to 4:00 P.M. Admission is Free, *but donations are accepted. Open year-round.*

Not only is the island a great place to view the zoo, but other forms of nature, too. The island is about 75 percent covered with hardwoods, including varieties of oak, silver maple, and dogwood. At the nature center, there are 3 miles of paved biking trails plus seasonal programs offered by park naturalists.

There's a hospital where injured wild

The First Tee (ages 6 and up)

Call (313) 852–4062 for tee times. The Belle Isle golf course has been redesigned and improved to bring the game to everyone. A public-private partnership between Ford Motor Company, the city, and the World Golf Foundation (part of the PGA) renovated the existing course into a new nine-hole course, with a training center for kids and adults, a driving range, and a putting green.

birds and other animals are brought by city residents to heal. Outside the zoo, the park is its own nature center, actually supporting upward of 120 European fallow deer in the island's wooded interior. You'll often see some of the herd along the inner routes.

 BELLE ISLE AQUARIUM (all ages)
On the island's southeast side; operated by the Detroit Zoo from its headquarters in Royal Oak, P.O. Box 39, Royal Oak 48068; (313) 852–4141. Open daily from 10:00 A.M. to 5:00 P.M. Admission is $2.00 for ages thirteen and older and $1.00 for ages two to twelve. Fee also covers admission to the adjacent Whitcomb Conservatory. Web site: www.detroitzoo.org.

This ninety-one-year-old facility—the nation's oldest freshwater public aquarium—displays more than a hundred types of species found in Michigan's lakes and streams or imported from around the world. Among the highlights are a freshwater stingray and an electric-eel exhibit that draws kids like a magnet. There's also a small exhibit on coral reef fish.

WHITCOMB CONSERVATORY (all ages)
Adjacent to the aquarium; (313) 852–4064. Open daily from 10:00 A.M. to 5:00 P.M. Call for details on upcoming flower shows and hours. Admission is $2.00

Detroit Grand Prix (ages 8 and up) Tickets start at $20

general admission, which actually buys you just a place to stand and try to peer over the guardrails and fences. Be prepared to balance your kids on your shoulders to let them see. It actually allows you to see little of the race. The best way to view the action is a grandstand seat at $40 to $115. The Friday before the race is a qualifying day, and admission is always Free. Paddock, or pit, passes are extra and get you closest to the cars and your favorite drivers. Bring earplugs for yourself and the kids, as the cars are loud. For information call (800) 338-7648. Web site: www.grandprix.com.

In early June, the racing world focuses on Belle Isle as the best Indianapolis-style race car drivers from the United States and Europe converge on its twisty track to see who can best the others. Following a few days of practice and qualifying, the grounds around the track come alive on race day Sunday as more than 170,000 spectators jam onto the island, arriving by foot, by bus, or by shuttle from downtown restaurants (the MacArthur Bridge is closed to regular auto traffic).

Enjoy the sights of brightly colored, finely crafted race cars and the smells of rubber and burning gasoline—not to mention all that greasy concession food. The race lasts two hours and fifteen minutes or 145 laps, whichever comes first.

On the Saturday before the Grand Prix is run, the fun starts as the Indy Lites cars, similar to Indy racers but with smaller engines, also run the course, usually along with a fun race by local celebrities.

for adults, $1.00 for seniors and ages two to twelve,and Free *for children younger than two. Ticket fee includes admission to the aquarium. Web site: www.bibsociety.org.*

Surrounded by grounds from which you can see giant oceangoing and lake freighters pass by in the Detroit River, the domed conservatory houses a unique display. It's a great place to explore the world of plants through more than 2,000 species, from dessert settings for cacti to tropical humidity for ferns, palms, and banana trees. The conservatory's annual winter orchid and mum shows, two of six special events mounted here annually, are spectacular.

DOSSIN GREAT LAKES MUSEUM (all ages)

On the southwest side of the island, on the river; (313) 852–4051. Open Wednesday through Sunday from 10:00 A.M. to 5:00 P.M. Admission is $2.00 for ages thirteen to sixty-one, $1.00 for ages sixty-two and older, and **Free** *for ages twelve and younger. Admission is* **Free** *on Wednesday.*

This is a city treasure. While the marine radio crackles with the sounds of river traffic, kids can stand in the working wheelhouse of a former Great Lakes ore carrier in the Ford fleet. Marvel at the Gothic Room, with more than seven and a half tons of hand-carved oak work taken from a 1912 Great Lakes steamer, and see the first boat to break the 100-miles-per-hour barrier on a closed course. There's a great model display, too, along with terrific views of passing vessels during the summer shipping season.

Street Festivals

The annual racing events on Belle Isle are just the prelude to two weeks of festivities in Detroit that celebrate the world's longest peaceful international border, in both length and years.

DETROIT-WINDSOR INTERNATIONAL FREEDOM FESTIVAL (all ages)

Running from mid-June through July 4 each year; (313) 923–7400. Many events are **Free**. *Detroit's sister city across the river, Windsor, hosts an annual downtown carnival, and rides are extra. Fun on the Detroit side includes activities revolving around the Detroit Institute of Arts and Children's Museum, and events on the waterfront for all ages. Web site: www.theparade.org.*

Freedom Festival activities include taking the kids to Canada—possibly their first visit to a foreign country—via the Ambassador Bridge or the Detroit-Windsor Tunnel. They can enjoy the carnival in downtown Windsor, other festival activities, or a meal at a sidewalk restaurant. They'll also enjoy the excitement on July 1, Canada Day, that country's version of our July 4. Windsor celebrates with what's billed as Canada's largest parade, plus crazy antics like the Great Bed Race downtown.

On the U.S. side you'll find a children's carnival and food fair in front of Ford Auditorium, the annual tugboat race on the river, and daily events on Hart Plaza, ranging from an international tug-of-war across the river against a team in Windsor to concerts for teens. The festival goes out with a bang of fireworks.

The **Free** Hudson's International Freedom Festival fireworks actually begin around 10:00 P.M. along the downtown riverfront, usually the week before the Fourth of July weekend. Popular viewing spots are located up and down the river, including right downtown at Hart Plaza. Other folks cross the river into Canada. Many rent rooms at a riverside hotel for the night, as traffic coming back across the bridge and through the tunnel can be monumental. This is the biggest family event of the year in downtown Detroit, and it is said to be the largest pyrotechnic display in North America.

MEXICANTOWN MERCADO

During the Freedom Festival and every weekend from mid-June through Labor Day in Detroit's Mexicantown area north and west of the Ambassador Bridge, Detroit 48202; (313) 967–9898. On Sunday from noon to 6:00 P.M., planners stage an array of family activities at Plaza Fiesta, located at the corner of Bagley and Twenty-first Street. Admission is **Free***. To reach Mexicantown, exit I–75 southbound at Clark Street, take the service drive to Bagley, and head west a few blocks and look for the banners along Bagley. From northbound I–75, exit at Springwells, head north to Vernor, and turn right. From I–96, exit at Michigan Avenue and take the southbound service drive to either Vernor or Bagley. Web site: www. fami.com.*

You can let the kids pour on the hot sauce over authentic Mexican fare and test their palates, find a toy among the craftspeople, or join in the folk dancing demonstrations during this annual event in the heart of the city's Latin community. Children's pastimes include petting miniature goats, horses, and even cows—and it's all **Free**. Every weekend, kids can participate in crafts, such as making musical instruments, or they can also learn traditional Hispanic games.

Have them join in on the fun when one of the children, blindfolded, finally breaks a holiday piñata, scattering candy and gum all over for the rest to gather in a headlong rush of sneakers and hands. Meanwhile, you can enjoy live music, check out cooking demonstrations given by famous Mexican-cookbook authors or chefs from the local restaurants (who explain how to can those hot chiles from the garden safely), or chat with local and Mexican artisans, who live north of Mexico City and are famed for the papier-mâché work, selling their crafts for adults and giving demonstrations. And don't forget the great restaurants for inexpensive Latin fare that's as mild or wild as you wish (see Where to Eat).

Spirit of Detroit Thunderfest (ages 8 and up) The races

usually take place in early July. Race day tickets range from $10 to $100, for a "super fan, all-week, all-race pass for a grandstand seat." If you're lucky and early enough, camp out along the northern shoreline of Belle Isle. Those spots are Free. Pit passes to see the giant boats lifted in and out of the water and see the crews and drivers up close also are available at extra cost. If you can afford it, it's a great way to show kids these complex machines. If you're near the course, earplugs might be a good idea, especially for younger kids. All ages are welcome, but older children may be more interested. Call (313) 331–7770 for updates on future dates, or via Internet at www.thunderfest.com.

Every summer, Belle Isle is taken over by race mania—both on land and on water. For the water race, the fun shifts to the stretch of the river between the island and the city, where the river's tricky waves are tested by up to a dozen Unlimited-class hydroplanes. An estimated 400,000 fans come to watch these boats, turning the event into a giant picnic beside the water. With tall rear tails and race car–like fins to create downforce and keep the stern in the water, they're built to skip across the river surface with a high-pitched whine, shooting giant columns of water called "rooster tails" into the sky.

During the race, drivers navigate a difficult course, encapsulated in cockpits like jet fighter pilots. They compete in several heats around a 2½-mile modified oval, running up to 225 miles per hour in the straights. Boats compete on both Saturday and Sunday, with qualifying heats starting before noon. Top finishers rack up race points, and those with the highest totals earn a spot in the afternoon championship heat. Smaller, Grand Prix–class boats powered by automobile engines take to a shorter course at the same site, in between the Unlimited heats, but they're nothing to be ignored either, running at up to 150 miles per hour.

AFRICAN-AMERICAN WORLD FESTIVAL (all ages)

At Hart Plaza the third weekend in August. Hours are noon to 11:00 P.M. Friday through Sunday during the festival. Admission is Free. *For specifics and events for each year's festival, call the Museum of African American History at (313) 494–5800. Web site: www.detnews.com/maah.*

With the beat of the drum and live performances of music from jazz to Motown, this annual festival is billed as southeastern Michigan's largest **Free** event. More than 200 vendors from around the world gather to sell their wares. There's African, Caribbean, and Haitian cooking. Storytellers, performers, and activities are in the Children's Village.

DETROIT FESTIVAL OF ARTS (all ages)

On the streets in the vicinity of Wayne State University, near Warren and Cass Avenues, Detroit 48201, held the third weekend of September; (313) 577–5088. To reach the area via I–75, exit at Warren and go west 1 block past Woodward. Admission is **Free**.

This annual celebration attracts more than 250,000 fairgoers and more than 130 artists and craftspeople from across the country. A major component of the fest is the huge children's fair, with more than seventy groups providing activities and educational experiences. At IBM's children's fair, for example, kids can try their hands on a computer. Also, a literary-arts program features poetry reading just for youngsters. Other programs just for fun feature fire eaters, tightrope walkers, children's song performers, puppeteers, and other street performers. Lots of "make and take" crafts activities are included, too.

For teens and parents, more than fifty performers entertain on the main stages. At various times you might see a New Orleans break-dancer or someone playing the spoons, while at another spot you can clog to bluegrass or limbo to the beat of a Haitian steel drum. In between, shop for a painting, basket, or item of handmade clothing among the artists' booths. And don't forget the international food stalls as well as special exhibits at the Cultural Center museums, plus historic tours.

Theatrical Adventures

Just up the street from the Coney emporiums (see Where to Eat), mostly along Woodward Avenue, a miniature renaissance is taking place in what once was Detroit's glittering theater district.

Detroit is home to a surprising number of venues that offer plays from classical to the avant garde. If your youngest kids can sit still for performances such as these, it's a grand way to widen their horizons in music and the arts as early as possible. However, be considerate of fellow concertgoers and judge whether your child should attend accordingly. If you bring your family here just once for a movie or concert, their visit to these restored complexes will stay with them the rest of their lives.

FOX AND STATE THEATERS (all ages)

Next to each other at 2115 Woodward Avenue, Detroit 48201; (313) 961–5450.
The Fox Theater is the world's largest surviving 1920s movie palace. From the gold-leafed lobby set off by magnificent simulated columns that evoke a scene from the movie *The Ten Commandments* to the huge, 5,000-seat auditorium with gargoyles and other characters staring down from everywhere under a tentlike dome, the Fox is a tribute to its architect, C. Howard Crane, and those who rescued this beauty from sure ruin. Your kids will instantly recognize that this is no mall multiplex.

Holiday children's shows draw crowds, such as ongoing Christmas performances by Radio City Music Hall's Rockettes, as do big-screen movie epics shown each summer.

The Fox's success has led another theater, geared to youths, to open across the street. The State Theater presents everything from irreverent movies like the Monty Python comedies to local and nationally famous alternative rock groups. On other nights it turns into a young people's nightclub called Club X.

MUSIC HALL CENTER (all ages)

It is at 350 Madison Avenue, Detroit 48075, at Brush; (313) 963–7622. Take I–75 and exit at Madison Avenue. The theater is 3 blocks to the left. Web site: www.youtheatre.org.
Part of the time, the Music Hall takes on a different moniker— Detroit Youtheater—when it's set aside just for kids from the wiggle set on up. From October through May the Youtheater presents weekend programs to introduce youngsters to all types of performing arts at the 1,700-seat facility.

There are two series of shows. The first, appropriately called the Wiggle Club, is for youngsters ages three through six. The Movin' Up Club is for kids age seven and older. More than a dozen different productions are presented each season, ranging from plays like *The Little Prince* and *Amelia Bedelia* to the return of Ishangi, the West African dance company that visits each February as part of Black History Month (the troupe has appeared for thirty straight years!).

Michi-fact: Despite what you might think, metro Detroit is still the world's motor capital, accounting for more vehicles manufactured than any other city.

In about half of the productions, performers answer questions from the audience after the shows. The Youtheater also offers performance workshops that help young people learn the fundamentals of acting and dance. Theater tickets are $7.00 each in advance or $8.00 at the door. Workshops cost $8.00 per person.

FISHER THEATER (all ages)

West Grand Boulevard and Second Avenue, Detroit 48202, at the heart of the city's "New Center," across from the original General Motors building; (313) 872–1000. Web site: www.fisherdetroit.com.

Located inside the art deco Fisher Building, this is one of the city's premier theater showcases, where touring Broadway companies often present their best, as well as other shows that come into town.

MASONIC TEMPLE (all ages)

Just west of Woodward; turn west at Temple and go 2 blocks to Cass, Detroit 48201; (313) 832–2232. Parking is adjacent, either on the street or in a lot; expect to pay about $5.00. Web site: www.masonicdetroit.com.

Another of the city's old theater landmarks is this huge hall owned by the Masons that is home to Broadway musicals, concerts, and other entertainment. Recent plays here have included *Phantom of the Opera* and a revival of *Showboat!*

HILBERRY THEATER (all ages)

4743 Cass, Detroit 48201, at Hancock, a block south of Warren, on the Wayne State University campus; (313) 577–2972. Exit I–75 at Warren and head west to the campus, then south on Cass.

Plays feature Wayne State drama students, and a great way to introduce kids to live theater. Plays here have included Agatha Christie's *The Mouse Trap* and other classics, including Shakespeare.

BONSTELLE THEATRE (all ages)

3424 Woodward, Detroit 48075, ½ block south of Mack; (313) 577–2960. From I–75, exit at Warren and head west to Woodward. Turn south.

Also featuring budding drama students from Wayne State University, this larger, traditional theater presents several plays in repertory. Plays recently performed here include *Dracula* and other contemporary classics.

CHENE PARK (all ages)

On the river off Atwater, south of Jefferson, at Chene; (313) 393–7827. From Jefferson, turn south on Chene.

Under a giant tent, up to 5,000 persons can enjoy outdoor concerts in summer.

Auto Shows

NORTH AMERICAN INTERNATIONAL AUTO SHOW (all ages)

Held in mid-January at Cobo Center downtown; (248) 643–0250. To reach Cobo, take the southbound Lodge Freeway (Michigan 10) downtown and follow the exit signs to the Jefferson exit; rooftop or underground parking at the convention center. Parking is also available in street-level lots. Crowds can be heavy on weekends, so it might be wise to plan a weeknight visit. And because of the crowds and the excitement, be sure to keep track of your kids, or arrange to meet the older ones periodically at predetermined sites. Tickets are about $8.00. Children twelve and younger accompanied by a parent are admitted **Free**. *Web site: www.dadanet.com.*

Visiting this show is like entering the world's largest new-car show-room, as each maker hires dancers, singers, and models and carts out glitzy rides that kids and grown-ups alike stand in line to try. Everywhere, kids walk by with bags full of advertising brochures and line up for a chance to sit behind the wheel of a new Mustang, Camaro, or other sporty model, while their parents check out the minivans.

Other showstoppers include the concept cars that are always introduced at this event, exhibits that show youngsters how auto engineers work to design next year's models, and drawings of concept cars done by local college and high school students. A recent example was Chrysler Corporation's unveiling of a space-age fuel cell to power vehicles, reducing greenhouse gases and increasing mileage.

On Cobo's lower level the kids will also be able to bounce on the sofa beds and try out the TVs in the latest van conversions or grab a snack at the concession area.

AUTORAMA (all ages)

Held in mid-February at Cobo Center; (248) 650–5560. See directions under North American International Auto Show. Admission: $12.50 for adults and $5.00 for children twelve and younger. Discount tickets are available before the event at area stores. Web sites: www.autorama.com or www.worldofwheels.com.

Bill's Top Family
Adventures in Detroit

- **Museum of African American History, in the Cultural Center.** A great addition to the area that's unique in the nation.

- **Belle Isle Park, in the Detroit River.** A unique island park; a wonderful facility with zoos to beaches.

- **Detroit's Coney Islands, on Lafayette Avenue.** Bite into a Coney dog, and you've tasted the essence of the city.

- **Auto Shows, Cobo Center.** What else says more about Detroit than cars?

- **Detroit's Cultural Center, near the Wayne State University Campus.** One of the nation's leading universities surrounded by the symphony, art, and historical museums.

Everyone from preteens to grown-ups will marvel at seeing favorite custom cars that have appeared in national auto magazines. Lacquered hot rods with gleaming chrome engines, side pipes, and wheels—pinstriped beauties that run the gamut from 1934 Fords and 1969 Corvettes to modified Mercedes—are polished and awaiting the car aficionado's review. Up to 500 custom models cover the display floor at Cobo.

Most of the entries are the pride and joy of average shade-tree mechanics who've worked on the cars in their own garages for a chance at showing them off. The show also features special exhibits, such as a display of nearly a hundred Harley-Davidson motorcycles and specialty cars from recent movies. Got a hankering to own a piece of Detroit muscle? There's a car corral with vehicles for sale by private owners as well.

Along with the stars of steel, stars of sports and television are present to sign autographs. Past appearances have included nationally known soap opera stars and sports celebrities such as football superstar Desmond Howard, Detroit Pistons basketball stars, and television celebrities signing autographs for the kids, and some for baby boomers. Best of all, with your admission comes the chance to pick out a favorite car and vote for it as best of the show. Other judges award trophies to winners in each class.

Cultural Center Attractions

Located adjacent and within a few blocks of Wayne State University, one of the nation's largest urban higher-education schools, Detroit's Cultural Center attractions are some of the best of their kind in any city. The area is reached by exiting I-94 at Woodward Avenue/John R and heading south on either John R or Woodward about ½ mile to Kirby. From I-75, exit at Warren Avenue and head west to Woodward, then go 2 blocks north.

DETROIT HISTORICAL MUSEUM (all ages)

5401 Woodward Avenue, Detroit 48202, at Kirby; (313) 833–1805. Hours are 10:00 A.M. to 5:00 P.M. Tuesday through Sunday. Closed Monday. Admission is $4.50 for adults, $2.25 for seniors and students, and Free *for children eleven and younger.* Free *admission for all on Wednesday. Parking is available on the street and on nearby lots and costs about $5.00. Web site: www.detroithistorical.org.*

This museum's focus on the city's past and future is made especially appealing for youngsters, who have fun while exploring the city's history at the same time.

The museum's trademark is on the lower level. In a darkened streetscape lit by "street lamps," visitors walk the cobbled streets of a mock-up of what the city looked like in the 1800s, before the automobile transformed it forever. You can peer into the homes and businesses, almost expecting the mannequins to come alive as they sit, counting out the day's receipts, or make purchases.

After a fire destroyed the original, a new 12-by-34-foot miniature train layout was built, which delights kids. There are four continuously operating 600-foot loops of track. The layout changes regularly and may depict a small-town scene, circus trains, or even a rodeo coming to town. A new feature is its "train-cam," a miniature camera mounted in the engine that displays its view on a nearby television monitor. In conjunction with the layout, there's also an annual train show in late December.

On the first floor is "The Motor City," an interactive display that includes a 70-foot section of the assembly line of the old General Motors Detroit Cadillac assembly plant, with an operating "body drop," where the body of a car is slid onto the chassis. Also included is an exhibit where kids can actually crank and start a replica Model T Ford.

Check into the series of tours to historic Detroit sights hosted by the museum. Historic churches and strolls through communities and sites along both Detroit's and Windsor, Ontario's, segment of the Underground Railroad (across the Detroit River) are among those available. The museum publishes a list of events, programs, and tours twice a year. Some last all day, so small children probably wouldn't last.

DETROIT INSTITUTE OF ARTS (all ages)

Kitty-corner from the historical museum at the corner of Woodward and Farnsworth, Detroit 48202; (313) 833–7900. Parking is behind the building and underground on the south side. The Detroit Film Theater, in the institute's auditorium, shows avant garde, European and other movies Friday through Monday. Call for what's showing, along with other special programs and concerts there. Hours are 11:00 A.M. to 4:00 P.M. Wednesday to Friday and 11:00 A.M. to 5:00 P.M. Saturday and Sunday. Tours take place at 1:00 P.M. Wednesday through Saturday and 1:00 and 2:30 P.M. Sunday. Recommended admission is $4.00 for those age fifteen and older, $1.00 for age fourteen and younger. You may pay what you wish, but you must pay something to enter. There are Brunch with Bach concerts every third Sunday for $21, but the series isn't recommended for children not used to sitting quietly. Food is served on paper plate—not to be economical, but to reduce table noise during the music. Web site: www.dia.org.

Now before the kids wrinkle their noses up at the uncool thought of going to an art museum, tell them to be patient. This one is different. While many museum employees gulp when they see kids coming, the DIA has plenty of exhibits that invite youngsters to touch and explore on their own and that start them on the road to appreciating art in all its forms.

There are several sure-bet draws for kids inside, says William H. Peck, curator of ancient art at the DIA: armor, mummies, a spiral staircase, the American house, the "donkey," and a special treasure hunt game, "The Mystery of the Five Fragments." The game motivates young visitors to discover the museum and its art with enthusiasm, overcoming any reluctance by sending them throughout the galleries in search of clues to solve the mystery. Another way to get the kids involved while you enjoy works from Warhol to Rembrandt is through the DIA's interactive computer programs. Two art games and a history time line allow young people and older folks alike to correlate art from, say, the same time period in Egypt, as art from Asia and North America.

The bronze, 30-inch-tall donkey, by German artist Renee Sintenis, welcomes kids to climb, hang, and otherwise play all over it till their energy's spent. The most popular exhibit for kids, however, is the display of ancient Egyptian art and artifacts. Included is a beautifully preserved, gilded, masked mummy. It is now in a display case with four jars once used—get this, kids—to store the mummy's internal organs.

In the recently renovated Great Hall, museum-goers can see up to a dozen suits of armor dating from the thirteenth to the eighteenth centuries, now lit by fiber optics to highlight the craftsmanship, while another case features swords, daggers, and other edged weapons.

 ## DETROIT SCIENCE CENTER (all ages)

5020 John R at Warren Avenue; (313) 577–8400. From I–75, exit at Warren and go west to Brush. Turn right, then go left. The center is open from 9:30 A.M. to 2:00 P.M. Monday through Friday, 10:30 A.M. to 5:00 P.M. Saturday, and 12:30 to 5:00 P.M. Sunday. Omnimax shows are presented hourly. Admission of $6.75 for adults and $4.75 for young people three through seventeen and seniors sixty and older includes the theater and all demonstrations. Admission to the theater only is $4.00 per person, and admission to the exhibits only is $3.00 for adults and $2.00 for children and seniors. Parking is available in the adjacent lot for $3.00. Web site: www.sciencedetroit.org.

After you finish exploring the Detroit Institute of Arts, walk behind 1 block on the DIA's south side and visit the colorful Detroit Science Center, which offers fun for everyone from toddlers on up. One of the highlights is taking a seat before the three-and-a-half-story-high Omnimax Theater screen, reached after traveling through a rainbow of neon colors on the 80-foot-long escalator tunnel to the lower level. Then, on the huge domed screen, lights dim as sixteen loudspeakers erupt, and you are taken on a seat-of-the-pants flight aboard the space shuttle, on a flight skimming over a canyon frothing with white water, on a 200 mph ride in an Indy racing car with Mario Andretti, or on some other spectacular film excursion. You'll leave awed but ready for the next adventure, just upstairs on the upper floor.

In late 1999, the Science Center announced a major expansion and renovation of the facility to be completed in May 2001. The museum will become even more interactive, fun, and educational for youngsters. As a result of construction, some science exhibits and floors may be closed throughout the period. Also because of the work, admission rates may vary due to fewer areas being open. Look for bigger and better when construction is completed.

 ## MUSEUM OF AFRICAN AMERICAN HISTORY (all ages)

315 East Warren Avenue, Detroit 48202, directly east of the Detroit Science Center; (313) 494–5800. Parking is adjacent. Admission is $5.00 for ages

thirteen and older, $3.00 for ages twelve and younger. Memberships available. Hours are 9:30 A.M. to 5:00 P.M. Tuesday through Sunday. During the holidays there's always a special presentation on Kwanza. Web site: www.detnews.com/ maah/.

This museum features some of the most extensive interactive exhibits of any museum in the nation. At a hands-on location, kids can learn by doing what it feels like to lift a thirteen-gallon bucket of water from a simulated 98-foot-deep well.

Detroit's African-American roots run deep, and visitors' introductory image will be the sight of a nearly full-scale replica slave ship. On its surface appear 2,500 names of ships that carried Africans across the Atlantic to the Americas as part of its core exhibit, "Of the People: The African American Experience." Children can push a button on a time line of video screens and learn about African life before the slave trade and how slaves were placed on the auction block if they survived the crossing. The exhibit traces the diverse history of African-Americans to the present day, including the space suit worn by Mae Jemison, the first African-American woman to fly on the space shuttle. She flew in 1992. Visitors will also learn about the Underground Railroad, the series of safe houses through which escaped slaves fled the South to freedom in the North before the Civil War. The network had many so-called stations, and one of its most active terminals was Detroit, where the refugees were transported across the Detroit River into Canada.

Other exhibits highlight the 1960s civil rights movement. Audio programs also include African-American and African music and its connection with present American music, folktales, opera and symphonic works, and, of course, the Detroit Motown Sound. An African-American history time line contains 264 panels that chronicle African-American history from 1310 through 1995.

DETROIT CHILDREN'S MUSEUM (ages 5–10)

67 East Kirby, Detroit 48202, across the street from the Detroit Institute of Arts' north wing and a block away from the Museum of African-American Art and the Detroit Science Center; (313) 873–8100. Run by the city's public schools, the museum is Free *and open to the public from 1:00 to 4:00 P.M. Monday through Friday, 9:00 A.M. to 4:00 P.M. Saturday October through May only, and noon to 4:00 P.M. daily late June through early August. There are special activities just for kids during events such as the Freedom Festival in June.*

This museum is mainly keyed to allow the younger crowd to take their imaginations to the limit. A visit here is a good accompaniment either before or after exploring the Detroit Science Center, a block away. On Saturday there are two **Free** shows in the museum's thirty-two-seat planetarium that are geared to children and parents who may not be familiar with the night sky. The museum is one of the focal points during Detroit's annual Freedom Festival Children's Day. Kids can try their hand at painting on easels set up outside, along with face painting, creating silk-screened T-shirts, and other activities.

Permanent exhibits, like a full-size example of a Bengal tiger, teach children about animals, while others focus on cultures as varied as those of Alaska's Inuit and the peoples of Indonesia and Africa. Toddlers will find plenty of fun in the Children's Discovery Room, where they can test their skills with blocks and other toys that also teach. Be sure to ask for the treasure hunt game (similar to the DIA's) that takes kids on a discovery safari through the building. In the museum's art gallery, the work of some of Detroit's best artists are on display in a collage depicting the city's African-American heritage since the 1950s, and its industrial heritage is represented by the museum mascot—a horse fashioned from 900 pounds of chrome auto bumpers on the museum's front lawn.

LAFAYETTE AND AMERICAN CONEY ISLANDS

Lafayette Coney Island, 118 West Lafayette, Detroit 48226 (313–964–8198); American Coney Island, 115 Michigan Avenue, Detroit 48226 (313–961–7758). From the southbound Lodge Freeway (Michigan 10), exit at Howard Street, continue 1 block, and turn left onto Lafayette. The restaurants are 3 blocks apart, 1 block east of the U.S. courthouse. They're open twenty-four hours a day, every day. $

Home of the "Coney Island dog," which has been imitated by others, but if you're in the Motor City, the Lafayette and American Coney Islands are the places to try 'em. Since 1918 both eateries have served millions of tube steaks in a bun, slathered in a meaty chili that's just spicy enough, then layered with onions and topped with mustard that's deftly applied by the grill man with a wooden spoon. It's been that way for generations of Detroiters who've pounded down Coneys accompanied by orange soda or other pop.

Grab a seat and order a chili dog or two accompanied by a bowl of chili, or try something completely different: a Coney burger, loose ground beef in a bun and again, smothered in chili and onions. Then listen as the waiter sings out the song of the Coney: "Six on four, one no onions, four Cokes." Translation: two plates with two Coneys on each and two with one each. And these are real skin-on franks that pop when you bite into them. Those brave enough to risk a be-chilied shirt pick them up, while the more practical and the suit-and-tie crowd cut them with a fork.

Holiday Traditions and Other Pastimes

AMERICA'S THANKSGIVING DAY PARADE (all ages)

Annually each Thanksgiving Day starting around 9:00 A.M., running along Woodward Avenue from the Cultural Center to Jefferson downtown; (313) 923–8259, or for shuttle transportation information, call (888) d–dotbus. For the best view, buy a ticket for a grandstand seat for about $15. Or get there early—by 6:00 A.M.—to watch free *at streetside.*

It may be officially called America's Thanksgiving Parade, but veteran Detroiters still remember it as the Hudson's Parade, named for the downtown department store that once sponsored the entire event. The store may have moved to the suburbs, but for many Detroiters and surburbanites, this is *the* parade.

Televised nationwide, the nearly seventy-year-old event signals the traditional kickoff to the holidays. The excitement of floats, marching bands, and balloons amid the city skyscrapers on a crisp November morning—and finally, the sight every child waits for, Santa's sleigh—is all here. The fun starts at 9:15 A.M. at Woodward and Mack, near the Cultural Center. The parade then heads downtown on Woodward, to Hart Plaza at Jefferson Avenue.

Detroit's Rising Star: Rivertown District The district is just east of the Renaissance Center, south of Jefferson, along Atwater between Rivard and Joseph Campau. From Jefferson, turn south at Rivard, and go east.

This is an area unique to the city—a former industrial area that is coming back as a chic entertainment district. Pubs, microbreweries, restaurants, and more are sprinkled throughout the area, and especially at the ends, along Orleans, Riopelle, Rivard and Joseph Campau, the location of Stroh River Place. Now there's Foxtown, Greektown, Mexicantown, the Warehouse District. These clusters of new businesses and entertainment popping up around the city only give more hope to an eventual linking of these separate entities to bring downtown back to its former grandeur. Count Detroit out, and you're making a big mistake.

INDOOR AMUSEMENT PARK (all ages)

In conjunction with the holiday festivities, at Cobo Center, Detroit 48226, Thanksgiving Day through mid-December; (313) 923–8259. Admission is Free, *but amusement ride tickets are sold separately. You can purchase an all-day pass for around $14.00. Discount coupons worth $4.00 are available at any Detroit mini–city hall location, and proceeds go toward supporting the parade.*

Sponsored as a fund-raiser for the Thanksgiving parade, this is a chance for kids to visit Santa and Mrs. Claus and to romp in an indoor amusement park with carousels and other rides you'd expect to find here only in summer.

 MOTOWN HISTORICAL MUSEUM (all ages)

2648 West Grand Boulevard, Detroit 48208, on the south side of the road; (313) 875–2264. Admission is $6.00 for adults and $3.00 for children age twelve and younger. From the Lodge Freeway (Michigan 10), exit at the Milwaukee/West Grand Boulevard exit and head west on Grand Boulevard.

Want a museum with a different beat? Check out one of Michael Jackson's famed sequined gloves and the cramped studio where the likes of Diana Ross, the Temptations, Marvin Gaye, the Four Tops, and Stevie Wonder put Detroit on the world's music map. In two side-by-side homes, composer and producer Berry Gordy lived and produced hits for those and scores of other performers from Detroit's neighborhoods who went on to recording glory in the studios he named "Hitsville, USA." With Motown hits playing in the background, guided, handicapped-accessible tours lead past the gift shop and other rooms where the raw talent Gordy discovered was refined to the point that it eventually was performed in front of heads of state worldwide.

 COMERICA PARK (all ages)

2100 Woodward Avenue, Detroit 48201; (313) 962–4000. From Lodge Freeway, take it downtown to Woodward, and turn north. Go about 1½ miles to the park. There is parking around the new ball park. Web site: www.detroittigers.com.

From opening day in early April to the last game in the fall, the 40,000-seat stadium is a magical place where the smells of steamed hot dogs and peanuts mix with the crack of the bat and the roar—or boos—of the crowd.

Comerica Park debuted in April 2000, a brand-spanking-new replacement for the old Tiger Stadium, which still stands along Michigan Avenue to the west. This is a cozy, state-of-the-art park with a scoreboard that promises to light the sky when the home runs fly. Home base looks out toward Detroit's skyline, and passersby can even catch a glimpse of the game from outside.

Seats range from the venerable bleachers to expensive corporate sky-boxes and even to special seats for die-hard Tiger fans who will pay extra to be in those spots. In the plaza outside, there's even a Ferris wheel and carousel and several restaurant choices. The Tigers beefed up the team but haven't forgotten the kids inside, either. Watch for the special promotional days when youngsters get free Tigers gear ranging from hats and beach towels to gloves and backpacks.

Paws, the Tiger mascot, is usually found roaming the plaza before the game and heads into the stands during play to cheer on or cheer up the crowd, depending on who's winning.

And, of course, everybody joins in singing "Take Me Out to the Ball Game" during the seventh-inning stretch. The Tigers were at the city's Old Ball Park since the early twentieth century. Look for them to be here for a long, long time, too.

New Lions Stadium

You watched—or heard about it—as the new Tiger Stadium, officially named Comerica Park, rose from the ashes of a rebounding downtown Detroit. Now, watch out, NFL. The new Detroit Lions stadium, already named Ford Field for its Ford Motor Company family owners, is next. The domed facility is expected to host up to 60,000 fanatical fans of the Silver Rush when the Lions leave the Pontiac Silverdome to return to downtown, where they last won the NFL championship nearly fifty years ago. They've at last come close, finishing high enough to at least gain a first round in the playoffs for several years, but have never grabbed the ring yet. All fans can do is watch the edifice rise and hope.

REDFORD THEATER (all ages)

17360 Lahser Road, between Grand River Avenue and Seven Mile Road; (313) 537–2560. To reach it, exit the Southfield Freeway (Michigan 39) at Grand River and turn west to Lahser, then head north. Movie tickets are a steal at just $3.00 each; occasional special shows range from $8.00 to $15.00. Theater tours also are available. Call for a recorded schedule, or watch the Detroit News *or the* Free Press *movie guides.*

It's the amazement at hearing the throaty blasts of a nearly seventy-year-old theater organ introducing a Laurel-and-Hardy comedy classic.

It's watching Humphrey Bogart in *Casablanca* or *The African Queen* on the big screen, or the spectacle of *Lawrence of Arabia*. It's blithely "nyucking" along with the crowd at the antics of the Three Stooges. Enjoying classic movies in an old-time, neighborhood theater setting is a practice that's still alive and well here. The Redford caters to families with its series of ageless flicks.

Before each feature, the kids will get a kick out of encountering something they—and possibly you—have never experienced: a thirty-minute concert performed on the giant 800-pipe, ten-rank Barton Golden Voice theater organ that can imitate everything from a tuba to a classical orchestra.

Michigan State Fair (all ages)

Taking place annually the last week of August and ending on Labor Day, the fair at the State Fairgrounds at Woodward and Eight Mile Road on the city's northern border (313–369–8250) is one of the nation's oldest and has recently undergone a face-lift to upgrade facilities and to make it more family-friendly. Admission is $9.00 for adults, $2.00 for ages eleven and younger, Free for ages two and younger. Most concerts are Free, although special front-row reserved seating is available for special concerts for about $10.00 per person. Hours are 10:00 A.M. to 10:00 P.M. daily, although the midway stays open until midnight. Visit the birthing area, where kids can see baby farm animals from chicks to larger critters get their first glimpse of the world. There are contests for the best livestock and even home-brewed and microbrewed beers. Midway rides and food from corn dogs to those flat, sugar-coated fried dough pieces called elephant ears are fare of the day here. A highlight of the fair is the Free concerts by nationally known groups from rock to gospel at the outdoor bandshell.

JOE LOUIS ARENA (all ages)

Just west of Woodward and Jefferson Avenues, Detroit 48226, along the Detroit River; (313) 983–6606. With its imposing figure of the Brown Bomber in classic boxing stance in its lobby, the arena plays host to the NHL Detroit Redwings hockey team from fall through late spring.

RENAISSANCE CENTER (all ages)

On Jefferson Avenue, Detroit 48243, just east of Woodward and adjacent to Hart Plaza; (313) 568–5600.

The dream of Henry Ford II, who helped push construction of these five glass towers, the Ren Cen's office towers have ironically been taken over by General Motors. GM plans to make its shops and multiscreen theater more user-friendly by eventually tearing down the imposing berm that some say symbolized a separation of sorts between the Ren Cen and the city. Also planned are a new garden atrium on the river side of the Ren Cen with more restaurants and shops, along with walking and bike paths along the river. In the middle is the seventy-story Westin Hotel, which overlooks the river and the city. A common complaint ever since the complex opened is that it's hard to find your way around. GM hopes to improve that.

GREEKTOWN (all ages)
On downtown's near east side, between Beaubien and St. Antoine, about 2 blocks north of Jefferson Avenue; (313) 202–1800. Watch for signs to the area along Jefferson just east of Woodward and across from the Renaissance Center.

Learn the meaning of "Ooopa!" here when you order a flaming cheese appetizer at any of several Greek restaurants in this lively downtown entertainment district. There's shopping for Greek treats like baklava in neighborhood stores, as well as other specialty shops.

DIAMOND JACK'S RIVER TOURS (all ages)
Tours depart Hart Plaza at Woodward and Jefferson downtown, and St. Aubin Park Marina, east of the Renaissance Center at the end of St. Aubin, Detroit 48214; (313) 843–7676. Take Jefferson past Beaubien and turn right on St. Aubin. Tours begin May 30 through August 31 and leave Tuesday through Sunday at 1:00 and 3:30 P.M. from Hart Plaza and fifteen minutes later from St. Aubin Park Marina. Tickets are $12.00 for adults, $11.00 for seniors, and $9.00 for ages six to sixteen. Children under six ride Free. Web site: www.diamondjack.com.

Two-hour tours aboard the *Diamond Jack* take in the history, both past and present, of the city and its Canadian neighbor, Windsor. Among the sites, the boat will pass under the Belle Isle Bridge and along the Windsor waterfront before turning at the Ambassador Bridge, just upstream of the mills that made Detroit the Arsenal of Democracy, Historic Fort Wayne, and the Detroit skyline, before returning.

PEOPLE MOVER AND TROLLEY (all ages)
The People Mover is an automated elevated monorail that links downtown. In fact, a ride's a good way to get acquainted with various parts

of the area, from the entertainment and restaurants of Greektown to a trip through the vast exhibit space of Cobo Center. Fare is 50 cents; kids five and younger ride **Free**.

The trolley, a restored antique red electric street car, runs from May through November along Washington Boulevard, past Cobo Center. For more information on these modes of transportation, call (313) 962-7245.

Where to Eat

Carl's Chop House. *3020 Grand River Avenue, Detroit 48216, just off the Lodge Freeway downtown; (313) 833–0700. Watch for the sign from the southbound Lodge at the Grand River exit. Open Monday through Thursday 11:30 A.M. to 11:00 P.M., Friday 11:30 A.M. to 11:00 P.M., Saturday 11:30 A.M. to midnight, and Sunday 10:30 A.M. to 10:00 P.M.* A classic steak house known for its huge portions of succulent prime rib, steaks, and lobster. If you savor beef, this is the place. It can be noisy and crowded evenings and during game nights, so a good time with kids is often Sunday afternoon. $$$

Elwood Bar & Grill. *At the corner of Adams and Brush downtown, Detroit 48201; (313) 961–7485.* "Bar" may be in its name, but the Elwood is suitable for all family members. Booths and tables are available. City landmarks don't have to be big. A shining example of art deco in Detroit, the Elwood was moved, like the Gem Theater, by owner-developer Chuck Forbes, to make room for new stadiums for the Detroit Tigers and Lions. Its claims to fame include not only its great burgers, but also its flashy architecture. And lucky for it, it'll be right near both stadiums. Call for current hours. $$

Evie's Tamales. *3454 Bagley in Mexicantown, Detroit 48216; (313) 843–5056. Open Monday through Saturday 8:00 A.M. to 6:00 P.M. and Sunday 8:00 A.M. to 3:00 P.M.* Serves inexpensive authentic Mexican lunch and dinner items daily. $

Fishbone's Rhythm Kitchen Cafe. *400 Monroe, Detroit 48226, at the corner of Brush; (313) 965–4600. Open Sunday through Thursday 6:30 A.M. to midnight and Friday and Saturday 6:30 to 2:00 A.M. No one under twenty-one allowed after 10:00 P.M. Friday and Saturday.* A bit of New Orleans in the Motor City, right down to the alligator tail and crawfish appetizers, hot sauces, and that bread pudding. Fun and noisy for breakfast, lunch, or dinner. Children's menu available, too. $$$

Majestic Cafe. *4130 Woodward, Detroit 48201; (313) 833–0120. Open Monday through Friday 11:00 to 2:00 A.M., Saturday 4:30 P.M. to 2:00 A.M., and Sunday 11:30 to 2:00 A.M.* Join Wayne State University students popping in for a bite from campus a few blocks north. Great varied menu from Southwest to Middle East. The music theater adjacent often hosts bands and is one of the last places the late blues great Luther Allison played. $$

Rhinoceros Club. *265 Riopelle, Detroit 48207, at Franklin, east of the Renaissance Center; (313) 259–2208. Open Friday and Sunday 11:00 A.M. to 11:00 P.M.; Monday, Wednesday; Thursday, and Saturday 5:00 to 11:00 P.M.; closed Tuesday.* Sunday brunch and a children's menu featuring pasta to some Cajun-style dishes. $$

Sinbad's. *Upper Detroit River at East Jefferson and Marquette, Detroit 48214; (313) 822–8000. Open Monday through Sunday 11:00 to 1:00 A.M.* Watch for the sign for the Roostertail and turn south from Jefferson onto Marquette and follow it to 100 St. Clair. Watch the boaters come and go in summer, or enjoy the river's quiet other times for lunch or dinner and Sunday brunch. Children's menu. Specializes in steak and seafood. $$$

Traffic Jam and Snug. *511 West Canfield, Detroit 48212, at Second; (313) 831–9470. Open Monday 11:30 A.M. to 3:00 P.M., Tuesday and Wednesday 11:30 A.M. to 9:00 P.M., Thursday 11:30 A.M. to 11:30 P.M., Friday 11:30 A.M. to midnight, and Saturday 5:00 P.M. to midnight.* From the Lodge freeway, exit at Warren and head east to Second, then south to Canfield. Parking is across the street. Dine beneath the barnlike timbers while rubbing elbows with professors from nearby Wayne State University. Take home bread baked on premises and enjoy dishes from traditional to vegetarian. Children's menu, too. $$

Union Street. *4145 Woodward, Detroit 48201, just south of the Wayne State University campus; (313) 831–3965. Open Monday through Friday 11:30 A.M. to midnight, and Saturday 5:00 P.M. to 1:00 A.M.* In a wonderful old building with a pressed tin ceiling, enjoy a large choice of casual dining options for lunch or dinner, from sandwiches to seafood and pasta. Large imported beer list, too. $$

Xochimilco. *3409 Bagley, Detroit 48216, in Mexicantown; (313) 843–0179. Open 11:00 to 2:00 A.M. daily.* You can't go wrong with any of the restaurants in this part of town if you enjoy food from south of the border. This restaurant, in the heart of Mexicantown, has great authentic Mexican food. $$

Where to Stay

Downtown Detroit's array of hotels and motels is about to get a giant boost in choice with the construction of lavish new accommodations connected with downtown casinos opening in the next two to three years. Here's a glimpse of what's available now.

Atheneum Suite Hotel and Conference Center. *1000 Brush and Lafayette, Detroit 48226, in the Greektown entertainment district; (313) 962–2323.* This property has 174 suite-style rooms, exercise facilities, and dining. Also adjacent to Fishbone's and other Greektown restaurants. $$$$

Blanche House Inn. *506 Parkview Drive, Detroit 48124; (313) 822–7090.* From the I-75/Jefferson Avenue exit, head east on Jefferson about 3½ miles, then south on Parkview. Possibly Detroit's only B&B with six rooms in a 1905 former mansion a block from the river. $$$

Courtyard by Marriott. *333 East Jefferson, Detroit 48226; (313) 222–7700.* Located across from and connected via walkway to the Renaissance Center in the Millender Center, this hotel has 255 rooms with indoor pool and exercise area, racquet and tennis courts. It's also a few blocks south of Greektown. A modern, very nice hotel for the money. $$$

Crowne Plaza Pontchartrain Hotel. *2 Washington Boulevard, Detroit 48226, at Jefferson Avenue, near Cobo Center; (313) 965–0200.* This property has 437 rooms, outdoor pool open in summer, exercise room, and restaurant. $$$

Holiday Inn Fairlane/Dearborn. *Ford Road and the Southfield Freeway (Michigan 39), Detroit 48228; (313) 336–3340.* Located much closer to Dearborn attractions than downtown's but still in the Detroit city limits, this property has 347 rooms, a large atrium lobby, indoor and outdoor pools, and an exercise room. Kids age eleven and under eat **Free**, and under nineteen stay **Free**, with dining room and sports bar and other restaurants adjacent. **Free** shuttles to Greenfield Village and Henry Ford Museum. $$$

Hotel St. Regis. *3071 West Grand Boulevard at Cass, Detroit 48202; (313) 873–3000.* Located in the New Center area near the General Motors Building and Fisher Theater, the St. Regis has 232 rooms with exercise room. An elegant building with a good restaurant. Near New Center restaurants, too. $$$

River Place. *1000 River Place, Detroit 48207; (313) 259–9500.* From downtown, head east on Jefferson about 1½ miles and turn south on McDougall. The property has 108 rooms on the Detroit River with a good restaurant and others nearby. $$

Shorecrest Motor Inn. *1316 East Jefferson, Detroit 48207; (313) 568–3000.* A short walk east of the Renaissance Center, this small, well-kept property on the outskirts of the Rivertown district has fifty-four rooms and a restaurant. $$

For More Information

Metro Detroit Convention and Visitors Bureau, *100 Renaissance Center, Suite 1950, Detroit 48243; (800) 338–7648. Web site: www.visitdetroit.com.*

Northwest and Northern Detroit Suburbs

This region of southeastern Michigan skirts metropolitan Detroit's northern suburbs, taking in parts of western Livingston, eastern Wayne, and Oakland, Macomb, and St. Clair Counties, at the base of Michigan's Thumb. In summer this is the region's "concert central," home of outdoor venues that bring in some of music's greatest stars. In contrast, though, it also offers visits to the baronial mansions of auto pioneers as well as beautiful beaches and parks that entertain families year-round.

Farmington Hills

This northwest Detroit suburb of chic office buildings and clusters of shops also has an attraction unique to Michigan and perhaps the region.

MARVIN'S MARVELOUS MECHANICAL MUSEUM (all ages)
31005 Orchard Lake Road, Farmington Hills 48334; (248) 626–5020. To reach it, take Orchard Lake Road north from I–696. Turn left into the Hunter's Square shopping center at 14 Mile Road. Hours are 10:00 A.M. to 10:00 P.M. Monday through Thursday, 10:00 A.M. to 11:00 P.M. Friday and Saturday, and 11:00 A.M. to 9:00 P.M. Sunday. Free *admission. Web site: www.marvin3m.com.*

It's a great name for one of the most interesting and peculiar collections of things that whir, click, toot, and tick that you'll ever see. Started by Marvin Yagoda, a pharmacist with a definite fascination for things mechanical, the museum is filled with seemingly every coin-operated nickelodeon or other carnival coin-swallowing machine that's ever been made. See what your future holds according to Madame Zelda, a 1917 fortune-telling machine, or bat against the baseball players of yesteryear

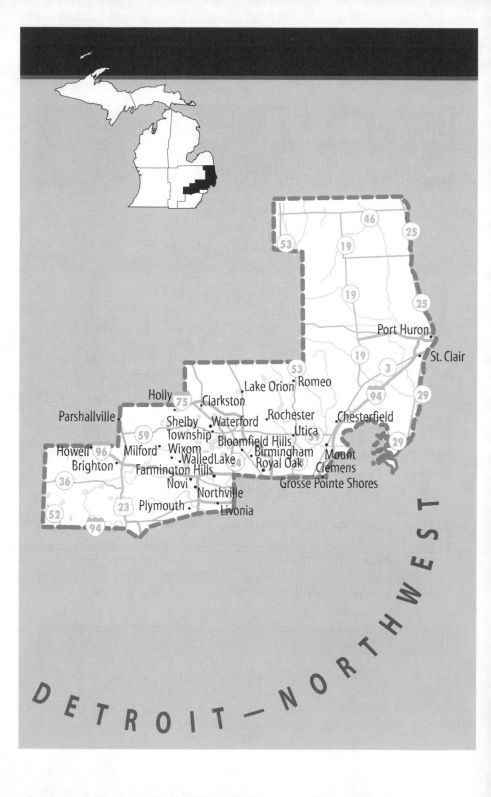

Port Huron
St. Clair
Lake Orion Romeo
Holly Clarkston
Parshallville Rochester Chesterfield
Shelby Waterford Utica
Township Bloomfield Hills
Howell Milford Wixom Birmingham Mount
Brighton WalledLake Royal Oak Clemens
Farmington Hills
Novi Grosse Pointe Shores
Northville
Plymouth Livonia

D E T R O I T — N O R T H W E S T

in a 1937 World Series game. There's even a forty-seven piece nickelodeon band and a "mechanical brain."

Admission is ꟻree, but Yagoda's no fool. You'll have to drop a quarter into most devices to operate them.

Where to Eat

Kerby's Koney Island. *21200 North Haggerty Road, at I–275 and Eight Mile, Northville 48167; (248) 449–7088.* One of a number of coney dispensers modeled after those in downtown Detroit but with larger menus. Great dogs and loose burgers and Greek salads for lunch or dinner. $

Max and Erma's. *30125 Orchard Lake Road, Farmington Hills 48334; (248) 855–0990.* Good selection of family fare like burgers, pasta, salads, and steaks. Children's menu. $–$$$

Where to Stay

Best Western Executive Hotel and Suites. *31525 West Twelve Mile Road, just north of I–696 and Orchard Lake Road, Farmington Hills 48334; (248) 553–0000.* Modern hotel with easy access to freeway has indoor pool and whirlpool, and restaurant. Several other restaurants adjacent. $$$

Comfort Inn Farmington Hills. *30715 Twelve Mile Road, Farmington Hills 48334, at the I–696/Orchard Lake Road exit; (248) 471–9220.* This hotel has 135 rooms, continental breakfast, and in-room movies. Restaurants nearby. $$

Radisson Suite Hotel. *37529 Grand River Avenue, Farmington Hills 48335, at I–96 and I–275; (248) 477–7800.* Take the Grand River exit off I-96. This hotel has 137 rooms, indoor pool, exercise area, and dining room. $$$

Red Roof Inn—Farmington Hills. *24300 Sinacola Court, Farmington Hills 48335; (248) 478–8640.* From I-96, take the Grand River exit. This property has 108 rooms. Coffee and papers available in the lobby. Restaurant nearby. Typical Red Roof, comfortable. Children under eighteen stay ꟻree. $$

Plymouth

Located on Wayne County's western borders, the city may have undergone lots of changes since its farmlands became expensive subdivisions, but it works hard to live up to its founders, who named it for the Massachusetts town of their ancestors. Quaint shops cluster around a great downtown park. A second, smaller downtown, called the Old Village, is just north of the main shopping district.

PLYMOUTH INTERNATIONAL ICE SCULPTURE SPECTACULAR (all ages)

Held annually in mid-January downtown; (734) 459–9157. To reach Plymouth, follow I–275 to Ann Arbor Road, then turn west and go about 1½ miles. Turn north on Main Street, find a parking spot, and follow the crowds downtown. Everything's **Free** *and open twenty-four hours a day until the festival closes. Web site: www.oeonline.com/plymouthice.*

Imitated but never duplicated, the festival draws more than 500,000 persons to the streets of this normally placid colonial downtown to ogle hundreds of sculptures carved from 400-pound blocks of ice. The event is one of the best of its kind, as carvers come to chip, chop, smooth, grind, and buff their way through town as they form more than 250 works of fleeting, crystalline art from more than 400,000 pounds of the stuff.

Away for the Weekend

Enjoy a leisurely early American weekend getaway in the cities of Plymouth and Northville. Great shopping, unique downtowns—with a large city park in Plymouth and cute shops lining the streets in Northville—cozy little restaurants, and movie theaters, plus bed and breakfasts and hotels make them a great place to relax.

Adjacent to the main display, a special exhibit for kids usually includes up to twenty fantasy ice sculptures.

PLYMOUTH ORCHARDS AND CIDER MILL (all ages)

10865 Warren Road; (734) 455–2290. West of the city in the rolling farmland. From the Plymouth-Canton area, take Ford Road west to Ridge Road and follow the signs. Open during harvest season, usually September through early November. **Free** *admission.*

Treat the family to a hayride, let the kids pet farm animals from horses to turkeys, pick apples from dwarf trees, and end the outing by sipping some freshly squeezed cider with a sugar-cinnamon doughnut or two. For the perfect sugar overload, top it off with a caramel apple. It's a fall tradition. The petting zoo is **Free**, as are trips into the orchards, but picking price varies by the season, as does the price for cider, sold in quarts, half gallons and gallons, and by the cup. Picnic-table seating is inside.

Where to Eat

Cafe Bon Homme. *844 Penniman, Plymouth 48170, west of Main, downtown; (734) 453–6260.* Consistently voted one of the region's best restaurants for French-style cooking. Inappropriate for very young children. $$$$

Dinersty. *447 Forest, Plymouth 48170, in the former Cloverdale Dairy; (734) 459–3332.* Inexpensive Chinese food for lunch and dinner. $$

Jack Dunleavy's Grill. *340 North Main, Plymouth 48170, just north of the railroad tracks; (734) 455–3700.* Upscale dining in this former part of a BB gun factory. Prime rib, seafood, and other dishes please the palate here. Children's menu available upon request. $$$

Soda Jerk. *1456 Sheldon Road, Plymouth 48170, in the strip mall at the corner of Ann Arbor Road; (734) 459–6182.* Inexpensive fare from hot dogs or burgers in a soda shop decorated with 1950s-style memorabilia. Sundaes and sodas. Good spot for a quick bite for lunch or dinner. $

Station 885. *885 Starkweather, Plymouth 48170, in the Old Village area of shops; (734) 459–0885.* Take Main Street north from downtown and turn north on Starkweather. Trains rumble by this replica of the old city passenger station as you enjoy your lunch or dinner. Besides steaks and seafood, the house specialty is the Veal Station 885, sautéed veal with garlic olives and shrimp, for $18.95. There's a children's menu and Sunday brunch, too. $$$–$$$$

Uncle Frank's Chicagos and Coneys. *In the Westchester Square Mall at 550 Forest, Plymouth 48170, downtown; (734) 455–4141.* This is about as kid-friendly as you can get, and this is the only place around where you can sink into a true Chicago-style hot dog, an all-beef weenie, or fourteen other types, from Italian to turkey and even tofu. Nothing's more than $5.00. $

Where to Stay

Plymouth Hilton Garden Inn. *14600 Sheldon Road, Plymouth 48170; (734) 420–0001.* One hundred fifty-seven rooms with free movies, restaurant, indoor pool, and exercise room. Kids under eighteen stay free in parents' room. $$$

Quality Inn. *40455 Ann Arbor Road, Plymouth 48170, just off I–275; (734) 455–8100.* This property has 123 rooms and an outdoor pool. Several restaurants are nearby. $$

For More Information

Plymouth Chamber of Commerce, *386 South Main Street, Plymouth 48170;* *(734) 453–1540. Web site: www. plymouthchamber.org.*

Bill's Favorite Events

in Northwest and Nothern Detroit Suburbs

- **Plymouth Ice Sculpture Spectacular** (January), downtown Plymouth, (734) 459-9157

- **Winter Craft Show** (February), Metro Beach Metropark, (810) 658-0440

- **Camper and RV Show** (February), Novi Expo Center, Novi, (517) 349-8881

- **Greater Detroit Sportfishing Expo** (March), Palace of Auburn Hills, directly off I-75, between Pontiac and Clarkston, (216) 529-1300

- **Spring Festival** (April), Kensington Metropark, Milford, (810) 685-1561

- **Art in the Park** (July), Kellogg Park in downtown Plymouth, (734) 454-1540

- **Blue Water Festival** (July), Port Huron, (810) 987-8687 or (800) 852-2828

- **Art in the Park** (July), Memorial Park in Royal Oak, (248) 544-6680

- **World's Second Largest Garage Sale and Antique Show** (July), Royal Oak, (248) 547-4000

- **Armada Fair** (August), Armada, (810) 784-5488

- **Howell Melon Festival** (August), downtown Howell, (517) 548-1795

- **Michigan Renaissance Festival** (August), Holly, (800) 601-4848

- **Victorian Festival and Art Market** (September), downtown Northville, (248) 349-7640

- **Plymouth Fall Festival** (September), downtown Plymouth, (734) 453-1540

- **Michigan Peach Festival** (September), downtown Romeo, (810) 752-6082

- **Chili Cook-Off** (October), Kellogg Park in downtown Plymouth, (734) 453-1540

- **Fantasy Lights Parade** (November), downtown Howell, (517) 546-3920

- **Rochester Community Christmas Parade** (December), (248) 651-6700

- **Christmas Walk** (December), downtown Northville, (248) 349-7640

Northville

Plymouth's twin sister to the north, built on a hill and settled in the 1830s, is now known for its compact old downtown's quaint shops and fine homes, some of which are now restaurants, and some unique attractions. To find Northville, exit I–275 at Eight Mile Road and head west; turn south at Center Street.

MARQUIS THEATER (ages 3 and up)

135 East Main Street, Northville 48167; (248) 349–8110. Tickets are $7.50.

Got a budding child actor in the house? This might be his or her chance to break into the big time. Since 1983, in a facility nearly a century old in quaint downtown Northville, the unique theater has been producing drama that makes stars out of children.

Owner-producer Inge Zayti began the Marquis featuring adult actors but later found her niche introducing children to the stage. In addition to spending the summer working with would-be actors, she presents children-oriented plays from March through December. Recent performances have included *The Princess and the Pea, Peter Pan,* and *Heidi,* all performed by children between eight and eighteen. In summer Zayti cultivates new talent by offering a two-week day camp that features acting and singing activities for kids who want to give the bright lights a whirl. She's assisted by five instructors. Zayti also plans to open a live-in children's summer theater camp.

MILL RACE HISTORICAL VILLAGE (all ages)

On Griswold south of Eight Mile Road, Northville 48167; (248) 348–1845. Exit I–275 at Eight Mile Road and go west to Griswold, then head south. Grounds are open year-round except when private functions are taking place. The buildings are open Sunday 1:00 to 4:00 P.M. from June through October. Informational signs outside give some of the history when the buildings are closed. Admission is
Free.

You can't miss the nine white clapboard homes and buildings of this replica community, created in 1972 on the site of a former gristmill. All structures except the gazebo looking over the branch of the Rouge River were moved here from various nearby locations. The New School Church, for example, was built in 1845. The Cady Inn was believed to have been a tavern and stagecoach stop, and possibly a station on the Underground Railroad for runaway slaves. Wash Oak School is one of the state's last surviving one-room schoolhouses, built in 1873. Another building was the waiting room at Newburgh and Eight Mile Roads for the Interurban, a rapid, electric mass transit rail line. Call for information on special events that often take place here.

MAYBURY STATE PARK (all ages)

On Eight Mile Road, Northville 48167, west of Beck road, west of Northville; (248) 349–8390. For this state park a motor-vehicle entry permit is required. Admission fee is $4.00 daily or $20.00 annually. Open 8:00 A.M. to dusk daily, year-round.

Michigan's first urban state park is 70 percent covered in forest, making it a wonderful spot to bring the family any time of year. Cross-country ski or hike in winter, horseback ride ($20 per hour weekends, $16 weekdays) in summer, and enjoy the colors of fall or the rebirth of spring. There are 6 miles of dirt hiking trails and 4 miles of paved bike trails, plus naturalist-led hikes and activities. Pamphlets help you teach youngsters to identify trees and plants along the way. There is no camping, however.

Also here is a turn-of-the-twentieth-century farm that features a children's petting area. In early October, there's a harvest festival, when guests can even try working the crops themselves.

HINES PARK (all ages)

To reach the park from downtown Northville, take Center south to Seven Mile Road and turn east, then veer to the right, and you're at the entrance. For park information call the Wayne County Parks, (734) 261–1990. Open year-round. **Free**. *Web site: www.waynecountyparks.com.*

This 16-mile-long park offers picnic areas, swings, slides, softball diamonds, and three artificially created lakes (unfortunately, they are not open for swimming). Since the passage of a new millage, the park is being dramatically improved. Farther east, Newburgh Lake was literally scraped clean of toxins in a multimillion-dollar demonstration project. It is now stocked with game fish. Rest-room facilities are being renovated as well. New facilities will include an in-line skating rink off Sheldon Road near Northville, plus another at the eastern end of the parkway.

From summer through fall, a portion of the park is closed to vehicles, and only bicycles and other nonmotorized vehicles are allowed during "Saturdays and Sundays in the Park." If you miss the weekend, try the recently completed bicycle trail, which covers the entire length of the park. Near Nankin Mills in Westland, summer activities include outdoor movies. The mill is being turned into a nature center with naturalist-led hikes and other activities planned, including bicycle rental. A canoe rental at Nankin Mills operates in summer.

In winter, sledding is available at Cass Benton and many other hills along the park when the snow allows, as is cross-country skiing.

Where to Eat

Genitti's Hole in the Wall. *108 East Main Street, Northville 48167; (248) 349–0522. Web site: www.genittis.com.* You can let the kids get a bit rowdy in this eatery, which began as a grocery. A hole was knocked out of one of the building's walls when the restaurant opened, hence the name. Expansions brought more and more for the seven-course Italian, please-pass-the-pasta family-style dinners that include antipasto, Italian sausage, chicken, pork, dessert, soup, and yes, pasta. Genitti's Little Theater features interactive performances where audience members get in on the act with a professional cast. Comedy acts and other kids' shows also are featured. All ages. $$$

Guernsey Farms Dairy. *21300 Novi Road, Northville 48167; (248) 349–1466.* From downtown Northville, go north on Center, then east on Eight Mile Road about ¼ mile to Novi Road and turn north. The dairy is about ½ mile on the right. What might be the best ice cream on the planet comes in fifty-five great flavors ranging from creme de Novi, a minty chocolate chip blend, to that kids' favorite, Superman, a blend of strawberry, marshmallow, and blue "fruity berry." Yum. There's a restaurant, too, that serves meals from breakfast on. $

MacKinnon's. *126 East Main Street, Northville 48167; (248) 348–1991.* Open for lunch and dinner and specializing in wild game dishes. It was at one time rated one of the country's top 250 restaurants by *Conde Nast Traveler.* It may be expensive, but treat your family. A children's menu is available upon request if the kids won't eat wild game. $$$$

Where to Stay

See Novi listing.

Livonia

One of the first towns to have been hit by the home-building boom of the 1940s and 1950s, Livonia is not about to forget its past, either.

JEEPERS! AT WONDERLAND MALL (all ages)
Corner of Plymouth Road and Middlebelt, Livonia 48150; (800) 533–7377. From I–96, exit at Middlebelt Road and turn south to Plymouth Road. Hours are 11:00 A.M. to 9:00 P.M. Monday through Thursday, 10:00 A.M. to 11:00 P.M. Friday and Saturday, and 11:00 A.M. to 8:00 P.M. Sunday. Ride for $9.99, $6.00 all day for youngsters under 36 inches. [Note: weekends and school days are same rates.] ℱ𝓻ℯℯ *admission for parents except for games and bumper cars. (There are two other locations in the Detroit area, the Macomb Mall, at Gratiot and Masonic in Roseville and Great Lakes Crossing in Auburn Hills along I–75.) Web site: www.jeepers.com.*

A year-round indoor amusement park located in one of the region's oldest shopping malls. Six rides, including bumper cars, are available along with video games and a climbing area to rid kids of excess energy. Tickets won can be redeemed for small prizes. Food is available, too. It's a perfect place to drop the kids with one parent while the other shops.

Where to Eat

City Limits. *38500 Ann Arbor Road, Livonia 48150, at exit 28 off I–275; (734) 454–0666.* A casual restaurant with a varied menu from seafood to ribs and a children's menu. $$$

Family Buggy Restaurant. *11502 Middlebelt Road, Livonia 48150, 1 mile south of the I–96 Middlebelt Road exit; (734) 427–8360.* Good selection of family fare in a turn-of-the-twentieth-century atmosphere. Children's menu. $$

Where to Stay

Embassy Suites Hotel. *19525 Victor Parkway, Livonia 48152; (734) 462–6000.* From I-275 take Seven Mile Road east, then head north on the parkway. This five-story hotel's 240 rooms feature microwaves and refrigerators. Dining room and indoor pool on premises. $$

Marriott Hotel–Livonia. *17100 Laurel Park Drive North, Livonia 48152; (734) 462–3100.* From I–275, take Six Mile Road east about a ¼ mile, then turn north into the Laurel Park shopping and business area. The hotel has 140 rooms, indoor pool and exercise facility, and restaurant. Adjacent to Laurel Park Mall. $$$

For More Information

Livonia Chamber of Commerce,
15401 Farmington Road, Livonia 48154;
(734) 427–2122.

Northville Chamber of Commerce,
195 South Main Street, Northville 48167;
(248) 349–7640. Web site: www.discsite.
com/northvillecoc.

Novi

This community is located at the intersection of Novi Road, Grand River Avenue as it makes its way from Detroit west, and I-96. Interesting name, eh? It's actually derived from Roman numerals. "No. VI" used to be stagecoach stop number six between Detroit and Lansing. The name was even further abbreviated to Novi, and the town is now one of the state's fastest-growing bedroom communities surrounding Detroit.

NOVI'S EXPO CENTER (all ages)

43700 Expo Center Drive, Novi 48375, at the southwest corner of the freeway interchange; (248) 348–5600. To get to the Novi Expo Center, leave I–96 at exit 162, Novi Road, go south about 1 block, look for the signs, and turn west. For Comic Con information, call (248) 350–2633 for show hours and exact dates.

This 204,000-square-foot, rectangular, one-floor center hosts exhibits throughout the year. Several events often occur simultaneously. There are plenty of rest-room facilities.

The annual Comic Con, or comic-book convention, is an event where father, mother, son, and daughter are on equal footing if they're like the rest of the crowd here: eager to pore over the more than 120,000 square feet of comics and memorabilia assembled in the center. It's just one of numerous family-oriented shows taking place here each month, from antique car auctions to Native American powwows and home improvement shows.

MOTORSPORTS MUSEUM AND HALL OF FAME OF AMERICA (all ages)

The hall of fame (248–349–7223) is located at the Novi Expo Center (see preceding entry). It is anticipating a move to larger headquarters in 2001. Hours are 10:00 A.M. to 5:00 P.M. daily except major holidays. Admission costs $3.00 for seniors and children younger than twelve and $5.00 for others. Web site: www.mshf.com.

69

This compact museum pays tribute to all motor sports. If you follow racing, a stop here is a must during any Detroit-area visit.

Challenge your companions to a run on the hall's four-lane slot car track, where scale model electric-motor stock cars held onto the course by a pin inside a slot (hence the name) race around a track; or climb into the coin-operated video simulation race car that pits you against another driver.

Inside the main exhibit area, changing displays include thirty-five racing vehicles, from current Indy-style cars, stock cars, and drag strip models to turn-of-the-twentieth-century vehicles, including motorcycles, powerboats, and a racing airplane.

Kids can have their picture taken in the driver's seat of a real Winston Cup stock car—a treat they'll remember for a long time. Four video screens play race footage throughout the display area, while a gift shop supplies everything from die-cast model cars to T-shirts and other wearables, collector cards, videos, and more.

Where to Eat

Don's of Traverse City. *48730 Grand River, Novi 48374, just east of Wixom Road, between Novi and Wixom; (248) 380–0333.* Music from the 1950s and 1960s, malts, and burgers rule here in this dinerlike incarnation of the original drive-in in Traverse City. $

Jonathan B Pub. *27302 Novi Road, Novi 48377; (248) 349–3950. Located inside the Twelve Oaks Mall.* Choose from fish and chips, burgers, and deli sandwiches in a publike setting. Children's menu. $$

Where to Stay

Doubletree Hotel Novi/Detroit. *27000 Sheraton Drive, Novi 48375, at I–96 and Novi Road, across from Twelve Oaks Mall; (248) 348–5000.* This property has 217 rooms, indoor and outdoor pools, exercise area, and restaurant. $$$

Novi Hilton. *21111 Haggerty Road, Novi 48375, at the northwest corner of I–275 and Eight Mile Road; (248)* 349–4000. You can't miss this white edifice rising seven stories. There are 239 rooms with indoor pool, exercise room, and dining. $$$

Wyndham Garden Hotel. *42100 Crescent Boulevard, Novi 48375, at the I–96 and Novi Road exit; (248)* 344–8800. This property has 148 rooms, indoor pool, and dining room. $$

NORTHWEST AND NORTHERN DETROIT SUBURBS

For More Information

Novi Chamber of Commerce,
43700 Expo Center Drive, Novi 48375;
(248) 349–3743.

Bill's Top Family
Adventures in Northwest
and Northern Detroit Suburbs

- **Motorsports Hall of Fame of America, Novi.** Speed demons can get their fill of track history. *Note:* The museum is scheduled to relocate in 2001.

- **Detroit Zoological Park, Royal Oak.** A great family institution open year-round.

- **Huron-Clinton Metroparks.** They're headquartered in Milford but are scattered all around the region. Kensington Metropark celebrated its fiftieth anniversary in 1998.

- **Skiing! At Mt. Brighton, near Brighton; Alpine Valley, Milford; Pine Knob, Clarkston; and Mt. Holly, Holly.** On any night, the family can have dinner and be skiing in an hour's time from nearly anywhere in metro Detroit.

- **Pine Knob and Meadow Brook Summer Music series.** Brings the best of recording entertainment to the city.

Walled Lake

This community was once the home of southeast Michigan's best amusement park. The lakeside park is long gone, but the homes built along this lake have given rise to the same suburban boom hitting other parts of the region.

MICHIGAN STAR CLIPPER TRAIN (ages 7 and up)

840 North Pontiac Trail, Walled Lake 48390; (248) 960–9440. From I–96, take Wixom Road north, then head east on Pontiac Trail about 4 miles. Web site: www.michiganstarclipper.com.

A three-hour, slow train trip with dinner aboard and served in 1950s dining cars, with American food a specialty.

Departure times are Tuesday through Thursday and Saturday at 7:00 P.M., Friday at 7:30 P.M., and Sunday at 5:00 P.M. Boarding time is an hour before departure. Cost is $69.50 per person, including meal and entertainment. Children under age twelve aren't recommended for the dinner train due to the length of the trip and the adult content of some of the shows. Be sure to ask about the show before booking your trip.

The Coe Rail Scenic Train, part of the same company, is a better bet for the wee ones since they don't have to sit for dinner. It takes one hour scenic trips from the same station on Sunday from April through October. Tickets cost $8.00 for adults, $7.00 for ages two through seventeen and for seniors. Kids one and under ride **Free**.

Where to Eat and Stay

See Novi listing.

Wixom

Wixom is another small farming community that is fast becoming a community of subdivisions. Prior to the boom, the biggest thing here for years was the Ford plant, which is still a top draw.

FORD MOTOR COMPANY WIXOM ASSEMBLY PLANT (ages 12 and up)

Just off I–94, north of the Wixom Road exit, Novi 48393; (248) 344–5358. Tours take place Friday only and as a result are in constant demand. If you plan to visit the area, write to reserve one of the forty-five spots at least six months in advance or, plant officials say, you'll probably miss your chance. Tours are **Free***. Children must be at least age twelve. To reserve your space, write Plant Tours, Ford Motor Company Wixom Assembly Plant, 28801 Wixom Road, Wixom, MI 48393–0001.*

Regardless of their age or gender, kids love things mechanical, and in metropolitan Detroit you're in one of the prime places to introduce them to the world of manufacturing by touring an auto plant. You'll see as steel, glass, and rubber become Lincoln Town Cars, Continentals, and LS models at the only factory in the country that produces them. The cars are put together in this far western Detroit suburb.

Usually lasting two hours, tours start with a fourteen-minute video previewing the steps it takes to build a car.

PROUD LAKE STATE RECREATION AREA (all ages)

From I–96, take Wixom Road north about 6 miles; (248) 685–2433. A state park vehicle permit is required for entry, $4.00 daily or $20.00 annually. Camping is extra.

Including a portion of the upper Huron River, the park contains more than 3,600 acres. There are more than 21 miles of trails offering warm-weather hiking. Part of the trails are open for cross-country skiing. There is a beach and swimming on a portion of the river, canoeing as well as camping and a boat launch area on Proud Lake. The area also is the site each spring of a release of large hatchery rainbow and brown trout available for catch and release until opening day of trout season (always the last Saturday of April).

ALPINE VALLEY SKI AREA (all ages)

Located on the north side of Michigan 59 at 6775 East Highland Road, White Lake 48383; (248) 887–4183. From I–96, take Milford Road exit north to Michigan 59 and head west. The ski school can accommodate children ages 6 and older. There isn't, however, child care available for younger children. Alpine Valley has cafeteria-style food.

Here is a Southeast Michigan ski area with a true "up north" feel due to its treed slopes along many of its twenty-five runs. Recent additions include a new chairlift, new rental equipment such as the "shaped" skis that helps all levels improve their skills. The facility offers snowboard rentals so skiers can try their hands—and whatever else hits the snow when they're learning—at it.

Where to Eat and Stay

See Novi listing.

Royal Oak

Let's jump east a few townships to this unique community. From I–696, take the Royal Oak exit and head north on Woodward to North Main into downtown. Lost in the doldrums of urban sprawl for decades, Royal Oak is suddenly one of southeast Michigan's hot spots to live and play. Restaurants line streets like Main and Washington, and in between are chichi shops next door to vintage clothing stores. While there are some concerns that all the upscale eateries are driving up rental prices and driving out longtime retailers, chances are that this, too, shall pass, and the city will continue to thrive with a good mix.

A new amenity is trolley service through town. Kids ride **Free** on Saturday when accompanied by an adult. Look for the red, white, and black trolley stop signs. There are eighteen locations throughout the city.

DETROIT ZOOLOGICAL PARK (all ages)

West Ten Mile Road and Woodward Avenue, Royal Oak 48068; (248) 398–0900. From I–75, take I–696 west and watch for the zoo directional signs near the Woodward Avenue exit. The park is open year-round, and hours vary by season. Admission is $7.50 for ages thirteen to sixty-one, $5.50 for seniors and children ages thirteen to eighteen with student i.d., and $4.50 for children ages two to twelve. Under two admitted **Free**. *Parking is $3.00. There's a picnic grove west of the Penguinarium, where grills are allowed, along with playscape playground for kids. Web site: www.detroitzoo.org.*

Wise planners placed this 125-acre park here in 1928, the first in the nation to use barless exhibits, place animals in settings as close to their natural environment as possible, and confine them using dry or water moats for an unobstructed view.

One of the zoo's most popular features isn't an animal at all. It's the Detroit Zoo Miniature Railroad. On weekends, the train transports nearly a half million passengers per year. It's 1¼ miles from the Main Station near the front gate, through a tunnel, to Africa Station, at the farthest corner of the park.

Other popular attractions include the bear dens; the Holden Museum of Living Reptiles and Amphibians; the Wilson Aviary Wing, a large free-flight building with a waterfall and hundreds of live plants that create a junglelike environment for more than thirty species of birds; the snow monkeys' hot-tub antics in winter; the Chimps of Harambee, where you can view chimps in forest, meadow, and rock-outcropping settings, all resembling their natural habitat; and the Penguinarium, with its underwater views of the flightless birds.

One of the newest major exhibits is an $8.2-million wildlife interpretive gallery that includes an aquarium of Pacific fish offering a diver's-eye view by minicams, a butterfly and hummingbird garden, and a theater. The National Amphibian Conservation Center was opened in 1999.

The zoo's also a great place for a family picnic in its large wooded grove. Adult roller chairs and "kid kabs" are available for rent year-round at the entrance near the gift shop. Cost is $5.00.

BLUEWATER CHAPTER OF THE NATIONAL RAILWAY HISTORICAL SOCIETY (ages 6 and up)

Since the society has no museum or other headquarters to visit, getting there, in this case, is all the fun. For information on all trips, call 248–541–1000. Web site: www.bluewaterNRHS.com.

Take your family back to the time when railroad passenger service was the only way to travel with a series of historic train trips offered by the National Railway Historical Society. You don't have to be a member of the society to join the thousands who have traveled with the group since 1983 in their own classic restored passenger cars behind vintage steam and diesel locomotives.

Trips range from a few hours to overnight journeys with stays and meals at charming hotels in some of the prettiest towns Michigan and surrounding areas have to offer. Many of the single-day trips include special events and tours. Some are multiday events to Canada, California, and New England.

Clay Invitational It takes place in mid-June downtown, centered along Washington Avenue, one of the streets closed to traffic for the two-day weekend event. The name is what it is: Michigan's only show featuring pottery and ceramics exclusively, from more than 130 artists. An accompanying Tastefest features nearly a dozen restaurants selling food, plus live music, children's art activities and more. Admission is Free.

Trips vary in price, depending on accommodations chosen and the particular excursion. Costs range from $34 for adults and $25 for children twelve and younger, to more than $100, depending on the trip you choose.

Where to Eat

If you like food, you've come to the right place. Royal Oak has exploded with restaurants of all types. Check out restaurant row on the parallel streets of Main and Washington.

Brazil Coffee House. *305 South Main, Royal Oak 48067; (248) 399–7200.* Wide variety of flavored coffees and herbal and black teas. Sandwiches and desserts also served. Open 11:00 A.M. to midnight Sunday through Thursday and 11:00 A.M. to 2:00 A.M. Friday and Saturday. $

Gayle's Chocolates. *417 South Washington, Royal Oak 48067; (248) 398–0001.* Did someone say chocolates? Hand-dipped masterpieces mixed with less-cholesterol-laden menu items mirror the mix of the city. Good selection of coffees, fresh juices, teas, sandwiches, and soups, too. $

Memphis Smoke. *100 South Main, Royal Oak 48067; (248) 543–4300.* With a name like that, ribs have got to be the featured meal, and they are. That, and turkey and others roasted over wood. Children's menu available for lunch and dinner. There's late-night blues entertainment, too. $$$

Mongolian Barbeque. *310 South Main, Royal Oak 48067; (248) 398–7755.* Open for lunch and dinner. Make your meal your way. Step along the offerings, scoop 'em on your plate, and take it to the huge wok, where cooks prepare your food. You can have it vegetarian, too. If you don't want to improvise, there are suggested combinations of goodies posted. $$$

Where to Stay

Sagamore Motor Lodge. *Woodward and Thirteen Mile Road, Royal Oak 48067; (248) 549–1600.* This property has seventy-nine rooms, many with kitchens. These are economy accommodations. $

See also the listing for Birmingham.

For More Information

Royal Oak Chamber of Commerce, *200 South Washington, Royal Oak 48067;* *(248) 547–4000 or (248) 544–EVENTS. Web site: www.virtualroyaloak.com.*

Bloomfield Hills

Consistently ranked among the top five or ten wealthiest communities in the nation, Bloomfield Hills has long been the retreat for auto barons from the 1920s. Gracious, and not always large, homes line streets where many southeast Michigan residents enjoy driving past and ogling the fancy digs.

CRANBROOK INSTITUTE OF SCIENCE (ages 6 and up)
1221 North Woodward Avenue, Bloomfield Hills 48304, in the Cranbrook complex; (248) 645–3200 or (877) 462–7262. Hours are 10:00 A.M. to 5:00 P.M. Monday through Thursday, 10:00 A.M. to 10:00 P.M. Saturday Memorial Day to Labor Day and 10:00 A.M. to 5:00 P.M. other times, and 10:00 A.M. to 5:00 P.M. Sunday. Admission is $7.00 for adults and $4.00 for children ages three through seventeen and seniors. The observatory, weather permitting, is open Saturday Memorial Day to Labor Day from 10:00 A.M. to 5:00 P.M. and on Friday from 8:30 A.M. to 10:00 P.M., and admission is free *with paid museum admission. Web site: www.cranbrook.edu.*

Things won't ever be the same at Cranbrook, which in 1999 opened after a $31 million renovation to its buildings and displays. Four new exhibits feature informative looks at geology and other aspects of the earth sciences. There's even a new full-size skeleton of a tyrannosaurus rex dinosaur along with displays on physics and biology that will knock every kid's socks off. The venerable Gem and Mineral Hall, where kids have peered at the ultimate rock collection, has been retained and updated.

In November the museum presents its annual Native American Days Festival. And in March, Cranbrook's annual Maple Syrup Festival is always a big hit, when visitors can see the sap flowing from sugar maple trees before it's taken to the sugar shake and boiled down into sweeter-than-sweet maple candy.

THE PLANETARIUM (ages 5 and up)

Inside the Institute of Science, Bloomfield Hills 48304; (877) 462–7262. Planetarium shows are on the hour from 7:00 P.M. to 9:00 P.M. Friday, with laser shows at 7:00 and 9:00 and an astronomy show at 8:00. Saturday and Sunday shows are at 11:30 A.M., 12:30 P.M., and 3:00 P.M. (astronomy) and 2:00 P.M. and 4:00 P.M. (laser). Admission is $2.50 per adult, $1.50 for children ages three through seventeen and seniors. Astronomy shows are $2.00 per adult, $1.50 ages three through seventeen and seniors. Children under three are admitted free. *Take the confusion out of planning a trip and call for current shows, or explore the Web site: www.cranbrook.edu.*

Young children may remember for the rest of their lives their first steps into the Planetarium at the Institute of Science. As the lights slowly melt to darkness in the seventy-five-seat theater, the star guide takes you on a journey around the Milky Way galaxy. Shows change several times a year, so chances are your next visit will hold something completely different. The Planetarium also presents annual special holiday programs, special events that introduce the heavens to children, and weekend music and spectacular laser shows set to music that are especially popular.

Where to Eat and Stay

See Birmingham listing.

Birmingham

One of the Detroit area's ritziest suburbs, Birmingham and neighboring Bloomfield Hills and West Bloomfield are consistently ranked among the richest communities per capita in the nation, due mainly to auto money. It has a great downtown shopping area; stores range from T-shirt shops to high fashion. Parking is available on the street or in covered lots for about $1.00 per hour. If you choose the street, beware that the meter maids are always watchful here.

Where to Eat

Main Street Cafe. *166 West Maple, Birmingham 48009; (248) 644–4000.* The former Amer's Deli has expanded to offer a wide variety of both American and Mediterranean foods. Introduce the family to the most popular dish, the combination platter, featuring chicken and beef kabobs, kefte (ground beef, parsley, and onion), hummus, tabouli, and stuffed grape leaves with salad or rice. On the deli side, items include spinach pie and other Mediterranean delicacies. $-$$ lunch, $$-$$$ dinner.

Max & Erma's. *250 Merrill, Birmingham 48009; (248) 258–1188.* A large variety of dependable entrees available from steak to pasta, seafood to burgers. Children's menu includes corn dogs, pasta, chicken fingers, and grilled cheese. $-$$$

Where to Stay

Hamilton Hotel. *35370 North Woodward, Birmingham 48009; (248) 642–6200.* This hotel has sixty-four rooms with fitness center, ℱree breakfast, and other restaurants nearby. $$$

Holiday Inn Express. *34952 Woodward Avenue, Birmingham 48009, at Woodward and Maple Road; (248) 646–7300.* Located near the main city shopping district. It has 126 rooms with ℱree movies. No pool. $$$

Grosse Pointe Shores

LAKE SHORE DRIVE (all ages)
Runs through the five Grosse Pointes: Park, Pointe, Farms, Woods, and Shores 48236. ℱree.

See where the rich and some famous, some not, live in this cluster of communities that has been known since the mid-1800s as Detroit's

Gold Coast. The area was settled in the 1700s as strip farms developed by French settlers. Then the English moved in, followed by the then nouveaux riches of America. While many of the mansions have been torn down to make room for more, somewhat smaller homes, a number still exist, and it's worth a drive along Lake Shore to gawk at the expensive homes and catch glimpses of the mini–Great Lake, Lake St. Clair.

Where to Eat

Jimmy's. *123 East Kercheval Avenue, Grosse Pointe Farms 48236, next to Grosse Pointe Shores; (313) 886–8101.* Casual, upbeat tavern that is a very kid-friendly place. All children's menu items are $3.95 and include beverage, meal, and dessert. $$$

Where to Stay

See Detroit listing.

Rochester

This region of rolling, forested hills wasn't recently discovered by those looking for a home in the 'burbs. It has been a favorite country playfield of the rich and famous of Detroit industry since the early twentieth century. One home in particular still draws attention year-round. The city is also the home of several of the region's most popular cider mills.

MEADOW BROOK MUSIC THEATER (all ages)

On the grounds of Meadow Brook Hall, Rochester 48306. From I–75, exit at University Drive. Turn right onto Walton and drive to Adams Road. Turn right onto Adams and drive about ¼ mile to the entrance to the east campus of Oakland University. Turn right and watch for signs; (248) 475–5668. Cost varies by performer, but it is usually $20 to $30 for pavilion seats and $10 to $20 for lawn seats. The season runs roughly from Memorial Day through late September.

Meadow Brook's lawn-seating atmosphere is genteel, restful, and family-oriented. Families heading for the 5,300 lawn seats—actually just a grassy place to spread your blanket—may carry in food and beverages, stretch out, and enjoy music by former Motown greats; folk songs from the likes of Peter, Paul, and Mary; and performances by other popular artists, plus occasional concerts by the Detroit Symphony. The uncovered pavilion seating holds 2,200. Specific concerts at Meadow Brook cater to families, with 𝐅𝐫𝐞𝐞 lawn admittance for children age twelve and younger when accompanied by an adult for select concerts. Picnicking on the lawn is one of the best, laid-back aspects of concerts here. Don't pass it up.

PAINT CREEK MILL AND RESTAURANT (all ages)

4480 Orion Road, Rochester 48306; (248) 651–8361. From Rochester, head north, the go 2 miles northwest on Orion Road.

Although they don't press cider here anymore, you can still buy it in season and enjoy dinner on the banks of Paint Creek, which in some spots of the area is a trout stream. The restaurant operates year-round and is open for lunch and dinner. It specializes in wild game, including great venison and pheasant breast. Children's menu, too. $$ lunch, $$$ dinner.

ADDISON OAKS COUNTY PARK (all ages)

1480 West Romeo Road, Leonard 48367, 9 miles north of Rochester; (248) 693–2432. From Michigan 59 in downtown Rochester, head north on Rochester Road, then west on Romeo Road. Open year-round. Web site: www.co.oakland. mi.us.

This scenic and convenient 794-acre park features two lakes with swimming, boating, camping, and four log cabins available to rent, an eighteen-hole disc golf course, plus 12 miles of cross-country ski trails, including one lighted for night touring and special events.

Where to Eat

Family Buggy Restaurant. *In the South Hills Shopping Plaza at 879 South Rochester Road, Rochester 48307. The restaurant is 2½ miles north of Michigan 59 and Rochester Road; (248) 656–0850.* Casual family dining with American cuisine. Children's menu. $$

Monterrey Cantina. *2601 South Rochester Road, Rochester 48307, about 2½ miles south of downtown; (248) 853–6800.* Serving good traditional Mexican food in a family atmosphere. Children's items available, too. $$

Where to Stay

See Rochester Hills listing.

For More Information

Rochester Chamber of Commerce,
*71 Walnut, Suite 110, Rochester 48307;
(248) 651–6700. Web site: www.
downtownrochestermi.com.*

Rochester Hills

YATES CIDER MILL (all ages)

*1990 East Avon Road (Twenty-three Mile Road and Dequindre), Rochester Hills
48307; (248) 651–8300. Open August through November daily from 9:00 A.M.
to 5:00 P.M. except Thanksgiving Day.* Free *admission.*

Up to 600 dozen doughnuts an hour come through the 8 feet of
cooking vats at this mill. Oh, and there's great cider, too.

GOODISON CIDER MILL (all ages)

*42965 Orion Road, Rochester Hills 48307; (248) 652–8450. From I–75, exit
north on Michigan 24, then head east on Silver Bell Road to Goodison. Open during the fall crushing season, usually from early September through mid-November.*
Free *admission.*

This mill is along the beautiful Paint Creek trail (see detailed entry
on the trail in Lake Orion section).

Where to Eat

See Rochester listing.

Where to Stay

Best Western Concorde Inn. *1919 Star-Batt Drive, Rochester 48309, at the junction of Michigan 59 and Crooks Road, only a few miles southwest of downtown Rochester in Rochester Hills; (248) 299–1210.* The inn has 124 rooms with indoor pool and cafe with **Free** and pay movies. Packages available. $

Red Roof Inn. *2580 Crooks Road, Rochester Hills 48309, at the junction with Michigan 59 in Rochester Hills; (248) 853–6400.* The inn has 111 rooms with **Free** and pay movies. Pets okay. $

Lake Orion

To reach Lake Orion, leave I–75 at exit 81 and go north on Michigan 24. Once considered too far outside metro Detroit as a suburb, it's rapidly become that with the advancement of metro Detroit toward it.

OLDE WORLD CANTERBURY VILLAGE (all ages)

2369 Joslyn Court, Lake Orion 48360; (248) 391–5700 or (800) 442–9627. From I–75, take exit 83 (Joslyn Road) north about 3 miles to Waldon. The village is open every day from 10:00 A.M. to 5:30 P.M. except Christmas and New Year's Days, Easter, and Thanksgiving. Web site: www.canterburyvillage.com.

A registered state historic site, this mall with a combination of gift, Christmas, and specialty shops was once the Wildwood Farm estate of publishing magnate William E. Scripps in the early 1900s. Canterbury Toy World is every boy's and girl's dream, filled with educational toys and books with hands-on testing and demos, while the Canterbury store has toys for big boys and girls including antiques, replica armor, and novelty items. The Fudge Shop tempts with twenty-four flavors, along with locally made Ray's Ice Cream.

BALD MOUNTAIN STATE RECREATION AREA (all ages)

Headquarters are at 1350 Greenshield Road, Lake Orion 48360; (248) 693–6767. To reach the park area, exit I–75 at Michigan 24 and head north to the first unit. Another section of the park is east of downtown Lake Orion. This is a day-use area only, no camping available. Entry is with state vehicle permit, $4.00 daily or $20.00 annually.

It's hard to believe that a touch of northern Michigan can be found so close to metropolitan Detroit, but here it is. Encompassing more than 4,600 acres, the recreation area straddles Michigan 24. At the southeastern section is Lower Trout Lake, called by many the best swimming beach for children in the region because of its long, sandy, gradual slope. There are canoe, paddleboat, and horse rentals, too.

Hikers can find nearly 14 miles of trails, and anglers will find bass and panfish. Fly fishermen may be amazed that there are brown trout in Trout and Paint Creeks.

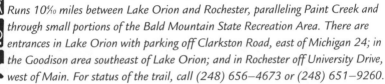

PAINT CREEK TRAIL (all ages)

Runs 10⁷⁄₁₀ miles between Lake Orion and Rochester, paralleling Paint Creek and through small portions of the Bald Mountain State Recreation Area. There are entrances in Lake Orion with parking off Clarkston Road, east of Michigan 24; in the Goodison area southeast of Lake Orion; and in Rochester off University Drive, west of Main. For status of the trail, call (248) 656–4673 or (248) 651–9260.

Actually a former railroad grade, the trail meanders through fields, woods, and some of the highest elevations in southeast Michigan. Use on foot, on a bike, on horseback (in certain areas only), or on cross-country skis (in winter). There are access points along the trail to try fishing for Paint Creek's trout.

Where to Eat and Stay

See Rochester and Rochester Hills listings.

For More Information

Orion Area Chamber of Commerce,
P.O. Box 236, Lake Orion 48361; (248) 693–6300.

Romeo

Located along Michigan 53 and Thirty-two Mile Road in northwest Macomb County, Romeo was founded in 1838. This little village retains its small-town atmosphere, thanks in part to attaining National Historic District stature. Lots of fine antiques shops grace the old downtown, which features brick-paved sidewalks.

WOLCOTT MILL METROPARK (all ages)

Southeast of Romeo between Twenty-nine and Thirty Mile Roads; (810) 749–5997, (810) 752–5932, or (800) 477–3175. From Michigan 53, head east on Twenty-eight Mile Road. Continue east to Jewell Road, and then head north to Twenty-nine Mile Road and then east 6 miles to Kuntsman Road, to the mill. The Farm Learning Center is on Wolcott Road, north 1½ miles off Twenty-nine Mile Road. It's open daily from 9:00 A.M. to 5:00 P.M. and 9:00 A.M. to 5:00 P.M. Wednesday through Sunday in winter. On weekends park admission is $3.00 daily or $15.00 annually per vehicle. Entrance is Free during the week. Web site: www.metroparks.com.

Wolcott Mill is an 1847-era gristmill that was operational until 1967. It was developed into the Huron-Clinton Metroparks system's only historical facility. Millstones grind as the history of milling in the area is explained. Special events include a Civil War Muster.

The park's Farm Learning Center is a real, modern operating farm that shows visitors the importance of farming today. See a dairy herd during their daily 10:00 A.M. milking, sheep flocks, and demonstration vegetation plots that even area farmers come to inspect for pointers. Special events also take place here. Call the park for information.

Armada Fair (all ages) Armada is off Michigan 53, northeast of Romeo in Macomb County. Every August this small town, at the base of Michigan's Thumb, welcomes upward of 50,000 visitors to what's generally regarded as Michigan's best county fair. The Armada Fair has been crowding 'em in for more than 125 years now, and depending on who's bragging, it's either the third- or fourth-oldest county fair in the state. The fun includes everything county fairs should include, from judging the best 4-H sheep, steers, and other four-footed farm inhabitants to the big midway with enough flashing lights to make any child's eyes open wide. But there's more that this fair also brings to the table. Up-and-coming country-and-western stars and other top-name acts entertain in the grandstands each evening, and there are always tractor pulls and other contests. Admission is $6.00 for those older than thirteen and Free for those two and younger. Parking is $2.00. For information on the next edition of the fair, call (810) 784–5488.

Where to Eat

Juliet Chocolates. *66870 Van Dyck Street, Romeo 48095; (810) 752–4335.* Now who could resist stopping by, with a name like that? More than eighty varieties of handmade chocolates. $

Office Pub & Cookery. *128 South Main Street, Romeo 48065; (810) 752–6680.* Serving pitas, burgers, and the like for lunch and dinner. $

Romeo Coney Island. *130 South Main Street, Romeo 48065; (810) 752–5730.* When the suburbs expanded, Detroiters took their likes with them, including downtown-style coneys. Breakfast and lunch. $

Where to Stay

Hess Manor Bed and Breakfast. *186 South Main Street, Romeo 48065; (810) 752–4726.* **Free** movies, a hot tub available, and full breakfast complement this home. Built in 1854, it features five rooms. There's also a gift shop, Country Touches and More, on the grounds, with items from antiques and reproduction furniture to cards, dolls, and the ubiquitous candles. $$

Prospect Hill Bed and Breakfast. *439 Prospect, Romeo 48065; (810) 336–1527.* From M–53, turn west onto West St. Clair Street, go 3 blocks to Prospect, then turn north. This 1870s-era mansion features feather beds and full breakfast. $$

For More Information

Romeo Washington Chamber of Commerce, *106 West St. Clair Street,* *Romeo 48065; (810) 752–4436. Web site: www.rwchamber.com.*

Milford

Named for the mills that once churned along the Huron River, Milford is now yet another bedroom community for metro Detroit. Along I-96, west of Novi, Milford is the site of several canoe liveries that offer day and overnight trips on the Huron.

KENSINGTON METROPARK (all ages)

The entrance is just off I–96, one exit past Milford at 2240 West Bund Road, Milford 48380; (248) 685–1561. The park is open from 6:00 A.M. to 10:00 P.M. daily. Another entrance is off Milford Road. Admission fees are per vehicle, and entry permits cost $3.00 on weekends, $2.00 on weekdays, or $15.00 annually. On Wednesday, entry is free. *Call for a locator map of all Metroparks and their facilities, including seven eighteen-hole golf courses. Web site: www. metroparks.com.*

Kensington Metropark, in the far western Detroit suburbs, is a 4,300-acre gem. Located on a 1,200-acre artificial lake backed up by a dam on the Huron River, it's a year-round family attraction that by itself draws millions of visitors annually. Where else can you sled and toboggan or take cross-country ski lessons in winter, swim and sunbathe in summer at two beaches, and launch your own boat or rent one of several types, including sailboats? In the fall you can enjoy Michigan's sweeping autumn color show by driving or biking (rentals available) roads overlooking the lake, exploring secluded nature trails on your own, or joining daily naturalist-guided hikes. You can also climb aboard the sixty-six-passenger *Island Queen* paddle wheeler (unfortunately, the *Queen* doesn't operate during the peak of the season here in mid- to late-October, because the lake is lowered to winter levels). There is great fishing here, too, for warm-water species like bass and panfish, and the entire lake is under a no-wake rule. In spring, take the children to witness the annual rite of the season as thousands of waterfowl return to the park's outdoor center. Kids can feed the animals at its petting farm as well. The petting farm admission is included in the entrance fee.

Golfers will enjoy a 6,300-yard, eighteen-hole course laid out along the southern shore of the lake. In winter, sleigh rides are offered, too, as long as there's a 4- to 6-inch base of snow.

Where to Eat and Stay

See Brighton listing.

Brighton

Brighton is located along I–96 at U.S. Highway 23. There are exits to the city on both freeways. Brighton was settled in the 1830s. Until only a few years ago, it was just another farm and resort lake community on the route between Lansing and Detroit—until it was discovered by suburbanites.

BRIGHTON RECREATION AREA (all ages)

Located at 6360 Chilson Road, Howell 48843; (810) 229–6566. From I–96, take exit 145 at Brighton and head south to Brighton Road. Turn west and drive about 1½ miles to Bauer Road. Turn south and head 2 miles to Bishop Lake Road, then turn west and follow the signs to the park. A state-park motor-vehicle entry permit is required, $4.00 daily or $20.00 annually. Camping is extra.

This is one of the most popular recreation areas in the region. Bishop Lake is a longtime favorite for metro-area swimmers, with two beaches, one there and another on Chilson Pond. There are four campgrounds that include primitive cabins. You can fish in several lakes for panfish, and in Appleton Lake for trout. Hiking, snowmobiling, and cross-country skiing also are available.

IMAGINATION STATION (all ages)

In downtown Brighton at the Mill Pond; (810) 227–5086. **Free**.

While you explore the shops of downtown, the kids can explore this 10,000-square-foot wooden castle and fortlike structure adjacent to the pond that once powered the town's mill and feed the pond's waterfowl. Next to the Imagination Station, Tridge, the three-pronged bridge, crosses part of the millpond. Sunday in summer, there are **Free** concerts in the nearby gazebo.

Where to Eat

See also subsequent entries for Howell, a city near Brighton.

E. G. Nick's. *11600 East Grand River Avenue, Brighton 48116; (810) 227–2131.* Open weekdays for lunch and dinner, weekends for dinner, including ribs, steaks, and fish. $$

Grecian Island. *9994 East Grand River Avenue, Brighton 48116; (810) 229–3101.* Open for breakfast through dinner daily. Inexpensive Greek food. $

Mount Brighton Ski Area (ages 7 and up)

Mount Brighton is reached by exiting I–96 at the Old Grand River Road exit in Brighton. Turn south, and at the first stoplight past the freeway, turn right. You'll see the ski area on the left. Contact Mount Brighton for conditions by calling (810) 229–9581. Rental equipment is available. Lift tickets are about $18.00 for adults and $14.00 for children up to age sixteen.

Metropolitan Detroit is blessed with plenty of things to do when winter arrives, including skiing at four downhill slopes, this being one. Ski areas like Mount Brighton are popular because they make it a point to cater to families, whether they're just starting on the bunny hill or are tackling the toughest black-diamond runs.

If you've never skied before, sign up for the state's "Discover Michigan Skiing" days. This annual program takes youngsters onto the slopes at Brighton and nearly two dozen other areas around the state for beginner lessons. Since the program is geared to first-time and neophyte skiers, the package also represents a great value. In January, they can quickly advance their skills, progressing through beginner-level lessons taught by a professional instructor during a ninety-minute session. You can even try out snowboarding. Cost includes all rental equipment and beginner-lift tickets. The package price is far less than the cost of a lift ticket alone, and renting your equipment the first few visits allows you to try out the sport with hardly any investment. Lesson and rental packages with Discover Michigan Skiing are about $25.00 for adults, $15.00 for ages seven to fourteen, and $35.00 for snowboarding lessons regardless of age. It's not recommended for youngsters younger than age seven.

A large and well-trained ski school staff will have your family up and shuffling around on slats within minutes. There are plenty of novice and gentle intermediate runs where you can hone new skills.

Intermediate and advanced skiers also will find plenty of challenging terrain over twenty-six runs. Experienced snowboarders may want to try the expert bumps and pipes in Brighton's terrain park, and there are children's learn-to-ski programs, too.

Nearly two dozen other Michigan resorts—including Alpine Valley, near Milford; Mount Holly, near Holly; and Pine Knob, in the southeastern part of the state—also participate in the program. To learn more, call the Michigan Travel Bureau at (888) 784–7328. Web site: www. michigan.org

Where to Stay

Courtyard by Marriott. *7799 Confer-ence Center Drive, Brighton 48114; (800) 321–2211 or (810) 225–9200. From I-96, take exit 145, Old Grand River Avenue. This property has ninety rooms, with indoor pool and breakfast. Restaurant adjacent. Children ages eleven and younger stay* **Free***. $$*

Holiday Inn Express. *8079 Challis Road, Brighton 48116; (800) 465–4329. From I-96, take exit 145. This property has 107 rooms and indoor pool. Restaurant nearby. Children ages eleven and younger stay* **Free***. $$*

See also subsequent Where to Stay list-ings for the nearby city of Howell.

For More Information

See subsequent For More Information section for Howell, a nearby commu-

nity that is headquarters for the Livingston County Visitors Bureau.

Parshallville

 PARSHALLVILLE CIDER MILL (all ages)
8507 Parshallville Road; (810) 629–9079. The cider mill is in what's called downtown Parshallville, even though the mill and a few other buildings are about all that's there. From Brighton, head north on U.S. Highway 23 to the Clyde Road exit. Head west, then north on Old U.S. Highway 23 to Parshallville Road, then go west about 1 mile to the mill. **Free** *admission.*

In the center of this tiny hamlet founded in 1835 by Isaac Parshall, North Ore Creek still is dammed up to power the gristmill, which was purchased by the Walker family in 1880. The family milled grain there until 1960. Cider making began several years later. Parshallville remains one of two historic mills in the state that can still operate using water power. Besides the pressing operations, there's a small store that sells baked and canned items. Enjoy your cider along the millrace below the building.

SPICER ORCHARDS (all ages)
10411 Clyde Road, Fenton 48340; (810) 632–7692. From Brighton, head north on U.S. Highway 23 to the Clyde Road exit. Turn east about ¼ mile. The mill and store are on the left. Admission is **Free***.*

In a modern setting compared with its neighbor in Parshallville, the farm also features apple picking in fall and late summer. The orchards also hosts a **Free**, early September car show, with pony rides and other activities for the kids.

Howell

Howell was founded in 1834, and in the last decade it has become a meeting point for community families heading west to Lansing and east to the Detroit area. Most of the downtown, however, still retains its rural, country feel. Located along I–96, just west of Brighton at exits 133 or 137.

 KENSINGTON VALLEY FACTORY SHOPS (all ages)
On Burkhart Road, Howell 48843; (517) 545–0500. From I–96, exit at Michigan 59 (exit 133) and head west. Turn right on Burkhart Road. Shops are open daily from 10:00 A.M. to 9:00 P.M. Monday through Saturday and 11:00 A.M. to 7:00 P.M. Sunday. From January 1 through February 28 it is open 10:00 A.M. to 7:00 P.M. Monday thorugh Thursday, 10:00 A.M. to 9:00 P.M. Saturday and Sunday, and 11:00 A.M. to 5:00 P.M. Sunday. Web site: www.kensingtonvalley.com.

It's Michigan's newest outdoor outlet mall, with more than ninety name-brand shops that offer wares from spatulas to men's and women's suits at discount prices. A food court is set in the middle of the stores.

Where to Eat

Tomato Brothers. *3030 West Grand River Avenue, Howell 48843; (517) 546–9221.* Good Italian lunches and dinners. $$

See also previous Where to Eat listings for Brighton, which is nearby.

Where to Stay

Best Western of Howell. *1500 Pinckney Road, Howell 48843; (517) 548–2900.* From I–96, take exit 137, then head south on County Road D–19. This property has sixty rooms, outdoor pool, and restaurants nearby. Kids ages eleven and younger stay **Free**. $$

Kensington Inn of Howell. *124 Holiday Lane, Howell 48843; (517) 548–3510.* This inn has 104 rooms, outdoor pool, and restaurants nearby. Kids age nineteen and younger stay **Free**. $$

See also previous Where to Stay listings for the nearby city of Brighton.

For More Information

Howell Chamber of Commerce, *123 Washington Street, Howell 48843; (517) 546–3920. Web site: www.howell.org.*

Livingston County Visitors Bureau, *123 East Washington Street, Howell 48843; (517) 548–1795 or (800) 686–8474. Web site: www.htnews.com/lcvb.*

Michigan Challenge Balloonfest

The sport of hot-air ballooning takes over the skies of southern Michigan each June. Besides a number of festivals, you'll find places where you can book a flight or two yourself.

In the small town of Howell, about 20 miles east of Lansing, nearly 60,000 ballooning fans converge for the festival that takes over the area around Howell High School the third weekend of every June. Skydiving demos, stunt kites, art exhibits, music, antique cars, and fireworks are topped off by mass ascensions of nearly sixty giant, colorful balloons each evening as they compete for the Michigan Challenge Trophy.

To reach Howell, take I–96 exit 137 or 141 and follow the signs. Parking is just $8.00 per carload each day or $12.00 for the weekend. Call (800) 686–8474.

Clarkston

 PINE KNOB MUSIC THEATER (all ages)
Pine Knob is reached from several exits off Interstate 75 north of Pontiac, the most popular of which is northbound Sashabaw Road, Clarkston 48346; (248) 377–0100. Open mid-May through late September. If sitting in the covered pavilion, bring along ear protection, especially for children. Prices all vary by the show, but count on paying around $16.50 per person for lawn seats or around $23.00 for covered pavilion seating. Parking is $6.00. Handicap-accessible. Web site: www.palacenet.com.

Pine Knob's covered pavilion seats more than 6,400, and the "cheap seats" on the lawn hold more than 8,000. For many concerts, especially the loudest ones, families prefer the lawn seating. Get there early to stake out a spot, spread out a blanket, and chow down on dinner. The season usually runs from mid-May through late September, featuring the gamut from eardrum-breaking hard rock for the teens to blues, country and western, New Age, and folk. Small beach chairs and picnic baskets are allowed, but drinks must be purchased in the park if you're eating on the hill. Otherwise, head for one of its picnic areas, or enjoy your own picnic and refreshments at a tailgate party in the parking lot before the show. The seasonal lineup usually is announced in late April or early May.

Where to Eat

The Clarkston Union. *54 Main Street, Clarkston 48346; (248) 620–6100. From I–75, take the Michigan 15 exit and go south about a mile into downtown. Open Monday through Wednesday 11:00 A.M. to midnight, Thursday through Saturday 11:00 to 2:00 A.M., and Sunday 9:00 A.M. to 2:00 P.M. and 3:00 to 9:00 P.M.* Set in a refurbished nineteenth-century church, this restaurant features pub-style food. It's especially known for macaroni and cheese made with sharp cheddar and penne pasta, baked with bread-crumb topping. Parents can sample any of the thirty-five American, European, and Japanese beers on tap as well as teas and coffees. Children's menu. $$

See also Waterford listing for more restaurants.

Where to Stay

See Waterford listing.

Holly

MOUNT HOLLY (ages 7 and up)
13536 South Dixie Highway, Holly 48442; (248) 634–8260 or (800) 582–7256. From I–75, take the Dixie Highway exit and head north on Dixie, or take the Fenton exit and follow the signs. The season generally runs from December through late March or snowmelt. Plan on spending about $36 per person per day for rental equipment and ski passes. You can buy cafeteria food or bring your own.

Eighteen ski runs of fun with the region's first high-speed, four-seat chairlift, along with one designed just for beginners. Rentals, a lounge and food, and a ski shop also are on the premises.

MICHIGAN RENAISSANCE FESTIVAL (all ages)
To reach the grounds, turn off I–75 north at exit 106 near Grand Blanc, Holly 48442. Go 2 blocks and turn south onto Dixie Highway for 2 miles. Festival grounds are 1 mile north of Mount Holly. Discounted advance tickets are on sale at area

supermarkets. Tickets are $13.95 at the gate and about $11.00 in advance for teens and adults. You pay $5.95 ($5.00 in advance) for children age five through twelve, and kids age four and younger enter **Free**. *Seniors sixty and older pay $10.75. Ticket prices include all entertainment, but you pay extra for food and souvenirs. The fair is open rain or shine. Parking's* **Free**. *Phone (800) 601–4848, or (248) 634–5552 for more information. Web site: www.members.aol.com/renfestmi.*

For seven weekends each year beginning in mid-August, the woods come alive with strolling minstrels, knights in shining armor, lords and ladies dressed to the hilt, and plenty of roasted turkey legs, soup in hollowed bread loaves, and other finger food to gnaw on Henry VIII–style (remember, this is the sixteenth century: no utensils). You don't have to come in costume, but it helps everyone get into the mood, especially if you come dressed as a noble family and make the "serfs" bow and scrape as you go by.

More than 150 craftspeople sell their wares, including beautiful walking sticks with sorcerer-like faces and other fantasy toppings that are made on the spot. Promenade to the competition ring and watch as knights in more than ninety pounds of armor climb onto horses and stage a mock jousting tourney or engage each other in a one-on-one contest on foot, as the festival's king and queen look on from their royal booths and courtiers nod approvingly at Upson Downs.

A portion of the park is set aside just for children, including human-powered rides to provide not only a laugh but a slight historical insight into what city fairs of yesteryear Europe must have been like. There are daily show performances, games, crafts, puppet shows, and more, including daily sightings of a friendly dragon. Entertainment on the festival's eight theme stages includes jugglers, storytellers, a sword swallower, and 200 other costumed performers.

Waterford

Once a sleepy village in the heart of north Oakland County's lake country, Waterford has grown up to become a suburb of metro Detroit, Pontiac, and Flint to the north. It was settled in 1819 and was named for the area's abundant lakes.

THE FRIDGE AT WATERFORD OAKS COUNTY PARK
(not for babies and toddlers)

On Scott Lake Road, Waterford 48327, between Dixie Highway and Pontiac Lake Road, near Waterford; (248) 858–0906. To get to the park, leave I–75 at Dixie

Highway and head south to Scott Lake Road. Turn south and follow it to the park. Cost is $6.00 per person for county residents and $8.00 for nonresidents. Hours are 4:00 to 10:00 P.M. Monday through Friday, 10:00 A.M. to 10:00 P.M. Saturday, and 10:00 A.M. to 8:00 P.M. Sunday, weather permitting. The runs are open New Year's Eve and Day but are closed Christmas Eve and Day. When you call, you can also receive a guide to the ten other Oakland County parks. Web site: www.co.oakland.mi.us.

It's like hopping on a giant ice cube at Michigan's first refrigerated toboggan run, at Waterford Oaks County Park north of Pontiac. A unique refrigeration system ices two flumes of water that drop riders 55 feet before they travel another 1,000 feet, flying over hills, straights, and dips. You don't need anything except warm clothes and a readiness to have a blast. Each of the park's 200 toboggans holds four riders (riders must be at least 43 inches tall; those age ten and younger must be accompanied by an adult) and are transported by park staff from the finish back to the start. There's a warming building with a fireplace, a viewing area, concessions, and rest rooms.

In summer, the park entertains with a wave pool, a five-and-a-half-story-tall raft complex, a BMX bicycling course, and tennis courts.

Where to Eat

For fast food check exits along I-75 between Pontiac and Clarkston. For other eateries see Clarkston listings.

Where to Stay

Best Western Concorde Inn of Waterford. *7076 Highland Road, Waterford 48327, at the junction of Michigan 59 and Airport Road; (248) 666-8555. From I-75, head south about 6 miles on U.S. 24 to Michigan 59, then go west 6 miles. The* hotel has 111 rooms with movie and game rental and an indoor pool with game room. $$

McGuire's Motor Inn. *120 South Telegraph Road (U.S. 24), Waterford 48328, 2 blocks south of Michigan 59; (248) 682-5100. The* hotel, which is 3 miles north of The Fridge, features forty rooms with an outdoor pool and a restaurant nearby. Small pets okay. $

Shelby Township

The township is one of the fastest growing in southeast Michigan, with farm fields disappearing into subdivisions' basements. It is also close to recreation on Lake St. Clair.

JOE DUMARS'S FIELDHOUSE (all ages)

45300 Mound Road, Shelby Township 48317, just north of Michigan 59; (810) 731–3080. To reach it, exit I–75 at Michigan 59 and turn east to Mound Road. Hours are 8:00 to 2:00 A.M. daily. You can rent an indoor volleyball hard court for $7.00 per person for two hours, or an outdoor beach volleyball court for $5.00 per person April through September.

In the off-season you might just catch a glimpse of Detroit Pistons great Joe Dumars at his namesake, a combination play-and-exercise center for both adults and children in this northern Detroit suburb.

If you're in shape, you could participate in ten sports in a row at this 70,000-square-foot complex. In addition to six full-size and three half-court hardwood-floor indoor basketball courts, there is minigolf, laser tag, batting cages, and a rock-climbing wall. The fieldhouse also houses five hardwood volleyball courts. Or, play touch football, or learn golf, rollerblading, or even cheerleading. Outdoors, beach volleyball courts are open in summer.

The fieldhouse has a full-size roller-hockey rink, complete with leagues for kids from ten and younger to dads and moms thirty-five and older. After the game, head for a workout in the training center run by Beaumont Hospital for an additional charge.

Once you've had enough, offer the kids a meal at Eat at Joe's (810–731–1503), a restaurant inside that serves reasonably priced family fare such as submarines, burgers, and pizza, or head for the sports-themed restaurant-bar and pick up a souvenir at the pro shop on the way. Food prices range from $2.00 to $9.00.

RIVERBENDS PARK (all ages)

From Michigan 59, head north on Mound Road for 1 mile; it becomes Auburn Road. Follow Auburn Road to Ryan Road, and turn north to the first unit. For the other unit, continue on Ryan Road to Twenty-two Mile Road and go east 1 mile to the picnic unit. Both units are parts of the same park, but they are divided by the river, and unfortunately there is no bridge. Phone (810) 731–0300. Park hours are 8:00 A.M. to 8:00 P.M. or dusk (whichever comes first) from May through

October, 8:00 A.M. to 5:30 P.M. from November through February, and 8:00 A.M. to 6:30 P.M. March and April. **Free**.

Originally part of a state recreation area, this park is a tribute to Michigan's history and that of the canal-building era of the mid-1800s. Officials, eager to put their young state on the map in 1838, began an ambitious project to link Lake St. Clair with Lake Michigan with a shipping canal between the Clinton River and west Michigan's Kalamazoo. However, an economic depression soon forced the end to the dream. Today, remnants of the 12 miles of canal that was dug are evident, especially in the unit off Ryan Road. Explore the canal and its tow path, walk a dozen miles of hiking and cross-country ski trails, or have a picnic. One unit also features an archery and gun range used for a fee.

Where to Eat and Stay

See listings under Mount Clemens.

Mount Clemens

Once famous for its mineral baths, the seat of Macomb County is located off I–94. And although it's located a few miles from Lake St. Clair, its soul feels connected with the water.

METRO BEACH METROPARK (all ages)

Reached at the eastern end of Metropolitan Parkway, Mount Clemens 48036, off I–94; (810) 685–1561 or (800) 477–2757. Entry permits, either $3.00 per vehicle daily on weekends and holidays or $2.00 weekdays (or $15.00 annually), are required. **Free** *entry on Wednesday. Swimming hours are 10:00 A.M. to 8:00 P.M. Monday through Friday and 10:00 A.M. to dusk on weekends and holidays. Unfortunately, a series of alerts in recent years led to several closings of the beachfront after heavy rains. Regional and local officials are working to rectify the pollution problem, which can be laid at the feet of the area's urban sprawl, old septic systems, and other factors. Water is tested daily. Web site: www.metropark.com.*

Another example of the Huron-Clinton Metropark system is this 770-acre lakeside beauty. On a typical steamy summer weekend day, you'll see thousands of suntan-lotion-soaked bodies on its large beach.

A trackless train shuttles families to and from the parking lot and along the 6,600-foot-long boardwalk. Other activities here include the tot lot, where kids as young as age three can ride their bikes without fear of running over a grown-up, to the east along Lake St. Clair. There's also an Olympic-size heated pool. Naturalist programs start at the park's nature center, where there are seasonal exhibits, displays of waterfowl inhabiting the area, and activities for kids.

Special events include the spring and fall Boat Show USA at the marina, one of the country's largest in-water shows.

MORLEY CANDY MAKERS (ages 6 and up)

23770 Hall Road (Michigan 59), Mount Clemens 48036; (810) 468–4300. Exit Interstate 94 at the Selfridge Air National Guard Field exit, or Hall Road. Turn west to Gratiot, the first light. Cross Gratiot and look for the signs at the Bavarian Tudor–style building. Free *group tours are between 10:00 A.M. and 1:00 P.M. Monday through Friday. Call before you visit to see if there will be a group your family can join for a guided tour with video. If not, your visit will be self-guided and won't include the video. Web site: www.morleycandy.com.*

What child isn't ready anytime to tour a candy factory? Morley's is one of Michigan's largest candy emporiums because of its popularity among charity fund-raising groups. Morley's cooks its chocolate goodies gallons at a time in huge, old-fashioned copper kettles, just like founder Ervin Morley did in 1919, when he created confections out of his original store in Detroit.

On hourlong tours of the facility, visitors walk along a 175-foot observation hallway and bask in the aromas of sugar and cocoa as employees and machines dip and mold each of the chocolates, which will eventually be boxed and ready for sale. Visitors learn that caramel is actually the controlled burning of milk, sugar, and cream and that those swirly marks on top of each chocolate identify what kind of center it has. A video also shows what raw cocoa beans and other ingredients look like.

Where to Eat

Paul's River House. *24240 North River Road, Mount Clemens 48043, just west of the I–94 River Road exit; (810) 465–5111.* $$ A local favorite, with children's menu and outdoor dining in warm weather.

Where to Stay

Comfort Inn. *1 North River Road, Mount Clemens 48043, about a mile west of I–94 at the River Road exit; (810) 465–2185.* The inn features ninety-eight rooms and a restaurant. $$

For More Information

Macomb County Chamber of Commerce, *49 Macomb Place, Mount Clemens* *48043; (810) 463–1528. Web site: www.central-macomb.com.*

Utica

Utica is a typical southeast Michigan bedroom community. It was settled in 1817 and named after Utica, New York, by settlers from that area.

FOUR BEARS WATERPARK (all ages)
3000 Auburn Road, Utica 48315, between Ryan and Dequindre; (810) 739–5860. Take I–75 to Rochester Road, head north on Rochester for 5 miles, and then turn east on Auburn Road. Go 2½ miles, and you'll find the park on the right side. There are no refunds if the lines are long and no rain checks. Four Bears is alcohol-free and is open from Memorial Day through Labor Day. Hours are 10:00 A.M. to 3:00 P.M. Monday through Friday and 11:00 A.M. to 7:00 P.M. Saturday and Sunday before June 15, and then 11:00 A.M. to 7:00 P.M. daily thereafter through Labor Day. Admission is $12.95 for those over 48 inches tall, $6.95 for those under 48 inches. Children ages two and younger as well as adults ages sixty-five and older enter Free. In addition, almost daily discounts make Four Bears an even better bargain. Web site: www.fourbearswaterpark.com.

Combine one of the state's largest collections of water slides, a sandy beach on a fifty-six-acre artificial lake, and other waterborne fun, and you've got one of Michigan's most popular summer family attractions. Thousands of families converge here every year to escape the heat and frolic at this watery amusement park less than an hour from downtown Detroit.

Four Bears entertains with miniature golf and a triple-chute water slide that sends kids on a 50-foot-long ride, ending in a splashy landing. Try your hand at the paddleboats or bumper boats, too. Special slides for nonswimming youngsters also help parents teach kids to lose their fear of water.

Out-of-the-water fun for a slight surcharge over regular admission includes go-carts ($3.00 for five laps) for kids, and batting cages ($1.00 for twenty pitches). You may also enjoy kids' carnival rides or head for the petting zoo to see the zebras, llamas, chimps, and toucans. There's even a sea lion performance and a bird show. Then, come lunch or dinnertime, grill out at the four-acre picnic grounds. Don't want to cook? Stop at the Honey Bear restaurant for burgers or chicken.

Where to Eat

Filippa's Wine Barrel. *45125 Mound Road, Utica 48315, at the corner of Hall Road (Michigan 59); (810) 254–1311. Hours 11:00 A.M. to 11:00 P.M. weekdays, 11:00 A.M. to midnight Saturday, and noon to 9:00 P.M. Sunday.* A local favorite with mostly American cuisine. Children's menu. $$$

Ristorante Piccirilli. *52830 Van Dyke, Shelby Township 48316, just south of Twenty-four Mile Road; (810) 731–0610. Open 11:30 A.M. to 2:00 P.M. and 4:30 P.M. to 10:00 P.M. weekdays, 4:30 P.M. to 10:00 P.M. Saturday, and 2:00 P.M. to 10:00 P.M. Sunday.* Classic Italian meals with a children's menu. $$$

Where to Stay

Baymont Inns and Suites. *45311 Park Avenue, Utica 48315, at Van Dyke (Michigan 53) and Hall Road (Michigan 59); (810) 731–4700.* The inn features 102 rooms and an indoor pool. Pets okay. $$

Comfort Inn. *11401 Hall Road (Michigan 59), Utica 48315; (810) 739–7111.* The inn has 104 rooms and **free** continental breakfast. $$

For More Information

Sterling Heights Area Chamber of Commerce, *12900 Hall Road, Sterling Heights 48313; (810) 731–5400.*

Chesterfield

Chesterfield is another former collection of farms fast turning into subdivisions north of Detroit. It was settled in 1830.

LIONEL TRAINS VISITOR CENTER (all ages)

26750 Russell Smith Drive (23 Mile Road), Chesterfield 48051; (810) 949–4100 (ext. 1454 to plan a visit). Take I–94 to exit 243 and then head left 1 mile to the second light. 𝐅𝐫𝐞𝐞 *tours are given at 10:00* A.M. *and 3:00 and 4:00* P.M. *Wednesday and Thursday; 10:00* A.M.*, 1:30, and 2:30* P.M. *Friday; and 9:00, 10:00, 11:00* A.M.*, and noon Saturday. The gift shop is open from 1:30 to 4:30* P.M. *Monday through Friday and 10:00* A.M. *to 12:30* P.M. *Saturday. Web site: www.lionel.com.*

Within a few miles of Joe Dumars's Fieldhouse there's a model railroader's heaven where you can see up to ten trains running on 1,000-plus feet of track.

𝐅𝐫𝐞𝐞 one-hour tours by reservation are offered Tuesday through Sunday. A ten-minute historical video recounts the company's founding in New York by its namesake and also takes visitors through each step in the process of making the trains. Then, kids, wearing their new 𝐅𝐫𝐞𝐞 engineer's caps, can join other model train buffs to gawk at the 14-by-40-foot layout with more than 1,000 feet of track supported by 5,000 railroad ties cut and painted by hand. Up to ten trains move simultaneously, switching scale-model rail cars, crossing bridges, and traveling through tunnels and past villages. Visitors can control the action with buttons, working water towers, rail car loaders, and other parts of the intricate layout. There is also a smaller 6-by-8-foot layout that the kids can run themselves.

Where to Eat and Stay

See Mount Clemens and St. Clair listings.

St. Clair

Located along scenic Michigan 29 on the St. Clair River, this picturesque river town has great shops downtown and is famed for its downtown inn and restaurant overlooking the swift St. Clair. It's also part of a great driving trip on Michigan 29. Michigan 29 parallels nearly the entire length of the St. Clair River. Exit onto Michigan 29 from I–94 north of Mount Clemens for the longer scenic route. To get to the city, exit I–94 at Rattle Run Road. The river is visible starting near Algonac.

ALGONAC STATE PARK (all ages)

Between St. Clair and Algonac along Michigan 29, St. Clair 48079, just south of Marine City; (810) 765–5605. For camping reservations call (800) MI–4PARKS. Entry fees are $4.00 daily or $20.00 annually.

Take a lawn seat for this 1,023-acre park's main event, watching the St. Clair River traffic, from oceangoing "salties" to hulking 1,000-foot-long lake freighters riding low with cargoes of train cars, iron ore, or coal. There are nearly 300 campsites, which get heavily used in summer, but most are small. The park makes a great weekend getaway, especially for anglers after the river's walleye. There are several trails that lead through a primitive prairie area, and there's cross-country skiing available in winter.

RIVER CRAB (all ages)

1337 North River Road (Michigan 29), St. Clair 48079, a few miles north of St. Clair; (810) 329–2261 or (800) 468–3727.

A wonderful intimate waterfront restaurant that features great seafood and fresh Great Lakes fish dishes for lunch and dinner. There's a children's menu and Sunday brunch available. Each April, the restaurant also participates in the annual River Crab Salmon Stakes, a fishing tournament that raises money for family counseling and child abuse centers statewide. Tickets sold at this and other restaurants formerly owned by the late C. A. Muer fund the services. Each ticket you purchase entitles you to an equal amount off a meal at a Muer restaurant, so it basically costs nothing to enter.

Michi-fact: Michigan's reputation for spectacular fall foliage is growing. The number of hardwoods in the state has leaped in the last few decades, and maples make up the majority of trees you'll see. Since they're the most colorful, it makes for great fall seasons that rival anything New England can offer.

Where to Eat

River Crab. *1337 North River Road (Michigan 29), St. Clair 48079, a few miles north of St. Clair; (810) 329–2261 or (800) 468–3727.* Great seafood, fresh fish lunch and dinners, Sunday brunch, children's menu available.

St. Clair Inn. *500 North Riverside Drive, St. Clair 48079; (810) 329–2222.* Boardwalk dining in warm weather on the St. Clair River. $$

Where to Stay

Blue Water Inn. *Adjacent to the River Crab; (810) 329–2236.* This cozy inn has twenty-one comfortable rooms. $$

St. Clair Inn. *500 North Riverside Drive (Michigan 29), in downtown St. Clair 48079; (810) 329–2222.* This

Tudor-style inn has seventy-eight rooms, many overlooking the river traffic. Other amenities include indoor pool and whirlpool. In the inn's restaurant, there's outdoor dining waterside in warm weather. $$$

For More Information

St. Clair Chamber of Commerce, *P.O. Box 121, St. Clair 48079; (810) 329–2962. Web site: www.stclairchamber.com.*

Port Huron

Located at the eastern end of I–94 on the St. Clair River, Port Huron is a city that's one of Michigan's three portals to Canada in Detroit, its near southern neighbor—that's right, by a quirk of geography, part of Ontario actually is south of metropolitan Detroit. Port Huron is one of the state's oldest cities, founded in 1686. Originally a fort to protect the entrance to the lower Great Lakes and the French fur trade, it sits where all Great Lakes water funnels into the narrows at the start of the St. Clair River under the Blue Water Bridge. Near it stands a statue dedicated to Thomas Edison, the town's most famous resident.

PORT HURON MUSEUM OF ARTS AND HISTORY (all ages)
1115 Sixth Street, Port Huron 48080, on the south edge of downtown; (810) 982–0891. From I–94, exit at Business I–69 until it ends. Make a left. Go 6 blocks to Wall Street. Turn left, and watch for the directional signs. Admission is $2.00 for adults, $1.00 for seniors, and $1.00 for students ages seven and older. Kids six and younger get in **Free**. *Museum hours are 1:00 to 4:30 P.M. Wednesday through Sunday.*

Port Huron counts Thomas Edison—inventor of the electric light, the movie projector, and the phonograph—among its native sons. Edison once sold newspapers on the train between the city and Detroit. To clue your kids in on local history, stop at this museum where a collection of Edison memorabilia is on display. It includes artifacts unearthed from the site of the house where he lived as a boy and performed his first experiments. For example, there are bottles believed to be used by young Edison to store chemicals. Equipment the inventor used in later life at his lab in Menlo Park, New Jersey, including a microscope and bamboo used to make an experimental bulb filament, are also on display. One of the first electric ranges and a light used to celebrate the light bulb's first century also are included. Note: A new museum dedicated to Edison should open in 2001 at the old city railroad depot where Edison worked. It will be on Edison Parkway in the shadow of the Blue Water Bridge.

Summer Fun on the Water

If you're a sailing family, plan to be here in mid-July in downtown Port Huron to participate in the annual Blue Water Festival, which culminates in every sailor's dream race—the Port Huron–Mackinac Island Sailboat Race. The evening before the starting cannon is fired, the Black River Harbor becomes one big floating party as visitors board and mingle with the crew. Late-night prerace events along the Black River can get a little rowdy at times. Other city events include one of the zaniest regattas on the Great Lakes. The Cardboard Regatta takes place in mid-August on the Black River. All boats must be made of the flimsy material, and this isn't a case of you've seen one, you've seen 'em all. All manner of craft, from elaborate designs that resemble pirate ships to dinghies that don't make it past the dock, try to float down the Black. Before its fateful journey, each entry is displayed downtown.

Both events are Free for spectators. Call (800) 852–2828 for more information.

LIGHTSHIP *HURON* MUSEUM (all ages)

Located at Pine Grove Park, Port Huron 48060, along the St. Clair River; (810) 982–0891. Follow I–94 to its end. At the light, follow Hancock Street, then go south on Pine Grove to the park. The lightship is open 1:00 to 4:00 P.M. Wednesday through Sunday in July and August. Admission is $2.00 for adults, $1.00 for seniors, and 50 cents for students ages seven and older. Children six and younger are admitted Free. Web site: www.phmuseum.org.

The same address of the museum is that of the retirement home of the *Huron,* moored along the St. Clair River north of downtown in Pine Grove Park. Until 1970 the *Huron,* actually a floating lighthouse, stood guard to direct ships past shoals north of the St. Clair's treacherous below-bridge currents. Kids can explore the ship to see how its crew of eleven lived aboard the vessel for twenty-one days at a time and learn where else the *Huron* served in its half century on the lakes. While you're there, the family can also scramble aboard the coast guard cutter *Bramble* for tours.

RUBY TREE FARM AND CIDER MILL (all ages)

6567 Imlay City Road, Ruby 48049, just west of Port Huron; (810) 324–2662. From I–94, follow I–69 west to exit 96. Turn north and follow the signs. The cider mill is open weekends 11:00 A.M. to 5:00 P.M. from August through Halloween, and tree-cutting is on weekends 11:00 A.M. to 5:00 P.M. from November through December.

You can make your children's Christmas even more magical when you take them on a trip to a cut-your-own tree farm like this one. Michigan is one of the nation's leading growers of Christmas trees. At this farm and others like it around the state, borrow a hand saw—no axes or power saws allowed—and for about $20 to $40, haul back your own tree. Many farms will wrap trees for easier transport and will also shake out dead needles there so you won't have to pick them out of your carpet later.

Ruby's version also is a cider mill, and during pressing time, there are carnival rides including a carousel open through Halloween, a wax museum featuring a presidential display, a Christmas gift shop, and a petting zoo.

DIANA SWEET SHOPPE (all ages)

307 Huron, Port Huron 48060, downtown; (810) 985–6933. Open 7:30 A.M. to 6:00 P.M. Monday through Thursday, 7:30 A.M. to 7:45 P.M. Friday, and 7:30 A.M. to 6:45 P.M. Saturday. Closed Sunday except for the last four weekends before Christmas, when it's open from noon to 4:00 P.M. in order to accommodate downtown shoppers.

The shop has been pleasing many a sweet tooth since 1926, and entering the small storefront is like stepping back in time. Bill and brother Leo Deliganis now run the shop begun by their father and uncle, tantalizing with nineteen different kinds of sundaes, topped with sauces made right in the store's big copper pot. The shop features an old-fashioned fountain with booths for enjoying sweet sensations like a chocolate sundae with vanilla ice cream, chocolate sauce, whipped topping, and a cherry in a souvenir plastic Detroit Tigers cap. You'll drool over store-made pastries and vanilla, lemon, and orange sodas. Enjoy breakfast, lunch, and dinner as well, including vegetarian items. One specialty is the roast chicken dinner, at only $4.10. Enjoy the antique Mills Violano–Virtuoso music box.

Where to Eat

The Fogcutter. *511 Fort Street, Port Huron 48060, atop the Port Huron Office Center downtown; (810) 987–3300.* Great views of the river and lake beyond for lunch and dinner, which include steak and seafood. Children's portions. $$$$

Thomas Edison Inn. *500 Thomas Edison Parkway, Port Huron 48060; (810) 984–8000.* Just south of the Blue Water Bridge, adjacent to Thomas Edison's statue, and located inside the city's main lodging of the same name is this upscale restaurant. Look out on the St. Clair River traffic and enjoy prime rib, paella, and other menu items for dinner. Breakfast and lunch also is served. Children's menu. $$$$

Where to Stay

Comfort Inn. *1700 Yeager Street, Port Huron 48060; (810) 982–5500.* Leave I-94 at the Water Street exit. This property features eighty rooms and an indoor pool. Continental breakfast served. There is other dining nearby. $$

Days Inn. *2908 Pine Grove Avenue, Port Huron 48060; (810) 984–1522.* At the end of I–94. The property has 106 nice rooms and an outdoor pool. Restaurant nearby. $

Fairfield Inn by Marriott. *1635 Yeager Street, Port Huron 48060; (810) 982–8500.* Leave I-94 at the Water Street exit. Marriott quality for a family budget. The inn has sixty-three rooms with indoor pool and whirlpool. Dining nearby. $

Thomas Edison Inn. *500 Thomas Edison Parkway, Port Huron 48060; (810) 984–8000.* See directions in Where to Eat section. The inn has 149 rooms, many looking over the St. Clair River. Amenities include indoor pool and exercise area with sauna and whirlpool. $$

For More Information

Blue Water Convention and Visitors Bureau, *520 Thomas Edison Parkway, Port Huron 48060, in the old railroad train station next to the Thomas Edison Inn;* *(810) 987–8687, (800) 852–2828, or (800) 852–4242. Web site: www. bluewater.org.*

East Michigan—South

EAST Michigan, which stretches from the Ohio border to the Straits of Mackinac, is the state's breadbasket. Within its borders farmers tend crops on some of the richest land on Earth—giant expanses where flat fields that once were home to the world's largest deciduous forest now grow more white, navy, and other beans than anywhere else on our planet. To the north are some of the state's richest natural resources, from trout-laden streams and reborn forests to the largest limestone quarry on Earth. To make it easier, we've split the region into north and south, using Michigan 46, which runs east and west, as the dividing line. This chapter covers the south part, the next chapter the north.

Irish Hills

Located along U.S. 12, between Michigan 52 on the east and Coldwater on the west. The region was named, legend has it, by an Irish immigrant minister for its resemblance to his homeland. The Irish Hills, located in Michigan's south-central Lower Peninsula, have, since the 1930s, been a one-stop vacation attraction for families. Everything from outdoor fun to quirky, tourist places can be found within a few miles of one another.

 PREHISTORIC FOREST (all ages)
On U.S. 12, ¼ mile west of Michigan 124;. (517) 467–2514. Open Memorial Day to October. Hours are 10:30 A.M. to 7:00 P.M. daily from Memorial Day through Labor Day, 10:00 A.M. to 7:00 P.M. May 1 to Memorial Day and September and October. Admission is $6.00 for adults and $4.00 for ages four through sixteen and for ages sixty and older. Ages three and younger are admitted Free. *Other attractions are extra: trampolines $3.00, maze $2.00, and batting cage $1.00.*

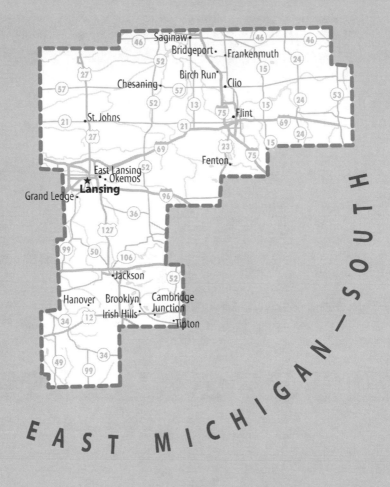

Saginaw
46
Bridgeport
Frankenmuth
52
24
Birch Run
Chesaning
57
Clio
15
27
57
57
52
13
15
24
53
St. Johns
21
75
Flint
21
15
24
27
69
21
69
23
East Lansing
52
75
Okemos
Fenton
★ Lansing
Grand Ledge
96
36
127
99
50
106
Jackson
52
Hanover
Brooklyn
Cambridge
Junction
Irish Hills
34
12
Tipton
34
49
99

E A S T   M I C H I G A N — S O U T H

Hop off after a forty-minute miniature "train ride" under a waterfall and see depictions of more than fifty life-size dinosaurs, including some that move and bellow. Kids can run through a maze and find the three dinosaurs that lead to the way out to the water slide, maze, trampolines and batting cages. It's part of the complex that includes the next two attractions, and combination tickets can also be purchased for all three.

 ### JUNGLE RAPIDS WATER SLIDE (all ages)

A ¼ mile west of Hayes State Park; (517) 467–2514. Open daily in summer. All-day rides on the water slide cost $6.00. Ages three and younger are admitted Free. *Younger children can slide with their parents.*

Take a thrilling ride down a 400-foot-long water slide. The slide is near Prehistoric Forest and Mystery Hill. There are combination tickets available.

MYSTERY HILL (all ages)

8108 U.S. 12, Onsted 49265, opposite the entrance to Hayes State Park; (517) 467–2517.

Mystery Hill tour guides take you to a spot where you'll see water running uphill and other illusory feats. Admission price varies by activity. Other fun kid things to do in the Hill include prerequisite go-cart and bumper-boat attractions.

Bill's Top Family Adventures in East Michigan—South

- **The Cascades at Sparks Foundation Park, Jackson.** Great fun with splashing colored water and other events like the big Civil War Muster.

- **Michigan Space Center, Jackson.** Michigan's best science museum.

- **State Capitol and Michigan Historical Center, Lansing.** The magnificently restored capitol and the Legislature, and all there is to know about Michigan, rolled into a few blocks.

- **Irish Hills, U.S. Route 12.** A fun ride through part of the nation's history.

- **The town of Frankenmuth.** Chicken dinners, a great list of festivals starting with the Bavarian Fest, great window shopping, and a grand hotel.

IRISH HILLS TOWERS (all ages)

*A mile west of U.S. 12 and Michigan 124; (517) 467–2606. Open from 10:00
A.M. to 10:00 P.M. daily from June through Labor Day and 10:00 A.M. to 8:00 P.M.
daily from mid-May to early June and from the day after Labor Day through October 31. Admission is $1.00 for adults, 50 cents for kids ages four through eleven.
Play miniature golf for $4.00 per adult, $2.00 per kid ages four through eleven.*

Climbing the old twin Irish Hills Observation Towers to admire the
scenic views has been a visitor tradition since the area first became a
tourist destination before the 1930s. The legend goes that one was built
just a bit higher to spite a mother-in-law. A recent addition is the miniature golf course with waterfall and streams coursing through it.

STAGECOACH STOP USA (all ages)

*7203 U.S. 12, Onsted 49265, near Michigan 124; (517) 467–2300. Admis-
sion is $10.00 for adults, $6.00 for children ages four through ten, and* **Free**
*for tykes ages three and younger. The attraction is open weekends only in May, and
Tuesday through Sunday from June through Labor Day.*

Always one of the most popular attractions for families making the
short drive from central Michigan and metropolitan Detroit is Stagecoach Stop USA, where more than 100,000 visit annually. This re-
created frontier town is themed to resemble a Michigan city of the early
1800s, with more than 10,000 antiques gathered by the Bahlau family,
from leaded-glass fixtures and a dome that once was the entrance to a
downtown Chicago haberdashery to fifty antique carriages, period furniture, and an antique gasoline engine display. Three times a day, the
century-old Pawson sawmill, relocated from nearby Devils Lake, fires up
to show how wood was cut. Other features include a chapel from the
Kentucky hill country.

Stop by the general store for bulk items from candies to peanuts
while the kids linger at the petting zoo. Entry to the petting zoo is
included in the admission fee. Several times in the summer, country-and-
western concerts are presented in the 2,000-seat outdoor amphitheater.

Where to Eat

Big Boy. *329 South Main Street, Brooklyn
49230, about 3 miles north of U.S. 12;
(517) 592–3212. Open 6:00 A.M. to
11:00 P.M. Sunday through Thursday and
6:00 A.M. to midnight Friday.* Chain
restaurant serving family meals from
spaghetti to its trademark triple-decker
burger. $

Golden Nugget. *7305 U.S. 12, Brooklyn 49230, 500 feet from Hayes State Park entrance; (517) 467–2190. Open 5:00 to 11:00 P.M. Tuesday through Friday, noon to 11:00 P.M. Saturday, and noon to 9:00 P.M. Sunday.* An Irish Hills landmark since 1975, the Nugget caters to vacationing families with items from burgers to lobster and a salad bar. Children's menu. $$

Jerry's Pub. *650 Eagan Highway, Brooklyn 49230; (517) 467–4700. Open 11:30 A.M. to 9:30 P.M. daily.* A cozy place frequented by locals and vacationers alike. It overlooks Wampler's Lake and offers outdoor dining in warm weather. Specialties include pizza, ribs, seafood, and pasta. Children's menu. $$

Where to Stay

The Irish Hills area does not provide many places to stay. For large, modern accommodations, see listings under Jackson, which is just to the north. Also see listings for Tipton.

Brooklyn Hotel. *131 North Main (Michigan 50), Brooklyn 49230, about 3 miles north of U.S. 12; (517) 592–0700.* A renovated 1860 hotel and stage stop with four rooms, two of which are kitchenette suites. Rooms are upstairs from two restaurants. $$

Lakeside Motel. *110 U.S. 12, Brooklyn 49230, 4 miles west of Hayes State Park; (517) 467–2536.* On Wolf Lake, the motel has seven rooms with kitchenettes. Dockage for boats is available, and there is a good beach at Hayes State Park. $

Brooklyn

Located just north of U.S. 12, it's one of several small communities nestled in the hills named by immigrants because they reminded them of Ireland.

MICHIGAN SPEEDWAY (all ages)

12626 U.S. 12, Brooklyn 49230; (517) 592–6672 or (800) 354–1010. Ticket prices range from $30 to $75 per person. For area camping and motel information, call (800) 543–2937 or (517) 764–4440. Web site: www.penskemotorsports.com.

For up to seven weekends each summer, the roar of finely tuned stock and Indy car engines that produce more than 900 horsepower each echoes through the heart of Michigan's Irish Hills region, a 2-mile, D-shaped track that rivals anything the South has to offer. One of the biggest draws is the Michigan 500, the Motor State's version of the Daytona 500 that's billed as the fastest 500-mile race in history. Other races are in June and August.

Tickets range in price from $30 per person for infield, look-over-someone's-shoulder viewing to between $30 and $75 for seats in the main grandstands on the front straightaway. There's also a special wheelchair platform, as well as a chance for fans who are eighteen and older to walk the pits for $45 (shirt and shoes must be worn, and shoulders and legs must be covered). Seats to witness practice and qualifying heats are a lot less.

Area accommodations include a field across from the speedway; camping is **Free** but strictly primitive here, with only central cold water and portable rest rooms, so you must be pretty self-sufficient. You can also purchase a pass to the limited, primitive camping area in the infield for $25 per vehicle plus regular daily admission for each person.

HAYES STATE PARK (all ages)

Entrance is located on U.S. 12 at the intersection of Michigan 124 and U.S. 12, Onsted 49265; call (517) 467–7401 for information, (800) 447–2757 for reservations. A $4.00 daily or $20.00 annual state motor-vehicle permit is required for entry. Camping is $15.00 per night.

One of the most popular state parks in lower Michigan, Hayes's 650 acres encompasses parts of two lakes: smaller Round, open to fishing and with camping nearby; and Wampler's, with a large swimming beach. There are boat launches on both lakes, and in fact, you can go from one to the other via a small canal. It's a great spot to bring the kids because the beach deepens very gradually. There's a 210-site campground as well.

Where to Eat

See restaurants in Jackson, Brooklyn, and Tipton.

Where to Stay

Greenbriar Golf and Campground. *14820 Wellwood Road, Brooklyn 49230, near Wampler's Lake, 1¾ miles north of U.S. 12 on Michigan 124; (517) 592–6952.* One hundred campsites, some with water and electricity. Heated pool and playground. $

See also listings under Jackson, Brooklyn, and Tipton.

Cambridge Junction

 WALKER TAVERN STATE HISTORIC COMPLEX (all ages)

At the corner of U.S. 12 and Michigan 50; (517) 467–4414. Open Memorial Day through Labor Day from 11:30 A.M. to 6:00 P.M. Wednesday through Sunday. **Free**.

You can get an inkling of what nineteenth-century stagecoach travel must have been like on the six- to eight-day run along the old Chicago Road (now known as U.S. 12 between Detroit and Chicago) at this restored former overnight inn that's also known as Cambridge State Historic Park.

For years the original inn was known for its famed "Murder Room," the purported scene of what one owner described as a particularly gruesome crime involving a stolen money belt. The cash was later reported to have been buried on the grounds and was the object of scores of secretive nighttime searches by locals—netting nothing but holes in the yard. According to the same owner, the inn hosted such famous guests as frontier author James Fenimore Cooper and Daniel Webster. State officials later surmised that these tales were hoaxes perpetrated by the inn's proprietor, who thought they'd be good for business. (He was right, of course.)

Annual events include a Civil War encampment and, in mid-August, Industry Days, which shows how settlers lived and produced their own goods on what then was the western frontier. A movie at the visitor center on travel in the 1840s depicts a young boy's journey from New York to Chicago, including an overland ride on a much more rugged U.S. 12 than today's paved version.

Where to Eat and Stay

See Tipton, Brooklyn, and Jackson listings.

Hanover

CHILDS'S PLACE BUFFALO RANCH (all ages)

12770 Roundtree Road, Hanover 49241; (517) 563–8249. Take U.S. 12 to Moscow Road, go north to Mosherville Road, and turn west to Roundtree; then follow the signs. The ranch is open from 9:00 A.M. to 4:00 P.M. Tuesday through Sunday from Memorial Day through Labor Day. A visit with the herd costs $4.00 per person. Horseback rides are $18.00 per person per hour. The rodeo is $8.00 for adults and teens, $5.00 for children ages six through twelve, and Free *for children five and younger.*

Here's a chance to show your kids a bit of living American history. In the late 1800s the American bison, or buffalo, was on the edge of extinction, reduced in an ongoing slaughter from the thirty to fifty million that once roamed the continent in nearly every region to fewer than 1,000. The future of the buffalo is now secure, however, thanks mostly to private herd ranchers like Gary Childs, owner of the Childs's Place Buffalo Ranch in the heart of Michigan's Irish Hills, which is home to up to 120 "buffs."

Visitors can climb aboard a hay wagon hitched to a tractor and ride into his pastures to help feed the huge animals ears of corn, and kids can actually reach out from the wagon to touch them.

Childs also sells buffalo meat, which he calls nature's original health food. In addition to the animal's meat, Childs uses just about everything else but the grunt, much as Native Americans once did on the plains. Bones are sold for jewelry, hides for coats, moccasins, and rugs. Native Americans often visit to purchase ceremonial items.

Like the Native Americans who sang songs of praise to the buffalo, Childs hosts a real, old-fashioned, two-day rodeo in mid-August that draws more than 200 competitors and upwards of 2,000 fans. Childs also offers hayrides and horseback riding.

Where to Eat and Stay

See listings for Brooklyn, Jackson, and Tipton.

Tipton

Founded in 1831, this tiny town was first named Tripp Town after its founder, and was shortened to Tipton a few years later. It's in the heart of the Irish Hills on Michigan 50, a few miles south and east of the intersection with U.S. 12.

 HIDDEN LAKE GARDENS (all ages)

Located 2 miles west of Tipton on Michigan 50, Tipton 49287; (517) 431–2060. Admission is $3.00 per person from April through October and $2.00 per person from November through March. Hours are 8:00 A.M. to 4:00 P.M. November through March and 8:00 A.M. to dusk the remainder of the year.

It's said that Michigan State University's East Lansing campus is one of the nation's most beautiful because of its greenery, and the university continues that tradition in Hidden Lake Gardens, just east of the other Irish Hills attractions. Inside this 755-acre complex, a 6-mile one-way drive takes you through a lush arboretum featuring thousands of trees, nearly all of them labeled; one-hundred-plus acres of plants and shrubs; and displays of special dwarf evergreens.

Under a tropical greenhouse dome, walk past plants from around the world or explore the gardens' 5 miles of nature trails, one of which accommodates wheelchairs. There's also a picnic area.

Where to Eat

Cruise Inn. *6400 U.S. 12, Tipton 49287; (517) 431–2770. Open year-round, 3:00 P.M. to 2:30 A.M. Monday through Thursday, 11:00 A.M. to 2:30 P.M. Friday and Saturday, and noon to 2:30 A.M. Sunday.* An old-fashioned restaurant. The inn features indoor dining with a menu that includes stacked ham, barbecue chicken sandwiches, and steaks. $$

Where to Stay

Ja Do Campground. *5603 U.S. 12, Tipton 49287; (517) 431–2111.* Five miles west of Michigan 52 and 6 miles east of Michigan 50, this facility has 130 campsites, some with electricity and water. Playground also available. $

Juniper Hills Campground. *13500 U.S. 12, Brooklyn 49230; (517) 592–6803 or (888) 396–8300.* This campground offers a number of amenities, including a fish pond, a playground, nature trails, volleyball, basketball, a video room, and a convenience store.

For More Information

**Brooklyn–Irish Hills Chamber of
Commerce,** *221 North Main, Brooklyn*

*49230; (517) 592–8907.
Web site: www.brooklynmi.com.*

Jackson

Founded in 1830 and named after Andrew Jackson, the city is the Jackson
County seat and remains a manufacturing center. Nicknamed the Rose City for
its annual rose festival downtown in mid-June, it was at the crossroads of an
old Native American trail and the upper Grand River. It also became one stop
on the Underground Railroad to help fugitive slaves reach freedom. In the early
twentieth century, twenty autos were made here. While many cities lay claim to
the title, Jackson citizens say the Republican party was formed here in 1854
underneath some spreading oak trees downtown, and they have a historical
marker there to prove it. The city also lays claim to the dubious distinction of
the home of Jackson State Prison, the world's largest walled home for the
notorious.

CASCADES AT SPARKS FOUNDATION COUNTY PARK
(all ages)

 *Exit I–94 at exit 138, go south on West Avenue, and follow the signs; (517) 788–
4320. The fountain runs from 7:30 P.M. to 10:45 P.M. nightly from Memorial Day
through Labor Day. Park admission is $5.00 per person; children ages four and
younger are admitted* Free.

Fountains and other watery displays have always been a part of
Michigan's towns, and one of the most spectacular in the state is here.
The oldest of its type in the Western Hemisphere, the 500-foot-long, 64-
foot-high structure has delighted families since 1932 as it gushes water
over sixteen falls and three main pools, while lights color the tableau
with an unending changing palette, all set to music.

The park also contains two golf courses, minigolf, picnic areas, batting cages, paddleboats, and the Cascades Museum, where photos trace
the history of the building of the fountain.

A Civil War Muster takes place at the Cascades in late August. It
includes battle reenactments between Union and Confederate soldiers,
with artillery and infantry demonstrations, living history docents, and
more in a show billed as the Midwest's largest.

Another fun event at the Cascades is the Classic Car Show in early June. For more information call (517) 787–2065.

 ELLA SHARP MUSEUM (all ages)

3225 Fourth Street, Jackson 49203; (517) 787–2320. Take exit 138 or 139 off I–94. Follow the green "trailblazer" signs south to the museum. Museum hours are Tuesday to Friday from 10:00 A.M. to 4:00 P.M. and Saturday and Sunday from 11:00 A.M. to 4:00 P.M.; closed Monday and holidays. Admission is $4.00 for adults, $3.00 for seniors and children ages five through eighteen, and **Free** *for children under five. A restaurant inside the original farm granary is open for lunch Tuesday through Saturday.*

It's only a 2-mile drive from the Cascades to the museum of nineteenth-century farm life, a 530-acre site filled with historic local structures and living history demonstrations around the home of Ella Sharp, who willed the property to the city. There's a one-room school, woodworking shop, and other buildings that have been moved to the site, including a log house and doctor's office. Special seasonal events are held in March, October, and December, when the Sharp residence is decorated for a Victorian Christmas. The visitor center connects to a modern-art gallery; entry to the gallery is included with admission.

MICHIGAN SPACE AND SCIENCE CENTER (all ages)

2111 Emmons Road, Jackson 49201; (517) 787–4425. To get to the space center from I–94, take exit 142, head south on U.S. 127, and go 6 miles to the Michigan 50 exit. Turn west onto McDevitt Avenue to the first traffic light, then turn south onto Hague Avenue, travel 2 miles to Emmons Road, and follow the signs to the center, which is on the campus of Jackson Community College. Hours from May 1 through October 31 are 10:00 A.M. to 5:00 P.M. Tuesday through Saturday and noon to 5:00 P.M. Sunday. From November through April, hours are 10:00 A.M. to 5:00 P.M. Tuesday through Saturday. Admission is $4.00 for adults and $2.75 for students with ID and seniors. Children younger than five are admitted **Free**. *Web site: www.jackson.cc.mi.us/spacecenter.*

Why a space center in Michigan, and particularly in Jackson? It was dedicated in 1977 to honor the several astronauts and other Michigan citizens who have played prominent roles in the nation's space program.

Kids can climb inside a mock Mercury capsule, the type America's first astronauts rode into low Earth orbit. In the theater you'll see either *Reflections*, a film based on the Apollo 9 flight, or, if the space shuttle is orbiting Earth, live broadcasts direct from the crew's quarters. Recently added exhibits include a display of a University of Michigan "sounding" rocket, a bulletin board of what's happening in space, and the suit astronaut Jerry Linenger wore aboard the Russian space station Mir during its troubles, which included a fire.

Bill's Favorite Events in East Michigan–South

- **Shrine Circus** (January), Saginaw, (517) 759-1330
- **Zehnder's Snowfest** (February), downtown Frankenmuth, (517) 652-6106
- **Sugaring and Shearing Festival** (March), Ella Sharp Museum, Jackson, (517) 787-2320
- **Easter train rides** (April), Huckleberry Railroad, (810) 736-7100
- **Storytelling Festival** (May), Jackson, (517) 784-8827
- **Frankenmuth Bavarian Festival** (June), Frankenmuth, (517) 652-6106
- **Michigan Challenge Balloonfest** (June), Howell, (517) 546-3920
- **Rose Festival** (June), downtown Jackson, (517) 764-4440 or (800) 245-5282
- **Hot Air Jubilee** (July), Jackson County Airport, (517) 782-1515
- **Car Capital Celebration** (August), downtown Lansing, (517) 372-0529
- **Civil War Muster** (August), Jackson, (517) 788-4320
- **Michigan Festival** (August), East Lansing, (800) 648-6630
- **Outdoor Craft Show** (September), Spicer Orchards, Fenton, (810) 629-2119
- **Country Autumn Folk Art Festival** (October), Chesaning, (517) 845-3055 or (800) 255-3055
- **Olde Fashioned Christmas** (December), downtown Holly, (248) 634-1900
- **Christmas at Crossroads** (December), Flint, (800) 648-7275

NITE LITES (all ages)

Jackson County Fairgrounds, 200 West Ganson Street, Jackson 49201; (800) 245–5282 or (517) 788–4405. From I–94, take exit 139, Cooper Street. Turn left and head downtown. Turn west on Michigan to Ganson. Open 6:00 to 10:00 P.M. Wednesday through Sunday from Thanksgiving through December 25. There is a $5.00 donation per vehicle, which helps purchase more lights and compensate the groups who volunteer to stand in the cold.

More than 100,000 lights twinkle on a 1-mile drive through the fairgrounds over the holidays. The auto route is lined with red lights and guides you through "Candyland," with lights depicting holiday scenes. Vehicles then enter the religious part of the display, which is complete with an animated manger scene. At the end of the trip, each rider receives a candy cane.

PHYLLIS HAEHNLE MEMORIAL SANCTUARY (all ages)

According to sanctuary caretakers there is no street address as there are no buildings at this location. Just follow the directions, and you'll get there: From I–94, take exit 147 and head north on Race Road 2 miles. Turn west on Seymour Road about 1½ miles, and the parking lot is on the north side of the road; (517) 769–6891. **Free.**

The woods, ponds, and wetlands are the site of the state's largest fall gathering of sandhill cranes. On any given day in October, more than 2,000 cranes can be seen returning to the marshlands for the night. The 930-acre property is owned by the Michigan Audubon Society.

DAHLEM ENVIRONMENTAL EDUCATION CENTER (all ages)

7117 South Jackson Road, Jackson 49201; (517) 782–3453. From I–94, head south at exit 138 on West Avenue. Go east on High, then south on Fourth. Follow Horton Road west to South Jackson, then turn south to the center. Open from 9:00 A.M. to 5:00 P.M. Tuesday through Friday and noon to 5:00 P.M. Saturday and Sunday. Trails open daily 8:00 A.M. to sunset. **Free.** *Web site: www.jackson.cc.mi.us.*

A bit of nature just outside the city. Five miles of hiking trails to explore fields, forests marshes, and ponds, including a ½-mile-long "special needs" trail. All-terrain wheelchairs are available on request. The Nutshell gift shop features books, clothing, bird feeding supplies, and other items. Cross-country skiing is available, weather permitting.

THE PARLOR AT THE ALL-STAR DAIRY

1401 Daniel Road, Jackson 49202; (517) 782–7141. To reach the dairy, leave I–94 at exit 138 and go south seven stoplights. At the seventh, turn west onto Wildwood, go two more lights, and veer to the right onto Daniel. The parlor opens at 11:00 A.M. daily. It closes at 11:00 P.M. Friday and Saturday, as well as every night from Memorial Day to Labor Day; the rest of the time it shuts down at 9:00 P.M. Sunday through Thursday and 10:00 P.M. Friday and Saturday.

After you're through giving the kids lessons in history and space, it's treat time. Jackson proclaims proudly that the Republican party was founded there. Now what can be more American than that? Ice cream, of course. According to voters of all political persuasions, one of the state's best places to sink your teeth into a triple-decker chocolate-banana sundae is the Parlor, on the city's northwest side.

The huge menu lists nearly two dozen different sundaes and fountain specials, parfaits, and splits—you name it, they'll make it. The pièce de résistance, if you dare, is twenty-one different flavors topped with every-thing in the place, for $15.20. A "single" cone, actually two scoops, is $1.27, plus tax. You can purchase ice cream by the half gallon, too, to take home. $$

Where to Eat

Cascades Manor House Restau-rant. *1970 Kibby Road, Jackson 49203, at the corner of Denton Road; (517) 784–1500. Open from 11:00 A.M. to 2:30 P.M. Wednesday and Sunday for brunch. It caters to private functions other days.* Over-looking Cascades Park, the Manor House features reasonably priced items for lunch or Sunday brunch. Dishes include two carved meats and four other entrees including fish, pasta, omelets, and shrimp cocktail. Cost is $11.95 for adults, $5.95 for ages six to twelve, and $3.95 for those five and younger. $$

Finley's American Restaurant. *1602 West Michigan Avenue, Jackson 49202, at the corner of Michigan and Brown; (517) 787–7440. From I–94, take Business 94 to Brown.* Open for inexpensive lunch and dinner, which feature chicken and ribs. Children's menu. $$

Gilbert's Steak House. *2323 Shirley Drive, Jackson 49201, at I–94 and U.S. 127 at exit 138; (517) 782–7135. Web site: www.gilbertsteakhouse.com.* A fifty-year Jackson dining tradition. Open for lunch and dinner. Children's menu. $$$

Red Lobster. *2400 Shirley Drive, Jackson 49201; (517) 787–7820.* Good, inexpen-sive seafood. The menu also has steaks and chicken. Children's menu. $$

Where to Stay

Baymont Inn. *2035 North Service Drive, Jackson 49202; (517) 789–6000. From I–94, exit northbound on U.S. 127. It's on the west side of the highway.* This chain property has sixty-five good rooms with continental breakfast. $

Cascade Falls Inn. *2505 Spring Arbor Road, Jackson 49203; (517) 784–0571. From I–94, exit at Robinson Road (exit 136), south to Spring Arbor Road, turn left, and drive ¾ mile. It's on the south side of the road.* A fourteen-room inn on two acres of land a short distance from the Cascades and Cascade Golf Course. $

Fairfield Inn. *2395 Shirley Drive, Jackson 49202; (517) 784–7877. From I–94, take exit 138 north a ½ mile to Springport Road, and then head south to Shirley.* This inn has fifty-seven rooms with an indoor pool. Restaurant nearby. $$

Greenwood Acres Family Campground. *2401 Hilton Road, Jackson 49202; (517) 522–8600. From I–94, exit at Race Road, exit 147. Go south to Ann Arbor Road, then west to Portage. Turn south to Greenwood, then east, then turn north on Hilton.* One of Michigan's largest campgrounds, if not the largest, with 1,160 campsites, many with electricity and water. Pool, beach, tennis, nine-hole golf course and minigolf, restaurant, recreation center, and weekend activities. $

Holiday Inn. *2000 Holiday Inn Drive, Jackson 49202; (517) 783–2681. From I–94, exit at U.S. 127, Springport Road, and head north.* This 184-room property has an indoor pool as part of an indoor recreation area with miniature golf and arcade, exercise room, and restaurant. Small pets allowed in rooms for $15 extra. $$

Motel 6. *830 Royal Drive, Jackson 49202; (517) 789–7186. From I–94, head south on U.S. 127.* This basic chain motel has ninety-five clean rooms. Restaurant nearby. $

For More Information

Jackson Convention and Tourist Bureau, *6007 Ann Arbor Road, Jackson 49201; Call (517) 764–4440 or (800) 245–5282. Web site: www. jackson-mich.org.*

East Lansing

The hometown of Michigan State University runs the gamut of family fun, from festivals to strolling one of the nation's most beautiful campuses. Michigan State University, founded in 1855, was the nation's first land-grant university. The campus is located just to the south of Grand River Avenue—yes, the same Grand River that begins in downtown Detroit.

MICHIGAN STATE UNIVERSITY (all ages)

To reach East Lansing and the MSU campus, take I–96 to I–496 north and follow the signs to the main campus exit, Trowbridge Road, East Lansing 48823. The general university phone number is (517) 355–1855. There are no special parking provisions, other than some lots open to faculty only, and meter maids are not stingy with tickets.

And you thought college campuses were only for eighteen- to twenty-one-year-olds. Think again. If you've got a precollege-age child who's ready to pick a school, or you just want to go back and relive a bit of your youth, a visit to East Lansing's 5,200-acre campus, with one of the largest student bodies in the nation, makes a perfect weekend getaway. It's considered one of the nation's most picturesque and beautiful college venues. Some liken it to going to school in an arboretum, so majestic are the huge oaks, maples, and pines that cover the old part of the campus. Classrooms and older dorm buildings are draped in ivy for that perfect campus look. The Red Cedar River flows between the buildings. You can join the students taking a study break along the riverbank or rent a canoe for a leisurely float. For a map of the campus area, contact the Greater Lansing Convention and Visitors Bureau (see For More Information under Lansing).

*S*hopping East Lansing

In downtown East Lansing, stores along Grand River Avenue that cater to students sell everything from MSU-logo clothing to books. Several good restaurants are in the area as well. For **Free** information on the entire Lansing–East Lansing region, call (800) 968–8474.

MSU HORTICULTURAL DEMONSTRATION GARDENS AND TEACHING GREENHOUSE (all ages)

Bogue and Wilson Road, East Lansing 48824; (517) 355–0348. Admission is **Free***, and parking is $1.00 weekdays,* **Free** *weekends and holidays. The gardens are open dawn to dusk May 1 through November. Tours, scheduled from June 1 through September 10 by appointment, are best for groups. Minimum charge is $15.*

One of MSU's newest gardens, this one of seven and three-tenths acres includes 18,000 square feet of perennials and the All America Trial Garden, a test site used by companies for annuals that include more than 1,000 varieties.

MSU CHILDREN'S GARDEN (all ages)

On Bogue Street, East Lansing 48824, behind the Plant and Soil Science Building, adjacent to the Horticultural Gardens; (517) 355–0348. Admission is **Free**, but there's a $1.00 charge to park at the nearby lot during weekdays. Evenings, holidays, and weekends, parking is **Free**.

Kids get a kick out of the sixty-three themed gardens here, from the Pizza Garden, featuring everything that goes on a pizza; and the Peter Rabbit Garden, with green chewy items favored by the make-believe bunny; to the Sensation Garden, where all plants can be sensed by smell. There's also a treehouse and other fun.

MSU DAIRY STORE (all ages)

On Farm Lane, East Lansing 48824, in the middle of campus; (517) 355–8466.

Join the kids in an ice cream or yogurt or take home some cheese from the store where all products come from animals raised in the university's dairy barns. Is two scoops of creamy delight less than $2.17 cheap enough?

MSU FARMS (all ages)

On the south campus. Open from 8:00 A.M. to 5:00 P.M. Monday through Friday. Closed during lunch hour. Call the Department of Animal Science at (517) 355–8383 for specific visiting times.

MSU originally was strictly an agricultural college, and the presence of the school's animal research and teaching, from veterinary science to farming research, remains a big part of the campus. Many of the buildings are open for touring. There are farms for sheep, cows, horses, and swine. Milking takes place each afternoon at the cow barn. Call first to learn specific times.

BUTTERFLY HOUSE (all ages)

In the teaching greenhouses, next to the Plant and Soil Science building at the corner of Bogue and Wilson, East Lansing 48824, adjacent to the Children's Garden; (517) 355–0348. Tours are $1.00 for students and $2.00 for adults, but visitation on your own is **Free**. Nearby parking is $1.00 from 7:30 A.M. to 5:30 P.M. Monday through Friday. Hours are 8:00 A.M. to 5:00 P.M. daily from June 1 through September 30.

Butterflies flutter, fly, and land on visitors as you walk through hundreds of species, from zebras and stately monarchs to julias, swallowtails, and others, all raised on the premises. Displays show caterpillars feeding on plants grown just for them. June is usually the most active time.

BUG HOUSE (all ages)

Rooms 146 and 147 of the Natural Science Building, on the northeast corner of Farm Lane and East Circle Drive, East Lansing 48837; (517) 355–4662. Programs presented here take about an hour. **Free**. *Web site: www.ent.msu.edu.*

Ever see a cockroach hiss? We hope not, but you will witness that variety from Madagascar, as well as hundreds of other species at the Bug House, including giant Florida lubber grasshoppers twice the size of normal ones, walking sticks, millipedes, and more.

MSU MUSEUM (all ages)

West Circle Drive, East Lansing 48824. Once on campus, follow the signs to the museum; (517) 355–2370. Hours are 9:00 A.M. to 5:00 P.M. Monday through Friday, 10:00 A.M. to 5:00 P.M. Saturday, and 1:00 to 5:00 P.M. Sunday. Admission is **Free**. *Web site: www.museum.cl.msu.edu.*

Great exhibits on three floors focus on the state's natural history, including fossils and Michigan history. There are exhibits on everything from wildlife art to the now extinct passenger pigeon, which once darkened the skies over parts of the state. There's a good gift shop, too, with jewelry and educational gifts for kids.

BEAUMONT TOWER (all ages)

West Circle Drive, East Lansing 48824, near the MSU Museum on the MSU campus. **Free**.

The forty-nine-bell carillon here is at the site of the Old College Hall, the first building in the nation built for agricultural instruction. There are weekly concerts in summer.

KRESGE ART MUSEUM (all ages)

Auditorium and Physics Roads, East Lansing 48824; (517) 355–7631 or (517) 353–9834. Hours are 9:30 A.M. to 4:30 P.M. Monday through Wednesday and Friday, noon to 8:00 P.M. Thursday, and 1:00 to 4:00 P.M. Saturday and Sunday from September through May; 11:00 A.M. to 4:00 P.M. Monday through Friday and 1:00 to 4:00 P.M. Saturday and Sunday in June and July. Closed in August. Admission is **Free**. *Web site: www.msu.edu/unit/khmuseu.*

A visit here is like getting an education in 5,000 years of art at MSU's collection, including avant-garde works. There are works by artists including Dali, architect Louis Sullivan, and Warhol, as well as unknown artists who fashioned Grecian urns and bowls, Russian icons, and other works from long ago.

WHARTON CENTER FOR THE PERFORMING ARTS (all ages)

On the campus's east side, at the corner of Wharton and Center, East Lansing 48824; (517) 432–2000 or (800) 942–7866. Web site: www.web.msu.edu/wharton.

Named for one of the university's former presidents, the center's two auditoriums almost always offer an evening concert or play. One is more suited to smaller productions, while the larger grand stage was the site of one of the 1992 presidential debates. There are **Free** backstage tours at 2:00 P.M. on Sunday.

ABRAMS PLANETARIUM (all ages)

Corner of Shaw Lane and Science Road, East Lansing 48824, on the MSU campus; (517) 355–4672 or (517) 355–4676. Open at 8:00 P.M. Friday and Saturday, 2:30 P.M. and 4:00 P.M. Sunday. For information on what you'll see in the real current sky, call (517) 322–7827. Admission: $3.00 for adults, $2.50 for seniors and students, and $2.00 for children younger than twelve. Tickets are sold a half hour before each show.

The planetarium's sky theater presents star shows using a state-of-the-art computerized star projector. Various themes are presented, and there are special shows for the holidays.

Although the shows are for all ages, preschoolers should be taken to a special family show at 2:30 P.M. Sunday.

MSU Tours There are two different tours, one for prospective university students and their parents if they're along, and another for those who want a basic walking tour of one of the nation's most picturesque campuses. The student tours are at 10:00 A.M. and 1:30 P.M. Monday through Friday and 10:30 A.M. Saturday. The regular walking tour is at 12:30 P.M. Monday through Friday when classes are in session. Student tours meet in room 250 of the Hannah Administration Building in the north-central campus area on Circle Drive. The regular tours meet at room 108 of the MSU Union Building at Grand River and Abbott. To book a student tour, call (517) 355–4458. **Free**.

You can become even more familiar with what the campus offers by "renting" a student for a **Free** tour. Tours are led by specially trained MSU students who can probably stump all but the most educated MSU fan with their knowledge of the campus and the university's history. All the major sites are covered.

Where to Eat

Beggar's Banquet. *218 Abbott Road, East Lansing 48823; (517) 351–4573.* From I-69/U.S. 127, take the Michigan Avenue exit. Go 3 miles east, then turn north on Abbott. Restaurant is in a rustic natural wood setting. Excellent breakfast. Lunch and dinner feature chili and vegetarian items in very large servings. Children's menu, too. $-$$

Evergreen Grill. *327 Abbott Road, East Lansing 48823; (517) 337–1200.* Just north of the MSU campus, off Grand River Avenue. Serving lunch and dinner in the former city post office. A great spot for casual dining. $$

Hershey's Steak & Seafood. *2682 East Grand River, East Lansing 48823; (517) 337–7324.* Open for lunch and dinner Monday through Saturday, plus Sunday brunch. Great prime rib and seafood. $$$

MSU Union. *Corner of Abbott and Grand River, East Lansing 48824; (517) 355–3460.* Fast food to go in a food court and cafe on the MSU campus. $

Where to Stay

East Lansing Marriott at University Place. *300 M.A.C. Avenue, East Lansing 48823; (517) 337–4440.* Across from the MSU north campus area. From I-496, exit at Trowbridge Road, go east, and turn north on Harrison, then east on Michigan 43 to Grand River. The property features 180 rooms, indoor pool, exercise area, and restaurant. $$$

Kellogg Hotel and Conference Center. *East Michigan and Harrison on the MSU campus, East Lansing 48824; (517) 432–4000 or (800) 875–5090.* A unique hotel that provides students at the university's hospitality school a firsthand look at hotel management, from folding sheets to working the front desk, and cleaning up juice spilled by the kids at breakfast. There are 165 rooms and suites, with access to a pool, tennis, exercise area and golf, and dining on the premises. $

For More Information

See the Lansing listing for how to get more information on the East Lansing area.

Lansing

Lansing's place in state history was assured when legislators, trying to decide on a proper state capital because the then-capital of Detroit was too near Canada, someone laughingly suggested this tiny town, which consisted of a sawmill and not much else. When it was approved, they all stopped laughing, knowing they'd have to travel through almost impenetrable woods to conduct business. Nevertheless, the legislature and the state survived. Later, Lansing became one of Michigan's industrial powerhouses and is still the home of Oldsmobile.

IMPRESSION 5 SCIENCE CENTER (all ages)

200 Museum Drive, Lansing 48933; (517) 485–8116. Open from 10:00 A.M. to 5:00 P.M. Monday through Saturday. Admission is $4.50 for adults and $3.00 for seniors and for children ages three to eighteen.

The Impression 5 Science Center is the state's largest hands-on children's museum and was judged one of the country's top ten. There's something here for everyone, from tots to teens, with demonstrations on computers, natural sciences, medicine, and physics, including a special exhibit on the fish of the Grand River, which flows just outside. Kids can freeze their shadows on a wall, try to grab a hologram, or explore their senses among the more than 150 exhibits.

Kids can make their own funny putty or television slime, explore the world of electricity, or have their hair stand on end, literally. There are daily floor demonstrations plus talks on subjects of displays. Educational programs including camp-ins and displays of children's art help students explore the worlds of science and art.

PLANET WALK (all ages)

Starts outside the Impression 5 Science Center and ends near Potter Park Zoo; (517) 371–6730. **Free.**

Take a tour of a scale model of the solar system as you stroll on a sidewalk. The walk begins with the sun, which is 20 inches in diameter, and then 179 feet away you'll find Earth, the size of a pencil eraser. In a little less than an hour, your family will have strolled over five billion scale miles. Total walking distance is about 2 miles. Every footstep will cover a million scale miles.

LANSING LUGNUTS (all ages)

The team plays at Oldsmobile Park, at the corner of Michigan Avenue and Cedar, Lansing 48912, 2 blocks from the capitol; (517) 485–4500. The regular season runs from early April through early September. The team hosts about seventy home games. Tickets are $5.50 for general admission, $6.50 for reserved seats, and $7.00 for box seats. Park in city lots nearby. Web site: www.lansinglugnuts.com.

What better way to finish a tour of the capital than with a ball game? The state capital now rings with the crack of the bat and howl of the crowd as the city welcomes its own baseball team, curiously named after the bolts put on the tires at the nearby Oldsmobile assembly plant. The stadium is big, seating 11,000, and that's a good thing, because the 'Nuts have become one of the hottest places to be in summer, not only to enjoy inexpensive, quality baseball, but because of the crazy name. Lugnuts caps and such are valued by collectors.

One of the most fun aspects of a game is seeing the hot dog cannon in action. The hydraulic-powered cannon shoots tube steaks into the crowd from the field, just for the fun of it.

POTTER PARK ZOO AND ZOOLOGICAL GARDENS (all ages)

1301 South Pennsylvania Avenue, Lansing 48912; (517) 483–4222. From Michigan Avenue downtown, head east to Pennsylvania and go about 1 block south of the I–496 underpass. Open 9:00 A.M. to 5:00 P.M. from April 1 through October 31 and 10:00 A.M. to 5:00 P.M. from November 1 through May 31. Admission is $1.00 for children ages three to fifteen, $5.00 for adults, and $3.00 for seniors. Parking is $1.50.

Pony rides, even camel rides, and canoe rentals are offered at the compact but well-stocked zoo. Some of the 400 other animals living there include rhinos, penguins, lions, and farm animals. Picnicking and food are available, too.

LANSING CITY MARKET (all ages)

333 North Cedar Street, Lansing 48912, on the banks of the Grand River next to Riverfront Park; (517) 483–7460. From Michigan Avenue downtown, head north on Cedar about 2 blocks. Open year-round 8:00 A.M. to 6:00 P.M. Tuesday, Thursday, Friday, and Saturday. Admission is **Free**.

Your chance to stock up on fresh veggies, in season, from local farms, along with baked goods, ethnic foods, and crafts in a market built as a Depression-era project in 1938.

APPLE SPORTSPLEX FAMILY ENTERTAINMENT CENTER (ages 6 and up)

3700 Lansing Road, Lansing 48917; (517) 485–7070. Open 10:00 A.M. to 10:00 P.M. Monday through Saturday and 10:00 A.M. to 7:00 P.M. Sunday. Cost is $3.00 for minigolf and $5.50 for skating plus $2.00 rental.

Indoor sports arenas for Rollerblade sports, along with a minigolf course, batting cages, video arcade, snacks, and a new skateboard park.

FENNER NATURE CENTER (all ages)

2020 East Mount Hope Road, Lansing 48910; (517) 483–4224. Open year-round from 9:00 A.M. to 4:00 P.M. weekdays and 11:00 A.M. to 4:00 P.M. weekends. 𝓕𝓻𝓮𝓮.

The city's nature center features self-guided trails through woods and around ponds, a visitor center and gift shop, and programs throughout the year that help introduce youngsters to such activities as making apple butter in fall and maple syrup in spring.

ADADO RED CEDAR AND GRAND RIVER WALK (all ages)

Winding along the rivers from 300 North Grand River, Lansing 48933; (517) 483–4277. Pick up the walk anywhere from access sites in downtown Lansing. 𝓕𝓻𝓮𝓮. *Paved and accessible for strollers and wheelchairs.*

Traveling over the water in places and in others alongside it, the river trail winds for about 6 miles along the waterways.

BRENKE RIVER SCULPTURE AND FISH LADDER (all ages)

Along the River Walk near the intersection of Turner and Grand River, Lansing 48933. Open daily. 𝓕𝓻𝓮𝓮.

In fall, see spawning salmon that have made it all the way from Lake Michigan miles away fight their way upstream. The event repeats each spring when steelhead, a lake-run rainbow trout, make the journey.

MALCOLM X HOMESITE HISTORICAL MARKER (all ages)

At the corner of Vincent Court and Martin Luther King Jr. Boulevard, Lansing 48933, downtown; (517) 487–6800. MLK Boulevard is 6 blocks west of the capitol. Vincent is to the south. 𝓕𝓻𝓮𝓮.

Now a registered historical landmark, this site has a historical marker and is where the home of one of the civil rights movement's most influential spokesmen used to be.

PEANUT SHOP (all ages)

117 South Washington, Lansing 48933; (517) 374–0008. Near the State Capitol. Open from 9:30 A.M. to 5:30 P.M. Monday through Saturday. Closed Sunday.
    A cute little shop that features more than thirty-six varieties of nuts, roasted on the spot, along with popcorn and other goodies to treat the kids to after your capitol tour. The shop has been here since 1948. Even the governor is known to stop by and buy a pound or two.

 LANSING FACTORY OUTLET STORES (all ages)

At the U.S. 27 exit from I–496 north of the city; (517) 669–2624. Open 10:00 A.M. to 9:00 P.M. Monday through Saturday, noon to 5:00 P.M. Sunday.
    More than thirty stores, selling at discounts, for everyone in the family. Stores include Oshkosh, Carters, and Toy Liquidators. There's also a small deli in the mall.

Where to Eat

Bill Knapp's. *5010 West Saginaw Highway, Lansing 48917, adjacent to the Lansing Mall; (517) 321–0931.* Good, inexpensive food for lunch and dinner. If someone has a birthday, they receive a corresponding percentage off their bill. $

Clara's Lansing Station. *637 East Michigan Avenue, Lansing 48912; (517) 372–7120. Just east of the Grand River and State Capitol. Open for lunch and dinner*

daily. The food's good and so is the atmosphere, inside a restored former train station where the freights still rumble by outside. The menu takes in many food styles. The chicken Caesar salad is great, as are the malts. $$

Hobie's Downtown. *115 South Washington Square, Lansing 48912, downtown; (517) 482–1383.* Open for breakfast through dinner, along with a separate ice cream parlor. $$

Where to Stay

Always ask about special group discounts, package plans, and weekend and children's rates, as many offer **Free** lodging for kids.

ASKME House. *1027 Seymour, Lansing 48906, downtown; (517) 484–3127*

or (800) 275–6341. Web site: www.askmehouse.com. A B&B built in 1911 with two guest rooms. The unusual name is a combination of the owners'—a husband and a wife—initials. Full breakfast is provided. $$

Holiday Inn West. *7501 West Saginaw Highway, Lansing 48917; (517) 627–3211.* From I-96, take the Michigan 43 exit and head east on Saginaw. The inn has 244 rooms, indoor pool, restaurant, and indoor recreation area including a whirlpool. $$

Harley Hotel. *3600 Dunckel Road, Lansing 48910; (517) 351–7600.* From I-96, head north on I-496/U.S. 127 to Jolly Road, then head east. This property, on the southern outskirts of Lansing and East Lansing, has 149 rooms with indoor and outdoor pools, exercise area, tennis courts, restaurant, and a game room. $$

Lansing Cottonwood Campground. *5339 South Aurelius Road, Lansing 48910; (517) 393–3200.* From U.S. 127, take the Jolly Road exit. Go 1 mile southwest on Dunkel Road, ½ mile west on Jolly, then head south on Aurelius. Open May 1 through October 31. This campground has 110 sites, with fishing, canoeing, paddleboat rental, and a pool. $

Radisson Hotel–Lansing. *111 North Grand Avenue, Lansing 48906, downtown; (517) 482–0188.* An easy walk 2 blocks east of the capitol and near Lansing's Museum Row. The hotel has 257 rooms in eleven stories with an indoor pool, sauna, exercise room, and dining. Downtown Lansing's best and most convenient accommodations. $$$

Sleep Inn. *1101 Commerce Park Drive, DeWitt, 48820; (517) 669–8823.* Just north of the intersection of U.S. 27 and I-69, 6 miles north of the Capitol Building. The inn has fifty-nine rooms with outdoor pool, and complimentary continental breakfast. Dining nearby. Only a ½ mile from the Lansing Factory Outlet Mall. $

Sleepy Hollow State Park. *On Lake Ovid, near St. Johns; (517) 651–6217.* From U.S. 27, head east on Price Road about 6 miles. Lake Ovid is an artificial lake, part of the Little Maple River, with a great ½-mile-long sand beach with concession stand and picnicking. There are 181 modern campsites in the 2,600-acre park. There also are about 16 miles of trails through the park's woods, and mountain biking is allowed. The lake is perfect for small-boat anglers, as there is no wake allowed. Boat rental is available, too. $

For More Information

Greater Lansing Convention and Visitors Bureau, *1223 Turner Street, Lansing 48912; (517) 487–6800 or (800) 648–6630. Web site: www.lansing.org.*

Grand Ledge

Named for the 300-million-year-old sandstone ledges along the Grand River, Grand Ledge is a popular Lansing bedroom community with a historic downtown.

 FITZGERALD AND OAK PARKS AND CLIMBING IN GRAND LEDGES (all ages)

 Fitzgerald Park is at 133 Fitzgerald Park Drive, Grand Ledge 48837. From I–96, take exit 93A and head west on Michigan 43 about 6 miles to Jefferson Street. At the sign for Fitzgerald Park, take a right, and the park is down the road on the left about a ½ mile. Call (517) 627–7351 for Fitzgerald Park information. The parks are open to all ages, but rock-climbing courses are for ages eight and older. There is a $2.00 motor-vehicle entry fee for Fitzgerald Park from April through October. Wednesdays are **Free***. Fitzgerald Park is open 8:00* A.M. *to dark daily.*

At Fitzgerald take a self-guided twenty-minute walk along the base of the ledges. There's also a connecting trail to the Island Park in downtown Grand Ledge.

Oak Park is on Front Street, across the river from Fitzgerald Park, and entry is **Free**. It's open from sunrise to sunset. For climbing information at Oak Park, call Vertical Ventures at (517) 336–0520. A basic learning course is $75 and runs from 9:00 A.M. to 5:00 P.M. Kids must be at least eight years old to participate and are placed in their own classes.

J&K STEAMBOAT LINE (all ages)

The Michigan Princess *runs February 19 through December 31 from various spots on the Grand River, including Lansing's Grand River Park. For schedule information call (517) 627–2154. Rates vary by what type of cruise you take. Prices range from $15 for an entertainment cruise to $54 for a dinner theater cruise including a five-course meal. Ages three through twelve are half price. A special kids' spectacular cruise, for children up to eleven or twelve, features the ride, music, magic, balloons, and punch for $8.00, with accompanying adults at the same price. Children younger than three are admitted* **Free***. Schedule for the spectaculars varies, so call ahead.*

It may be headquartered in Grand Ledge, but the three riverboats, *Spirit of Lansing, Princess Laura,* and *Michigan Princess,* sail the Grand and Red Cedar Rivers during festivals and also provide other entertainment from sight-seeing cruises and dinner theater to concerts. Largest is the *Michigan Princess,* with three levels.

Where to Eat and Stay

See Okemos, Lansing, and East Lansing listings.

Okemos

A bedroom community for the Lansing and East Lansing area, Okemos is the location of one of its largest shopping centers, the Meridian Mall, along Grand River Avenue.

 MERIDIAN MALL (all ages)
1982 West Grand River Avenue, Okemos 48864; (517) 349–2030. Open 10:00 A.M. to 9:00 P.M. Monday through Saturday, noon to 5:00 P.M. Sunday.
One of the state's largest malls, with 130 stores, including Sears, J. C. Penney, Hudson's, and Mervyn's. There is also a food court and stores that cater to families, including KayBee Toys. Stroller rentals are available.

Where to Eat

B. D.'s Mongolian Barbecue. *2080 East Grand River Avenue, Okemos 48864; (517) 347–3045. Reached by taking the I–96 Okemos exit to Grand River Avenue and heading east.* The restaurant is on the north side of Grand River. Open for lunch and dinner. Make up your own meal or use the suggested combinations on the big menu board, and watch as cooks prepare it on a large cooking table. Pay one price for all you can eat, if you wish. $$$

Traveler's Club International Restaurant and Tuba Museum. *2138 Hamilton Road, Okemos 48864, downtown; (517) 349–1701. From I–96, take the Okemos Road exit and head downtown. It's at Okemos and Hamilton.* Open for breakfast through dinner. An eclectic restaurant that serves ethnic foods, with evening entertainment from folk to jazz. $$

Where to Stay

Fairfield Inn by Marriott. *2335 Woodlake Drive, Okemos 48864, off I–96 at exit 110. Go north on Okemos Road* about ¼ mile; *(517) 347–1000.* This hotel offers seventy-nine rooms and an indoor pool. $$

Holiday Inn Express. *2187 University Park Drive, Okemos 48864. Off I–96 at exit 110, head north about ¼ mile on Okemos Road, then east on University Park* *Drive; (517) 347–6690.* This hotel has ninety rooms. $$

See also entries for Lansing and East Lansing.

St. Johns

St. Johns is the seat of Clinton County, north of Lansing along U.S. 27, which became Old U.S. 27 when the new stretch of freeway bypassing the town opened. The town was infamous in past years for the huge summer holiday traffic jams, one of the reasons for the expressway extension. The county and another town in it, Dewitt, were named after former New York governor Dewitt Clinton, under whose stewardship the Erie Canal was opened, which enabled many of the area's pioneers to settle here.

This is a big agricultural area, with mint among the largest crops, hence its nickname, Mint City, U.S.A. In downtown St. Johns, in the second weekend of August, more than 60,000 visitors come to enjoy the St. Johns Mint Festival, which includes arts and crafts sales, food vendors, a parade with 170 entrants, kids rides and games, a professional rodeo, and more.

UNCLE JOHN'S CIDER MILL (all ages)

8614 North U.S. 27, St. Johns 48823; (517) 224–3686. The mill is 7½ miles north of St. Johns on the east side of the highway. Watch for the signs. Open from 9:00 A.M. to 6:00 P.M. daily May through August and November and December; 9:00 A.M. to 8:00 P.M. daily in September and October. Exact dates vary by season. **Free** *admission; extra charges for tours and special attractions. Web site: www.ujcidermill.com.*

In the Beck family for more than a century, the cider mill and farm have been an attraction for area families since 1972. There's something taking place at the farm and mill nearly every weekend. In May, there's a garden shop with plants for sale. Summer finds fresh fruit, and starting approximately September 1, it's apple season, culminating with pumpkins in October. There also is a gift shop, plus a mile-long nature trail that winds past three ponds and a picnic area. Events include an annual car show the last Sunday in August, with more than 500 antique, classic, and collectible cars on display, **Free** tractor rides through the orchard on September and October weekends, an orchard tour ($1.00 per person on weekends), a Halloween fun house ($1.50 per person admission), and a petting zoo in October ($1.25 per person admission).

MAPLE RIVER STATE GAME AREA (all ages)
Located 8 miles north of St. Johns along U.S. 27 (old), St. Johns 48823. For more information, including maps, call the State Department of Natural Resources Rose Lake Wildlife Research Center at (517) 373–9358.

Take the kids on a "soft" eco-adventure to this 10,000-acre game area, the largest single wetland complex in mid-Michigan and home to thousands of ducks, geese, swans, and other animals throughout the year. Portions of the wetland are created by diking parts of the Maple River, and visitors are welcome to walk the dikes to view the wildlife. There's also a barrier-free hunting-photo blind and trail, reached just north of the U.S. 27 bridge in Unit B of the area. There's also an observation tower visitors can climb to look out over the complex. A few words of caution, however. Canals throughout the area are deep, so watch younger children. Trails can get muddy in spring, and the area is open to hunting in fall.

Where to Eat

St. John's Big Boy. *1408 South Old U.S. 27, St. Johns 48879, in town; (517) 224– 6828. Open 6:30 A.M. to 11:00 P.M. Monday through Saturday, 6:30 A.M. to midnight Sunday.* Chain restaurant serving a variety of foods, from salad bar to its trademark Big Boy triple-decker burger. $

Sable Point. *Downtown at 314 North Clinton Avenue, St. Johns 48879, west of Old U.S. 27. Turn west on Michigan 21 to Clinton Avenue and turn north; (517) 227–1600. Open 11:00 A.M. to 8:00 P.M. Tuesday through Thursday, 11:00 A.M. to 10:00 P.M. Friday, and 11:00 A.M. to 9:00 P.M. Saturday. Open on Sunday only for private parties.* Barbecue ribs are a specialty along with the walleye. Children's menu. $$

Where to Stay

Capri Motel. *1204 Business U.S. 27, St. Johns 48879, south of Michigan 21; (517) 224–4239.* This motel has twelve cozy units with heated indoor pool. Restaurants nearby. $

St. Johns Motel. *1508 North U.S. 27, St. Johns 48879; (517) 224–2321.* Located just north of the city on the west side of the road, near the intersection of Michigan 21. A quiet, renovated country motel with ten rooms, including two whirlpool suites. Restaurants nearby. $

For More Information

St. Johns Area Chamber of
Commerce, 201 East State Street,
St. Johns 48879; (517) 224–7248.

Fenton

Now travel to the east, to this suburban town smack in the middle between Flint and northern metro Detroit. Originally settled in 1830s as the end of the line for railroad freight traffic from Detroit, Fenton later counted on using the cement and aggregate business to make its way. Fenton, in Genesee County, also is site of one of the area's larger lakes, Lake Fenton.

BALLOON QUEST INC. CAPTAIN PHOGG BALLOON RIDES (all ages)

2470 Grange Hall Road, Fenton 48430; (248) 634–3094. To get to Captain Phogg, take I–75 to exit 101, Grange Hall Road. Turn west, go about 4 miles to Holly, and continue through the traffic light. Watch for a traffic light at Fish Lake Road; the entrance is 200 yards past the light on the south. Captain Phogg flies twice daily, seven days a week, except Christmas Day, weather permitting. Web site: www.balloonride.com.

Take your family walking the winds and get a bird's-eye view of the state's scenic landscape, lakes, and wildlife the way the pros do aboard an aerial nature trek with Captain Phogg. The most popular package is "the traditional." From a private launch field on Grange Hall Road, up to eight persons can join the pilot on an hour-long flight wherever the winds take you, setting down in another field and ending with a ballooning tradition, a champagne celebration back at the headquarters. The traditional flight is $199 per person. Got a hankering to get into the sport yourself? Lessons are available, and balloons also are for sale.

Where to Eat

Elias Brothers Big Boy. *3401 Owen Road, Fenton 48430. Take the Owen Road exit off U.S. 23. The restaurant is just to the east. (810) 629–0541. Open Sunday through Thursday 6:00 A.M. to 11:00 P.M.,* *Friday and Saturday 6:00 A.M. to 1:00 A.M.* Chain restaurant that serves a variety of foods, from a salad bar to the Big Boy burger. $

John's Pizzeria. *1492 North Leroy Street, Fenton 48430. From U.S. 23, head east on Silver Lake Road into town to Leroy Street. Turn north and go about a mile. (810) 629–5060. Open Sunday through Thursday 11:00 A.M. to 11:00 P.M., Wednesday and Thursday 11:00 A.M. to* *midnight, and Friday and Saturday 11:00 to 1:00 A.M. Sit-down restaurant with pizza and pastas. Children's menu.* $

See also Flint and Fenton listings for more eateries and places to stay.

Where to Stay

Best Western Fenton. *3255 Owen Road, Fenton 48430, at the U.S. 23 and Owen Road exit; (810) 750–1711. Chain* property has eighty-two rooms with an indoor pool. Restaurant nearby. $$

For More Information

Fenton Area Chamber of Commerce, *207 Silver Lake Road, Fenton 48430; (810) 629–5447.*

Flint

This community rests at the intersection of I–75, U.S. Highway 23, and Interstate 69. The whole of this city's modern history is tied in some way to the wheel. Once it outgrew its simple existence as a river ford, the city was on the road to become a major manufacturing center. First there were the carriage shops of downtown, which gave birth to the largest automotive company in the world. General Motors remains a presence in this town, nicknamed the Vehicle City, despite being hit hard by closings. Visitors might wonder about some addresses in Flint that begin with the letter G. This denotes locations outside the city of Flint, but in Genesee County. It's a little confusing, especially when a few addresses might carry identical numbers, except for the G, denoting one as outside the city. As long as you understand that, you won't have trouble getting around.

FLINT INSTITUTE OF ARTS AT DEWATERS ART CENTER (toddlers and up)

1120 East Kearsley, Flint 48503, in the Flint Cultural Center; (810) 234–1695. Hours are 10:00 A.M. to 5:00 P.M. Tuesday through Saturday and 1:00 to 5:00

P.M. Sunday. Admission is *Free*, and donations are appreciated. This is a great spot to introduce youngsters to art, but be mindful when bringing small children who may not appreciate a visit here. Strollers are welcome. Web site: www.flintarts.org.

Flint Cultural Center

This complex is located along East Kearsley Street and Longway Boulevard. Take I–475 to Longway Boulevard, head east to Walnut, and then head south. The road dead-ends at the parking lot for the Cultural Center area. The center features several attractions, including the Flint Institute of Arts, Robert T. Longway Planetarium, and Sloan Museum.

Nearly 5,000 works of art on display make this one of the largest privately owned museums in the state. Art includes works from the eighteenth-century onward, including a unique collection of antique French paperweights. The museum hosts seasonal art fairs, and there's also a gift shop.

ROBERT T. LONGWAY PLANETARIUM (ages 6 and up)

1310 East Kearsley, Flint 48503, in the Flint Cultural Center; (810) 760–1181. The building is open from 9:00 A.M. to 4:00 P.M. Monday through Friday and 1:15 to 4:30 P.M. Saturday and Sunday. The display area is Free. *Planetarium and light shows are $3.00 to $6.00 per person. The planetarium itself has laser light shows Friday and Saturday and astronomy shows at 1:00 and 2:30 P.M. Saturday and Sunday. Web site: www.flint.org/longway.*

Since they may not understand or like sitting in the dark for the shows, very young children should probably not accompany you to these excellent shows on the night sky. Special holiday shows are also offered.

 ## FLINT CHILDREN'S MUSEUM (ages 3–10)

1602 West Third, Flint 48504, on the city's northwest side; (810) 767–5437. To reach the museum, take I–475 to Longway Boulevard. Turn west, and go about a mile to Saginaw Street. Head south to Third, and then head west about 1 mile. Open from 10:00 A.M. to 5:00 P.M. Monday through Saturday and noon to 5:00 P.M. Sunday. Admission is $3.00 for ages one and older and is Free *for children younger than age one. There's also a $12.00 family pass.*

More than one hundred hands-on exhibits, from carnival-style crazy mirrors to create-your-own buildings at a Lego table and a real storybook coach. Activities are designed so children can learn while having fun. During the holidays, kids can make presents and enjoy their own New Year's Eve party. There's also a gift shop.

🏛 HISTORIC CROSSROADS VILLAGE AND HUCKLEBERRY RAILROAD (all ages)

G-6140 Bray Road, Flint 48506; (800) 648–7275. Exit I–475 off either I–75 or I–69 to Saginaw Street, exit 13. Take it north to Stanley Road, and then follow the signs to go east on Stanley to Bray and south to the village. There also are signs along the way to direct you. The village is part of the Genesee Recreation Area and is open pretty much year-round. Regular summer hours are 10:00 A.M. to 3:00 P.M. Monday through Friday and 11:00 A.M. to 5:30 P.M. Saturday and Sunday from May 18 through June 12 and on Memorial Day. Hours from June 14 through September 7 are 10:00 A.M. to 5:00 P.M. Monday through Friday and 11:00 A.M. to 5:30 P.M. Saturday, Sunday, and holidays. The village is also open weekends in September for special events, from a harvest jubilee to a juried quilt competition. Christmas at Crossroads runs November 27–29 and December 3–6, 10–23, and 26–30. Hours are from 3:30 to 9:30 P.M. Regular-hours admission for the train ride and village is $8.75 for adults, $5.75 for children ages four through twelve, and $7.75 for seniors. Children ages three and younger get in **free**. *Village-only admission costs less, but the train ride is worth it for the kids' reactions alone. Special dates, including the Ghost Train during October weekends, the Bunny Train prior to Easter, and Christmas at Crossroads, vary. Web site: www.jonra.com/ village/carousel.htm.*

History of the 1800s in Michigan and elsewhere comes to life at this village alongside Mott Lake, a dammed portion of the Flint River. Everything from a steam-train ride through the countryside—complete with a visit by mock robbers every hour—to a look at what everyday life in the Flint area was like back in the 1860s is in store here. The complex is part of the Genesee County parks system. Inside, craftspeople demonstrate blacksmithing, spinning, woodworking, and how mothers managed cooking with the right temperatures on woodstoves. Twenty-nine historic buildings make up the village. Kids will especially enjoy the 1910-era Ferris wheel and 1912 carousel.

The park is also the site of the annual Fastest Mule in Michigan Race, usually coinciding, hopefully just coincidentally, with Father's Day weekend. It's one of fifteen weekend events scheduled in summer. During the holidays, the village is festooned with more than 300,000 twinkling lights during Christmas at Crossroads, weekends from Thanksgiving through December 30. There's also a Valentine Dinner and an ice harvest on the lake, re-creating the days when such harvests took place throughout Michigan, and the ice was stored for summer use.

STEPPING STONE FALLS (all ages)

G-5161 Branch Road, Flint 48506, at the dam forming Mott Lake; (800) 648–7275; From Crossroads Village, head south on Bray Road, and then east at the end of the lake on Carpenter Road to Branch Road. Head north on Branch to the falls. Open 8:00 A.M. to 11:00 P.M. daily. 𝐅𝐫𝐞𝐞.

The falls impounds 600-acre Mott Lake and features colored-lighting evenings between Memorial Day and Labor Day. It's also site of the docks for the *Genesee Belle*. This sight-seeing boat departs from Stepping Stone Falls and Crossroads Village, offering forty-five-minute cruises on the lake. Call (810) 736–7100 or (800) 648–7275 for specific times and prices.

PENNY WHISTLE PLACE (ages 1 and up)

G-5500 Bray Road, Flint 48506, next to Crossroads Village; (810) 736–7100. Open from 10:00 A.M. to 6:00 P.M. Monday through Saturday and noon to 6:00 P.M. Sunday from late May through August 31. Admission is $3.00 per person, with adults accompanied by kids ages two and younger admitted 𝐅𝐫𝐞𝐞.

If the kids need a place to unwind, head to this creative outdoor playground with climbing nets, water play area, a punching bag forest, and more.

Where to Eat

Flint contains a multitude of dining opportunities, including a couple of must-dos and some family favorites.

Angelo's Coney Island & Grill. *1816 Davison Road, Flint 48506; (810) 238–3761. Open daily almost around the clock.* Some argue this is the home of the epitome of Coney Island hot dogs. One thing's for sure, it is popular with Flint-area residents and those traveling through. $

Bill Knapp's. *Three locations: 3140 Miller Road, Flint 48507, just off I–75 exit 117, (810) 239–4609; 4418 West Pierson Road, Flint 48504, at I–75 exit 122, (810) 732–2240; and 1401 East Hill, Grand Blanc 48439 (take I–475 exit 2), (810)*

695–6722. Open Monday through Friday 11:00 A.M. to 10:00 P.M., Saturday and Sunday 11:00 A.M. to 11:00 P.M. Good, inexpensive American food such as hamburgers and macaroni and cheese. Children's menu. If it's your birthday, celebrate with a 𝐅𝐫𝐞𝐞 cake. $$

Bill Thomas's Halo Burger. *Six Flint locations: 800 South Saginaw, Flint 48506, downtown; 3410 Corunna Road, Flint 48430, on the northwest side; G-3388 South Linden Road, Flint 48504; G-4474 Richfield Road, Flint 48504, northwest of the city off I–475; 3805 East Court, Flint 48506, downtown; G-4415 West Pierson Road, Flint 48504, off I–75. Also at 11355 Saginaw, Grand Blanc 48509, and 1464*

North Leroy, Fenton 48430. A Flint area tradition since the 1920s and one of the best burgers you'll ever have, cooked to order the old-fashioned way. Take your choice of unusual toppings including one of my favorites, green olives. $

Walli's East. *G-1341 South Center Road, Burton 48509, just south of the I–69 and Center Road exit; (810) 743–9600.* Family restaurant for breakfast, lunch, and dinner. $$

Where to Stay

Holiday Inn Gateway Centre. *5353 Gateway Centre, Flint 48507; (810) 232–5300. Exit U.S. 23 at Hill Road and turn east. Or from I–75, head north 1 mile from the I–475 interchange, then 2 miles west on Hill Road.* This property has 173 nice rooms, huge lobby, restaurant, indoor pool, and exercise area. Convenient to the entire area's attractions. $$

Howard Johnson Motor Lodge. *G-3277 Miller Road, Flint 48507; (810) 733–5910. From I–75, exit at Miller Road and head west.* Chain property has 135 rooms and outdoor pool. Restaurants nearby. $

Red Roof Inn. *G–3219 Miller Road, Flint 48507; (810) 733–1660. From I–75, exit at Miller Road and turn west.* Inn features 107 simple, comfortable rooms. Restaurants nearby. $

Timber Wolf and Wolverine Campgrounds. Both are part of the Genesee Parks and Recreation Commission system, on portions of the dammed-up Flint River. Timber Wolf is at 7004 North Irish Road, Flint 48506, in the Genesee Recreation Area near Crossroads Village and Huckleberry Railroad; (810) 640-1600. Take I-75 to Mount Morris Road and head east about 10 miles to Irish Road. Go south 1 mile to the campground. Timber Wolf features 196 campsites open from early May to mid-September, with showers, laundry, and electricity. There's also a small boat launch to explore the Flint River and playground and hiking trails. $

Wolverine Campground is in Holloway Reservoir Regional Park at G-7698 North Baxter Road, Flint 48506; (810) 793-6613. Take I-75 to Mount Morris Road and head east about 14½ miles to Baxter Road. Head south to the campground. Wolverine, open from mid-May through early September, has 195 campsites on the 2,000-acre Holloway Reservoir and showers, electricity, and rustic tent camping, too. There's a boat launch and beach, too. $

For More Information

Flint Area Convention and Visitors Bureau, *519 South Saginaw Street, Flint 48502; (810) 232–8900 or (800) 253–5468. Web site: www.flint.org.*

Clio

For a tiny town, Clio, just off I–75 north of Flint, has a lot to offer. It has the largest park system in the county, including a 7-mile bike and jogging path along Pine Run Creek.

 CLIO AMPHITHEATER (ages 6 and up)
In downtown Clio 48420; (810) 687–7611. Web site: www.clioamp.org.
The 2,700-seat open-air theater offers big-name music performers and other **Free** or low-cost concerts all summer. Remember earplugs for you and the youngsters.

Where to Eat and Stay

See Flint listings.

Chesaning

Somewhat off the track of most tourists zooming up I–75, this community is worth a westward detour to check out. Downtown Chesaning and stores just west of the city center offer lots of fun for families, along with the famous *Showboat*.

 CHESANING SHOWBOAT (all ages)
In Showboat Park, Chesaning 48616, just southeast of downtown; (800) 844–3056. The festival takes place the second full week of July. Tickets range between $20 and $55.
Running for more than fifty-six years, this family-style variety show along the water features a big-name entertainer each year on the *Showboat* stage, when the words "Showboat's a-coming" ring out over the park. Past guests have included Frankie Valli and the Four Seasons, Roy Clark, and Lee Greenwood. The stage on land seats 7,000, and it's nearly always filled, so order tickets as early as possible.

Where to Eat

Chesaning Heritage House. *605 West Broad Street, Chesaning 48616, just west of downtown; (517) 845–7700.* A restored 1908 mansion that serves lunch and dinner. Children's menu. Casual dress. $$$

Showboat Restaurant. *244 West Broad Street, Chesaning 48616; (517) 845–2830.* Family-style cooking specializing in prime rib and fish. Breakfast through dinner served. $$$

Where to Stay

Colonial Motel. *9475 East Michigan 57, Chesaning 48616, ½ mile from downtown; (517) 845–3292. Web site: www. instantweb.com/colonial.* Fourteen rooms with breakfast included in the motel's breakfast room. $

See also lodging listings for Flint and Saginaw.

Birch Run

Only a few years ago, this tiny community was a local farming center. The biggest event to hit town was when the downtown grain elevator burned to the ground. I remember it, too, for years as the northern end to the I-75 freeway. From this point, travelers going north exited onto four-lane Dixie Highway to head through towns like Saginaw and Bay City on their way to resorts farther north.

That all changed, however, when suburbanites discovered the area, and the first portion of the megamall of discount stores opened here to make it one of the hottest tourist destinations in the state.

PRIME OUTLETS AT BIRCH RUN (all ages)

12240 South Beyer, Birch Run 48415; (517) 624–7467. This outdoor mall is open from 10:00 A.M. to 9:00 P.M. Monday through Saturday and 11:00 A.M. to 6:00 P.M. Sunday. Exit I–75 at Birch Run and follow the flying charge cards. There are often special sales and events, such as deer hunter's Widow's Weekend the first weekend on or after November 15. Web site: www.primeretail.com.

There are five other factory discount-outlet malls in Michigan, but for anyone's money, this one is by far the largest, offering markdowns on everything from books to toys to tools to brand-name clothes that you would otherwise find only at standard retail malls. True, some items are damaged and some are closeouts, but many are only last season's line or production overruns from this season.

Families, especially around the big summer holiday sidewalk sales, spend the entire day roaming more than 180 stores. You can pick up school shoes for the kids at Nike, luggage for your next trip at American Tourister, and book bags at Eddie Bauer, and then shop for clothes at scores of other stores that specialize in everything from knives to books. Some of the stores that specialize in exercise or stereo equipment don't discount at all, so it's a good idea to check prices at other stores before you head here for anything. While sale items at regular retailers may be better priced, most often you won't find name-brand items for less than you can here.

If you get hungry, there are shops that sell everything from real food to fudge—even one for Pepperidge Farm cookie aficionados. Open since 1986, the mall is not enclosed.

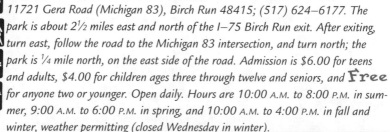

WILDERNESS TRAILS ANIMAL PARK (all ages)

11721 Gera Road (Michigan 83), Birch Run 48415; (517) 624–6177. The park is about 2½ miles east and north of the I–75 Birch Run exit. After exiting, turn east, follow the road to the Michigan 83 intersection, and turn north; the park is ¼ mile north, on the east side of the road. Admission is $6.00 for teens and adults, $4.00 for children ages three through twelve and seniors, and Free for anyone two or younger. Open daily. Hours are 10:00 A.M. to 8:00 P.M. in summer, 9:00 A.M. to 6:00 P.M. in spring, and 10:00 A.M. to 4:00 P.M. in fall and winter, weather permitting (closed Wednesday in winter).

Three miles to the east of the outlet stores, one of the best privately owned exhibits in the state introduces young children to the animal kingdom. More than sixty different species from around the world can be seen from gravel trails that weave throughout thirty-eight acres of woods at the park. Show your youngsters everything from black bears, which roam wild barely an hour's drive north; to coyotes; raccoons; otters; and porcupines.

More exotic types you'll see include lions, llamas, bison, and even a Siberian brown bear and Siberian tiger. There are two walking paths. A ½ mile trail takes you past the front part of the exhibits, while a back trail allows you to see many of the hoofed animals, such as elk and deer (you can see those in the wild in northern Michigan, too) that may be too shy to be seen from the other. You pay 50 cents per person to hop aboard the horse-drawn covered wagon that takes twenty visitors per trip on half-hour tours of the entire facility. In addition to a petting area where children can see, feed, and touch baby animals, there's also a small picnic area and playground.

NHL AT BIRCH RUN (all ages)

11600 Beyer Road, Birch Run 48415; (517) 624–5204. From I–75, exit at Birch Run Road and head west to Beyer, then drive north to the facility. Hours are 9:00 A.M. to midnight Monday through Friday and 7:00 A.M. to midnight Saturday and Sunday. Web site: www.nhlskatebirchrun.com.

A unique ice rink and teaching facility that also promotes the National Hockey League through its store. All twenty-six NHL teams are represented with hats, jerseys, and the like. Amateur hockey players can also purchase equipment. Video games allow even nonskaters in on the action. A full-service restaurant also is planned.

ALPINE MOUNTAIN MINI GOLF (all ages)

11873 Gera Road (Michigan 83), Birch Run 48415; (517) 624–4848. From I–75, exit at Birch Run and head east, then north on Michigan 83. Admission costs $4.50 for eighteen holes of minigolf, $4.00 for five minutes on go-carts, and $6.00 for unlimited use of paddleboats. Open 10:00 A.M. to 10:00 P.M. daily from Memorial Day through Labor Day.

After shopping all day, here's a fun spot to burn off some energy for the kids and adults, too. Besides minigolf, there also is a go-cart track and bumper boats. Go-karts feature single and double seating so young children can go. Single-seat drivers must be at least nine years old and 4-feet, 8 inches tall. Six-year-olds can pilot a bumper boat.

Where to Eat

Besides the national chain fast-food restaurants at the exit, here are some local favorites:

Bill Thomas's Halo Burgers. *9130 East Birch Run Road, Birch Run 48415; (517) 624–5441. From I–75, take the* Birch Run exit and head east to the driveway. Open from 7:00 A.M. to 10:00 P.M. Saturday through Thursday, 7:00 A.M. to 11:00 P.M. Friday, and 10:30 A.M. to 9:00 P.M. Sunday. The same great fixed-to-order, old-fashioned burgers available at several locations in Flint.

145

Tony's. *Birch Run Road, Birch Run 48415, just west of I–75, on the north side of the road; (517) 624–5860.* Humongous servings and low prices. Order a BLT, and you'll get a pound of bacon with lettuce and tomato packed between Italian bread a quarter of a loaf thick. Other items, like famous Italian sausage sandwiches, are equally huge. Serves breakfast, lunch, and dinner. $$

Varsity Diner. *11740 Gera Road (Michigan 83), Birch Run 48415; (517) 624–1355. From I–75, exit at Birch Run and head east on Birch Run Road, then north on Michigan 83. You'll see the neon sign on the west side of the road. Hours are 7:00 A.M. to 8:00 P.M. Monday through Thursday and Sunday, and 7:00 A.M. to 9:00 P.M. Friday and Saturday.* Treat the kids to a meal inside a real East Coast diner, built in 1955 and opened here in 1994. Waitresses in nostalgic uniforms serve comfort food from goulash and meat loaf to burgers and chicken pot pie. On select Tuesdays, prices are rolled back, with 60-cent burgers and 20-cent Cokes. $$

Where to Stay

Best Western Market Street Inn. *At the Birch Run–I–75 exit, Birch Run 48415; (517) 624–9395.* This property has 153 rooms with restaurant and indoor pool. It's the original motel serving mall shoppers. $$

Super 8 Motel. *9235 East Birch Run Road, Birch Run 48415; (517) 624–4440.* From I–75, exit at Birch Run and head east. A basic place with 107 rooms. Restaurants nearby. $$

For More Information

Birch Run Chamber of Commerce, *P.O. Box 153, Birch Run 48415;* *(888) 624–9193. Web site: www. birchrunchamber.com.*

Bridgeport

Founded in 1836 and named for the bridges that crossed the Cass River here, Bridgeport has become a suburb of Saginaw.

JUNCTION VALLEY RAILROAD (all ages)

7065 Dixie Highway, Bridgeport 48722, at Junction Road; (517) 777–3480. Open from 10:00 A.M. to 6:00 P.M. Monday through Saturday and 1:00 to 6:00

P.M. *Sunday from Memorial Day weekend through Labor Day weekend. The train operates from 1:00 and 5:00* P.M. *on weekends only from the day after Labor Day through October 8. Admission is $5.00 for adults and teens, $3.25 for children ages two through eleven, and $3.75 for seniors. To reach the rails, exit 144 off I–75 and head south on Dixie Highway 2 miles to the first flashing traffic light.*

Rain or shine, after or before hitting Birch Run, treat the kids to a ride on the world's largest one-quarter-size railroad, Junction Valley, just east of the Saginaw suburb of Bridgeport. Climb aboard the miniature cars as one of eight scale-model diesel locomotives pulls you on the 2-mile ride through woods, over 865 feet of trestles, including the only "diamond crossing trestle" in the world, and even through a 100-foot-long tunnel. There's also a picnic area and a playground. The season starts the weekend before Memorial Day, and special events take place regularly. Halloween "spook train" rides pass thirty-five different scenes, to the light of more than 250 trackside jack-o'-lanterns. A Christmas program features more than 100,000 twinkling lights. For those rides, the train stops halfway through the route at a warming house and gift shop where kids can make simple decorations.

Where to Eat

Freeway Fritz. *6560 Dixie Highway, Bridgeport 48722; (517) 777–8730. From I–75, exit southbound on Dixie Highway. It's in the Shell station complex on the* south side of the road. Pick up a bucket of chicken on your way up north, along with desserts and other items. $$

Where to Stay

Baymont Inn. *6460 Dixie Highway, Bridgeport 48722; (517) 777–3000. From I–75, head north on Dixie Highway.* Basic property with 104 rooms. Restaurant nearby. $

Days Inn–Frankenmuth/Bridgeport. *6379 Dixie Highway, Bridgeport 48722; (517) 777–1611. From I–75, exit northbound Dixie Highway.* The inn has 123 rooms with indoor pool and whirlpool and exercise room. $$

Heidelberg Inn Motel. *6815 Dixie Highway, Bridgeport 48722; (517) 777–2195. From I–75, exit southbound onto Dixie Highway and drive about 1 mile.* There are fourteen rooms in this well-kept motel that date from the days when Dixie Highway was the main route north and south. Dining is nearby at the I–75 interchange area. $

Frankenmuth

Barely five minutes east of the Junction Valley Railroad, Frankenmuth is the realm of *gemütlichkeit,* that untranslatable German word that can mean everything from hospitality to down-home friendly. Whatever your interpretation, Frankenmuth will supply. Founded in 1845 by fifteen young German Lutherans who came to this then-wilderness to preach to Native American tribes, the town has held onto its German past while transforming itself into Michigan's top tourist destination. Many towns have tourist attractions. Here, just about the entire town is one. There are two ways to get to Frankenmuth. From the Birch Run exit, head east to Michigan 83 and take it north straight into town. From the Bridgeport exit, head south on Dixie Highway to Junction Road, then go east about 5 miles.

BAVARIAN FESTIVAL (all ages)

Throughout the city in mid-June; (517) 652–6106. **Free**.

Whatever the season or the reason, it seems there's almost always a celebration going on in town. This is the one that started it all and put the city on the map for tourists, a weeklong mid-June celebration that draws more than 100,000 for food, parades, and lots of polka music. All events take place in Heritage Park, a short walk across the authentic wooden covered bridge from downtown's restaurants and other fun. Dance the polka in one tent or enjoy other music in another. Knock back a bratwurst sausage with a glass of your favorite beverage and join in the fun.

BRONNER'S CHRISTMAS WONDERLAND (all ages)

25 Christmas Lane, Frankenmuth 48734; (517) 652–9931 or (800) 255–9327. Just off Michigan 83 at the south end of town; you can't miss it. Open nearly every day of the year. Hours are 9:00 A.M. to 9:00 P.M. Monday through Saturday and noon to 7:00 P.M. Sunday from June through December; 9:00 A.M. to 5:30 P.M. Monday through Thursday and Saturday, 9:00 A.M. to 9:00 P.M. Friday, and noon to 5:30 P.M. Sunday from January through May. Admission is **Free**. *Web site: www.bronners.com.*

Be ready to share your visit to what's billed as the world's largest Christmas store with lots of folks. They come here by the busload to view the Christmas ornaments, trees, nativity scenes, and more that are up year-round inside, along with a great light display outside. Owner Wally Bronner started the business downtown as a sidelight to his sign business. When it outgrew the two buildings being used, Bronner moved into this huge structure. Things are a mite pricier here than at the local discount store, but what the heck, it's Christmas here even when it's ninety degrees outside. Rest a bit at the store's refreshment area, take in the short slide show that tells the Bronner story, or view the 500-piece Hummel collection.

At the south end of the Bronner's parking lot, be sure to see the Silent Night Memorial Chapel, a replica of the chapel in Oberndorf, Austria, where the famous Christmas song was penned.

FRANKENMUTH RIVERBOAT TOURS (all ages)

445 South Main Street, Frankenmuth 48734; (517) 652–8844. Departs daily starting at 12:30 P.M. from May through October. Admission costs $6.00 for adults, $3.00 for children ages three through eleven.

Take a scenic forty-five-minute cruise on the Cass River as the captain of the *Riverview Queen* narrates a short history of the area.

ZEHNDER'S (all ages)

730 South Main Street, Frankenmuth 48734; (800) 863–7999. Open 11:30 A.M. to 9:30 P.M. daily all year. Web site: www.zehnders.com.

There are a lot of other items you can order off its menu, but at Zehnder's, most opt for its renowned family-style, all-you-can-eat chicken dinner, which comes complete, from bread and soup to veggies and dessert and platefuls of fried chicken. Be sure to get a side order of the zesty chicken livers. $$

Frankenmuth Means Friendly I consider Frankenmuth one of Michigan's friendliest cities. Case in point. Before I was drafted into the Army, I lived in the city. Two years later, I returned with a friend. Along the banks of the Cass River, which flows through town, I just happened to recognize my former postman nearby. Striking up a casual conversation, I said that I used to live in town. "I remember," he replied. "You lived off Flint Street opposite the brewery." I was dumbfounded that he remembered an apartment dweller who lived here about six months. That's the kind of town this is. Scratch beneath the touristy surface, and there's a genuinely honest, friendly atmosphere, where German is still taught in schools, and when folks say "Hi," they mean it.

BAVARIAN INN (all ages)
713 South Main Street, Frankenmuth 48734; (800) 228–2742. Open year-round from 11:00 A.M. to 9:30 P.M. Saturday and 11:00 A.M. to 9:00 P.M. weekdays and Sunday. Web site: www.bavarianinn.com.

Across the street, the Bavarian Inn also serves chicken, but it's most famous for serving German-style meals. Outside, entertain the kids first with a performance of the inn's Glockenspiel clock tower, which tells the Pied Piper story in music. Each restaurant, incidentally, is owned by Zehnder family members. Be sure to check out the lower-level gift shops in both restaurants. In the Bavarian Inn, have a doll made for your children in about an hour. $$–$$$

Where to Eat

Tiffany's. *656 South Main Street, Frankenmuth 48734, just north of Zehnder's; (517) 652–6881. Open from 11:00 A.M. to 11:00 P.M. daily.* Where the locals go to ogle at the tourists waddling out of Zehnder's. Fresh pastas, pizzas, and grilled items. Children's menu. $$$

Zehnder's Snow Fest (all ages) This event in the first week of February brings thousands of people out into the cold to view massive snow sculptures thrown up around the town's two famous downtown restaurants. There are paths around the works in front of and behind both the Bavarian Inn and Zehnder's restaurants, which are across the street from each other, and tents are available so you can duck in and out of the cold and, if you wish, grab something to eat or something hot to drink. Even if there's no snow on the ground, festival organizers will have plenty available for the champion carvers who sculpt figures out of blocks of snow. Snow sculptures also line Main Street, where there are nearly fifty shops, which sell everything from fresh-ground flour and hand-carved chess sets to made-while-you-shop dolls for the kids.

Where to Stay

Drury Inn. *260 South Main Street, Frankenmuth 48734, downtown; (517) 652– 2800.* The inn has seventy-eight rooms and indoor pool and complimentary breakfast. Within walking distance of downtown attractions. Restaurants nearby. $$

Frankenmuth Bavarian Inn Lodge.
*1 Covered Bridge Lane, Frankenmuth
48734, 1 block east of downtown across the
bridge; (517) 652–7200.* The lodge has
354 rooms along the Cass River in a
European-themed setting. A family fun
center includes five indoor pools and
three whirlpools, family suites, an eighteen-hole indoor minigolf center, jogging trails and exercise area, tennis
courts, and more. Two restaurants
inside. $$$

**Frankenmuth Jellystone Camp-
Resort/MiniGolf.** *1339 Weiss Street,
Frankenmuth 48734; (517) 652–6668.
Web site: www.frankenmuthjellystone.com.*
This facility has 250 sites open all year,
with playground, an outdoor pool,
game room, theme weekend fun, and a
minigolf course. $

Frankenmuth Motel. *1218 Weiss
Street, Frankenmuth 48734; (517) 652–
6171 or (800) 821– 5362. Web site:
www.bavarianinn.com/motel.sht.* This
motel has seventy inexpensive rooms
and is close to downtown. $

Zehnder's Bavarian Haus. *1365
South Main Street, Frankenmuth 48734, a
½ mile south of downtown; (517) 652–
6144.* The property has 137 rooms and
indoor and outdoor pools, exercise
room, and coffee shop for breakfast
only. $$

For More Information

**Frankenmuth Convention and
Visitors Bureau,** *(517) 652–6106.
A town visitor center is at 635 South Main
Street, Frankenmuth 48734, near Zehnder's*
*and the Bavarian Inn. Web site: www.
frankenmuth.org.* It has **Free**,
on-site hotel reservation assistance
and attraction information.

Saginaw

This former rip-roaring lumber town is a bit quieter than the days in the 1800s
when lumberjacks would drive log rafts down the Cass and Tittabawassee
Rivers to the city's sawmills. While it still owes much of its vitality to auto manufacturing, tourism is becoming a major part of its economy. The upper Saginaw and lower Tittabawassee Rivers are now famous among walleye anglers
nationwide. Each fall and winter, and again in spring, anglers gather to try for
walleye, which enter the river system from Lake Huron's Saginaw Bay to the
north. Local bait shops have the skinny on what's biting where. Best times are
usually in November, during ice-fishing season (in previous years, the Saginaw
River never froze, and the return of ice is a testament to cleanup efforts), and
early May.

JOHNNY PANTHER QUESTS (all ages)

A trip to introduce you to the upper Flint River is $80 per couple, plus $30 for each extra person. The Saginaw-area trip is $120 per couple, plus $50 for each additional passenger. Trips accommodate two to six people. Call (810) 653–3859.

If you've never taken your kids on a real adventure, there's one waiting just down the road, literally. For within a few minutes of leaving downtown Saginaw, you could be watching a bald eagle fly silently over the water, see roosting cormorant, hear calling geese and ducks, watch deer bounding through thickets, or hear the slap of a beaver's tail on the water in the unspoiled natural habitat that covers the thousands of acres of wetlands owner/guide Wil Hufton's pegged Michigan's Everglades.

Hufton motors his flat-bottomed boat into the wilds and then floats through the silence. Trips can accommodate any age, from more adventurous types who don't mind a portage to see the beauty to those who just want to float. He'll even let you off to quietly picnic for a few hours before he returns to pick you up in time for your very own sail into the sunset. You provide your lunch; he provides a cooler, ice, a bag of pistachios, and the silence. It's a great time.

 SAGINAW CHILDREN'S ZOO (all ages)

1720 South Washington, Saginaw 48605; (517) 771–4966. To get to the zoo, leave I-675 at the Fifth Street/Sixth Street exit and head south on Washington Avenue approximately 2 miles. The park is on the east side of the street. The zoo is usually open daily from Mother's Day-weekend through Labor Day. Zoo hours are Monday through Saturday 10:00 A.M. to 5:00 P.M; Sunday and holidays 11:00 A.M. to 6:00 P.M. Admission is $3.50 for ages thirteen to sixty-four, and $2.50 for seniors and children ages three through twelve. Children younger than three are admitted Free.

Keep that phone number handy, and stand by, as the zoo is undergoing major changes that officials say will make it the state's premier children's zoo as it reopens in segments. Officials weren't quite sure what shape exhibits would take at press time, so a trip here will be a real voyage of discovery. Rest assured, however, that the zoo that previously wowed area children for years will be reborn. Located in a grove of trees on the city's east side, it featured twenty-eight species of animals on its eight and a half acres, but that will change, too, as more exhibits are added and more acreage is as well. The Ibershoff Special, a miniature-train ride featuring a ½-mile loop around the zoo for 75 cents per person, is still part of the fun, as are a souvenir shop and playground. There also will be a new amphitheater for shows, and kids and adults alike can ride on the state's only locally hand-crafted carousel. When

Shiver on the River
When the temperature drops here, it's the signal for hundreds of locals and tourists to come into the cold during the annual downtown fishing festival, which not only celebrates renewed annual runs of hungry walleyes but includes a contest to catch the biggest walleye through the ice of the Saginaw River and its main tributaries. Each year the fish swim into the river from Saginaw Bay to winter and then spawn in spring. The contest usually runs between late January and early February.

There are usually top prizes that total nearly $4,100 for first through fifteenth place, and some years there's a special award for any angler who catches a fish that sets a state record. Walleyes up to ten pounds are often pulled up through the ice here. If you come for the fun of it or to teach your offspring this unique brand of fishing, all the equipment you'll need is a license, a stubby ice-fishing rod, an auger or spike to chip a hole through the ice, and warm clothes, including gloves or mittens and boots, and lots of patience to sit on the ice hoping for a bite. If you're in it for the money, get the rules and fill out an entry blank for $5.00 at local tackle shops, and head out.

Best fishing times are usually early morning and late evening, and most anglers use small jigs tipped with minnows. Weigh-ins are all conducted at a local outfitter or tackle shop named in the rules. For more information call (517) 776-9704.

completed, the carousel will have seating for twenty-nine persons on sixteen horses, two bunnies, two zebras, and two chariots. Painting boards will depict Saginaw County history. The carousel will be set inside a pavilion with stained glass windows created by local artists.

KOKOMO'S FAMILY FUN CENTER (all ages)

5200 Kokomo Drive, Saginaw 48604; (517) 797–5656. From I–675, exit at Tittabawassee Road and head west past Bay Road to Kokomo Drive, and then head north. Open 9:00 a.m. to 9:00 p.m. Monday through Thursday, 11:00 a.m. to 11:00 p.m. Friday and Saturday, and 11:00 a.m. to 7:00 p.m. Sunday. Prices for all activities range from $3.50 to $6.50, and a wristband good for three attractions may be purchased for $10.95. Web site: www.kokomos.com.

A nineteen-hole minigolf course, go-carts, bumper boats, laser tag, even an ice rink and snacks make a stop here fun. Golfers will find an enclosed driving range with thirty-four stations, indoor putting green, and golf pros to give you pointers. There also is "water wars," a water-balloon game.

Where to Eat

Forbidden City. *4024 Bay Road, Saginaw 48603; (517) 799–9340. In the Town Campus mall, set back on the east side of Bay Road (Michigan 84). From I–675, exit westbound on Davenport and then go north on Bay Road about 2 miles.* Excellent Chinese fare for lunch and dinner. $$

La Senorita. *3823 Bay Road (Michigan 84), Saginaw 48603; near the Fashion*

Square Mall; (517) 793–6312. From I–675, exit west at Tittabawassee Road, and then go south on Bay Road. Good Mexican food. Children's menu. $$

Sullivan's West. *5235 Gratiot (Michigan 46), Saginaw 48603; (517) 799–1940. From I–75, exit at M–46 and head west.* Good family dining. Children's menu for lunch and dinner. $$

Where to Stay

Four Points Hotel by Sheraton. *4960 Towne Centre Road, Saginaw 48604; (517) 790–5050.* At the junction of I-675 and Tittabawassee Roads, north of downtown, the hotel has 156 rooms, indoor and outdoor pool, fitness area, whirlpool/sauna, and dining rooms serving breakfast, lunch, and dinner. Near Fashion Square Mall. $$

Hampton Inn. *2222 Tittabawassee Road, Saginaw 48604, at the junction with I–675; (517) 792–7666.* A basic motel with 120 rooms with outdoor pool and dining nearby. Also close to Fashion Square Mall. $$

Montague Inn. *1581 South Washington, Saginaw 48601; (517) 752–3939. From I–675, exit downtown and head west to*

Washington, then head south about 1½ miles. Web site: www.montagueinn.com. The inn has eighteen rooms. What might be one of the best bed-and-breakfast experiences you'll have in the state is waiting inside this former lumber baron mansion overlooking Lake Linton, a lagoon of the Saginaw River. Great Victorian atmosphere as well as a restaurant serving both breakfast and elegant dinners. Choose from two buildings to stay, and make arrangements to take a Johnny Panther wilderness tour with a stay here. $$

Red Roof Inn. *966 South Outer Drive, Saginaw 48601; (517) 754–8414. From I–75, exit at M–46 and head west to Outer Drive, then turn north.* A basic motel with seventy-nine comfortable rooms. $

For More Information

Saginaw County Convention and Visitors Bureau, *1 Tuscola Street, Suite*

101, Saginaw 48607; (517) 752–7164. Web site: www.saginawcvb.org.

East Michigan—North

The northern part of east Michigan drifts from the nation's "beanbasket," which produces more soy, navy, and other bean varieties than any other state, to some of the largest publicly owned tracts of forestland in the nation. The dichotomy amazes even well-traveled Michiganians, who keep coming back, drawn by the diversity. Here are just a few areas to explore:

Bad Axe

Bad Axe is at the intersection of Michigan Highway 53, which runs north and south from the Detroit area through the Thumb, and Michigan 142. A great way to tour the Thumb is along Michigan 25, which runs through many of the area's major communities, as well as along the Lake Huron shoreline in many areas. It is part of a designated scenic drive called the Lake Huron Circle Tour, which includes routes in Ontario, too. Native American rock drawings in Michigan? Yup—in the heart of the state's Thumb, the tip of which makes up Huron County. The county seat got its name innocently from an old ax found on the site by early surveyors.

SANILAC PETROGLYPHS STATE HISTORIC PARK (all ages)
Open Wednesday through Sunday from Memorial Day through Labor Day. Hours are 11:30 A.M. to 4:30 P.M. To find the park, turn east off Michigan 53 onto Bay City/Forestville Road, travel about 4 miles to Germania Road, and turn south. The park is ½ mile farther, on the west side. For more information contact the Michigan Historical Museum at (517) 373–3559. Admission is Free. *Web site: www. sos.state.mi.us/history/history.html.*

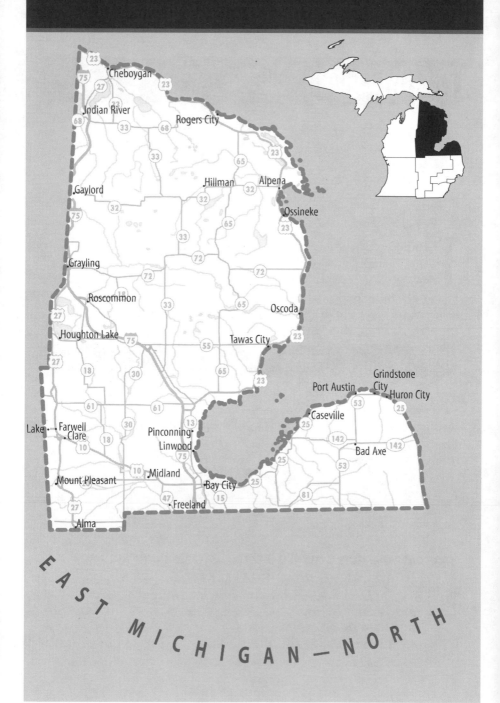

EAST MICHIGAN—NORTH

Estimated to be more than 1,000 years old, the rock carvings, or pet-roglyphs, were chiseled into the soft sandstone along the north branch of the Cass River. Kids will marvel at these characters, including the fig-ure of a hunter with a bow and arrow, and others that resemble ani-mals. Visitors can also walk a mile-long nature trail through the forested park, where you'll see more marked sites (plan on at least one hour, and take along bug repellent). Forty-five-minute guided presentations on the petroglyphs are given in summer. Special events include "Romancing the Stone," a mid-August presentation on Native American folklore.

BAD AXE MUSEUM AND LOG CABINS (all ages)

In Bad Axe City Park, downtown: (517) 269–8325. Open from 2:00 to 5:00 P.M. Sunday from Memorial Day to September 26. Free.

It's hard to believe when looking over the region that lumbering, not farming, was the major activity here one hundred years ago. Huge fires in 1871 (at the same time as the Chicago fire) and 1881 sent lumber-men elsewhere, and they began farming. You'll learn more about the area through the museum. Its log cabins are open by appointment. The cabins depict a pioneer home, school, blacksmith shop, chapel, store, and barn in the nineteenth century.

Bill's Top Family Adventures in East Michigan–North

- **Hartwick Pines State Park, Grayling.** Kids will be mesmerized by the size of the trees in the park and the history of Michigan logging.

- **Dinosaur Gardens Prehistoric Zoo, Ossineke.** Children come face-to-face with one of the great fascinations of kid-dom.

- **Fishing for salmon on Lake Huron in Oscoda, Alpena, or Rogers City.** With several ports to choose from, what could be better than spending a day fishing with your kids?

- **Higgins Lake South State Park, Roscommon.** A great place that kids enjoy because of its gentle, sloping beach, where they can get their toes tickled by minnows.

- **Renting a cabin for a week on Lake Huron, between Au Gres and Rogers City.** A great way for a family to vacation together.

Where to Eat

Elias Bros. *900 North Van Dyke (Michigan 53), Bad Axe 48413; (517) 269–9515.* Family restaurant with food from salad bar to trademark triple-decker burgers. $$

The Pasta House. *337 Main, Kinde 48445, east of Michigan 53 in Kinde, about 10 miles north of Bad Axe; (517) 874–4070.* Family-oriented Italian restaurant in the middle of this tiny farm community, across the street from the elevator. Open for lunch and dinner. $$

Where to Stay

The Franklin Inn. *1070 East Huron Avenue, Bad Axe 48413, 7 blocks east of Michigan 53 (Michigan 142); (517) 269–9951.* This inn has fifty-nine rooms and a restaurant on the premises. $

For More Information

Bad Axe Chamber of Commerce, *P.O. Box 87, Bad Axe 48413; (517) 269–6936.*

Huron City

HURON CITY MUSEUM (all ages)

To reach the museum, which is just about the entire town, take Michigan 25 east from Port Austin about 8 miles (it's on the north side of the road). For more information call (517) 428–4123. From July 1 to Labor Day, the museum is open Thursday through Monday from 10:00 A.M. to 5:00 P.M. The price of admission depends on which of two tours (the town, the lifesaving station, or both) you'd like to take. Tours of both the town and museum that includes the Point Aux Barques Lifesaving Station are $10.00 for adults, $5.00 for anyone ten through fourteen years old, and $8.00 for seniors. Children nine and younger enter **Free**. *Tours of Seven Gables or the museum separately are $6.00 for adults, $5.00 for seniors, and $3.00 for ages one through fourteen. The last tour of the day is at 4:30 P.M.; the last double tour leaves at 3:30.*

Catch a glimpse of what local life was like in the early twentieth century at the Huron City Museum, a restored town on the Lake Huron shore at the tip of Michigan's Thumb. From 1893 until 1938, Huron City was the summer home of William Lyon Phelps, a Yale professor, whose relatives created this unique museum.

Each summer families can join guides on one-hour tours of Phelps's restored home, Seven Gables, the restored general store, the church where Phelps preached, an 1837 log cabin, the town's Community House Inn, and the U.S. Lifesaving Station along the beach. The Lifesaving Service was the forerunner of the Coast Guard, and its crew's job was to save passengers and crew from foundering ships along the Thumb's reef-scarred shoreline.

Huron County Regional Information

For more information on the county, call the Huron County Economic Development Corporation at (517) 269-6431. Web site: www.huroncounty.com. Cellular phone users can dial *FISH for a fishing report, or *CHARTER for charter booking information. Besides cottages and resorts, some private beachfront homes also are rented seasonally. Call (800) 358-4862 for more information.

Where to Eat and Stay

See Port Austin listing.

Grindstone City

To get to Grindstone City, take Pointe Aux Barques Road east from Port Austin about 4 miles until it ends, turn north, and watch for the signs directing you to the harbor.

To get a little lesson in Michigan history and a big lesson in fishing for the "fightingest" fish in the Great Lakes, visit this tiny town, which once was the nation's grindstone capital. Located at the very tip of the Thumb, Grindstone City was famous nationwide for a century for producing some of the world's finest grinding stones, which were cut from its limestone quarries and sent to markets around the globe.

When other sharpening materials became popular during World War I, the town's two factories closed. Old grindstones ready for export can still be seen lining the roads and driveways in spots.

159

CHARTER FISHING (all ages)

For Grindstone City charter boat information, call (517) 738–5500.

The grindstone industry may be long gone, but now Grindstone is known for something else: what may be the best early-season salmon and trout fishing on the lakes. From a cozy, crescent-shaped harbor, up to a dozen charter boats take anglers on morning and afternoon trips in pursuit of chinook salmon, steelhead (a lake-living rainbow trout), and lake trout.

All gear—and instructions when you hook into a big one—is provided. All you need is a state fishing license (children ages sixteen and younger are exempt). The best salmon fishing runs from May to mid-June, and fish that are more than twenty pounds are not uncommon. In summer, lake trout fishing is tops, and by July 20 the salmon return, and fishing stays productive through early September. Charters are priced at around $250 for a half day (usually, morning fishing is best, starting at or before sunup) and take up to six persons, so the cost can be split among friends or family members.

Where to Eat and Stay

See Port Austin listing.

Port Austin

Located 8 miles west of Grindstone city on Michigan 53 at the intersection with Michigan 25. This resort town at the tip of the Thumb is pretty quiet, except in summer, when cottage renters and campers populate the environs, especially on weekends.

MISS PORT AUSTIN (all ages)

The Miss Port Austin *ties up at the foot of Michigan 53 in downtown Port Austin. To reserve a spot on the next voyage, call (517) 738–5271. Capt. Fred Davis charges about $28 per person for fishing trips, with a 20 percent discount for families and seniors on weekdays. Starting in July, the* Miss Port Austin *leaves the dock at 7:30 A.M. and 2:30 P.M. Call ahead for departures at other times of the spring and fall. If fishing is on the docket, you'll need a Michigan state fishing*

license (one-day permits are available from area tackle shops; children ages sixteen and younger don't require a license) and a cooler for drinks. Clean your catch at the fish-cleaning station at the dock. Chances are the boat's mate will help you clean for tips. If only sight-seeing's available, call for sailing times and prices.

For one of the best all-around family fun experiences on Lake Huron, sign up for a fishing cruise aboard the *Miss Port Austin*, captained by Fred Davis. Up to twice a day in summer, Davis takes up to twenty aboard his boat, moored at the public harbor in this summer vacation town, and steers a course toward fun. If the perch are in, Davis will head for the fishing grounds. If they're not, the boat also is available for historic and sight-seeing cruises along the rugged Lake Huron shore. Sight-seeing cruises will take you past rock outcroppings like Turnip Rock and caves along the shore near Broken Rock.

If he's fishing, Davis will use an electronic fish-finder that he'll be happy to show you. If you've never fished before and have no equipment, Davis will rent you a rod for the day. Then bait up with the minnows he provides, and the rest is up to you. If nothing's doing, Davis will try several spots until the fish start biting. It's a great way to introduce children to the joys of summer on the water, the bird life that typifies the area, and something they can take pleasure from the rest of their lives.

If the perch aren't biting, however, either tackle salmon or trout, or try for walleye later in Caseville.

SANDY DUNES ADVENTURE GOLF (all ages)

2755 Michigan 25, between Port Austin and Caseville; (517) 738–6066. Open daily in season from 10:00 A.M. to 10:00 P.M. One round costs $5.00 per person or $3.00 for children four and younger.

Besides a landscaped eighteen-hole minigolf course with waterfalls, there's a game room, dairy bar, and deli.

FAMILY GO-KARTS (ages 6 and up)

One mile south of Port Austin on M–53; (517) 738–5130. Open daily from Memorial Day weekend through Labor Day weekend. Hours are 10:00 A.M. to 10:00 P.M.

Go-carts for juniors, rookies, and adults are the featured attraction. You'll also find basketball hoop throws, a trampoline, and a gyro fitness test, among other fun activities.

161

Where to Eat

Besides these upscale places to eat, there are others in the area that aren't as hard on your pocketbook. But since most persons come here on vacation anyway, and many of us like to take the family out for a treat at least once during our stay, here are some in the area that will impress them all:

The Bank–1884. *On Michigan 25, Main Street, Port Austin 48467, 2 blocks south of the harbor; (517) 738–5353. Open April through October.* Built of brick to withstand any repeat of the 1881 fire that swept the Thumb, the bank is now a restaurant that serves great dinners on two floors. Enjoy a variety of entrees from prime rib to fresh walleye. Children's menu. $$$

The Farm. *699 Port Crescent Road, Port Austin 48467; (517) 874–5700. Two miles west of M–53 and about 3 miles south of Port Austin.* Since the restaurant is open only seasonally, here is its schedule: Open daily except Monday for dinner from Memorial Day to Labor Day, open weekends from Mother's Day to Memorial Day and from Labor Day through mid-October. Surprising dinners served in a one-hundred-year-old farmhouse and spiced with herbs and produce grown in their own five-acre garden. Whitefish, pasta, and made-on-premises desserts, breads, and soups. Children's menu. $$$

Sportsman's Inn. *8708 Lake Street, Port Austin 48467. In downtown Port Austin on the east side of M–25, just south of the traffic light; (517) 738–7520.* It may look like a bar at first glance, but there's a separate side entrance to a family dining room that serves pizza, fresh seafood, and ribs at inexpensive prices. $$

Where to Stay

If you're looking for a posh hotel or motel, this isn't the area to find one. The area prides itself on being one of the last bastions of family-run resorts in the state. If staying in a cottage, don't expect a mansion. There also is a good selection of campgrounds in the mix.

Kreb's Cottages. *3478 Port Austin Road, Port Austin 48467, 9 miles west of the city along Michigan 25. (517) 856–2876.* Eight cottages from one to four bedrooms, usually renting weekly. Featuring sandy beach on the lake, with grills. Rates start at $475 per week.

Lake Vista Motel and Cottages. *168 West Spring (Michigan 25), Port Austin 48467, ½ mile west of the town light; (517) 738–8612.* This facility has fifteen rooms in a motel setting along the beach next to Port Austin's harbor. $$

Oak Beach County Park. *3356 Port Austin Road, Port Austin 48467, west of downtown along Michigan 25; (517) 856–2344.* Here you'll find fifty-five campsites, a swimming beach, and tent and modern camping. $

Port Crescent State Park. *About 4 miles southwest of Port Austin along Michigan 25, Port Austin 48467; (517) 738–*

8663. *For reservations call (800) 543–2937. Motor-vehicle permits required to enter are sold at the gate for $4.00 daily or $20.00 annually.* Port Crescent is not only a place to stay but a place to enjoy on a vacation as well. It is one of the newest and most picturesque state parks in Michigan. At 565 acres, is also has one of the last undeveloped stretches of beach along the Thumb. Families can choose from among 138 campsites (try for number 89, a beachside gem nicknamed the "honeymoon site"), roam some of the finest examples of Lake Huron sand dunes in east Michigan, and go for an inland hike on the 6½ miles of nature trails that run along the beach and through the Thumb's surprisingly extensive hardwood forests. The park also includes a fitness trail, fishing access along the Pinnebog River for persons with physical disabilities, and a 3-mile-long beach for daytime use that often is virtually deserted. Port Crescent also features minicabin rentals by reservation. $

For More Information

Port Austin Hot Line, *(517) 738–7600 (twenty-four-hour recording) or (517) 738– 5271 (live person).*

Caseville

Caseville is a great little resort town nestled along the beach on Lake Huron with a large harbor. The city beach is a wide, popular spot in summer and has a boardwalk. In mid-May, the annual Dulcimer Festival and Art in the Park takes place in Sleeper State Park. The annual Auto Festival takes place in mid-July at Caseville Public School, featuring antique and classic cars and rods, and there's also a walleye tournament in July.

 WALLEYE FISHING (all ages)

Call charter captain Vern Metz at (248) 634–7988 or (517) 550–2301, and he'll show you how Saginaw Bay has of late become known nationwide for its walleye fishing.

It's estimated that up to a million legal-size fish are finning through the waters off the town. If you don't have a boat or the expertise, Metz will take you. He fits up to six anglers per trip to introduce them to the fish, considered one of the top-tasting freshwater fish around, up close and personal. Best action, he says, runs from mid-June through mid-September. A trip includes tackle and everything except beverages and onboard food.

Where to Eat

Bay Window. *6750 Main Street, Caseville 48725; (517) 856–2676.* Open for breakfast, lunch, and dinner. Outdoor dining in summer, with children's menu and family atmosphere. $$

Guiseppe's Pizzeria Italian American Restaurant. *6562 Main Street (Michigan 25), Caseville 48725;*

(517) 856–2035. Enjoy pizza for lunch or dinner with overlooks of Caseville's harbor area. $$$

Shaker's Diner. *6515 Main Street, Caseville 48725; (517) 856–9898.* Open for breakfast, lunch, and dinner. Family atmosphere, with children's menu. $$

Where to Stay

Albert E. Sleeper State Park. *Five miles northeast of Caseville on M–25; (517) 856–4411. The park is open all year; however, showers and flush toilets are only open from May 1 to mid-October. A valid motor-vehicle permit is required for use and is sold at the gate. Cost is $4.00 daily or $20.00 for an annual pass.* One of the oldest and most beautiful state parks in Michigan preserves 700 acres of woods and beachfront and features a walkway over Michigan 25 between the campground and the day-use-only beach area. Sleeper has 208 campsites and about 4 miles of nature trails that run through the woods, which actually are made up

of old dune areas from when the lake was higher long ago. Trails also are open to cross-country skiing in winter. Unsure about camping? Sleeper and Port Crescent also feature minicabin rentals by reservation. The cabins are handicapped-accessible and include electricity, bunk beds, and a table and chairs, as well as a grill and fire pit outside. $

Bella Vista Motel. *6024 Port Austin Road (Michigan 25), Caseville 48725; (517) 856–2650.* This cozy motel has sixteen rooms, pool, and a restaurant. Cottages also available for longer stays. Beach nearby. $$

For More Information

Caseville Chamber of Commerce, *6632 Main Street, Caseville 48725; (517) 856–3818 or (800) 606–1347.*

Bay City

To get to downtown Bay City, from I-75, take business I-75 east, which becomes Michigan 25. Cross the bridge and turn north on Washington, and you're in the heart of downtown. To reach the west side business district, turn north on Michigan 13 from Business I–75, then east on Midland Road and follow it there.

Lumbering and sawmills were so thick along the river in the nineteenth-century that even today, when workers lay foundations for new buildings nearby, they still run into piles of sawdust several feet deep. This former rip-roaring lumber town has settled down a bit from when bars along the Saginaw River held trapdoors waiting for unsuspecting lumberjacks who'd just gotten paid and had too much to drink. Today the excitement has shifted to more legitimate action. Bay City, with its scores of Victorian-era buildings and quaint downtown, is the setting for some of the region's best special events, recreational activities, and shopping. The city's business districts are divided east and west by the Saginaw River, and there's plenty to do on both sides.

The Bay City River Roar, a series of boat races held the third weekend of June on the Saginaw River downtown, draws more than 50,000 spectators to the shores to see hyrdoplanes powered by automotive engines roar around an elliptical course. A final heat determines the winner. The Fourth of July Fireworks Festival takes place on the riverfront downtown from July 2 through 4. Billed as the largest show in the region, the festival includes a Fourth of July parade. The day is capped by the **Free** fireworks show over the water at dusk on July 4 before more than 175,000 pyrotechnics fans.

DELTA COLLEGE PLANETARIUM AND LEARNING CENTER (all ages)

100 Center Avenue, Bay City 48708; (517) 667–2260. On the river's east side, in downtown. Head across the river on Business U.S. 10, then turn north on Saginaw. It's at the corner of Center and Saginaw. Shows take place at 4:00 and 6:00 P.M. Thursday; 2:00, 4:00, and 7:00 P.M. Saturday; and 2:00 and 4:00 P.M. Sunday. Afternoon shows are perfect for youngsters ages ten and younger, as the later ones are reserved for those older. Admission is $3.50 for adults, $3.00 for those ages eighteen and younger and sixty and older.

Funded by NASA, this place is a great one to introduce youngsters to stargazing of the noncelebrity kind. There's a rooftop observatory, along with a state-of-the-art planetarium, where occupants of the 130 seats can actually vote on what to see in the solar system.

ST. LAURENT'S NUT HOUSE (all ages)

1101 North Water Street, Bay City 48708, on the city's east side; (517) 893–7522 or (800) 289–7688. From Business I–75, head across the bridge to Saginaw, head north to Second, then west about a block. Open 9:00 A.M. to 9:00 P.M. Monday through Saturday and 11:00 A.M. to 5:00 P.M. Sunday.

The sign outside says NUTS SINCE 1904, and it's right. Stock up on the PB part of PB&J sandwiches here, where all-natural, regular or low-sodium, smooth or crunchy peanut butter is sold in tubs of up to five pounds. Go nuts at the nuts counter, too, while the kids are inside picking out some penny candies.

This area along Water Street, incidentally, was the city's most notorious, known in the nineteenth century as "Hell's Half-Mile" by even the roughest lumberjacks.

BAY CITY STATE RECREATION AREA (all ages)

Six miles north on the west side, at the end of Euclid Avenue, Bay City 48706; (517) 684–3020. To reach it from I–75, exit at Beaver Road (exit 168) and drive east 5 miles, or exit from the south at Michigan 25/15 to Euclid, then turn north and follow it to the park. Admission is by vehicle permit, $4.00 daily or $20.00 annually. Camping is $12.00 nightly.

Formerly Bay City State Park, the park's name was changed because of the great variety of activities it encompasses, including camping in 264 sites and a beach on the bay. Swimmers should be watchful of zebra mussels. Brought in from Europe to the Great Lakes by passing ships, the mussels are now a nuisance in one sense but good in another, as they have cleaned the bay's water. The shells are sharp, however, so swimming is confined to a nice beach at the park's northern end, featuring the gradual slope so attractive to families with small children. The day-use area features new playground structures as well.

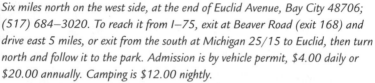

Sportfishing in the Bay

At least seven charter boats operate out of the Bay City area after fish from salmon to those famous Saginaw Bay walleye. Check out the list provided by the Bay Area County Convention and Visitors Bureau (see For More Information at the end of this section). If you have your own boat, there are several public boat-launch sites around Saginaw Bay, so you can follow the fish through the season.

The park also includes the Saginaw Bay Visitors Center (517–667–0717) across the road from the day-use area, with exhibits on the importance of wetlands to the bay's health. A paved nature trail including one with Braille signs leads to two towers with overlooks of the 1,700-acre Tobico Marsh. Bring bug repellent if you go on the trail in the evening. There are 5 miles of trails in all. The wetland is considered one of the best birding spots in the state.

Where to Eat

Krysiak's House Restaurant. 1605 Michigan Avenue, Bay City 48708; (517) 894–5531. From I–75, head east on Michigan 25/15 to Euclid and go south to M–13. Head west across the river to continue south. Turn east on Cass Avenue, and then south on Michigan. When in Bay City, do as the Bay Cityans do, and this is one spot this town with a large Polish heritage heads for. Made-on-premises Polish and American dishes. Children's menu for both lunch and dinner. Homemade fudge and ice cream. $$

Original Grampa Tony's. 1108 Columbus Avenue, Bay City 48708; (517) 893–4795. From Michigan 25/15, head east across the river. Take Washington south to Columbus and head east. It's on the south side of the road. Another Italian spot where Bay City folks head for pizza and other fare for lunch and dinner. $$$

Terry & Jerry's O Sole Mio Ristorante. 1005 North Saginaw Street, Bay City 48708, north of Third Street; (517) 893–3496. From Michigan 25/15, head over the bridge to the east side, then go north on Saginaw. The restaurant is on the west side of the street. If you like Italian, you'll love it here, as this is one of the best in the state. Great atmosphere for dinner. My favorite is the cannoli. Children's menu. $$$

Where to Stay

Bay Motel. 910 South Euclid, Bay City 48706; (517) 684–4100. From Michigan 25/15, head east to Euclid, and then turn south a ½ mile. The motel is on the west side of the road. Only eighteen rooms, but a clean, inexpensive place to stay. Dining is nearby. $

Bay Valley Resort Hotel. 2470 Old Bridge Road, Bay City 48706; (517) 686–3500. From I–75, exit at Michigan 84 and head west about ¼ mile, and then follow the signs north. A full-service resort with a Jack Nicklaus–designed golf course, indoor-outdoor pool, and 150 rooms in a country club–like setting. Restaurant on premises and other dining nearby. $$

Best Western Creekside Inn. 6385 West Side Saginaw Road, Bay City 48706; (517) 686–0840. At the junction of I–75 and Michigan 84, on the west side of the freeway. The inn has seventy-one rooms with outdoor pool, next to a Saginaw River tributary. Restaurant adjoins. $$

For More Information

Bay Area Convention and Visitors Bureau, 901 Saginaw Street, Bay City 48708; (517) 893–1222 or (800) 424–5114. Web sites: www.tourbaycity.com or www.baycityarea.com.

Freeland

Freeland is a small community along the Tittabawassee River and is the site of a ski area.

APPLE MOUNTAIN (ages 3 and up)

4519 North River Road, Freeland 48623; (517) 781–0170. From Saginaw, head west on Davenport. It becomes State Street. Follow State Street to a big curve. At the curve, turn to the west across the Tittabawassee River to a four-way stop. Turn north on River Road and drive about 4½ miles to a stop sign. At the sign is the entrance to Apple Mountain. Plan on spending about $30 for rentals and a lift ticket for adults and teens. A lesson, ski pass, and ski rental is $25 for children between ages of three and six. Web site: www.applemountain.com.

Built next to an apple orchard, this manmade ski hill has ten runs, with equipment rental, instruction and other amenities.

Where to Eat and Stay

See Saginaw and Midland listings.

Midland

The town that aspirin built has lots to offer the family, from plant tours to the arts to nature study. It has a great compact downtown along the Tittaba-wassee River, including a unique three-cornered bridge called the Tridge, just beyond the corner of Ashman and Main Streets.

MIDLAND CENTER FOR THE ARTS (all ages)

1801 West St. Andrews, Midland 48640; (517) 631–5930. From U.S. 10, take the Eastman Road exit 2 miles into town. It's at the corner of Eastman and West St. Andrews. Open daily from 10:00 A.M. to 6:00 P.M. Admission is Free *for Hall of Ideas; call ahead for rates for events. Web site: www.mcfta.org.*

One of the state's first children's museums is included in the galleries. The Hall of Ideas has do-it-yourself displays, computer games, and puzzles, most of which are hands-on activities. Also included are exhibits of the Midland Historical Society, which feature local history and prehistory. The gallery features art collected from around the world.

DOW GARDENS (all ages)

Adjacent to the Midland Center for the Arts, Midland 48640; (517) 631–2677. Open 10:00 A.M. to 9:00 P.M. daily except in winter when it closes at 4:15 P.M. Admission is $3.00 for adults, $1.00 for children ages six to seventeen, and Free *for children five and younger. Web site: www.dowgardens.com.*

More than one hundred acres of gardens include displays of rhododendrons, trees, and wildflowers. In season, 20,000 tulip bulbs and 10,000 bedding plants erupt in color along waterfalls and bridges

CHIPPEWA NATURE CENTER (all ages)

400 South Badour Road, Midland 48640; (517) 631–0830. To reach the center, take the Business U.S. 10 exit off U.S. 10 and turn south onto Cronkright. Go over the bridge and then north on St. Charles, the first street past the Tittabawassee River. Watch for the sign at the Y in the road, turn left, and drive about 3 miles farther, and you'll see the entrance. Admission is by donation. The center is open Monday through Friday from 8:00 A.M. to 5:00 P.M., Saturday from 9:00 A.M. to 5:00 P.M., and Sunday and most holidays from 1:00 to 5:00 P.M. Web site: www.chippewanaturecenter.com.

At the center, activities focus on humankind's interaction with the planet. One of its most popular events is the Maple Sugaring Weekend, which begins on the third Saturday in March. Families can tour the 1,000-acre center with a naturalist and follow the process that turns watery sugar-maple sap into thick, luscious syrup in the center's Sugar Shack. Other perfect family activities include nature walks through the center's 14 miles of trails, exploring a restored 1870s farm and log school, and naturalist-led programs such as insect, reptile, and flower identification in summer. There's a wheelchair-accessible trail as well. The Oxbow Archaeological District contains the site of a monumental territorial battle between two Native American tribes, the Ojibwa and Sauk. The burial ground was unearthed in the 1930s.

PERE MARQUETTE RAIL TRAIL (all ages)

From Midland, the trail begins at the Forks, location of the Tridge downtown, where the Chippewa River, coming from Mount Pleasant, and the Tittabawassee River, coming from the north, merge. The trail can be picked up at several parks and other sites along old U.S. 10. For information contact the Midland County Department of Parks and Recreation, (517) 832–6870, or the Midland City Parks and Recreation, (517) 835– 9071. Free. *Web site: http://users.mdn.net/fopmrt.*

Grab your bike or in-line skates or just walk a part or all of this 22-mile-long trail, which follows the old Pere Marquette Railroad right-of-way between Midland and Coleman and, eventually, all the way to Clare and even beyond. The paved portion runs between Midland and Coleman (population 1,295) along Old U.S. 10, through parks, and over rivers like the Tittabawasse and the Salt, the stream favored by Native Americans for its salt deposits, which supposedly gave Herbert Dow the idea for his operations. It crosses three old railroad trestles. Maps are available from the Midland Convention and Visitors Bureau (see For More Information at the end of this section). Traversing woods and farmland is a great way to explore the diversity of mid-Michigan.

Bill's Favorite Events in East Michigan—North

- **Winterfest** (January), downtown Gaylord, (800) 345–8621.
- **Camper and RV show** (February), Flint, IMA Arena, (517) 349–8881.
- **St. Patrick's Day Parade** (March), Bay City, (517) 684–7980.
- **Irish Festival** (March), downtown Clare, (517) 386–2442.
- **Maple Syrup Festival** (April), Shepherd, south of Mount Pleasant, (517) 828–5726.
- **Blacksmiths Weekend** (May), Crossroads Village & Huckleberry Railroad, (810) 736–7100 or (800) 648–7275.
- **Free fishing weekend on all Michigan Great Lakes and inland waters** (June, usually first full weekend), (517) 373–2842. No license needed this weekend only.
- **Corn Festival** (July), Auburn, (800) 424–5114.
- **East Tawas Antique and Classic Car Show** (July), East Tawas, (517) 362–8643 or (800) 558–2927.
- **Bluegill Festival** (July), St. Helen, (517) 389–3725.
- **Bay Port Fish Sandwich Festival** (August), Bay Port, (517) 656–3221.
- **Fall Art Fair** (September), Midland, (517) 662–4357.
- **Tawas Bay Fall Festival** (October), East Tawas and Tawas City, (517) 362–8643 or (800) 558–2927.
- **Festival of Lights** (November), Bay City, (517) 893–3573.
- **Holiday Walk** (December), Flint Cultural Center, (810) 760–1169.

Where to Eat

Bamboo Garden. *2600 North Saginaw Road, Midland 48640; (517) 832–7967. From U.S. 10, exit at Eastman Road and head 1 mile south and ½ mile west on Saginaw Road.* Very good Chinese food, specializing in spicy Szechuan and Shanghai cuisine for lunch and dinner. Children's menu. $$

Big Boy Restaurant. *1513 South Saginaw Road, Midland 48640; (517) 631–1059. From U.S. 10, exit at Midland Road toward town to Saginaw Road.* Inexpensive family fare, including trademark triple-decker burgers. Serves breakfast, lunch, and dinner. $

Damon's Place for Ribs. *6801 Eastman Road, Midland 48642; (517) 837–7427. From U.S. 10, exit at Eastman.* Sports atmosphere with ribs a specialty for lunch and dinner. $$

Pizza Sam's/Jim & Tony's. *Corner of Ashman and Main, Midland 48640, downtown; (517) 631–1934.* Pizza, sandwiches, and more in a family atmosphere for lunch and dinner. $$

Where to Stay

Best Western Valley Plaza Resort. *5221 Bay City Road, Midland 48642; (517) 496–2700 or (800) 825–2700. From westbound U.S. 10, take the Midland/Bay City Road exit. From eastbound U.S. 10, exit at Waldo Road. Head 2½ miles south on Waldo to Bay City Road, and then turn east and go about a mile.* The resort has 236 rooms with three indoor pools, even a beach and lake for summer swimming, plus bowling alley and billiards, four restaurants, exercise area, and movie theater. $$

Fairview Inn. *2200 West Wackerly Road, Midland 48642; (517) 631–0070 or (800) 422–2744. From U.S. 10, take the Eastman Road exit south to Wackerly, and then head west.* The inn has ninety-three rooms, indoor pool, and hot tub. Restaurants nearby. $$

Holiday Inn of Midland. *1500 West Wackerly, Midland 48640; (517) 631–4220. From U.S. 10, take the Eastman Road exit south to Wackerly, and then head west.* The property has 235 rooms, with indoor pool and recreation area, racquetball courts, and a restaurant. $$

For More Information

Midland County Convention & Visitors Bureau, *300 Rodd Street, Midland 48640; (517) 839–9901 or (888) 464–3526. Web site: www.maac.org.*

Alma

Alma, north of Lansing along U.S. 27, is a small town that up to the early 1900s lived in relative obscurity. As a byproduct of drilling brine wells for Midland's Dow Chemical, oil was discovered in the area, and the town became a refinery site. It's also the site of Alma College, founded by the Presbyterian Church in 1887.

ALMA HIGHLAND FESTIVAL AND GAMES (all ages)

To get to the festival area, take the Alma exit downtown to the Alma College campus. Festival hours are 9:00 A.M. to 5:00 P.M. on Saturday and Sunday. Admission is $8.00 for teens and adults, $5.00 for children ages six through twelve and seniors ages sixty-three and older; children ages five and younger are admitted Free. *For more information on the event and other Alma activities, call the area chamber of commerce at (517) 463–5525. Web site: www.almahighlandfestival.com.*

At the annual festival, you can show your kids that yes, Scotsmen really do wear kilts, even when they compete in contests such as the caber and stone toss—old training techniques dating from the times when the English would not let the Scots have weapons. In these contests of strength and skill, competitors see how far they can flip a piece of wood the size of a telephone pole, and how far they can push a heavy chunk of rock (sizes vary according to class).

Michi-fact: Just to the north of Alma, St. Louis is the geographical center of the state, marked by a historical plaque.

Scottish-style food, dancing demonstrations and contests, and lots of bagpipe music prevail the entire weekend, as does other fun, including sheep-herding demonstrations, and arts-and-crafts sales.

Since this is a small town, accommodations around the area fill fast, with some visitors even heading for dorm rooms here and at Mount Pleasant's Central Michigan University, so plan ahead if you intend to attend.

Where to Eat

Elias Brothers Big Boy. *7990 North Alger Road, Alma 48801; (517) 463–5039. Open Sunday through Thursday 6:00* A.M. *to midnight, Friday and Saturday 6:00 to 1:00* A.M. Family fare from salad bar to triple-decker burgers. $$

Where to Stay

Days Inn. *7996 North Alger Road, Midland 48801, at the junction of Michigan 46 and U.S. 27; (517) 463–6131. The inn* has fifty-one rooms with indoor pool. Restaurant nearby. $$

For More Information

Area Chamber of Commerce, *110 West Superior, Alma 48801; (517) 463–5525.*

Mount Pleasant

What a difference a few ringing bells and flashing lights make. Quite a few, in fact. Just to the north on U.S. 27, Mount Pleasant may not be on much of a mountain, but it is home to Central Michigan University and one of the largest gaming casinos east of the Mississippi, a few miles from where Amish farmers and craftspeople ply their wares to tourists, from baked goods out of a farm kitchen to hand-worked oak furniture and quilts.

Such is the dichotomy facing residents here today, and the choice facing tourists, who once would only gas up here on their way farther north. Now the area has reinvented itself as a tourist destination. Golfers will find some of the state's best public courses here, scattered along the Chippewa River.

MUSEUM OF CULTURAL AND NATURAL HISTORY (all ages)

On the Central Michigan University campus in Rowe Hall, at the corner of East Bellows and Mission Street (Business U.S. 27), Mount Pleasant 48859; (517) 774–3829. Open from 9:00 A.M. to noon and 1:00 to 5:00 P.M. Monday through Friday. Admission is Free. *Web site: www.museum.cmich.edu.*

It may not be the largest museum you've ever gone through, but it is one of the most interesting. Located inside a classroom building on campus, the museum explores Michigan's natural history through artifacts and fossils. One room focuses entirely on Native Americans of the Great Lakes, ending in the Native American Gallery, where wonderful contemporary works of art are displayed.

CHIPPEWA RIVER CANOEING (all ages)

Offered by Chippewa River Outfitters in Mount Pleasant; (517) 772–5474. From U.S. 27 northbound, turn onto Mission Road/Business U.S. 27. Turn west on Bloomfield Road to Lincoln, then turn north about ¼ mile to the store. From 27 North, exit at Pickard Road and go west to Lincoln, then south about 1¾ miles. Open May through October with reservations. One-hour trips cost $20; two-hour trips cost $22.

Roll—or in this case, paddle—on the river for one hour to an overnight trip on this section of the "Chip." There are no rapids, so bring along an inner tube (also available for rent). It's a great, relaxing float.

Where to Eat

You won't run out of choices here, from family food to fine dining. Here are a few of the city's more than forty restaurants:

The Embers. *1217 South Mission Street (Business U.S. 27), Mount Pleasant 48858; (517) 773–5007.* A city dining tradition. Famed for its marinated one-pound pork chop, it also serves lighter fare for lunch, dinner, and Sunday brunch. Children's menu. $$$

Jon's Drive-In. *1030 South Mission Street, Midland 48858, off the CMU campus; (517) 773–9172.* Treat the kids to a real drive-in like you used to enjoy, right down to the burgers and malts. $

Sweet Onion. *405 South Mission Street, Midland 48858; (517) 772–0801.* Good selection of family-style fare. $$

Where to Stay

Fairfield Inn by Marriott. *2525 South University Park, Mount Pleasant 48858, next to CMU off Mission Street; (517) 775–5000.* Marriott quality for the family budget. The inn has seventy-four rooms, indoor pool, and whirlpool. Restaurant and recreation nearby. $$

Holiday Inn. *5665 East Pickard Street, Mount Pleasant 48858; U.S. 27 and Michigan 20; (517) 772– 2905.* This reliable family inn has 184 rooms with indoor and outdoor pool, restaurant, tennis, and two eighteen-hole golf courses. Courseside accommodations available. $$

Shardi's Hide-Away Campground. *340 North Loomis Road, Mount Pleasant 48858; (517) 773–4268. From Mount Pleasant, head east on Michigan 20, then north on North Loomis Road.* Campground has 102 sites, pool, playground, and on-site cabin rentals year-round. $

Soaring Eagle Hotel. *On the Chippewa Indian Reservation, Mount Pleasant 48858, adjacent to the Soaring Eagle casino; (517) 775–7777. From U.S. 27, head east 1½ miles on Michigan 20 and south on Leaton Road.* The hotel has 512 rooms, pool, exercise area, restaurant, cafeteria and deli, and children's programs. $$

For More Information

Mount Pleasant/Isabella County Convention and Visitors Bureau, *114 East Broadway, Mount Pleasant*

48858; (517) 772–4433. Web site: www.mt-pleasant.net/cvb.

"Pleasant" Fests The city puts on lots of different faces throughout the year, many of them family-oriented. Admission is charged for most and varies by year. Call the convention and visitors bureau (see For More Information) for information. Here is a sampling of these activities:

- **Mount Pleasant Summer Festival.** Takes place the first weekend in June, with fun such as a custom car show, carnival, music all day, and evening fireworks.

- **Co-Expo World Championship Rodeo.** Takes place the third weekend in June at the Isabella County Fairgrounds, reached by taking the Michigan 20 exit west off U.S. 27 and then going west on Pickard to Mission; turn north onto Mission, then west onto Old Mission, which leads to the grounds. Cowpokes from across North America come to compete and rack up points in hopes of being recognized as the world's best in events from bull riding to barrel racing.

- **Little Elk's Retreat Indian Powwow.** Takes place the first weekend in August on the Chippewa Indian Reservation. Authentic foods, crafts, arts, colorful dancing, and storytelling.

Clare

This town is just north of Mount Pleasant, about 15 miles off U.S. 27. For decades, Clare, named for County Clare in Ireland, was known to travelers as "The Place Where the North Begins" so much that the town adopted the slogan. And it does, a few miles north of town.

A few years ago, Amish from Pennsylvania liked the area's low land prices and began moving in. Now, locals hardly take notice of the black buggies parked outside the local supermarket, which has built a spot just for the horses. The Amish residents have prospered not only through their farming, but with their craftsmanship as well. A map that features locations of Amish businesses is available from the Clare Chamber of Commerce downtown on Business U.S. 27, just north of the main stoplight. On typical weekends, at the commuter parking lot at the corner of Old U.S. 27, just north of the U.S. 27 freeway, local Amish gather to sell beautifully handcrafted quilts in all colors of the rainbow.

 ### AMISH COUNTRY BAKERY (all ages)

East of Old U.S. 27 on Colonville Road; Clare 48617. There is no phone. From downtown Clare, head north on Old 27 and turn east on Colonville Road. Watch for the sign at a farmhouse on the south side of the road. Open daylight hours except Sunday.

Inexpensive, home-baked coffee cakes, rolls, and other sweet treats. Step inside the house and enjoy some soft-spoken Amish hospitality.

 ### LEPRECHAUN SHOP (all ages)

Downtown on Business 27, Clare 48617, across from the Doherty Hotel; (517) 386–7599. Hours are 9:30 A.M. to 5:00 P.M. Monday through Saturday and 11:00 A.M. to 4:00 P.M. Sunday. Shortened hours in winter.

Clare likes to champion its Irish heritage, and no one is behind it more than Kristi Gollish, red-headed proprietor of this shop, which specializes in all things Gaelic, including bolts of cloth, tea and tea services, and Gaelic music.

 ### JAY'S SPORTING GOODS (all ages)

On Old U.S. 27, Clare 48167, north of the city; (517) 386–3475. Open daily.

A sportsman's paradise, Jay's is one of the largest stores of its kind in the Midwest. Here you can be outfitted for the woods or waters from the cap down.

Where to Eat

Downtown Danny's. *407 North McEwan, Clare 48617, 2 blocks south of Old U.S. 10 on Business U.S. 27; (517) 386–2051. Great homemade pastas and soups. Try the reuben soup. $$*

Where to Stay

Doherty Motor Hotel. *Corner of Old U.S. 10 and U.S. 27, Clare 48617; (517) 386–3441.* Here you'll find ninety-two hotel and motel-style rooms, indoor pool, whirlpool, golf and ski packages. Pets okay. There is a restaurant on the premises. $$

Budget Host Clare Motel. *1110 North McEwan, Clare 48617, 5 blocks north of Business U.S. 27; (517) 386–7201.* The motel has thirty-four rooms, outdoor pool, and whirlpool. Restaurants nearby. Small pets okay. $

For More Information

Clare Chamber of Commerce, *429 North McEwan, Clare 48617, across from the Doherty Motor Hotel downtown; (517)* *386–2442. Web site: www.claremichigan.com.*

Farwell

This small community is home to a renovated ski area.

 SILVER RIDGE RESORT (all ages)

Located just south of Farwell on 1001 Mott Mountain Road; (517) 588–7220. From downtown Clare, go west on Old U.S. 10 to Farwell. Turn south at the blinker and follow the signs. It's about 1½ miles away. The ski season runs from December through late March. Plan on around $36 per person for lift ticket and rentals. Restaurant open year-round.

New owners have put new funds into the area. It features nine runs with one chairlift and a new two-tier restaurant looking over the slopes, ski rentals, lessons, package stays and night skiing.

Where to Eat

Silver Ridge Restaurant. *At Silver Ridge ski area, separate from the main lodge, Farwell 48622; (517) 588–7220. Serves* lunch sandwiches until 3:00 P.M. and dinner thereafter, including fish, prime rib, shrimp, and other items. $$

Where to Stay

See Clare listing.

Lake

Along U.S. 10 west of Clare, this tiny resort community is in the midst of a fast growing area for retiring baby boomers because of its lakes. The tiny down-town was formerly a stop on a passenger rail line that ran across central Michigan. Snowmobilers now use the trail, which eventually may be linked with a paved trail in Midland.

BIG AL'S RESTAURANT (all ages)

In downtown Lake on Mystic Lake Road, one block south of U.S. 10; (517) 544–3502. Open 11:00 A.M. to 10:00 P.M. daily including Sunday.

"Big Al" Kuebler, a former Elvis impersonator, may even belt out a tune, or at least a few notes, as you enjoy his good, inexpensive fare for lunch and dinner, from fish to burgers. Elvis memorabilia and black velvet paintings decorate the walls. $$

Where to Stay

See Clare listing.

Linwood

On the shore of Lake Huron. From I–75, take Michigan 13 north at Bay City.

NATIONAL PICKLE FESTIVAL (all ages)

Takes place each third weekend of August in downtown Linwood, east of Michigan 13 at the stoplight. Call (517) 697–3790 or the local Citizens Bank branch at (517) 697–4418 for information.

I know, now you've heard everything. But there really is a reason. The extensive farm fields around Linwood, a few miles north of Bay City, still produce truckloads of cucumber pickles each summer, so why not a festival? Pickle companies bring in trucks full of fresh pickles. A $3.00 button gets you into the entertainment tent and a chance to win, yes, another jar of pickles. The Saturday pickle parade on Center Street through this tiny town features a 6-foot-tall float topped with Petunia Pickle and eighty to one hundred other units. On Sunday it's the kids' turn, with a bike parade and small floats, and there's plenty of food, carnival games, and other small-town craziness, just for the fun of it.

WILLIAMS CHEESE COMPANY (all ages)

998 North Huron Road (Michigan 13), Linwood 48634, south of Deer Acres; (517) 697–4492. Hours are 8:00 A.M. to 6:00 P.M. Monday through Thursday, 8:00 A.M. to 7:00 P.M. Friday, 8:00 A.M. to 6:00 P.M. Saturday, and Sunday hours are 10:00 A.M. to 6:00 P.M. Admission is Free.

The company produces 80 varieties of cheese and sells more than 180 types at the store in front of its cheese-making plant.

Where to Eat and Stay

See Bay City listing.

Pinconning

This east Michigan town may be nicknamed Michigan's cheese capital because its factories produce the cheddarlike Pinconning cheese, but there's nothing cheesy about its attractions.

DEER ACRES (all ages)

2346 Michigan 13, Pinconning 48650; (517) 879–2849. Deer Acres is reached from I–75 by taking exit 164 at Kawkawlin and going north on Michigan 13 for about 10 miles. Open daily from May 15 through Labor Day from 10:00 A.M. to 7:00 P.M., and after Labor Day until October 15 on weekends only from 10:00 A.M. to 6:00 P.M. Admission is $8.50 for teens and adults, $6.50 for children ages three to twelve, and $7.50 for seniors. Web site: www.deeracres.com.

Since 1959, this attraction, painted a bright chartreuse and located on the east side of Michigan 13, has attracted an average of 40,000 families each summer. Kids love to hand feed the herds of deer—and the deer love the attention, too. The deer have learned to come running when they hear the sound of the food dispensers clicking all over the park. In Story Book Village, kids can meet all their favorite Mother Goose and other storybook characters, like Peter Pumpkin and Jack, the beanstalk-climbing giant killer. Pack a lunch and use the grills and picnic tables, or head for the snack shop. Five amusement rides include a narrated trip past storybook characters and animals from llamas to monkeys with signs explaining how and where they live in the wild, and a narrated ½-mile-long miniature train excursion. There are characters roaming the park that welcome kids to have their pictures taken, too.

Where to Eat and Stay

See Bay City listing.

Tawas City–East Tawas

This community used to be the quintessential tourist town that buzzed with activity in summer and curled up by the fire for winter. Not so anymore. Summer is still a busy season, but nowadays winter also finds folks out on the trails, either snowmobiling or cross-country skiing. Many of the resort cabins and motels that used to shut down for winter are staying open. Until a few years ago, this was strictly a mom-and-pop resort town, but that's changed, too, with a beachfront hotel. Tawas Bay and Lake Huron are very good producers of walleye, perch, salmon, and lake trout. Check with the Tawas Chamber of Commerce (see For More Information at the end of this section) for a list of current charter boat operators. A Michigan fishing license is required for those ages sixteen and older. A daily license is $6.00 for residents, $7.00 for nonresidents. Tawas City and East Tawas are next to each other along U.S. 23.

Summer on the Water From the time I was young, my family vacationed along the shores of Lake Huron and Tawas Bay. Long mornings were spent soaking in the odors of creosote and minnows of the perch anglers along the boardwalk dock at East Tawas. I can still remember those moonlit nights aboard the old *Miss East Tawas* perch party boat, when the captain would place lights along the side of the boat to attract the fish, and we'd always come back with pails full of yellowbellies, as they're nicknamed, which we caught when we weren't munching on candy bars, untangling fishing lines, and watching the Tawas Point lighthouse guide boats safely by the shallow waters.

Long summer days were spent diving into the clear, cold lake with my cousin, interspersed by trips to the minigolf course at neighboring Oscoda or picnicking at the lakefront where my father now lives. We wouldn't have stayed in fancy condos then even if there were any—we didn't have to spend lavishly to have a good time—and had a grand time at a simple resort cottage. Do yourself and your family a favor and experience this kind of vacation, too. While condos are popping up like mushrooms and shutting out the views along parts of Tawas Bay, there are plenty of other places to enjoy the joys of a cottage vacation on this side of the state. You owe it to your family to try it before they're gone. It's the stuff of which memories are made.

CORSAIR SKI AREA (all ages)

218 West Bay Street, East Tawas 48730; (517) 362–2001. The trails are in Silver Valley, about 8 miles outside town along Monument Road. From U.S. 23, turn west on M–55 to Wilber Road. Follow it to Monument Road. Follow it about 7 miles to the Silver Valley and watch for the parking lot signs. Trails are Free, but because it costs money to groom routes and maintain equipment (a single pass through the Corsair trail system requires twelve hours of machine operation), skiers are expected to drop something into the donation tubes at the trailhead. Web site: www.skinordic.org.

When winter comes to the dense Huron National Forest, about 6 miles outside the twin cities of Tawas City and East Tawas, it signals an entirely new season of family fun. Some 35 miles of trails on both sides of Monument Road are rated among the best in the country. They beckon cross-country ski enthusiasts of all ability levels to the series of looping courses that always begin and end at the three large parking areas. Beginners can take always-groomed, mostly flat trails that wind through the dense woods around trout-filled Silver Creek, while intermediates and advanced types can be challenged by some pretty hilly terrain with some mean curves thrown in. Young nonskiers can be towed behind in a sled.

In summer, the area doubles as a great picnic and hiking spot, and where kids with an inexpensive fishing rod and a can of worms might have some luck catching a few brook trout in Silver Creek. Hunters walk the river valley in fall.

Gary Nelkie, owner of East Tawas's Nordic Sports shop, can outfit your family in inexpensive rental cross-country skis and shoes and will start you off with an in-store lesson if you ask. Plan on spending about $15 per person per day for all equipment.

PERCHVILLE USA (all ages)

This annual festival takes place on the ice and at shore sites the first weekend of February. Call (800) 55–TAWAS for information. You can combine skiing at Corsair with this festival on the ice at East Tawas.

Some 15,000 persons stroll about for fun, and many go after the schools of perch swimming underneath the bay ice. Fishing contests, arts and crafts, and a traditional demolition derby on the ice fill out the roster of events for one of the oldest winter carnivals in the state, which celebrated its fiftieth anniversary at the millennium.

One of the festival's most amusing events takes place near the state's longest wooden dock. A few hardy and normally responsible souls, who

181

might have been cooped up in their cabins a mite too long, jump into frigid Lake Huron through a hole chopped in the ice during the Polar Bear Swim. Other events include frozen softball and children's games, plus a Friday-night, all-you-can-eat perch dinner.

HUBIE'S WONDERGOLF (all ages)

On U.S. 23, East Tawas 48730, just north of McDonald's; (517) 362–8050. Open Memorial Day through Labor Day, 10:00 A.M. to 10:00 P.M. daily. Costs $5.00 for adults and $4.00 for children twelve and younger.

The course here has eighteen holes of minigolf, with streams, water-falls, and flowers. A fudge shop awaits as the nineteenth hole.

Where to Eat

Big Boy. *1222 North U.S. 23, East Tawas 48730, at the north end of town; (517) 362–4403.* Known for its burgers and buffet, it's a good, inexpensive family place. $

Genii's Fine Foods. *601 West Bay (U.S. 23), East Tawas 48730; (517) 362–5913.* A bayside fixture for more than thirty years that features family fare for breakfast, lunch, and dinner. $$

Marion's Dairy Bar. *111 East Bay, East Tawas 48730; (517) 362–2991.* An old-fashioned ice cream parlor with cones, malts, and sundaes in thirty-two fla-vors. Open Monday through Saturday 11:00 A.M. to 11:00 P.M., Sunday noon to 11:00 P.M. $

Where to Stay

There are scores of places to stay here along the beach, from old-time cottages and resorts (both south and north of both cities) to motels and small resorts in town. Most resorts rent by the week and fill quickly before summer, but occasionally nightly rentals are available. If you're coming up for a week, it's a good idea to drive up in spring to check out a resort to see if it's to your liking.

Bambi Motel. *1100 East Bay (U.S. 23), East Tawas 48730; (517) 362–4582.* A basic property with fifteen lakeside units. $

Bayview Resort. *1047 Bay, Tawas City 48730; (517) 362–4361.* Eight cottages on Tawas Bay with sand beach. $$

East Tawas City Park. *Along U.S. 23 at the foot of Newman Street, East Tawas 48730; (517) 362–5562.* When the state park moved to the point, the city moved into this ready-made facility. It has 170 paved campsites, with ¼ mile of sandy beach, playground, even sea-sonal cable TV. $

Stoney Shores Resort. *111 North Baldwin Resort Road, East Tawas 48730; (517) 362–4609. Located on Lake Huron* *north of town off U.S. 23.* Four cottages on the beach that usually rent by the week in summer. $$

Tawas Bay Holiday Inn Resort. *300 East Bay (U.S. 23), East Tawas 48730; (517) 362–8601.* This property has 103 rooms, an indoor pool, and a 900-foot beach on the bay with great swimming. Within walking distance of downtown East Tawas's shops and movie theater, with dining. $$

Tawas Point State Park. *At the tip of Tawas Point 48730; (517) 362–5041 or, for reservations, (800) 447–2757. From East Tawas, take U.S. 23 north, then jog onto Tawas Beach Road and follow it to the end. A $4.00 daily or $20.00 annual permit is required for vehicle entry. Camping is extra.* In summer take the family to the beach at Tawas Point, about 4 miles north of the twin cities, where there's also a working lighthouse and 205 very popular sandy campsites and two mini-cabins with rustic accommodations. A nature trail heads to the point and is popular with birders, especially during migration times. The park, in fact, is rated one of the nation's top spots for migration-watching in May. Campers have a choice of swimming in Lake Huron or warmer Tawas Bay. As the guide brochure to the hike of Sandy Hook Nature Trail explains, don't worry if the beach may look oily here and there. The dark substance is actually magnetite, iron oxide. Campers can hike past the lighthouse that's been here since 1876. Tawas Point Celebration Days, held the second weekend of June, offers family activities, arts and crafts, a fishing derby, guided hikes, and more. $

Wooded Acres Resort. *968 North U.S. 23, East Tawas 48730, 5 miles north of town; (517) 362–5188.* Fourteen cottages on Lake Huron, some with fireplaces. $$

For More Information

Tawas Area Chamber of Commerce, *402 East Lake Street (U.S. 23), Tawas 48764; (517) 362–8643 or (800) 558–2927. Web site: www.tawas.com.*

Oscoda

Only 15 miles up U.S. 23 from Tawas City and East Tawas, this beachside town offers even more summer fun. The city's population grows each summer as vacationers come up to enjoy both the nearby inland lakes and Lake Huron's great sandy beaches. They stay until fall, when salmon congregate at the mouth and fill the lower Au Sable. Charter boats usually leave from marinas around the mouth of the Au Sable River at Bunyantown Marina (517-739-2371) and Fellows' Marine and Tackle Shop (517-739-2525). Both marinas are near the mouth of the Au Sable River, and boats fish Lake Huron for salmon and trout.

THREE MILE BEACH PARK (all ages)

Along U.S. 23, Oscoda 48750, about 3 miles north of town; (800) 235–4625. **Free.** *The park closes at 10:00 P.M. daily.*

A unique roadside park that not only includes a great sandy beach, but a bit of nature, too. Birders head for this picnic area to watch migrating waterfowl. Wildflowers also are prevalent among the beach sands.

AU SABLE *RIVER QUEEN* (all ages)

Board in Foote Dam pond, just upstream of Foote Site Village; (517) 739–7351 or (517) 728–3775. Cost of the trip is $8.50 for teens and adults (for the fall-color tours, the price rises to $12.00), $5.25 for kids ages five to eleven, and $4.75 for children ages four and younger. There's also a 10 percent discount for seniors except during fall-color season. The boats run from Memorial Day weekend through the third weekend in October. Times vary, so call ahead.

Board an authentic paddle wheeler for a lazy trip through the impoundment on the river. The boat has been touring this section of river more than forty years. The 19-mile narrated trips run about two hours. Follow Captain Bill Norris's running commentary about the river's history and wildlife. The area is especially beautiful and popular in fall—reservations are required for fall trips—but a trip is a wonderful relaxing journey any time.

IARGO SPRINGS (all ages)

Along the Au Sable River Road Scenic Byway, Oscoda 48750, about 15 miles west of town; (800) 235–4625. Open daily, year-round. **Free.**

Kids and adults with stamina love to take the 227 steps down the high banks to a naturally flowing spring that Chippewa tribe members once used to quench their thirst. They also held ceremonies at the spring, which they believed had curative abilities. There's a walkway around the spring so the area won't be disturbed. There are more platforms over Cooke Dam Pond. To help you catch your breath on the way down, and especially on the way back up, there are viewing benches. The water flows at a near-constant temperature at around fifty degrees.

Where to Eat

Charbonneau's Family Restaurant. *700 Lake Street, Oscoda 48750; (517) 739–5230. Just west of U.S. 23, at the foot of the Au Sable River Bridge.* Serving breakfast, lunch, and dinner, including roasted chicken and a weekend seafood buffet. $$

Desi's Taco Lounge. *1945 West River Road, Oscoda 48750; (517) 739–7856. At Foote Site Village, about 6 miles west of Oscoda on River Road.* Desi's has been here serving traditional Mexican meals—and American items such as burgers, chicken, and seafood—for more than twenty years. Serves breakfast, lunch, and dinner. $$

Pack House. *5400 North U.S. 23, Oscoda 48750, downtown; (517) 739–0454.* In an 1878 home with affordable

fine dining for dinner. Ask about the ghost that's supposedly inhabiting the upstairs rooms. $$

Wiltse's Brew Pub and Family Restaurant. *5606 North County Road F–41, Oscoda 48750; (517) 739–2231. From U.S. 23, take F–41 northwest about 1 mile.* Chicken and steak cut to order and on-premises-brewed beers for those ages twenty-one and older to sample. Children's menu, too. Breakfast, lunch, and dinner. $$

Au Sable River Road National Forest Scenic Byway

Head west out of Oscoda by turning from U.S. 23 onto River Road in the center of town. The twentieth highway in the nation to be designated a scenic byway, it runs 22 miles through the Huron National Forest, on River Road and Michigan 65 along the south bank of the Au Sable River, where more attractions await. For more information on byway attractions, call (517) 362–4477, (517) 739–0728, or (800) 821–6263.

Where to Stay

This resort town has scores of beachfront and woodsy choices, from motels to cottage resorts both on Lake Huron and nearby inland lakes.

Acres & Trails KOA. *3591 Forest Road, Oscoda 48750; (517) 739–5115. Off U.S. 23, about 1½ miles south of town and ¾ mile west on Johnson Road, 1 mile south on Forest Road.* This campground has 143 sites with hookups available as well as tent sites and a fishing pond.

Monument Campground. *Just east of Lumberman's Monument on River Road, Oscoda 48750; (517) 362–4477.* This spot offers twenty sites with rustic camping.

Old Orchard Park. *Along River Road, Oscoda 48750, on Foote Dam Pond, just west of Foote Site Village; (517) 739–7814.* Michigan's largest county campground has 500 campsites, many with water, including showers, and electricity. Rustic tent sites available, too. Located on the backwaters of Foote Dam, one of six hydroelectric dams on this stretch of river.

Redwood Motor Lodge. *3111 North U.S. 23, Oscoda 48750, 2½ miles north of town; (517) 739–2021.* The lodge offers forty-five rooms, a restaurant, heated indoor pool, sauna, whirlpool, and Lake Huron beach access across U.S. 23. $$

Super 8. *4270 North U.S. 23, Oscoda 48750, 1½ miles south of the city; (517) 739–8822.* The inn has seventy-six   rooms on Lake Huron. Restaurant nearby. $$

For More Information

Oscoda Area Convention and Visitors Bureau, *4440 North U.S. 23,*   *Oscoda 48750; (800) 235–4625. Web site: www.oscoda.com.*

Oscoda Annual Events and Festivals

- **Art on the Beach.** Takes place the last weekend of June at Oscoda Beach Park, at the east end of River Road. Turn east at the stoplight to the park.

- **Au Sable River International Canoe Marathon.** Runs the last full weekend of July from Grayling to Oscoda, a distance of 120 miles. They say it's "the world's toughest spectator sport." It's unknown if that's because it's tough on the spectators to follow the canoeists downstream, or because it is so wearing on the participants that many collapse and have to be lifted from their canoes at the end of the race in Oscoda. In both cases, it takes dedicated spectators to follow their favorites downstream. Best places to view the race include bridges crossing the river east of Grayling, at the finish in downtown Oscoda, and the dams upstream from Oscoda (as the by-now bedraggled racers drag their canoes up and over the structures, then hop back in to continue paddling in their special racing canoes with oversize paddles). There's a hospitality tent near the finish line with refreshments, entertainment, and more. The race takes fourteen hours, starting at dusk in Grayling and running through the night until the teams finally make it to Oscoda the next afternoon.

Houghton Lake–Prudenville

These communities are located near the intersections of two of the state's major north-south routes, I-75 and U.S. Highway 27. With more than 31 square miles of surface, Houghton Lake is Michigan's largest inland body of water. Along its edges, the towns of Houghton Lake and Prudenville have been family vacation destinations for decades, and resorts, motels, and cottages practically encircle the lake. There are plenty of things to do when you're not at the beach, too, especially in the town of Houghton Lake, like go-cart rides and miniature and full-size golf.

Houghton Lake is one of the best places to take your family fishing. The lake abounds with panfish, pike, and walleye, with some of the best places to fish near shore, such as wild-rice weed beds. In addition, the Muskegon River, which begins on the lake's western shore, enters Reedsburg dam impoundment, also a good spot for anglers.

Tip-Up Town The fun doesn't stop in winter. Snow sculptures, ice-fishing contests, snowmobiling, and a frosty parade make up the annual winter carnival that draws upwards of 60,000 persons to Houghton Lake area during the last two full weekends in January. The event is named for a particular type of ice-fishing rod that tips up when a fish bites and has been a winter fixture here since 1950.

PINES THEATER (all ages)

4673 West Houghton Lake Road (Michigan 55), Houghton Lake 48629; (517) 366–9226. Two shows nightly from Memorial Day weekend through Labor Day. One show nightly after Labor Day to Memorial Day. Tickets are $5.00 for adults and $3.00 for children twelve and younger.

Be sure to take in a film in what is perhaps Michigan's most unusual movie theater. A handsome local landmark since 1941, it's Michigan's only movie house constructed completely of western Douglas fir logs. Inside the lobby are stuffed examples of Michigan wildlife, including deer, duck, and pheasant. Movie buffs will find such memorabilia as autographed posters of Hollywood star Charlton Heston, whose family has a cottage in nearby St. Helen and who often visited the theater. Still part of the auditorium's 500 seats are "love seats" that can fit two cuddlers.

ZUBLER'S INDIAN CRAFT SHOP AND POW WOW (all ages)

3282 West Houghton Lake Drive (Michigan 55), Houghton Lake 48629; From U.S. 27, take the Michigan 55 exit and head east around the lake. The store is on the north side of the road. Programs and demonstrations are Free.

Down the street from the Pines in Houghton Lake, at Zubler's the rhythmic sounds of drums and ancient chants once again echo each summer as they have for more than forty years. Every Thursday from June through August, Native Americans from the Swan Creek and Black River bands of Chippewa and Odawa travel from the Mount Pleasant area to demonstrate Native American dances and crafts inside a circle of permanent tepees next to the store. Often, dancers will coax young audience members to join in. Native American storytelling for kids includes tales of the wise Coyote and how ducks got their quacks. There are crafts for sale and more inside Zubler's, which specializes in Southwest Indian and Cherokee items.

FUNLAND AMUSEMENT PARK (all ages)

On Michigan 55, Houghton Lake 48629; (517) 422–5204. Reached from U.S. 27 off the Michigan 55 exit by heading east. Cost varies, starting from $3.50 for five minutes on a bumper boat. Open Memorial Day through Labor Day.

Batting cages, go-carts, and other activities made for kids of all ages. Snacks are sold on the premises.

*S*cenic Drives You've come to the right place for leisurely drives through the woods and exploring small communities. Try these on for size if you're looking for something to do. Old U.S. 27, the same highway that cuts through Clare, Mount Pleasant, and Lansing, among other cities listed earlier in this chapter, also runs along the western edge of Houghton Lake. It's a wonderful two-lane road that is forsaken by most travelers using the U.S. 27 freeway to the west or I-75 to the east. It edges both Houghton and Higgins Lakes, heads through wild scenic woodlands both north and south of town, and goes past public access points on both Houghton and Higgins Lakes that it seems only locals know about. And with state highway construction and repairs at their peak in summer, it's a good alternate to avoid what can be monumental traffic jams on weekends when the freeways are cut to one lane.

Another suggestion is a 32-mile loop drive around Houghton Lake. The route also gives you a good idea as to what's available for lakeside resort stays.

Where to Eat

There are more than two dozen restaurants ringing the lake in the towns of Houghton Lake and Prudenville. Here are some of our favorites:

Brass Lantern. *729 Houghton Lake Drive, Prudenville 48629; (517) 366–8312. On Michigan 55, just past the inter-section with Michigan 18. Well-prepared meals in a nice rustic atmosphere for lunch and dinner, including steak and seafood. $$$*

Coyles Restaurant. *9074 Old U.S. 27, Houghton Lake 48629; (517) 422–3812. Just north of Michigan 55 on the west shore* *of Houghton Lake.* Reasonably priced breakfast, lunch, and dinner with children's menu. $

Houghton Lake Big Boy. *On Michigan 55, Houghton Lake 48629, just west of the U.S. 27 exit; (517) 422–5193.* Family-style meals and buffet, with burgers a specialty. $$

Where to Stay

More than three dozen resorts, from inns and bed and breakfasts to lakeside cottages, ring the lake. They are conveniently arranged by zone in the local resort finder. Most on the northeast and western edges of the lake will be farthest from traffic. Some offer beaches, but others have breakwalls only for waterfronts, and some also feature pools, as the lake bottom is silty in some areas. It's wise to check out where you want to stay beforehand and make reservations, as accommodations fill rapidly during June, July, and August and for the Tip-Up Town festival in January.

Holiday Inn. *9285 West Houghton Lake Drive (Michigan 55), Houghton Lake 48629, just east of the junction of U.S. 27; (517) 422–5175.* Reliable chain property has 101 rooms with indoor pool and recreation area. Restaurant serves breakfast, lunch, and dinner. Small pets are okay. $$

Holiday on the Lake. *100 Clearview Road, Houghton Lake 48629; (517) 422–5195. On Old U.S. 27, ½ mile north of Michigan 55 on the western shore of Houghton Lake.* Not to be confused with the Holiday Inn chain, this independent property has thirty rooms, some with cooking facilities. There's also a restaurant on premises. This place features one of the best swimming beaches on the lake. Pets are okay at $15 per night. $$

Mazur's Skytop Resort. *5260 West Houghton Lake Drive (Michigan 55), Houghton Lake 48629, 4 miles east of U.S. 27; (517) 366–9107.* This resort offers nineteen rooms and ten two-bedroom cottages on the lake with swimming. Cottage rentals include a rowboat, and motors can be rented. Cottages can be rented weekly. $

Super 8. *9580 West Lake City Road (Michigan 55), Houghton Lake 48629, at U.S. 27; (517) 422–3119.* This basic property has seventy rooms. Restaurants nearby. $

For More Information

Houghton Lake Chamber of Commerce, *1625 West Houghton Lake Drive, Houghton Lake 48629; (517) 366–5644 or (800) 248–LAKE.*

Web site: www.houghtonlakechamber.com. Offerings include a cottage-and-resort guide and scenic drive suggestions.

Higgins Lake–Roscommon

Now we're talking vacation country. In the heart of the Huron-Manistee
National Forest, which stretches across northern Lower Michigan, Roscommon
is near what some say is the crown jewel of Michigan's more than 11,000
inland lakes. Summer, fall, winter, or spring, there's always something to do
here to enjoy the season. And Roscommon's a cute little town in its own right,
too. There are six golf courses within 15 miles of town and a small movie theater in town.

NORTH AND SOUTH HIGGINS LAKE STATE PARKS (all ages)

To reach both parks, exit I–75 at Roscommon Road; head south for Higgins Lake
South, or west on Roscommon Road to Higgins Lake North. Entry fee is $4.00
daily or $20.00 annually, and camping is extra. For park information call the south
unit at (517) 821–6374; the north unit at (517) 821–6125; or for reservations
call (800) 447–2757.

   Consistently ranked in Michigan reader polls as having the state's
favorite inland lake beach, these two parks are both located on a body
of water that members of the National Geographic Society once voted
the world's sixth most beautiful lake.

   Higgins Lake South is especially well liked by families with young
children, as knee-high kids can wade on its shelf of hard sand and
rolling bars up to 700 feet out before Mom and Dad have to worry too
much about the depth. Along with 512 modern campsites and plenty of
wooded picnic space, there are cross-country ski and hiking trails starting across from the park. The park store just off the beach rents boats
and pontoons and has picnic supplies.

   Higgins Lake North has as many family-friendly attributes.

CANOE TRIPS (all ages)

To reach downtown, take exit 239 off I–75 and turn north on Michigan 18 into
town. Go through the stoplight, and the river is about 1 block farther. Signs direct
you to other liveries in the area as well. Call (517) 275–8760 for a list of area liv-
eries. Cost varies by trip. Trips are usually offered Memorial Day through October.

   In downtown Roscommon you can take the family canoeing along
the south branch of the Au Sable River. This branch, which joins the
main stream about 20 miles north by water, is one of the most scenic,

as much of it flows through the Mason Wilderness Tract, a 16-mile stretch of pristine natural beauty. Wildlife from deer to bald eagles and coyotes can be seen along its banks. Liveries are located in and near Roscommon. Liveries provide drop-off and pickup service included in the rental fee.

For a real adventure, take an overnight trip. Some liveries, including Paddle Brave in Roscommon (517–275–5273 or 800–681–7092), will rent camping equipment. Paddle Brave also offers guided overnight trips. There is no camping in the Mason Tract, but Canoe Harbor forest campground is at the downstream boundary of the tract and has rustic sites.

CROSS-COUNTRY SKI HEADQUARTERS (all ages)

9435 North Cut Road (Roscommon County Road 100), Roscommon 48653; (517) 821–6661. Exit I–75 at Michigan 18, exit 239, then jog south 1 block to Robinson Lake Road, also known as County Road 103. Turn west and go 3 miles to the blinker light. Go north on North Cut Road for ½ mile. The store is open November through March. Plan on around $12 for rentals. Web site: www.cross-country-ski.com.

Cross-Country Ski Headquarters has gained a national reputation for excellence in ski rentals, sales, customer service, and its own network of trails that stretches 12½ miles around the store, including great night skiing on torchlit forest trails. The store is close to state-maintained trails as well, including the Mason Tract trail, which doubles as a hiking path in summer. It follows the river through the tract along the north shore. Lynne and Bob Frye will teach you if you don't know how. It's as easy as walking.

Where to Eat

Trapper's Restaurant. *4603 West Higgins Lake Drive, Roscommon 48653; (517) 821–7339. From I–75, take exit 239 west to County Road 100 south. Turn northwest on County Road 100, then north on County Road 200, or West Higgins Lake Drive.* Good local restaurant serving breakfast on Saturday and Sunday, lunch and dinner other days of the week. $$

Where to Stay

Besides the two state parks, there are plenty of accommodations to choose from. Rent one of several vacation cottages and homes along Higgins Lake by the week or longer. Prices range from around $425 up to $1,500. The Higgins Lake–Roscommon Chamber of Commerce has a complete rental list; (517) 275-8760. Others include:

Great Circle Campground. *5370 Marl Lake Road, Roscommon 48653; (517) 821–9486. From I–75, take exit 239 and jog south to County Road 103, and then head west. Turn south on County Road 101 and then west on County Road 104 to the campground. From U.S. 27, exit at Higgins Lake Road, County Road 104, and go east. The campground has forty-five sites, with tent sites available, too. Pets okay. $*

Great Escape Motor Lodge. *8097 North Harrison Road, Roscommon 48653;* *(517) 821–6343. From U.S. 27, take the Higgins Lake Road exit to Old U.S. 27 and turn north. The property has thirty rooms with indoor pool. Restaurants nearby. $*

Higgins Lake Family Campground. *2380 West Burdell Road, Roscommon 48653; (517) 821–6891. Take exit 239 from I–75, and go south on Michigan 18, then 3 miles west on County Road 103 and 1 mile north on County Road 100. This campground has sixty modern sites, tenting area, and bicycle rentals a mile from Higgins Lake. $*

Tee Pee Restaurant & Motel. *On the I–75 Business Loop, Roscommon 48653; (517) 275–5203 or (800) 420–5348. Fourteen rooms. Restaurant serves breakfast through dinner at inexpensive prices. Children's menu. $*

For More Information

Higgins Lake–Roscommon Chamber of Commerce, *P.O. Box 486, Roscommon 48653; (517) 275–8760. Web site: www.hlrcc.com.*

Grayling

Located just off I-75 and bisected by Business I-75 (formerly Old U.S. 27), Grayline is one of the most storied towns in the hearts of both state historians and trout anglers. In the midst of Michigan's vast white-pine forests, this town grew up named after the silvery fish that once inhabited the Au Sable River. Rapacious land practices destroyed the forests and caused silting in the rivers, and overfishing decimated the grayling so much that by the early 1900s, it was extinct from the river. Except for a remnant of the forests preserved forever, the trees around the area are the result of reforestation efforts in the early twentieth century.

The area survived to come back as a great vacation destination in every season, with skiing and snowmobiling in winter, fishing and waterfront fun in spring and summer, and fall color viewing and hunting in fall. It's one of my favorite towns in the north. Days will find my friends and me lounging on the beach at nearby Higgins Lake, or maybe walking through the pines at Hartwick Pines State Park. In the evenings, we'll join other friends, lose ourselves in the sunset's afterglow, and marvel at the hues of that impressionist canvas called the Au Sable River as we wait for the hatch and the rising trout it brings. You'll find me up here or on the river almost every summer weekend.

TROUT FISHING OR RIVER SIGHT-SEEING (all ages)

The cost of a float trip is about $275. For a list of guides, call the Grayling Chamber of Commerce at (517) 348–2921.

Become a part of Michigan floating history while fishing, bird-watching, or just enjoying the ripple of water and quiet of the day by heading out in an authentic Au Sable River Drift Boat. They've been part of the river scene here for more than a hundred years, first as supply craft for riverside lumber camps. Guides in the area include Bob Andrus, a retired Grayling school teacher. He and others will take you on a day-long, half-day, or night float on the river to either fish or just enjoy the scenery, which is especially beautiful in fall. Usually the riverboats are 20 to 24 feet long and take one or two persons plus guide. Passengers sit forward, and the guide steers from the stern. Part of the fun can be a shore lunch over a wood fire. Besides trout splashing after their dinners, you'll probably see beaver, deer, duck, muskrat, and an assortment of birds that might include herons and bald eagles.

CANOEING (all ages)

There are at least ten canoe liveries in town and downstream from Grayling. Most are in the city, just off Business I–75. Call (800) 937–8837 for information.

Michigan is filled with beautiful floatable rivers, but probably the best, most family-fun-oriented, and certainly the most popular in east Michigan is the upper Au Sable River, which flows through this former lumber town. You can canoe the main stream from several liveries in downtown Grayling. Each offers relaxing float trips as short as two hours and as lengthy as weeklong paddles to the mouth of the Au Sable in Oscoda. Depths in the upper river range from 1 to 5 feet, and flotation devices are provided. Canoeists also have a choice of trying the less-populous Manistee River, about 6 miles west along Michigan 72.

▥ WELLINGTON FARM PARK (all ages)

6940 South Military Road, Grayling 49738; (888) 653–3276. From I–75, take exit 251, Four Mile Road, and turn west to the end of the road. Turn south on Military Road and go about a mile. Parking is on the west side of the road. Admission costs
$2.00 for adults and
$1.50 for seniors and
students. There's also an
$8.00 family rate.

The park is a new
concept in historical,
environmental edu-
cation. It is a work-
ing replica of a
1930s Depression-
era farmstead. Farm-
ing activities are
conducted daily
using vintage tools
and practices, from
blacksmithing to
plowing and harvest-
ing. Special events

Rules of the River A few words

about river etiquette. In past years canoeists have been the scourge of the wading
trout angler, and vice versa, because a lot of
first-time paddlers don't understand that
trout anglers aren't just walking around in
the river to plague canoeists—that's how
they fish. Nowadays, liveries instruct canoeists so when they meet an angler they're not
sideways, backwards, tied in rafts, or underwater after encountering a hidden log or
after squirt gun battles with fellow paddlers. Actually, most anglers are off the
river when canoeists are on. But please,
respect their fun, and they'll respect yours.

include women's role on the farm, a walk through history showing farming from 1760 to 1932, and other events. There are self-guided nature
trails through the woods, too. The park gets its name from a tiny farming community that once existed in the area.

◿ SKYLINE SKI AREA (ages 7 and up)

4020 Skyline Road, Grayling 49738; (517) 275–5445. From I–75, take exit 251, Four Mile Road, head east to Old U.S. 27, then south 2 miles to Skyline Road. Follow it 1 mile to the hill. Open from 10:00 A.M. to 5:00 P.M. Friday through Monday, plus 6:30 to 10:00 P.M. Friday and Saturday. Plan to spend around $30 per day for adults and around $20 for children for tickets and rentals.

Ski on one of the few ski areas in the state reliant on all natural
snow. The area has ten runs with one chairlift and nine surface tows.
Rentals, lessons, and a ski shop are available.

GOODALE'S BAKERY (all ages)

500 Norway, Grayling 49738; (517) 348–8682. At the corner of Ottawa, 1 block south of Business I–75/Michigan 72, the town's main street. Open daily except Sunday, with extended hours Friday.

Famous for its baked goods made fresh daily, including wonderful cranberry oatmeal cookies, and its made-on-premises cinnamon and English muffin breads that are sent across the country to loyal customers.

GRAYLING FISH HATCHERY (all ages)

On North Down River Road, Grayling 49738; (517) 348–9266. Off I–75, take exit 254, follow I–75 Business Loop through town, and turn north at the Clark gasoline station; then follow the signs. Admission is $1.50 for adults, $1.00 for children ages five to seventeen. Ages five and younger are admitted Free. A family package is $6.00. The hatchery is open daily from Memorial Day through Labor Day between 10:00 A.M. and 6:00 P.M. Web site: www.hansonhills.org.

Along the Au Sable's tiny east branch, take the kids to feed trout from fingerling size to several pounds at this former state trout hatchery. Dating from 1914, it was closed for production of fish in the 1960s. It reopened as a tourist attraction in 1983. Currently, eleven ponds raise up to 45,000 trout to supply a local trout farm, and to delight kids. There's even a special area for youngsters who want to take home some. (Parents, you pay by the inch.) There are dispensers for fish food for a quarter or two, and it's great fun to watch as your youngsters sprinkle the pellets into the water and watch as the trout, from 6-inchers to six-pounders, gobble them up.

GATES AU SABLE LODGE (all ages)

To reach the lodge, take exit 254 off northbound I–75 and turn east on Michigan 72; follow it to Stephan Bridge Road and turn north. The lodge is at the bridge. For reservation information call (517) 348–8462. Web site: www. gateslodge.com.

Nestled by the river 6 miles east of the city, the Gates place will introduce you to the quiet joys of trout fishing up close. With sixteen rooms renting for reasonable prices, you'll get a large space with a picture-window view of the river through the trees that cover the property. Owner Cal "Rusty" Gates runs the fly shop where you can purchase equipment and your license while wife Julie manages the restaurant, which serves breakfast and dinner. If you're a new angler, come to the fly-fishing workshop held each spring; or arrange a float with one of the lodge's guides. Then take the kids down to the "bread hole" under a willow over the river, where huge trout gulp crusts. Gates also supports a group that looks after the river, so patronizing his place helps ensure that the Au Sable will remain a treasured stream for generations.

HARTWICK PINES STATE PARK (all ages)

To get to the park, take I–75 exit 264 and drive about 2 miles east on Michigan 93, Grayling 49738. A motor vehicle permit, $4.00 daily or $20.00 annually, is required to enter. Camping is extra. For information call (517) 348–7068. For reservations call (800) 447–2757.

Six miles north of Grayling, you'll see almost all that remains of the giants that once covered nearly all of Michigan more than a century ago in this unique 10,000-acre park, which many visitors revere as an outdoor cathedral to nature. Walk miles of trails covered by a canopy of huge white pines and hemlocks that block so much sunlight, hardly any vegetation grows on the forest floor.

There's a new entrance road leading to a one-hundred-site campground (shaded sites that were a feature of the old campground across the street are few at the new one) and the Michigan Forest Visitor Center at the edge of the pines. The center provides an excellent grounding in the history of logging in the state and how it has changed from being a destructive force to a mostly beneficial practice through scientific methods that benefit both wildlife and people.

A restored logging camp, complete with a "big wheel" (which was used to haul logs out of the forest; you'll also see a red one at the park's entrance), a bunkhouse, and a dining room, is set deep in the woods. In summer the camp comes alive twice a year as living-history portrayals explain what logging life was like in the old days.

Events take place during Wood-Shavings and Sawdust Days in July and Black Iron Days in August, and there are portrayals of lumber-camp life by costumed employees in character. The steam-powered sawmill is fired up, and other workers are on hand selling crafts. There's also a woodland chapel, an extensive network of mountain-biking trails, miles of great cross-country skiing in winter, a driving loop with numbered stops to follow on a guide, and also a Braille trail.

Where to Eat

Chief Shoppenagon Hotel. *On South Michigan Avenue, Grayling 49738, just south of the intersection with Business I–75/Michigan 72 downtown;* (517) 348–6071. Newly remodeled, the hotel is known more for its restaurant than as a place to stay. It's named after one of the area's last Native American residents. Menu ranges from burgers to chicken. $$

Patty's Town House. *On the west side of Business I–75, Grayling 49738, about 1 mile north on Business I–75 from exit 254 on I–75; (517) 348–4331.* Maybe the town's best restaurant, with steaks, fish, and other items on the menu for breakfast, lunch, and dinner. $$

Stevens Family Circle. *231 North Michigan Avenue, Grayling 49738; (517) 348–2111. Just north of the main stoplight at the intersection of Business I–75/Michigan 72 in downtown Grayling. Summer hours are 8:00 A.M. to 8:00 P.M. Monday through Thursday and 8:00 A.M. to 10:00 P.M. Friday and Saturday. Closed Sunday. Earlier closing in winter.* Rolls, soups, salads, sandwiches, and vegetarian meals are outshone by the old-fashioned soda fountain for outstanding phosphates, coolers, cones, and malteds, all served to 1950s tunes, with plenty of 1950s and 1960s memorabilia to enjoy in this onetime family drug store. You won't find a friendlier staff anywhere. Try the mulligatawny stew. $

Where to Stay

If you aren't staying at the unique Gates Au Sable Lodge, there are scores of motels in the Grayling area.

Holiday Inn. *2650 Business I–75, Grayling 49738; (517) 348–7611. From I–75, take exit 254. The facility is on the west side of the road.* It has 151 rooms, indoor playground area and pool, and cross-country ski shop in winter. Restaurant on premises serves break-fast, lunch, and dinner, and there are others nearby. $$

Hospitality House. *1232 North I–75 business route, Grayling 49738; (517) 348–8900. From downtown, head north on Business I–75. The motel is on the west side.* It has sixty-four rooms, indoor pool, and restaurant serving breakfast, lunch, and dinner. Other restaurants nearby. $$

For More Information

Grayling Area Visitors Council, *213 North James (Business I–75), Grayling 49738; (800) 937–8837. Web site: www.grayling-mi.com.*

Gaylord

Gaylord is located 20 miles north of Grayling along I-75. Either of two exits will bring you into town. Besides its reputation as a tourism center, Gaylord has also gained a reputation as the center of nearly two dozen of the state's best golf courses, which are sprinkled through the woods. Downtown Gaylord also is home to the annual Alpenfest event the third week of July. Swiss-inspired traditions such as the burning of the Boogg—where residents place all their troubles on pieces of paper and send them up in smoke—together with parades and the world's largest coffee break are part of the fun.

BAVARIAN FALLS PARK (all ages)

On Wisconsin Avenue, Gaylord 49735, adjacent to Call of the Wild; (517) 732–4087. Open from 9:00 A.M. to 10:30 P.M. (or later, depending on the crowds) from May through October.

Minigolf around waterfalls and hills. There are go-carts and rides for tots, too, along with Western gifts.

TREETOPS-SYLVAN RESORT (all ages)

Just east of downtown; (517) 732–6711. Take Michigan 32 to Chester Road and turn north, and then continue east on Wilkinson Road. Open for golf in spring through fall and downhill and cross-country skiing in winter. Golfing rates range from $22 to $86. For ski rentals and lift tickets, plan on around $36. Web site: www.treetops.com.

The ski area boasts nineteen runs and four chairlifts, with rentals and instructions in a family atmosphere.

Where to Eat

Sugar Bowl. *216 West Main Street (Michigan 32), Gaylord 49735; (517) 732–5524. From I–75, take exit 282, Michigan 32, and go east. The restaurant is on the north side of the road.* Great breakfasts, lunches, and dinners in one of the state's oldest family-run restaurants. Steak and fish are specialties. Children's menu, too. $$$

Where to Stay

Microtel Inn & Suites. *510 South Wisconsin, Gaylord 49735. Turn east from I–75 exit 282 on Michigan 32 to Wisconsin, then head about ½ mile south; (517) 731–6331.* This inn offers one hundred rooms and an indoor pool. $$

Super 8 Motel. *1042 West Main Street, Gaylord 49735, just west of the I–75, Michigan 32 exit (exit 282); (517) 732–5193.* This motel has eighty-three rooms, an outdoor pool, and restaurants nearby. $$

For More Information

Gaylord Area Convention and Tourism Bureau, 101 West Main Street, Gaylord 49735; (517) 732–6333 or (800) 345–8621. Web site: www. gaylord-mich.com.

Indian River

Indian River is a summer and winter resort town located along I-75 north of Gaylord. In summer, Burt, Black, and Mullett Lakes beckon with resort cottages, while in winter, there are more than 180 miles of groomed snowmobile trails, not to mention miles of cross-country ski trails. The area also is near some of west Michigan's most popular ski areas. Be sure to check out the totem pole carved from a cottonwood tree planted by early settlers.

INLAND WATERWAY (all ages)

For pontoon boat rental information, call (231) 238–9325, or the Landings at (231) 238–9955. Cost is about $120 daily.

Rent a pontoon boat and float along all or part of Michigan's unknown canal, the Inland Waterway. This 68-mile, partly artificial, partly natural canal cut through the tip of Michigan's "mitt" takes you to some of the state's largest inland lakes and through two locks. The waterway was dredged in the 1800s to allow steamboats to reach the region's interior and was later improved in the 1950s.

Travelers can begin in Indian River and head all the way to Cheboygan on Lake Huron or to Crooked Lake, a few miles from Lake Michigan. While the waterway doesn't connect to the big lake, you can rent a trailer from a local marina to take your craft there.

Where to Eat

Cafe Noka. *On old U.S. 27, Indian River 49749, overlooking Mullett Lake; (231) 238–9103. From I–75, take exit 310 and head north on old U.S. 27 along the north shore of Mullett Lake, on the outskirts of Topinabee. The restaurant is on the north side of the road.* It serves excellent breakfasts and lunches in a tiny, knotty pine building. $

Michael's. *5200 South Straits Highway (Old U.S. 27), Indian River 49749; (231) 238–4987. Leave I–75 at exit 310. Go a mile west on Michigan 68, then ½ mile south on Straits Highway.* Good home-style cooking for lunch and dinner. $

Where to Stay

Burt Lake State Park. *On Burt Lake, Indian River 49749; (231) 238–9392 or (800) 447–2757. Leave I–75 at exit 310. Head west on Michigan 68 to Old U.S. 27. Go south less than a mile to the park entrance. A state motor-vehicle permit is required for entry, $4.00 daily or $20.00 annually. Camping is extra.* The park has 395 campsites with a great beach on Michigan's third-largest inland lake. $

Holiday Inn Express. *4375 Brudy, Indian River 49749; at exit 310 off I–75; (231) 238–3000.* The inn offers fifty rooms, indoor pool, and whirlpool. $$

Nor Gate Motel. *4846 South Straits Highway (Old U.S. 27), Indian River 49749; (616) 238–7788. Leave I–75 at exit 310. Go 1 mile west on Michigan 68, then ½ mile south on Straits Highway.* This little property has fourteen rooms. Restaurant nearby. $

For More Information

Indian River Resort Region Chamber of Commerce, *3435 South Straight Highway, Indian River 49749; (800) 394–8310. Web site: www.irmi.org.*

Hillman

Hillman is about 45 miles east of Gaylord and about 20 miles west of Alpena along Michigan 32. In fall the distinctive bugling of Michigan's elk herd can be heard for miles through the Pigeon River State Forest between Gaylord and Hillman. The herd of more than 1,000, the largest east of the Mississippi, inhabits some of the wildest forest in Lower Michigan. In summer some of the best places to spot the elk are in one of several clearings they're known to frequent especially at dusk. For information on an elk sight-seeing ride, call (517) 742–4502 or (800) 729–9375.

Where to Eat

See Gaylord and Alpena listings.

Where to Stay

Thunder Bay Golf Resort. *27800 Michigan 32, Hillman 49746, just south of town; (517) 742–4502 or (800) 729–9375.* The resort has thirty rooms in condo units, including some two- bedroom units. Whirlpool in separate building. Great golf in summer and cross-country skiing in winter, and a restaurant for breakfast, lunch, and dinner. $$

Ossineke

Ossineke was settled in the 1840s by lumbering interests. Its name was transformed by settlers from the Indian, *Wasineke*. It is on the southern edge of Alpena's Thunder Bay.

DINOSAUR GARDENS PREHISTORICAL ZOO (all ages)

11160 U.S. 23, Ossineke 49766; (517) 471–5477. Open from 9:00 A.M. to 6:00 P.M. daily from Memorial Day through Labor Day. Admission is $5.00 for adults, $4.00 for children younger than twelve, and $3.00 for children younger than six.

A bit to the east is a low-key tourist destination that has attracted families to its wooded setting for more than a half century—Dinosaur Gardens has been entertaining and educating youngsters since 1938. It took original owner Paul Domke thirty-eight years to sculpt the twenty-six life-size dinos set amid the pines and hardwood forest that line the winding Devil River. Storyboards at each exhibit tell visitors what scientists believe the lives of these magnificently fearsome animals were like. In one scene a towering tyrannosaur battles a horned triceratops, and in another an animal roars in frustration after being trapped in a lake of tar. A gift shop sells souvenirs, including plastic dinosaur models. It's a great exhibit and was a favorite of my kids when they were small.

Where to Eat and Stay

See Alpena listing.

Alpena

Built on sawmills powered by the area's abundant pine forests in the nine-teenth century, Alpena is now northeast Michigan's largest city and has a great waterfront, fishing and scuba diving opportunities in Thunder Bay, and wildlife viewing along the lower Thunder Bay River.

JESSE BESSER MUSEUM (all ages)

491 Johnson Street, Alpena 49707; (517) 356–2202. From U.S. 23, go through town on Chilshom (U.S. 23) to Alpena General Hospital. Turn right onto Johnson Street and go 300 feet. The museum is on the left. Open 10:00 A.M. to 5:00 P.M. Tuesday through Saturday and noon to 5:00 P.M. Sunday. Planetarium shows are at 1:00 and 3:00 P.M. Sunday in July and August. Admission is $2.00 for adults, $1.00 for seniors and kids ages five through seventeen, and **Free** *for children ages four and younger. Planetarium shows are $1.00 per person extra; children ages five and younger are not recommended in the planetarium. Web site: www.oweb.com/up/upnorth/museum.*

The museum highlights local history, including the concrete-block-making machine perfected here as a result of the area's rich limestone deposits used in cement making. Nineteenth-century shops and cabins line a re-created street, and outside there's a cabin and log home.

Where to Eat

Hunan Chinese Restaurant. *1120 South State Street (U.S. 23), Alpena 49707, 1½ miles south of town; (517) 356–6461.* Great Chinese food for lunch and dinner. Children's menu and some non-Chinese food also available. $$

Where to Stay

Days Inn. *1496 West Michigan 32, Alpena 49707, 2½ miles west of U.S. 23; (517) 356–6118.* Another chain prop-erty with seventy-seven rooms, with indoor pool and whirlpool. Dining in Alpena. $$

Holiday Inn. *1000 U.S. 23, Alpena 49707, a mile north of downtown; (517) 356–2151.* This chain property has 148 rooms, indoor pool, and recreation area. Restaurant serves breakfast, lunch, and dinner. More restaurants nearby. Pets okay. $$

For More Information

Alpena Area Convention and Visitors Bureau, *235 West Chisholm Street, Alpena 49707; (517) 354–4181* or *(800) 425–7362. Web sites: www.xmission.com/~gastown/balaam/alpena.htm or www.alpena.com.*

Rogers City

Located just off U.S. 23, about 20 miles north of Alpena, Rogers City got its start in fishing, then turned to limestone mining, and is now back to fishing again, but this time as charter-boat action for salmon and steelhead. Rogers City also has become a hot spot for salmon fishing and is touted by some as the best in the state in mid- to late summer. Salmon plants by the state in the late 1990s have been some of the largest in the state. Fishing is good in early summer and only gets better starting in August. Plan on around $350 for a trip.

For the town's size, Rogers City has plenty to offer tourists. While other vacationers head to Michigan's west coast for everything from huge hotels to condoplexes, northeastern Michigan's main attraction is the lack of the same— just plenty of natural things to help you relax and keep you busy at the same time. One such area surrounds this city. At first glance the tiny town doesn't look like much, just another spot to gas up and go. But look closer.

HARBOR VIEW (all ages)

Watch for signs in downtown Rogers City directing you to the overlook. Open for daylight hours. **Free**.

Watch giant Great Lakes freighters pulling up to the docks to load before heading for steel mills in Indiana, Ohio, and Detroit. Take the kids into the former wheelhouse of the retired freighter *Calcite*.

PRESQUE ISLE LIGHTHOUSE MUSEUM (all ages)

To get to the museum, turn east off U.S. 23 at County Road 638 (East Grand Lake Road), travel past two stop signs, and turn right onto Grand Lake Road, Rogers City 49777. Follow it about 9 miles, and you'll see the lighthouse on the right-hand side. Admission is $2.00 for adults and teens and $1.00 for children ages six through eleven. Kids five and younger are admitted **Free**. *Open 9:00 A.M. to 7:00 P.M. daily from May 15 to October 15. Call (517) 595–2787 or (517) 595–2706 for more information.*

A few miles to the south of Rogers City on a spit of land between picturesque Grand Lake and Lake Huron is the old lighthouse. Built in 1840, it is filled with period antiques—and some say it's haunted by a former lightkeeper.

OCQUEOC FALLS (all ages)

Head west of Rogers City along Michigan 68 to reach the park, on the north side of the road. **Free**.

The falls, pronounced *ock-kee-ock,* are largest in the Lower Peninsula. There are hiking and cross-country ski trails along the river as well.

Where to Eat

The Buoy. *530 West Third Street, Rogers City 49779, on the waterfront downtown; (517) 734–4747.* Good selection of dishes for lunch and dinner. Children's menu available. $$

Where to Stay

Driftwood Motel. *540 West Third, Rogers City 49779; (517) 734–4777. Next to the Buoy restaurant downtown.* The motel has forty-four rooms looking over a sandy beach. Heated indoor pool with whirlpool. Lake swimming, too. $$

For More Information

Rogers City Chamber of Commerce, *292 South Bradley, Rogers City 49779; (517) 734–2535 or (800) 622–4148. Web site: www.lhi.net/chamber.*

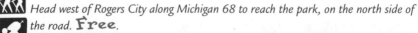

Cheboygan

Only 20 or so miles from the top of the Lower Peninsula, and the eastern terminus of the Inland Waterway, Cheboygan grew up on lumbering, like so many others in this area.

COAST GUARD ICEBREAKER *MACKINAW* TOURS (all ages)

Docked at the end of Coast Guard Drive, Cheboygan 49721. From U.S. 23 and Michigan 27, turn south on U.S. 23 and go across the bridge, then turn east on Coast Guard Drive. **Free**.

One of Cheboygan's claims to fame is that it's the home port of the *Mackinaw*. When the vessel is in port along the Cheboygan River, it's most always open for tours. Contact the Cheboygan Area Tourist Bureau, which appears at the end of this section, for more information.

CHEBOYGAN OPERA HOUSE (all ages)

403 North Huron, Cheboygan 49721, just west of U.S. 23; (231) 627–5432 for more information, or (231) 627–5841 for the box office to check the playbill. Plays are performed all year long. Open for guided tours from 1:00 to 4:00 P.M. Tuesday through Friday from June through September. Admission costs $1.00. Web site: www.theoperahouse.org.

A great example of structures built with lumber money in the north in the nineteenth century, the restored 1877 theater still plays host to local as well as national theater and musical groups.

GORDON TURNER PARK (all ages)

At the end of Huron Street, Cheboygan 49721, which is the extension of Michigan 27 east of U.S. 23.

The cattail marsh that borders Lake Huron is one of the Great Lakes's largest and has been set aside as a wildlife sanctuary. Climb the viewing platform, and to the north in the distance, you'll probably be able to make out the Mackinac Bridge.

CHEBOYGAN RIVER LOCKS (all ages)

Just south of Michigan 27 and east of U.S. 23, near the city's paper plant. **Free.**

Stop by to watch pleasure boats using the Inland Waterway being raised or lowered 12 feet. It's one of two lock systems on the waterway.

CHEBOYGAN COUNTY HISTORICAL MUSEUM (all ages)

At Huron and Court Streets, Cheboygan 49721, 1 block west of Main Street; (231) 627–5448 or (231) 627–9597. Hours are 1:00 to 4:00 P.M. Monday through Friday, 11:00 A.M. to 2:00 P.M. Saturday from June 15 to September 15. Admission is $2.00 for adults and **Free** *for preschool through high school children.*

This museum is in the former county sheriff's home, which doubled as a jail from 1882 to 1969 and still has eight cells.

Where to Eat

Boathouse. *106 Pine Street, Cheboygan 49721, downtown on the river, just off Michigan 27; (231) 627–4316.* Enjoy lunch and dinner alongside the Inland Waterway in a converted boathouse once owned by members of Detroit's infamous Purple Gang in Prohibition's rum-running days. Children's menu available. $$$

Elias Brothers Big Boy. *861 South Main Street (U.S. 27), Cheboygan 49721; (231) 627–3661. Open 6:00 A.M. to 11:00 P.M. daily.* Good family fare from salad bar to trademark triple-decker burger. $$

Hack-Ma-Tack Inn. *8131 Beebe Road, Cheboygan 49721; (231) 625–2919. From downtown Cheboygan, head west on U.S. 27 for 3¼ miles, then turn east ¼ mile on Michigan 33, and then follow the signs about 2 miles to the inn.* One of the best restaurant settings in the north, alongside the Inland Waterway at the eastern end of Mullett Lake. Sit in an 1894 lodge amid outdoor memorabilia. Prime rib and whitefish are not to be missed for lunch or dinner. $$$

Where to Stay

Best Western River Terrace Motel. *847 South Main Street (Michigan 27), Cheboygan 49721; (231) 627–5688.* The motel has fifty-three riverside rooms, indoor pool, and exercise area. Restaurants nearby. $$

Days Inn. *889 South Main Street, Cheboygan 49721; (231) 627–3126. From U.S. 23, head west on Michigan 27 about 1⅓ miles.* The inn has twenty-eight rooms on the river. Restaurants nearby. $$

For More Information

Cheboygan Area Tourist Bureau, *124 North Main Street, Cheboygan 49721; (231) 627–7183. Web site: www. cheboygan.com.*

West Michigan—South

Fruit orchards, sandy beaches, marinas, artist colonies, cities celebrating their ethnic heritage—west Michigan has a wealth of activities, spread from the Indiana state line to one of the state's most popular tourist destinations, Mackinaw City. The southern portion of this region is a great place to start your explorations.

Bridgman

Huge dunes seen on the west side of I–94 announce the area of Michigan that's been dubbed "harbor country." It's a favorite vacation spot not only for Michiganians, but for Chicago area residents as well. From here north, Lake Michigan's lakefront is nearly one big sand beach.

WARREN DUNES STATE PARK (all ages)

Take exit 16 off I–94 and go 2 miles south; (616) 426–4013. Entry is by state-issued vehicle permit ($4.00 daily or $20.00 annually). Camping is $15.00 nightly. Open year-round.

This is another one of those parks that is more than just a place to stay. Covering more than 2½ miles of beautiful Lake Michigan shore near the small town of Bridgman, the park has become one of the state's most popular, welcoming more than one million visitors annually.

Encompassing 1,507 acres, the park is known for its continually changing sand dunes that greet motorists as soon as they turn onto the entrance road. For many coming from Indiana or Illinois, it's the first glimpse of the magnificent Lake Michigan sand shore that stretches nearly the length of west Michigan.

WEST MICHIGAN — SOUTH

Walk the beach of sugary silica sand and tell your kids to shuffle through it. It literally squeaks. Head into the dunes along 6 miles of marked hiking trails. Watch for the tops of trees long ago covered by the shifting sands. There are nearly 200 modern campsites, as well as three cabins to rent. Parts of the park are heavily wooded, but there are hundreds of acres of high sand dunes, too.

JONES BLUEBARRY FARM (all ages)

9245 Gast Road, Bridgman 49106, exit 146 off I–94; (616) 465–4745. Picking usually runs July 4–Labor Day.

Southwest Michigan is also famous for its you-pick farms, and this is one example. In July, there are ten acres of blueberries to choose from. Plan about $1.50 per pint, or about $13.00 for ten pounds. The farm also sells picked berries, peaches, jams, jellies, and syrups. Farms with pick-your-own cherries and raspberries are also in the area. Ask the Joneses for directions.

Where to Eat

Hyerdall's Cafe. *9673 Red Arrow Highway, Bridgman 49106; (616) 465–5546. From I–94, take the Bridgman exit 16.* Head north on Red Arrow Highway about 1 mile. Serves breakfast, lunch, and dinner. Children's menu. $$

Where to Stay

See St. Joseph listing.

Buchanan

Settled in 1833 on a bend of the St. Joseph River, this tiny town was named for President James Buchanan. It is located north of U.S. 12 and west of U.S. 31.

BEAR CAVE (all ages)

4085 Bear Cave Road, Buchanan 49107; (616) 695–3050. From Buchanan, head north 4 miles on Red Bud Trail and watch for signs. Open daily from 9:00 A.M. to 4:00 P.M. from May 1 through Labor Day. Admission is $3.00 for adults, $1.50 for ages six through twelve. Children five and younger are admitted Free.

One of the few caves in Michigan accessible to the public. Small by spelunking standards, it's a 150-foot-long cave accessible by a winding stairway. Since the temperature inside is a constant fifty-eight degrees, wear suitable clothing. Also be forewarned that the cave contains bats. Generally they won't bother you if you don't bother them.

Where to Eat

See Niles and St. Joseph listings.

Where to Stay

Bear Cave Resort. *See aforementioned directions and phone number.* After you've seen Bear Cave, stay at its campground. There are eighty-five campsites and an outdoor pool, playground, movie room, and other amenities. $

See also listings for Benton Harbor/St. Joseph.

Berrien Springs

Across the river a few miles west of tiny Eau Claire, Berrien Springs has a few surprises for travelers, too.

CHRISTMAS PICKLE FESTIVAL (all ages)
Takes place in downtown Berrien Springs the first week of December. To get there, head south on U.S. 31 from I–94 into town. For more information call (616) 471–9680.

What better celebration to hang the annual downtown holiday doin's on than a pickle festival? According to the promoters, it's based on a tradition begun in Germany 200 years ago, when the first child to find the pickle hidden in the tree on Christmas morning got an extra present or could open hers first. From this tradition sprang Berrien Springs' version, with a parade, street lighting, and other fun including pickle tasting provided by local growers and packers.

 BERRIEN SPRINGS NATURAL HISTORY MUSEUM (all ages)
On the campus of the private Andrews University, just west of downtown; (616) 471–3243. Open by appointment Monday through Friday. **Free**.

The small, two-room museum features the only complete mastodon skeleton unearthed in Michigan plus other exhibits on local natural history with animal and insect collections.

Sportfishing on the St. Joseph River

When it's cold outside, the best salmon and steelhead anglers head inside—inside their boats, that is. Steelhead fishing on the St. Joseph River here from just below Berrien Springs dam downriver several miles stays hot all winter. The addition of Skamania steelhead, which spawn in summer, means some boats stay active on the river year-round.

Charter operators have specialized boats for fishing the river's holes and gravel runs. In the bow area, a glass cocoon heated by portable kerosene stoves keeps you warm until a fish hits one of the lines strung at the stern and extending downstream over productive areas. Salmon, steelhead, and walleye are the game. Cost per trip is about $260. To contact a guide like Mike Stowe of Niles, call either the Berrien Springs–Eau Claire Chamber of Commerce at (616) 471–9680, or the Southwestern Michigan Tourist Council at (616) 925–6301. Web site: www. swmichigan.org.

Where to Eat

Daybreak Cafe. *126 East Ferry (old U.S. 31), Berrien Springs 49103, downtown; (616) 471–5605.* Breakfast served all day, lunch and dinner at appropriate times. $$

See also listings for St. Joseph.

Where to Stay

More accommodations are located near Benton Harbor and St. Joseph.

Pennelwood Resort. *10652 Range Line Road, Berrien Springs 49103; (616) 473–2511. Web site: www.pennelwoodresort. com. From downtown, go south on U.S. 31 across the St. Joseph River. The first road to the right is Range Line. Turn south.* A one-hundred-year-old resort that includes meals with your stay, two outdoor

pools, playground, and tennis courts. $$

Shamrock Park Campground. *Operated by the village on the St. Joseph River, Berrien Springs 49103; (616) 473–5691. From downtown, head across the bridge at the north end of town, and watch for the sign.* Full-service and rustic sites. Many river fishing charters leave from here. No swimming. $

For More Information

Berrien Springs–Eau Claire Chamber of Commerce, *P.O. Box 177, Berrien Springs 49103; (616) 471–9680.*

Niles Area/Four Flags Tourism Council, *321 East Main Street, Niles 49120; (616) 684–7444.*

Coldwater

This town grew to prominence in the 1800s as a trading center for the region's farm families and because of its location on the then Chicago to Detroit turnpike, which is now U.S. 12. Located on the western edge of the Irish Hills, it has a great Victorian downtown courthouse and other historical buildings.

TIBBITS OPERA HOUSE (all ages)

14 South Hanchett Street, Coldwater 49036, south of U.S. 12; (517) 278–6029. **Free** *theater tours offered from 9:00* A.M. *to 5:00* P.M. *Monday through Friday by reservation only. Tickets for "Popcorn Theater" cost $5.00 for adults and $4.00 for children ages twelve and younger. Tickets for other productions start at around $9.00. Web site: www.discover-michigan.com/tibbits.*

Opened in 1882, the opera house still presents professional summer stock productions June through August, and community plays the rest of the year. There's also a small art gallery inside.

The Tibbets also presents "Popcorn Theater," made especially for children five and up. Productions such as *Thumbelina* and *Treasure Island* take place Friday and Saturday mornings at 10:00 A.M.

Where to Eat

Big Boy of Coldwater. *556 East Chicago Street (U.S. 12), Coldwater 49036; (517) 278–5762. Open 6:00 to 1:00* A.M. *daily.* A wide selection of family fare from salad bar to its trademark triple-decker burger. $$

Coldwater Garden. *432 East Chicago Street (U.S. 12), Coldwater 49036; (517) 278–3172. From I–69, head east on U.S. 12.* Daily specials for breakfast, lunch, and dinner. Ribs are a specialty. Senior discounts and children's menu. $–$$

There also are lots of places to eat just west of the I–69 exit to the city.

Where to Stay

Chicago Pike Inn. *215 East Chicago (U.S. 12), Coldwater 49036, downtown; (517) 279–8744.* Inside a huge, exquisitely restored 1903 Victorian home are eight rooms. $$

Little King Motel. *847 East Chicago (U.S. 12), Coldwater 49036; (517) 278–6660. From the U.S. 12 exit at I–69,* head east about 2 blocks. The motel has twenty-one economy-style rooms. Small pets okay. $

Super 8 Motel. *600 Orleans Boulevard, Coldwater 49036; (517) 278–8833. From I–69, go ⅓ mile west, a block north, and ½ block east.* The budget property has fifty-eight rooms. Small pets okay. $

Colon

Colon is 16 miles west of Coldwater along Michigan 86. If you say a visit to this tiny town is truly magical, you're right. Each year during the first weekend in August, thousands of professional and amateur magicians converge on the town to take part in the Magic Get-Together. For four days they pay homage to the memory of Harry Blackstone Sr., the former Colon resident who became world famous for his illusions. The festival and the famous Abbott Magic Company support Colon's claim that it's the Magic Capital of the World.

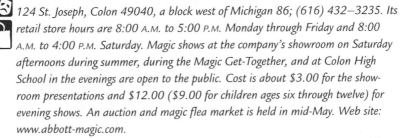 **ABBOTT'S MAGIC COMPANY (all ages)**
124 St. Joseph, Colon 49040, a block west of Michigan 86; (616) 432–3235. Its retail store hours are 8:00 A.M. to 5:00 P.M. Monday through Friday and 8:00 A.M. to 4:00 P.M. Saturday. Magic shows at the company's showroom on Saturday afternoons during summer, during the Magic Get-Together, and at Colon High School in the evenings are open to the public. Cost is about $3.00 for the showroom presentations and $12.00 ($9.00 for children ages six through twelve) for evening shows. An auction and magic flea market is held in mid-May. Web site: www.abbott-magic.com.

Faster than you can say "abracadabra," the kids and the rest of the family can disappear inside the Abbott's Magic Company to seek out items for Halloween and tricks to dazzle their friends back home. Lacquered Chinese boxes, black top hats, magic wands, rubber chickens, and fake raccoons are among the more than 2,000 products Abbott's sells to magicians around the globe. It's the world's largest producer of handmade illusions.

Bill's Favorite Events in West Michigan–South

- **Discover Michigan Skiing** (January), at various ski areas including those in southwest lower Michigan, (810) 620–4448.

- **Icebreaker Festival** (February), downtown South Haven, (616) 637–5252. Web site: www.southhaven.org.

- **Home & Garden Show** (March), Grand Center, Grand Rapids, (616) 530–1919.

- **Derrick Edwards Bicycle Safety Program** (April), Kellogg Arena, Battle Creek, (616) 963–4800.

- **Blossomtime Festival** (May), Benton Harbor and St. Joseph, (616) 926–7397. Web site: www.blossomtimefestival.org.

- **Berrien Auto Fair** (June), Berrien County Youth Fairground, Berrien Springs, (616) 463–5532.

- **Coast Guard Festival** (July), downtown Grand Haven, (616) 846–5940.

- **Krasl Art Fair** (July), Lake Bluff Park in downtown St. Joseph, (616) 926–0271.

- **Kustom Kemp of America Street Custom Car Show** (August), on Windmill Island in Holland, (616) 394–0000 or (800) 506–1299.

- **Celebration on the Grand** (September), downtown Grand Rapids, Ah-Nab-Awen Park, (616) 456–1613.

- **International Festival of Lights** (November), downtown Battle Creek, (616) 962–2240 or (616) 963–3830.

- **Holiday parade** (December), St. Joseph, (616) 983–6739.

- **Christmas Pickle Festival** (December), Berrien Springs, (616) 473–1188.

Where to Eat

See Coldwater listing.

For More Information

Branch County Chamber of Commerce, 20 Division Street, Coldwater 49036; (517) 278–5985.

Stevensville

Another lakeside town named for a former resident, Stevensville is perched atop the now-grassy dunes, just off I–94 and just south of St. Joseph.

RED ARROW HOBBIES (all ages)

5095 Red Arrow Highway, Stevensville 49127; (616) 429–8233. Open Saturday and Monday through Thursday 10:00 A.M. to 6:00 P.M., Friday 10:00 A.M. to 7:00 P.M., and Sunday noon to 5:00 P.M. Web site: www.goos.com/~hobbies.

Got a budding rocket scientist in the house? Head to the store that caters to kids of all ages. Model-rocket supplies, science education kits, stamp and coin collecting supplies, and more are inside.

GRAND MERE STATE PARK (all ages)

On Red Arrow Highway; (616) 426–4013. From I–94, take the Stevensville exit and go south to Thornton Road. It soon becomes Willow Road. The park entrance is about ½ mile away. Warren Dunes State Park administers the facility. Entrance is by state park permit, which costs $4.00 daily or $20.00 annually.

This stately old park (*grandmere* is French for "grandmother") offers a glimpse of what the lake's sand dunes were like before towns and cities sprang up along the shore. Mostly undeveloped, the park has hiking trails through tree-covered and bald dunes and is a great place for bird-watching and enjoying the seclusion.

Where to Eat

Grand Mere Inn. *5800 Red Arrow Highway, Stevensville 49127; (616) 429–3591. From I–94, take exit 22 and go east.* Great view of Lake Michigan, with seafood and steak specialties. Children's menu available. $$$

Schuler's. *5000 Red Arrow Highway, Stevensville 49127; (616) 429–3273. Just off I–94, south of the Stevensville exit.* Casual dining and children's menu. The restaurant's decor and architecture is reminiscent of a log lodge. $$$

For less expensive fare, try the restaurant at Park Inn International (see Where to Stay) or see listings under Benton Harbor/St. Joseph.

215

Where to Stay

Baymont Inns and Suites. *I–94, exit 23;* (616) 428–9111. Basic motel has one hundred rooms. Restaurants nearby. Two rooms are available for guests traveling with pets. $$

Park Inn International. *4290 Red Arrow Highway, Stevensville 49127;* (616) *429–3218. Just south of St. Joseph. Take I–94 exit 23 at Stevensville and go ½ mile north on Business I–94. The inn has* ninety rooms, indoor and outdoor pools, and exercise areas. Restaurant on premises serves moderately priced breakfast, lunch, and dinner. Pets okay. $$

Benton Harbor/St. Joseph

If you've got a Sears appliance in your home, chances are it came from these towns, home of the Whirlpool Corporation. This is indeed a tale of two cities. While Benton Harbor is attempting to lift itself up by its bootstraps, sister city St. Joseph, just across the St. Joe River bridge, is prospering. One-way brick streets route traffic past shops downtown. Down the hill toward the beach is the old part of town, with many historic homes and a great beach. The two towns are accessible just off I–94.

KRASL ART CENTER (all ages)
Corner of Lake Boulevard and Park Street, St. Joseph 49085, downtown; (616) *983–0271. Open from 10:00 A.M. to 4:00 P.M. Monday through Thursday, 10:00 A.M. to 1:00 P.M. Friday, 10:00 A.M. to 4:00 P.M. Saturday, and 1:00 to 4:00 P.M. Sunday. Admission is* Free. *Web site: www.krasl.com.*

The museum features regional artists and traveling exhibits with works from other museums around the country, such as the Detroit Institute of Arts. Exhibits change about every six weeks. There is also a permanent collection of sculpture on the grounds outside. There are occasional one-day workshops for children as well.

CURIOUS KIDS MUSEUM (all ages)
415 Lake Boulevard, in downtown St. Joseph; (616) *983–2543. Reach the museum by taking exit 27 off I–94 and heading north on Niles Avenue; turn west on Broad, go 2 blocks, and then proceed south on Lake Boulevard. Admission is $3.50 for anyone age one or older. The museum is open daily, but hours vary by season. Kids ages twelve and younger must be accompanied by an adult. Web site: www.curiouskidsmuseum.org.*

Southwest Michigan's own hands-on children's museum features interactive displays and ways for kids to learn about everything from serving customers to listening for a heartbeat in a teddy bear.

Where to Eat

Chesapeake Bagel Bakery. *Corner of Main and Broad, St. Joseph 49805, downtown; (616) 983–7646.* Great bagel sandwiches, soups, and coffees for meals throughout the day, starting at around 6:00 A.M. $

Clementine's. *1235 Broad Street, St. Joseph 49805, downtown; (616) 983–*0990. Looks over a marina and serves a wide variety of lunch and dinner items. Children's menu available. $$$$

Schu's Grill & Bar. *501 Pleasant Street, St. Joseph 49805, downtown; (616) 983–7248.* Good American-style food. Children's menu available for lunch and dinner. $$

Where to Stay

The shoreline between Indiana and Benton Harbor literally has hundreds of choices for travelers and vacationers, from bed and breakfasts to large motels and inns. Here are a couple of favorites:

Boulevard Inn. *521 Lake Boulevard, St. Joseph 49805; (616) 983–6600. From I–94, take exit 33 into Benton Harbor and across the bridge to St. Joseph. At the first light, turn left onto Main. Go to the next light and turn right onto Broad. Go to the second stop sign and turn left onto Lake. The* hotel *is 2 blocks down on the left.* The hotel offers eighty-three suite-style rooms and restaurant serving breakfast, lunch and dinner. $$$

Clarion Hotel. *100 Main Street, St. Joseph; (616) 983–7341. On Business I–94 just across the bridge from Benton Harbor.* The hotel has 149 rooms, indoor pool, whirlpool, and restaurant serving breakfast through dinner. Also close to downtown St. Joseph shopping, fishing piers, and beachfront. $$$

For More Information

Southwestern Michigan Tourist Council, *2300 Pipestone Road, Benton* Harbor 49022; (616) 925–6301. Web site: www.swmichigan.org.

Coloma

Founded in 1834, this village, once called Dickerville, was renamed after a west coast wildflower. It's now a familiar stop on I–94.

DEER FOREST (all ages)

Off the I–94 Coloma exit, then north 2½ miles; (616) 468–4961. Open daily from 10:00 A.M. to 6:00 P.M. from Memorial Day weekend through Labor Day. Admission, which includes rides on the train, Ferris wheel, child-size roller coaster, and more, is $12.00 for adults, $10.00 for kids ages three through eleven. Web site: www.deerforest.com.

More than 300 tame animals await the kids to pet and feed them. The kids also can ride a Ferris wheel and take a railroad ride through the woods or play on a huge playscape. Snacks and picnic area with grills available.

Where to Eat and Stay

See Benton Harbor/St. Joseph listings.

Battle Creek

While the city that cereal built no longer features tours of the Kellogg Company, Ralston Purina, and Post—protecting trade secrets was the reason, the companies said—Battle Creek throws a party by feeding its most famous product to all comers. To reach the festival area, take exit 98B off I-94 and go north into downtown.

CEREAL FEST (all ages)

Takes place throughout downtown the second Saturday in June. The Free feast runs from 8:00 A.M. to noon along Michigan Avenue downtown. For details call (800) 397–2240 or (616) 962–2240.

The festival starts with the World's Longest Breakfast Table. How long? How about 250 picnic tables end to end, groaning under boxes of cereal, milk, juice, doughnuts, and Kellogg's Pop Tarts to feed some 60,000 celebrants each year? On the Friday night before, a grand parade, including a costumed children's contingent, wends through downtown. On Saturday, children's activities ranging from face painting to rescue demonstrations and other entertainment fill up the time through midnight.

KELLOGG'S CEREAL CITY U.S.A. (all ages)

171 West Michigan Avenue, Battle Creek 49017; (616) 962–6230. From I–94, take exit 98B onto I–194/Michigan 66 and head north into town. Turn west at Michigan Avenue. Admission is $6.95 for adults, $5.95 for seniors, $4.95 for children ages three to twelve, and **Free** *for children two and younger. Open 9:30 A.M. to 5:00 P.M. Monday through Saturday and 11:00 A.M. to 5:00 P.M. Sunday, with slightly reduced winter hours. Web site: www.kelloggscerealcityusa.org.*

Exploring cereal from field to flakes and your table, this museum traces the development of the city's most famous export. It began with the health-food boom of the late 1800s that started Dr. John Kellogg's famous health resort, which prompted brothers W. K. and Harvey Kellogg, as well as their competitor across the city, C. W. Post, to prepare ready-to-eat grain cereals. There is a simulated working production line that takes the place of the discontinued factory tours, hands-on activities for kids on health, Kellogg's toys and characters, of course, and a theater presenting the history of the industry and its advertising.

TEAM U.S. NATIONALS BALLOON CHAMPIONSHIP AND AIR SHOW (all ages)

Takes place in early July at W. K. Kellogg Airport, Battle Creek 49014; (616) 962–0592. The airport is reached by exiting I–94 at Helmer Road and following the signs. Entry requires a parking fee of $4.00 per day for cars or $10.00 for RVs. Web site: www.bcballoons.com.

Each July, Battle Creek residents turn their eyes to the skies for eight days, starting the Saturday before the Fourth of July holiday. The competition draws up to 200 balloon fliers to the city for takeoffs, weather permitting. During the air show, see the likes of the Air Force's Thunderbirds or the U.S. Navy's Blue Angels perform precision maneuvers. Your kids will love the wing walkers and stunt planes, not to mention their chance to inspect aircraft up close during on-the-ground displays.

BINDER PARK ZOO (all ages)

7400 Division Drive, Battle Creek 49014; (616) 979–1351. The zoo is 3 miles south of I–94 exit 100. It is normally open from the last Saturday of April through mid-October. Hours are 9:00 A.M. to 5:00 P.M. Monday through Friday (until 8:00 P.M. on Wednesday only from June through August), 9:00 A.M. to 6:00 P.M. Saturday, and 10:00 A.M. to 6:00 P.M. Sunday. Admission is $7.95 for adults and teens, $5.95 for children ages three through twelve, and $6.95 for seniors. Stroller-accessible.

The zoo contains more than 80 animal exhibits with more than 250 animals in natural settings, including snow leopards, an interactive exhibit on insects, and the new Wild Africa exhibit. Eighty African animals roam free in a fifty-acre exhibit. There's a gift shop offering nature books, stuffed animals, and the like. A restaurant serves snacks and sandwiches indoors and out. There's also a hands-on playground at Miller Children's Zoo, part of Binder Park, and what's billed as one of the world's largest accurate dinosaur replicas.

LEILA ARBORETUM AND KINGMAN MUSEUM OF NATURAL HISTORY (all ages)

928 West Michigan Avenue, Battle Creek 49014, at Twentieth Street; (616) 965–5117 for the museum, (616) 969–0270 for the arboretum. To get there, take exit 95 off I–94 and travel north on Helmer for about 6 miles to West Michigan Avenue; from there, head east 1½ miles, then north into the arboretum. Museum hours are 9:00 A.M. to 5:00 P.M. Monday through Friday and 1:00 to 5:00 P.M. Saturday. Admission is $2.00 for adults and $1.00 for students. The arboretum is open daily from dawn to dusk and is Free.

The seventy-two-acre arboretum, built with the help of Post Cereal money in 1922, was left dormant during the Great Depression and remained that way until 1982, when it was revived once more. There are massive floral displays in season, a children's adventure garden, sunken garden, and a visitor center.

The site also is the home of the Museum of Natural History, which is run by the Battle Creek Public Schools and features three floors of exhibits. You can delve into the age of dinosaurs if you like or explore the universe in the planetarium.

MICHIGAN BATTLECATS (all ages)

1392 Capital Avenue NE, Battle Creek 49017; (616) 660–2255. Take exit 98B off I–94 and go north. The road becomes Capital Avenue, which will take you through town to Bailey Park and the stadium. Ticket prices are $8.00 for field box seats, $6.00 for box seats, $5.00 for reserved, and $4.00 for bleachers. Senior citizens and ages fourteen and younger pay $3.00. Many nights feature special promotions, such as Free *hats or balls, or fireworks. The team plays seventy games at home. Web site: www.michiganbattlecats.com.*

Like baseball? The Cats took to the field for the first time in 1995 in the 6,200-seat C. O. Brown Stadium, home of the annual Stan Musial World Series for high schoolers and the NCAA Championships. It is a Class A farm team for the Houston Astros. Special theme games include **Free** bats, and jersey giveaways. There are senior citizen discounts on Sunday.

FULL BLAST AND BATTLE CREEK YOUTH CENTER (all ages)

35 Hamblin Avenue, Battle Creek 49017; (616) 966–3667. From I–94, take I–194/Michigan 66 north into town. Turn left at the first light onto Hamblin, and you're there. Hours are 6:00 A.M. to 9:00 P.M. Monday through Friday, 8:00 A.M. to 9:00 P.M. Saturday, and 11:00 A.M. to 8:00 P.M. Sunday in summer. Gully Washer, the indoor water park, is open year-round from 3:30 to 7:00 P.M. Monday through Friday, 10:00 A.M. to 7:00 P.M. Saturday, and 11:00 A.M. to 7:00 P.M. Sunday. The same hours hold in summer for the outdoor water park, Flash Flood. Admission is $6.00 per person with water park entry ($5.00 in winter) or $3.00 per person without. Web site: www.fullblast.org.

One of the largest outdoor and indoor exercise areas in the state goes right along with the reputation of Battle Creek from its early days as a health-spa location. Included in the fifteen attractions are a full-service health club, an Internet cafe and teen nightclub, an indoor playground, a food court, and Gully Washer, an indoor park with two water slides, "river" float, and other amenities. Next to it is Flash Flood, for outdoor fun in summer, with two 200-foot water slides and playground. There's also a gym with three basketball courts.

Where to Eat

Arcadia Brewing Co. *103 West Michigan Avenue, Battle Creek 49017, downtown; (616) 963–9690. From I–94, head north on I–194/Michigan 66 to Michigan Avenue, and turn west.* Enjoy house-made brews with wood-fired pizza for lunch and dinner. $$

Clara's on the River. *44 North McCamly, Battle Creek 49017; (616) 963–0966. Web site: www.claras.com. From I–94, head north on I–194/Michigan 66 to downtown. Turn west on Michigan to McCamly and north to the riverside.* Large and varied selection of foods for lunch and dinner. Chicken Caesar salad is great. Children's menu. $$

Where to Stay

McCamly Plaza Hotel. *50 Capital Avenue, Battle Creek 49017, downtown; (616) 963–7050. From I–94, take I–194/Michigan 66 north. Turn west on Hamblin to Capital, then north.* The hotel has 242 rooms, indoor pool, exercise area, and restaurant serving breakfast through dinner. Small pets okay at extra charge. $$$

Super 8 Motel. *5395 Beckley Road, Battle Creek 49015; (616) 979–1828. From exit 97 on I–94, head east on Beckley. The* motel has sixty-two rooms. Restaurant nearby. Small pets okay. $

For More Information

Greater Battle Creek–Calhoun County Visitors Bureau, *77 East Michigan Avenue, Suite 100, Battle Creek* *49017; (616) 962–2240 or (800) 397–2240. Web site: www.battlecreekvisitors.org.*

Hickory Corners

Named after a hickory tree found in the 1840s, Hickory Corners is home to about 250 people.

GILMORE CLASSIC CAR CLUB OF AMERICA MUSEUM (all ages)

6865 Hickory Road, Hickory Corners 49060; (616) 671–5089. Take Michigan 43 north from Kalamazoo to Hickory Corners. Museum hours are 10:00 A.M. to 5:00 P.M. daily from May 1 through October 29. Admission is $6.00 for adults, $5.00 for seniors, and $3.00 for children ages seven through fifteen; kids six and younger get in Free. *Web site: www.gilmorecarmuseum.org.*

You'll find more than 140 preserved beauties that epitomize the term *rolling sculpture*. They're all on display in antique barns in the tiny town of Hickory Corners, just northwest of Battle Creek. The collection includes a rare 1899 Locomobile Steamer as well as Packards, Cadillacs, and cars made in Kalamazoo. Along with the autos and a replica of a 1930s Shell filling station, there's a narrow-gauge locomotive, plus picnic and playground areas where the kids can blow off steam. On at least two weekends a month in summer, the museum hosts shows highlighting vintage motorcycles, tractors, and cars from sports models to specific makes.

Where to Eat and Stay

See Battle Creek and Kalamazoo listings.

Kalamazoo

From maple sugaring in season to a walk-by history of aviation at its "Air Zoo" and a stroll through the campus of Western Michigan University, this city along I-94 delivers a memorable visit for the entire family. Sports fans can enjoy not only WMU's great football program, but also professional baseball and hockey.

KALAMAZOO NATURE CENTER (all ages)

7000 North Westnedge, Kalamazoo 49004; (616) 381–1574. Go north from I–94 at U.S. 131 and get off at exit 44 (D Avenue); drive east to Westnedge, and then south less than a mile. The visitor center is open from 9:00 A.M. to 5:00 P.M. Monday through Saturday and from 1:00 to 5:00 P.M. Sunday. The grounds are open one hour later. Admission is $4.50 for adults, $3.50 for seniors, and $2.50 for children ages four through seventeen. Web site: www.naturecenter.org.

A newly renovated interpretive center greets visitors to the 1,000 acres of dense hardwood forest awaiting exploration. Filled with lots of hands-on exhibits, kids can walk through tree trunks and learn about animals. There's also a butterfly house where you can watch the entire life cycle of butterflies, along with a hummingbird garden. The Delano pioneer homestead, with depictions of early Michigan farm life, operates during warm weather. The dense woodlands include a glen that was a favorite inspiration for nineteenth-century author James Fenimore Cooper.

KALAMAZOO AVIATION HISTORY MUSEUM (all ages)

3101 East Milham, Portage 49002; (616) 382–6555. Take I–94 exit 78 south onto Portage Road and go about 1½ miles to Milham Road; then head east ½ mile. Open June through August from 9:00 A.M. to 6:00 P.M. Monday and Tuesday; 9:00 A.M. to 8:00 P.M. Wednesday; and noon to 6:00 P.M. Sunday. From September to May, hours are 9:00 A.M. to 5:00 P.M. Monday through Saturday and noon to 5:00 P.M. Sunday. Admission is $10.00 for adults, $8.00 for seniors, $5.00 for kids ages six through fifteen, and Free *for children ages five and younger. Web site: www.airzoo.org.*

The "Air Zoo," as it's nicknamed, is one of the state's best. At times more than fifty aircraft are on display in a large hangar, an adjacent annex, and outside. Let the kids climb in and "fly" a flight simulator. At 2:00 P.M. Saturday and Sunday from May through October, you can ride in an antique Ford Tri-Motor for $35 per person, weather permitting.

You'll also see military uniforms and model aircraft, and there's a gift shop, too. In place of the annual air shows given in previous years, the museum presents summer weekend events highlighting aircraft and past air shows. Plans were recently announced for a major expansion of the museum to turn it into a theme park–style attraction by 2003.

KALAMAZOO VALLEY MUSEUM (all ages)

230 North Rose Street, Kalamazoo 49004; (616) 373–7990. From I–94, take the Westnedge Avenue exit north. Jog onto Park Street, then turn east on Michigan Avenue to Rose and head north. Hours are 10:00 A.M. to 6:00 P.M. Monday through Saturday (until 9:00 P.M. Wednesday) and 1:00 to 5:00 P.M. Sunday. Admission is Free*, but there are charges for special exhibits and programs; $2.00 per person for the Learning Hall; $2.00 per person for the planetarium; $2.00 for children ages eight through twelve and $3.00 for adults for the Challenger Learning Center. Web site: www.kvcc.edu.*

A hands-on science center for the kids is combined with local history lessons in this museum, created with the largest capital contribution campaign in the history of the city. More than 11,000 persons contributed to its construction. The core gallery features exhibits from the museum's collection of 45,000 local artifacts. There are also antiques.

A Trail of History explores local history with the help of items found in home attics. And, of course, there's the mummy, which has been part of a museum here since 1927. The mummy is that of a woman who lived more than 2,300 years ago. In the Interactive Learning Hall, a computer drives a fully interactive theater that creates programs based on audience ideas, while the Challenger Learning Center focuses on space exploration.

ECHO VALLEY (all ages)

8495 East H Avenue, Kalamazoo 49004; (616) 349–3291. To reach Echo Valley, take I–94 exit 85, Thirty-fifth Street. Turn right. At the first stop, turn left on Michigan 96 and drive to Thirty-third Street. Turn right and go 3 miles to H Avenue. Turn left. Toboggans are $8.00 per adult. An all-day pass costs $10.00, or inner tubing $7.00. Open in winter from 6:00 to 10:00 P.M. Friday, 10:00 A.M. to 10:00 P.M. Saturday, and noon to 7:00 P.M. Sunday.

The family fun in Kalamazoo doesn't stop for winter. Remember those butterflies in your stomach at just the moment your sled or toboggan moved down your neighborhood winter hill? You and your kids can experience the same roller-coaster thrill at Echo Valley, east of the city. Eight iced tracks await. You'll get to use a wooden toboggan. Load it onto one of the tracks, and you'll be launched down a 120-foot hill at

Theater Choices in the Kalamazoo Area

The Kalamazoo Civic Theatre (616–343–1313) is at 329 South Park Street at South Street downtown, just off Bronson Park, the only location where Abraham Lincoln spoke in Michigan, four years before becoming president. From I–94, take Westnedge downtown, then turn north onto Park.

The **Barn Theatre** (616–731–4121) is along M–96, west of downtown Kalamazoo in Augusta. From downtown, head east on Michigan 96. It features summer stock. The theater has been performing plays and musicals for local crowds more than fifty years.

The **New Vic Theatre** (616–381–3328) is at 134 East Vine. From I–94, head north on Westnedge to Vine and turn east. The theater is a professional stock company that produces and performs plays year-round except January. *A Christmas Carol* is performed each November and December. Tickets are $12.50 to $16.00 for all performances.

up to 60 miles per hour, more than ¼ mile of curves and straights. A rope tow gets you back to the top. Cold noses and toes can be warmed at the lodge while you sample the offerings at the snack bar. Then strap on a pair of rental skates ($4.00 for skating, rentals are $1.00) and try the 43,000-square-foot outdoor rink.

MICHIGAN K-WINGS (all ages)

The Wings play at Wings Stadium, 3620 Van Rick Drive, Kalamazoo 49002; (616) 345–5101. From I–94, take the Sprinkle Road exit and head south to Van Rick. Tickets run between $7.00 and $13.00 for adults. Children twelve and younger get in for $4.00. Admission for public skating is $3.00, and rentals cost $1.00. Web site: www.kwings.com.

Watch the Wings, a farm team for the Dallas Stars in the NHL, take on other International Hockey League teams in forty-one home games between October and April.

KALAMAZOO TORNADOES (all ages)

The team plays at the Edward J. Annen Sports and Recreation Complex, 200 Mills Street, off King Highway; (616) 323–0909 or (616) 349–5466. From I–94, take the Business I–94 at exit 81 west, then go west on King to Mills. Ticket prices are adults $5.00 general admission, $4.00 reserved seats, and $5.00 box seats. Web site: www.kalamazootornadoes.com.

Everybody's getting into the act for sports teams, including Kalamazoo. The city now has a minor league pro football team that won the

1998 American Football Association's national championship, and last year finished third. You can enjoy exciting Saturday evening family fun during the season from August through November.

Where to Eat

Antique Kitchen Family Restaurant. *6215 South Westnedge, Portage 49002, off I–94; (616) 327–4014.* Great for breakfast and lunch. $$

Bill Knapp's. *4315 West Main, Kalamazoo 49009; (616) 342–0227.* Great family fare from fish to burgers. $

Old Country Buffet. *5220 West Main, Kalamazoo 49009; (616) 344–6212. From U.S. 131 and Michigan 43, head 1 mile east to the Maple Hill Mall.* Serves inexpensive lunch and dinner. Self-serve buffet includes salads, soups, meats, vegetables, pasta, fruits, beverages, and desserts. Kids pay by their age (up to age twelve), and prices cover unlimited trips for refills. $$

Where to Stay

Radisson Plaza Hotel at Kalamazoo Center. *100 West Michigan Avenue, Kalamazoo 49007, at the junction of Michigan and Rose; (616) 343–3333.* Upscale hotel has 281 rooms with restaurants, health club, indoor pool, whirlpool, and sauna. Attached to shopping mall. $$$

Red Roof Inn West. *5425 West Michigan, Kalamazoo 49009, at I–94 and Sprinkle Road; (616) 375–7400.* This economical property has 108 rooms. Restaurants nearby. Small pets okay. $

Stuart Avenue Inn Bed and Breakfast. *229 Stuart Avenue, Kalamazoo 49007; (616) 342–0230. Web site: www.stuartaveinn.com. Located in the Stuart Avenue Historic District, which along with the South Street District, west of South Westnedge, and the Vine Historic District, just south and west of downtown, is in a historic walking tour brochure.* The B&B has seventeen rooms in two historic Victorian homes with English gardens. $$–$$$

For More Information

Kalamazoo County Convention and Visitors Bureau, *128 North Kalamazoo Mall, Kalamazoo 49007–3900;* *(616) 381–4003. Web site: www. kazoofun.com.*

Otsego

North of Kalamazoo off U.S. 131, Otsego is the location of another ski area.

 BITTERSWEET SKI AREA (ages 7 and up)
North of Otsego along U.S. 131; (616) 694–2032. The season generally runs from December through March. The ski runs are usually open until 11:00 P.M. Plan on spending about $35 for adult lift tickets and rentals and $25 for children.
Bittersweet features sixteen runs with five chairlifts, snowmaking, instruction, night skiing, and rentals. Food is available on the premises.

Where to Eat and Stay

See Kalamazoo listing.

South Haven

From I-196, take exit 20 west into this lakeside town, which will remind you a lot of New England. South Haven's businesses abut the Black River, which flows right through town. Harborfest, South Haven's annual summer festival, is in mid-June.

 CAPTAIN NICHOLS'S AND CAPTAIN CHUCK'S PERCH BOATS (all ages)
Leaves from downtown from March through October. To reserve a spot, stop at the booths at dockside downtown. Michigan fishing license is required for anglers older than sixteen. Cost is $30 for adults and $22 for children ages twelve and younger. On summer Fridays, kids go for half price with a paying adult. Licenses are sold at the dock and cost $6.00 daily for state residents, $7.00 daily for nonresidents. Annual licenses are also available. Call (616) 637–2507 for schedule on Captain Nichols's or (616) 637–8007 on Captain Chuck's.
If you've got a fishing license, don't miss the next departure. Boats take up to forty anglers per trip on daily fishing outings that leave the dock at 7:30 A.M. and in the afternoons. Adults pay $30 each, and the crews will even clean your catch for a small extra charge. Perch fishing in the last several years has taken a downturn, but Captain Nichols assures that the lake's cyclical population is on the rise again. Afterward, browse the quaint streets, or in summer head for the great Lake Michigan city beach.

Where to Eat

Black River Inn. *402 Phoenix Street, South Haven 49090; (616) 637–3040. Downtown at the corner of Kalamazoo and Phoenix.* Serves dinner and, in warm weather, lunch. Children's menu available. $$$

Magnolia Grille. *515 Williams Street, South Haven 49090; (616) 637–8435. In the Old Harbor Village area. From I–196,* head west at exit 20 on Phoenix Street, then go 1 block north on Center. Floating restaurant at Nichols Landing for lunch and dinner. Children's menu. $$$$

For less expensive fare, see area fast-food stops along I–94 or call the convention and visitors bureau at (616) 637–5252.

Where to Stay

Econo Lodge. *09817 Michigan 140, South Haven 49090, a mile north of exit 18 on I–196; (616) 637–5141.* This motel has sixty rooms, indoor pool, exercise area, and restaurant serving breakfast, lunch, and dinner. $$

Old Harbor Inn. *515 Williams Street, South Haven 49090; (616) 637–8480. From I–196, head west at exit 20 and go 1 mile on Phoenix, and then 1 block north on Center to Williams.* The inn has forty-four rooms downtown on the banks of the Black River in the Old Harbor Village shopping area. Indoor pool and whirlpool. Restaurant nearby. $$$

Seymour House Bed & Breakfast. *1248 Blue Star A–2 Highway, South Haven 49090; (616) 227–3918.* Seven miles north of town on Blue Star Highway, this B&B offers five rooms and two log cabins with swimming, fishing, and nature trails. $$$

Van Buren State Park. *23960 Ruggels Road, South Haven 49090; (616) 637–2788, or for reservations, (800) 447–2757. From South Haven, go south on Blue Star Highway (old U.S. 31) to Ruggels Road and head west. A $4.00 daily or $20.00 annual permit is required for entry. Camping is $12.00 nightly.* The park has 220 campsites, a picnic area, and its main attraction, the large, duned beach.

For More Information

South Haven/Van Buren County Convention and Visitors Bureau, *415 Phoenix Street, South Haven 49090;* (616) 637–5252 or (800) 764–2836. *Web site: www.southhavenmi.com.*

Saugatuck

Saugatuck is west of I–196 at exit 41 (also known as A–2, or the Blue Star Highway). Originally a lumber shipping town, it was discovered in the late 1800s by

Chicagoans who hopped quick passage on steamboats for the area's magnificent beaches and lakeshore inns. Saugatuck, which means "river's mouth" in Native American, still holds a quaint, quiet atmosphere and is now known as an artists' colony. Be sure to visit some of the area's twenty-four galleries for locally produced art. There are so many that the region bills itself as the Art Coast of Michigan.

Take the A–2 The A–2, also called the Blue Star Highway, is a wonderful alternative to the freeway grind. Many who travel it have labeled it Michigan's version of New England's U.S. 1. Traveling through tiny towns with frequent glimpses of sparkling Lake Michigan, the highway traverses some of the state's most picturesque country and passes country inns tucked in the woods, you-pick fruit farms, and roadside stands, which in summer brim with home-grown peaches, blueberries, and other goodies. If you have the time, take the drive, which runs from the Indiana state line nearly all the way north. Some of my best vacation finds have been on these forgotten former major highways. You won't be disappointed.

The annual Taste of Saugatuck/Douglas takes place in mid-June in downtown Saugatuck along Water Street. Up to thirty area restaurants take part in setting up booths to serve their best.

MOUNT BALDHEAD (all ages)

Along the river near Oval Beach. From Saugatuck, take Blue Star Highway across the river to Douglas, and then turn west on Center and north on Park.

Everyone has to climb the 279 steps up this giant dune for a view of the area and Lake Michigan beyond town.

STAR OF SAUGATUCK (all ages)

Leaves from 716 Water Street, Saugatuck 49453; (616) 857–4261. Operates from mid-May to late October. Costs $9.00 for adults and teens, $5.00 for kids ages three through twelve, and Free *for kids younger than two. Web site: www.saugatuckboatcruises.com.*

Take a scenic ninety-minute cruise on the Kalamazoo River with a short turnaround in Lake Michigan aboard this two-deck paddle wheeler. The eighty-foot boat offers snacks and drinks during the trip along with live narration. The craft conforms to all Coast Guard safety regulations; it's safe for smaller kids.

Where to Eat

Saugatuck is so compact, most of the places that serve meals don't even need a street address. Just watch for them. The main business district is along Water Street.

Coral Gables. *Overlooking the harbor downtown; (616) 857–2162 Web site: www.coral-gables.com.* Serves lunch and dinner—from burgers to chicken and seafood—seasonally, with dockside open-air dining in warmer weather. $$

Crane's Pie Pantry & Restaurant. *On Michigan 89 between Saugatuck and Fennville; (616) 561–2297.* As the name implies, Crane's specializes in fresh-baked pies and other items for lunch and dinner. $

Ida Red's Cottage. *On Water Street; (616) 857–5803.* Serves breakfast all the time and lunch from burgers to pasta. $

Where to Stay

The twin towns of Saugatuck and Douglas plus neighboring Fennville together hold one of the most extensive concentrations of Victoriana and early-twentieth-century bed and breakfasts and cottages in the state, as well as modern motels and campgrounds.

Goshorn Lake Family Resort. *3581 Sixty-fifth Street, Saugatuck 49453; (616) 857–4808 or (800) 541–4210. Web site: www.saugatuck.com/sbonline.htm. From I–196, take exit 41 and turn west to Sixty-fifth.* The resort offers nineteen housekeeping cottages on Goshorn Lake, a few minutes from downtown Saugatuck. Cottages usually rent weekly. $$

Lake Shore Resort. *2885 Lakeshore Drive, Saugatuck 49453; (616) 857–7121. From Highway A–2, head west on Wiley Road, and then a mile south on Lakeshore*

Drive. The resort offers thirty motel rooms on the lake as well as an outdoor pool. Restaurant nearby. $$$

Park House Bed & Breakfast Inn. *888 Holland Street, Saugatuck 49453; (616) 857–4535. From I–196, take exit 41 and go west.* This inn has eight rooms in a restored 1857 home plus four cottages. $$–$$$$

Saugatuck RV Resort. *On Blue Star Highway, Saugatuck 49453, west of I–196 exit 41; (800) 336–9724 or (616) 857 3315.* The resort has 175 wooded sites, five camping cabins, and one cottage with two beaches on Goshen Lake. $

Shangrai-la Motel. *6190 Blue Star Highway, Saugatuck 49453; (616) 857–1453. Web site: www.saugatuck.com/ sbonline.htm.* The motel has twenty rooms, with outdoor pool. $$

For More Information

See Douglas listing.

Douglas

Just across the mouth of the Kalamazoo River is this small town, home of one of the last great overnight steamers afloat in the Great Lakes.

CITY OF DOUGLAS (all ages)

From Memorial Day through Labor Day the City of Douglas leaves daily for lunch (about $16.50, fare included), afternoon sight-seeing ($9.00), and dinner cruises ($32.00) and also features Sunday brunch ($28.00 per person, children $3.00 off). Both vessels are located along Highway A–2, near the Saugatuck-Douglas bridge. Call (616) 857–2464 or (616) 857–2107 for more information.

The *City of Douglas* is a sight-seeing cruiser that offers lunch and dinner trips that include a sail on Lake Michigan if the weather's agreeable.

SAND DUNE RIDES (all ages)

6495 Washington Road, Saugatuck 49453; (616) 857–2253. Take exit 41 (Saugatuck) from I–196 and go south on Blue Star Highway about ½ mile. Price is $11.50 for teens and adults, $7.50 for kids ages three through ten, and **Free** *for kids two and younger. Rides start in May at 10:00 A.M. Monday through Saturday and at noon on Sunday; the last ride leaves at 5:30 P.M. In July and August there are extended hours. Rides run through mid-October.*

Visitors can take sight-seeing trips skimming over the nearby dunes in dune buggies that hold up to eighteen people. Trips last about thirty-five minutes and are safe for babies and tots.

Where to Eat

M&M's Ice Cream Treats & Stuff to Eat. *On Blue Star Highway, Saugatuck 49453; (616) 857–1030.* One of several sweet shops in the area. Ice cream, burgers, and other items served from breakfast onward. $

Spectators. *6432 Washington Road, Saugatuck 49453; (616) 857–5001.* Sports-themed restaurant. Children's menu. $$

For More Information

Saugatuck-Douglas Convention and Visitors Bureau, *303 Culver, Douglas 49453; (616) 857–1701.*

Holland

A visit to this quaint city gives you a taste of the area's history. As you'd guess by its name, it was settled by the Dutch in the nineteenth century. They brought all their customs with them, many of which remain today and are highlighted in the annual Tulip Time Festival in May. The city was also a famous furniture-making center—like its neighbor, Grand Rapids, 30 miles to the east.

WINDMILL ISLAND (all ages)

The thirty-acre island is downtown at Seventh Street and Lincoln Avenue, Holland 49423; (616) 355–1030. Open from May through October. Admission is $5.50 for teens and adults, $2.50 for children ages five through twelve, and Free for ages four and younger. Hours vary through the summer. Web site: www. windmillisland.org.

Cross an authentic Dutch drawbridge to see the 200-year-old De Zwann windmill, which still operates and produces flour sold at the park. There's also a miniature Dutch village where there are dancing demonstrations and guided tours in summer. A carousel and farm animals can entertain the kids, too.

DE KLOMP WOODEN SHOE AND DELFTWARE FACTORY AND VELDHEER TULIP GARDENS (all ages)

12755 Quincy Street, Holland 49424, at U.S. 31, 3 miles north of the city; (616) 399–1900. Admission to the shoe factory is Free. Admission to the gardens is $5.00 for adults and $3.00 for children ages three through fifteen. Hours are 8:00 A.M. to 6:00 P.M. Monday through Friday and 9:00 A.M. to 5:00 P.M. Saturday and Sunday from April through December; 9:00 A.M. to 5:00 P.M. Monday through Friday from January through March. Web site: www.veldheertulip.com.

Tulip Time Festival

The Holland area is a major producer of tulip bulbs, and its Dutch heritage is celebrated each May during one of Michigan's first warm-weather outdoor events. If you're planning to come for the event, make your reservations early, as this is a popular festival.

Each spring, the city's streets are lined with 8 miles of blooming tulips. Thousands of visitors come out to watch parades, which feature the traditional washing of the streets by costumed, dancing scrubbers. For information call (616) 396–4221 or (800) 822–2770.

As many as 90 percent of the locals you'll see are of Dutch descent, left from when the area was settled in 1846 by religious-freedom seekers. The immigrants brought their crafts with them, and two examples can be seen here. Artisans continue to create the blue-and-white delftware ceramics produced at De Klomp, the only delft factory in the nation, while in another area skilled experts gouge, carve, and shape blocks of wood into shoes. Next door at the gardens, more than a hundred varieties of tulips bloom in neat rows each spring along U.S. Highway 31, and visitors who stop can purchase bulbs. The best times to see the tulips in bloom are the last week of April and the first week of May. Veldheer is the largest tulip grower in the Midwest.

DUTCH VILLAGE (all ages)

At U.S. 31 and James Street, Holland 49423; (616) 396–1475 or (800) 285–7177. Open from 9:00 A.M. to 6:00 P.M. daily in July and August; 9:00 A.M. to 5:00 P.M. from mid-April through June and in September and October. Admission is $6.00 for adults, $4.00 for kids ages three through eleven, and **Free** *for ages two and younger.*

Wooden shoe carving, folk dancing demonstrations, and imported gifts are set amid Dutch architecture and gardens. Stroller access. Food is available on premises and nearby.

CRAIG'S CRUISERS FAMILY FUN CENTER (all ages)

U.S. 31 and Chicago; (616) 392–7300. Web site: www.craigscruisers.com. Open daily 9:30 A.M. to 11:00 P.M. during summer. Plan on about $3.50 for go-cart rides and $1.00 for batting cages. Minigolf costs $4.50 for adults and $3.50 for children twelve and younger and seniors. The indoor arcade is open all year. Food is available.

Go-carts, minigolf, carts for younger children, batting cages, and other fun activities are offered here.

Where to Eat

The Piper. *2225 South Shore Drive, Macatawa 49434, overlooking Lake Macatawa; (616) 335–5866. From U.S. 31, take Sixteenth Street west through town. It becomes South Shore Drive. Pastas and wood-fired pizzas are specialties for lunch and dinner. $$$*

Russ's Restaurants. *Three different locations in Holland: 210 North River, (616) 392– 6300; 1060 Lincoln, (616) 396–4036; and 361 East Eighth, (616) 396–2348 in Holland; all off those streets west of U.S. 31. Serves breakfast, lunch, and dinner. Traditional family fare from pancakes to burgers. Try the pie. $$*

Where to Stay

Most accommodations will be along or just off U.S. 31, which skirts the town's eastern edge.

Blue Mill Inn. *409 U.S. 31 South at Sixteenth Street in Holland; (616) 392–7073.* This inn has eighty-one rooms and offers morning coffee. Restaurant nearby. Pets okay. $$

Budget Host Wooden Shoe Motel. *465 U.S. 31 at Sixteenth Street, Holland 49423; (616) 392–8521.* The motel has twenty-nine rooms and outdoor pool. Restaurants nearby. $$

Holiday Inn and Conference Center. *650 East Twenty-fourth, Holland 49423, just east of U.S. 31; (616) 394–*

0111. This hotel has 168 rooms, indoor pool, sauna, exercise room, hot tub, recreation area, and restaurant. $$–$$$

Holland State Park. *Seven miles west of U.S. 31 on Ottawa Beach Road; (616) 399–9390. From U.S. 31, turn west onto Lakewood, then follow Douglas. It becomes Ottawa Beach Road.* The park has 142 campsites on mostly open area near the road, but the real draw is the park's Lake Michigan beach around the corner. Camping is available here, too, but there is little shade. The beautiful beach is what brings folks out. At sunset, be sure to bring your camera for stunning shots of the bright red lighthouse.

For More Information

Holland Area Convention & Visitors Bureau, *100 East Eighth Street, Holland 49423; (616) 394–0000 or*

(800) 506–1299. Web site: *www.holland.org/.*

Grand Rapids

While the rapids that gave name to this city are long covered under dams, you can see one of the state's minor-league baseball teams in action, explore a museum portraying the city's past, stroll through sculpture gardens, and perhaps even wet a fishing line downtown. The city is at the intersection of U.S. Highway 131, I–96, and I–196, named the Gerald R. Ford Freeway. Most of the addresses outside the city are divided by geographical quadrant, with *NE, NW, SE,* or *SW* after them meaning northeast, northwest, southeast, or southwest. Use those designations to help find locations of accommodations or attractions.

In the 1800s, Grand Rapids was the nation's capital of furniture design as it is today, with huge annual shows that drew buyers from across the country. Logs from the surrounding hardwood forests floated down the Grand River to mills that brought European craftsmen here to create the industry. Lots of office furniture is still made in town, but most of the home furniture factories have gone south.

PUBLIC MUSEUM OF GRAND RAPIDS AND VAN ANDEL CENTER (all ages)

272 Pearl Street, Grand Rapids 49504; (616) 456–3977. Hours are 9:00 A.M. to 5:00 P.M. Saturday and noon to 5:00 P.M. Sunday. Admission is $5.00 for adults, $4.00 for seniors, and $2.00 for young people three through seventeen. Located on the west bank of the Grand River. Barrier-free. Web site: www.grmuseum.org.

The $40-million complex traces the city from its start as a trading post to its peak as an industrial center known worldwide for furniture production. One of the first things you'll see, though, isn't furniture. It's a 76-foot-long finback whale skeleton hanging from the museum's three-story entrance Galleria. The museum shows the city's furniture-manufacturing heyday through artifacts, photos, and videos.

Inside, a huge flywheel of a 1905 steam engine powers a replica furniture factory, where docents explain the hours of work that went into making fine-crafted furniture that the "Furniture City" was known for. Antiques buffs will like the more than 120 types of finished furniture representing several periods, including pieces designed by Frank Lloyd Wright. Other exhibits include a re-creation of downtown at the turn of the twentieth century and one on west Michigan's first inhabitants, Native American Anishinabes.

For kids and the young at heart, a 1928 carousel is set in a pavilion over the river, accompanied by an old Wurlitzer organ, at 50 cents per ride. Also inside is a gift shop and cafe.

The museum also houses the Roger B. Chaffee Planetarium; (616) 456–3663. There's a $1.50 extra charge for planetarium shows and $5.00 for laser shows. The planetarium is not recommended for children ages three and younger, but your grade-schooler will enjoy it.

GERALD R. FORD MUSEUM (all ages)

303 Pearl Street, Grand Rapids 49504, on the west bank of the Grand River; (616) 451–9263. Open daily 9:00 A.M. to 5:00 P.M. Admission is $4.00 for adults, $3.00 for seniors sixty-two and older, and Free *for children younger than sixteen. From I–196, take the West Ottawa Street exit. Go south on Ottawa to Pearl. Go west on Pearl to the museum lot.*

This stunning mirrored-glass building, reflecting most of downtown and the Grand River, houses memorabilia of the private and public life of local boy made good, President Ford, who assumed office when

President Nixon resigned and to whom some credit was given as the leader who began the country's healing following years of conflict at home and overseas. Not only will you see glimpses into the Ford White House years, but also changing interactive exhibits on the life and times of America during that period of conflict and resolution. There's also a re-creation of the Ford Paint & Varnish Company where he worked as a boy.

MICHIGAN BOTANIC GARDEN AND MEIJER SCULPTURE PARK (all ages)

3411 Bradford NE, Grand Rapids 49525; (616) 957–1580. From I–96 take the East Beltline exit and go north to Bradford, and then turn east and drive about ½ mile. The gardens are open daily from 9:00 A.M. to 5:00 P.M. Monday through Saturday and noon to 5:00 P.M. Sunday. From June through August, they stay open until 9:00 P.M. Thursday. Admission is $4.00 for adults, $3.50 for seniors, and $1.50 for kids ages five through thirteen. Barrier-free. Web site: www.meijergardens.org.

Take in some greenery at the park commonly known as Frederik Meijer Gardens, a seventy-acre sanctuary of tropical and other plants from five continents named after the Meijer family, owners of one of the state's largest "superstore" chains.

At five stories tall, the indoor Lena Meijer Conservatory is Michigan's largest. Mixed in with coconut palms from the Pacific, ficus from India, and orchids from South America is a desert garden. In spring, butterflies flutter in the conservatory. Outside is a sculpture park with more than fifty sculptures by renowned artists, such as Michigan's own late Marshall Fredericks. The largest sculpture is the new, huge, DaVinci horse by Nina Akamu, with its own football field–size, open-air space. It's the world's largest horse sculpture.

Outdoor tours include tram rides ($1.00 for adults, 50 cents for ages five through thirteen, under five Free, weekends only) that focus on woodlands and wetlands. There's a gift shop and restaurant inside, too, plus Free tours and docents to answer questions.

WEST MICHIGAN WHITECAPS (all ages)

The Whitecaps's Old Kent Park is at U.S. 131 and West River Drive, Comstock Park 49321; (616) 784–4131. The exit is about 5 miles north of downtown. Season runs from April through September. Ticket prices are $7.50 for box seats, $6.00 for reserved, $4.00 for bleachers, and $3.00 for the lawn. Web site: www.whitecapsbaseball.com.

Old Kent Park isn't old at all. Completed in 1994, it's home to a Class A baseball farm team for the Detroit Tigers. Up to 10,000 fans can watch each of the seventy home games a year. Take your lawn chair and wait with the kids for that foul ball in a special grassy area set aside for folks who want to watch the game the way spectators did when it was invented. Special youth-oriented events include clinics and giveaway games, and there's even a new playground.

GRAND RAPIDS CHILDREN'S MUSEUM (ages 3–10)

11 Sheldon Avenue NE, Grand Rapids 49503, at the corner of Fulton and Sheldon Streets, east of the river on Fulton; (616) 235–4726. Open 9:30 A.M. to 5:00 P.M. Tuesday, Wednesday, Friday, and Saturday; 9:30 A.M. to 8:00 P.M. Thursday; and noon to 5:00 P.M. Sunday. Admission is $3.00 per person except on family night, Thursday, from 5:00 P.M. to 8:00 P.M. and admission is only $1.00 per person. $\mathbf{Free}$ *for children younger than two. Web site: www.grcm.org.*

Hands-on exhibits for kids to explore and learn, including the Rapids, where kids can try on waders or design a bridge across the river.

JOHN BALL PARK ZOO (all ages)

1300 West Fulton Street, Grand Rapids 49504; (616) 336–4300 or (616) 336–4301. East of I–196 and Michigan 45, 2 miles west from downtown on Fulton. Open daily from 10:00 A.M. to 6:00 P.M. from mid-May to Labor Day and from 10:00 A.M. to 4:00 P.M. daily the rest of the year. Admission is $3.50 for persons ages fourteen through sixty-two and $2.00 for seniors ages sixty-three and older and kids five through thirteen. Children ages four and younger get in $\mathbf{Free}$*—and so does everybody else from December through February, when the entrance fee is waived. Handicapped and stroller accessible. Web site: www.co.kent.mi.us/zoo.*

The 140-acre park is the state's second largest, with more than 800 animals from around the world. The zoo's VanAndel Living Shores Aquarium features penguins, sea birds, and underwater viewing. Be sure to see the lions, tigers, bears, wart hogs, and the African forest edge exhibit. There's also a petting corral with farm animals for kids, plus food and a gift shop.

Where to Eat

Downtown alone features nearly forty restaurants, from diner food to Spanish. Here's a selection:

Cottage Bar and Restaurant. *Fulton Street and LaGrave, Grand Rapids 49503, 5 blocks east of Monroe; (616) 454–9088.* Next door to One Trick Pony, it's the city's oldest bar and restaurant. Good burritos and chili, along with other items for lunch and dinner. $$

One Trick Pony. *136 East Fulton, Grand Rapids 49503, downtown; (616) 235–7669.* Pizza tops the list, along with Cajun and Caribbean fare for lunch and dinner. $$

Pal's Diner. *6502 Twenty-eighth Street SE, Grand Rapids 49546, off I–96; (616) 942–7257.* A 1950s stainless-steel diner that serves breakfast, lunch, and dinner all day. $$

Pietro's Ristorante. *2780 Birchcrest Drive SE, Grand Rapids 49507, off I–96 and the Twenty-eighth Street exit; (616) 452–3228.* Very good Italian food. Children's menu. $$

Where to Stay

Choose from among nearly fifty places to stay, including four bed and breakfasts in the historic Heritage Hill area. Here are some good bets for families:

Amerihost Inn Grand Rapids North. *2171 Holton, Walker 49544, south of the I–96 Walker Avenue exit in the suburb of Walker; (616) 791–8500.* The inn has sixty rooms and indoor pool. Restaurant nearby. $$

Amway Grand Plaza Hotel. *187 Monroe, Grand Rapids 49503; (616) 774–2000. At the corner of Pearl downtown, east of the U.S. 131 Pearl exit.* The hotel has 682 rooms in both renovated and new portions of the hotel. Indoor pool, racquetball and exercise area, six restaurants. $$

Days Inn Downtown. *310 Pearl Street, Grand Rapids 49503, at the U.S. 131 exit; (616) 235–7611.* The property has 175 rooms, indoor pool, and restaurants. Small pets okay. $$

Econo Lodge Grand Rapids. *At exit 43, Twenty-eighth Street, Cascade 49512, in the southwest suburb of Cascade; (616) 956–6601.* This budget motel has 102 rooms with small outdoor pool. Restaurants nearby. $–$$

For More Information

Grand Rapids/Kent County Convention and Visitors Bureau, *140 Monroe Avenue NW, Suite 300, Grand Rapids 49503–2615; (616) 459–8287 or (800) 678–9859. Web site: www. visitgrandrapids.org.*

Rockford

Just north of Grand Rapids off Michigan 44 and east of U.S. 131, Rockford's downtown is filled with interesting places to shop, browse, and dine.

CANNONSBURG SKI AREA (ages 7 and up)

6800 Cannonsburg Road, Cannonsburg 49317; (616) 874–6711.
The facility has ten runs with three chair lifts, lessons, and equipment rental. Cannonsburg offers ski school for all ages of learners. Food and drink are available in the cafeteria. There is no baby-sitting per se, but youngsters can sign up for lessons while their parents ski. There is both daylight and night skiing. Plan on spending around $36 per adult and $20 per child for lift tickets and rentals.

AAA CANOE RENTALS (all ages)

12 East Bridge Street, Rockford 49431, downtown; (616) 866–9264. The livery opens in mid-April and closes in late October after fall color-viewing season, starting at 9:00 A.M. daily. A two-hour paddle is $12.50 per person; there are four-hour trips available also. Kids five and younger ride Free. Life preservers are standard issue for young children, and flotation seat cushions are provided also. Children as young as two months have gone on the trip. Parents should judge as to whether they are competent enough paddlers to bring along the youngest children, since canoes can be tippy. The river is calm with no rapids.
Canoe on the Rogue River, a trout stream that runs through town. Near the end of the trip, a dam downtown halts the upstream spawning run of salmon in fall and steelhead trout in spring. Anglers catch them below the dam.

Where to Eat

Red Geranium. *7 Squires Street, Rockford 49341, downtown; (616) 866–7778. Open Monday through Saturday 6:00 A.M. to 3:00 P.M. and Sunday 8:00 A.M. to 2:30 P.M.* Specializes in big breakfasts, such as scrumptious omelets, and lunch items such as hamburgers. $$

Rosie's Diner. *4500 Fourteen Mile Road NE, Rockford 49431, downtown; (616) 866–3663. Web site: www.rosiesdiner.com.* Remember Rosie and her "quicker picker-upper" paper towels? The diner used in those TV commercials was moved here. Food includes classic pot roast and salads, plus malts. Breakfast served, too. $$

Where to Stay

See Grand Rapids listing.

For More Information

Rockford Area Chamber of Commerce, *P.O. Box 520, Rockford 49341; (616) 866–2000.*

Coopersville

This is a small community 15 miles west of Grand Rapids along I–96. Take the Coopersville exit, of course.

COOPERSVILLE & MARNE RAILWAY (all ages)

Departs from downtown Coopersville; (616) 837–7000. Summer train rides from mid-July through mid-September begin 1:00 and 3:00 P.M. Saturday. Tickets cost $7.50 for adults, $4.50 for kids ages three through fourteen, and $6.50 for seniors; two and younger ride Free.

Besides the summer rides, there are special theme rides for kids, including a Pumpkin Train on October weekends and a Santa train on December weekends. The train makes a slow tour to Marne, about 5 miles away, and returns on the same route, which runs through west Michigan's farm country. It's a chance for kids to experience rail travel in slow motion.

Where to Eat and Stay

See Grand Rapids listing.

Hastings

Named after a local landholder, Hastings was settled in 1836 on the banks of the Thornapple River. It's the seat of Barry Country.

CHARLTON PARK VILLAGE AND MUSEUM (all ages)

2545 South Charlton Park Road, Hastings 49058; (616) 945–3775. A quarter mile north of M–79 between Hastings and Nashville. Travel north from I–94 on Michigan 66, turn west on Michigan 79, and then head 2 miles south and 4 miles east on Michigan 79. From mid-May through September, hours are 9:00 A.M. to 4:30 P.M. daily. Admission is $4.00 for adults, $3.00 for persons ages fifty-six and older, and $2.00 for kids ages five through fifteen, four and younger admitted **Free.** *Special-events costs vary.*

Southeastern Michigan has Greenfield Village and the Henry Ford Museum. Flint has Crossroads Village. And Hastings, population only 6,500, has a historic village that is on par with the big boys. Seventeen buildings help re-create an 1890s Michigan town; in addition, you'll find a beach, a playground, and a boat launch, on more than 300 acres. In the village there's everything from a blacksmith's to a schoolhouse. Christmas is one of the most decorative times, as buildings are lit by candlelight, starting on the first two weekends in December from noon to 5:00 P.M.

Where to Eat

Besides concession stands at Charlton Park, local restaurants include fast food chains and:

Elias Brothers Big Boy. *915 West State Street, Hastings 49058; (616) 948–2701.*

Open Sunday through Thursday 7:00 A.M. to 10:00 P.M., Friday and Saturday 7:00 A.M. to 11:00 P.M. Serves a variety of family fare from salads to its trademark triple-decker burger.

Where to Stay

Parkview Motel. *429 North Broadway (Michigan 43), Hastings 49058, about ⅓ mile north of the town center; (616) 632–7177.* There are eighteen rooms in this economy motel. $

See also Grand Rapids listing.

For More Information

Hastings Area Chamber of Commerce, *118 East Court Street, Hastings 49058; (616) 945–2454.*

Cedar Springs

Cedar Springs is at exit 104 off U.S. 131, 15 miles north of Grand Rapids; head east 2 miles to downtown.

Lumberjacks wore 'em. So did some of the greatest comedy stars. And you, too, can own a pair of the original trapdoor red flannels that have been made at Cedar Springs since the turn of the twentieth century. It all started when a *New York Times* editorial fussed that red flannels were hard to find in winter. The local paper shot back that the town had plenty. To meet demand, a factory produced the union suits and other items, but now that job has been taken over by local residents.

 CEDAR SWEETS & SPECIALTIES (all ages)
4386 Fourteen Mile Road, Rockford 49341 (actually across the road from Cedar Springs); (616) 863–0460. Open 7:00 A.M. to 7:00 P.M. Monday through Friday, 9:00 A.M. to 5:00 P.M. Saturday. Web site: www.redflannel.com.

The exclusive seller of the original red flannels. Other items for sale at the store include nightshirts and boxer sets, popular with the college and high school crowd, plus old-fashioned nightshirts, granny gowns, and more. They also sell health food and deli items, fudge and chocolates.

 CEDAR SPRINGS HISTORICAL MUSEUM (all ages)
In Morley Park; (231) 696–3335. Hours are 10:00 A.M. to 5:00 P.M. Wednesday and Thursday and 1:00 to 4:00 P.M. Sunday from Memorial Day through Labor Day; 10:00 A.M. to 5:00 P.M. Wednesday and 2:00 to 5:00 P.M. Thursday the rest of the year. Admission is **Free**.

The museum features an entire section on the history of red flannels. It also has a restored one-room schoolhouse that will amaze your school-age kids when they compare it to where they go today.

Where to Eat

See Grand Rapids listing.

For More Information

Cedar Springs Chamber of Commerce, *P.O. Box 415, Cedar Springs 49319; (616) 696–3260.*

242

Red Flannel Festival

Red Flannel Festival On the last weekend of September and first weekend of October, the town pays its respects to the clothing that put Cedar Springs on the map. There are two parades on the first weekend of October, arts-and-crafts vendors, and even the crowning of a red-flannel queen. There is no admission fee for the festival except for individual events and special attractions. For more information call (616) 696–2662.

Grand Haven/Spring Lake

Grand Haven is reached by taking exit 9 (Michigan 104) off I-96 and heading west. The town is one of a successive string of beachside communities along Lake Michigan that help make this neck of the state one of the most appealing to summer vacationers from across the Midwest. Its simple, compact downtown is one of the most picturesque in the area as the end of the Grand River sweeps past boats moored in the harbor. U.S. Highway 31 acts as a second business district, and many motels are located along it. It's only a few blocks from the water. Walk the 2½-mile boardwalk along the river and lakefront, or take the trolley that runs all summer.

Spring Lake is mentioned in the same breath because it's right next to the town on the lake that is formed by the Grand River.

Sportfishing charters in the Grand Haven–Spring Lake area focus on big-lake fishing for salmon and steelhead from summer through fall. Call (616) 842–4910 or (800) 303–4096 for more information.

MUSICAL FOUNTAIN (all ages)

In downtown Grand Haven on the riverfront. Bursts to life nightly about 9:45 P.M. from Memorial Day through Labor Day and on September weekends. **Free.**

Families start gathering just before sundown, and by nightfall the grandstand, which holds 2,500, is usually filled. The harbor, where the Grand River ends its journey across lower Michigan at Lake Michigan, is dotted with boat lights as—suddenly—a dune erupts in color, water plumes, and music. They've come, as they have every summer for more than thirty years. The fountain spews jets of water up to 125 feet in the air—and best of all, the show's **Free.**

GRAND HAVEN/SPRING LAKE TROLLEY (all ages)

(800) 303–4096 or (616) 842–3200. Runs from 11:00 A.M. to 10:00 P.M. daily from Memorial Day through Labor Day, linking the towns of Grand Haven, Spring Lake, and Ferrysburg. Pick it up at several locations including the state park and Chinook Pier. Costs $2.00 for adults, $1.00 for children three through twelve, two and younger ride **Free**. *Web site: www.grandhaven.com/harbortransit.*

Trolleys, actually converted minibuses, transport visitors up and down the beachfront and through all three towns.

HARBOR STEAMER (all ages)

Board at the riverfront on Chinook Pier, 301 North Harbor Drive, Grand Haven 49417, about 8 blocks west of U.S. 31; (616) 842–8950. There are cruises daily at noon, 3:00, 4:00, 5:00, 7:00, 8:00, 9:00, and 10:00 P.M. from Memorial Day through Labor Day. Fares start at $5.00 for adults, $2.50 for ages two to eighteen; two and younger ride **Free**. *Web site: www.harborsteamer.com.*

Cruises on this tiny replica paddle wheeler take passengers for a tour of Spring Lake and the lower Grand River. Wheelchair accessible. Snacks and refreshments on board, or bring your own.

Great Lakes Kite Festival

Viewing the championships is **Free** with admission to Grand Haven State Park (see Where to Stay). If you come here in mid-May and someone in town tells you to go fly a kite, he or she just might be directing you to the golden sand beach, with blue Lake Michigan as the background, where you'll join up to 40,000 spectators to watch kites up to half a football field long fill the air during the annual event on the beach.

You'll see kites here that are a bit different than the ones you buy at the local hardware for your kids—you know, kites that eventually end up in your front-yard tree. The ones here include both wildly decorative models, to sport kites controlled by two lines that pilots use to steer. Individuals and teams fly the kites through maneuvers, executing some pretty spectacular aerial ballets.

Events run Friday through Sunday and include a Friday-night fly at which lights attached to the kites and lines create a spectacular show. Relive your childhood and try your own hand during **Free** stunt kite lessons for beginners. For more information call the event's sponsor, the Mackinac Kite Company, at (616) 846–7501. Web site: www.mackite.com.

HARBORFRONT PLACE (all ages)

*In downtown at Harbor Drive and Washington Street, Grand Haven 49417;
(616) 846–5711. Open 10:00 A.M. to 6:00 P.M. Monday through Saturday.
Some stores open on Sunday.*

Built out of the relic of a century-old piano company, this enclosed, three-story contemporary shopping and dining mall is one of the reasons for the city's revitalization. There are more than a dozen shops, Porto Bello Restaurant (see Where to Eat), and a coffee house. Later take the kids to Imagination Station (at Harbor Drive and Y Drive), a playscape designed by kids.

MACKINAC KITE COMPANY (all ages)

106 Washington Street, Grand Haven 49417; (616) 846–7501. Open Monday through Saturday 10:00 A.M. to 8:00 P.M. and Sunday noon to 5:00 P.M. Web site: www.mackite.com.

You can pick from more than a hundred types of kites, from indoor models that take only a whiff of air to fly to the newest trend, power kites, with up to 55 square feet of surface. You can even try your hand at a 150-foot-long dragon kite with a mouth 15 feet in diameter. (If you can't make it to Grand Haven, stop by owner Steve Negen's other store in Mackinaw City during Father's Day weekend for the annual Mackinaw City Kite Festival. Family fun runs from 𝐅𝐫𝐞𝐞 kites for the kids to demonstrations of Japanese fighting kites battling to cut opponents out of the sky.)

Where to Eat

Bil-Mar Restaurant. *1223 Harbor Avenue, Grand Haven 49417, on the beach; (616) 842–5920. Web site: www.grand-haven.com/~bil-mar.* Lake perch is the specialty at lunch and dinner. Outdoor seating available. Children's menu. $$$

Porto Bello. *41 Washington Street, Grand Haven 49417, west of U.S. 31, in Harbourfront Place (aforementioned); (616) 846–1221.* Italian food for lunch and dinner. $$

Stable Inn. *118880 U.S. 31, Grand Haven 49417, 5 miles south of town; (616) 846–8581.* Serves lunch and dinner, with Mexican food a specialty. Children's menu. $$

Where to Stay

Days Inn. *1500 South Beacon, Grand Haven 49417; (616) 842–1999.* This economical motel offers one hundred rooms, indoor pool, and restaurant. $$

Fountain Inn. *1010 South Beacon (U.S. 31), Grand Haven 49417; (616) 846–1800 or (800) 745–8660.* The inn has forty-seven rooms and is 1½ miles from the beach. $

Grand Harbor Resort & Yacht Club Haven. *940 West Savidge (Michigan 104), Spring Lake 49456, just east of U.S. 31; (616) 846–1000.* This property has 121 rooms overlooking the river and Spring Lake, indoor and outdoor pools, exercise area, and restaurant. $$$

Grand Haven State Park. *1001 South Harbor Drive, Grand Haven 49417, on the beach; (616) 798–3711 or, for guaranteed reservations, (800) 447–2757. A $4.00 daily or $20.00 annual permit is required for* vehicle entry. Camping is $14.00 nightly. Web site: www.dnr.state.mi.us/www/parks/ index. Like your camping sandy and close? This is the place. It's one of the state's most popular campgrounds despite the fact there's little shade. You're camping right on the beach sand at any of the 174 sites. $

Lakeshore Bed & Breakfast. *11001 Lakeshore Drive, Grand Haven 49460; (616) 844–2697 or (800) 342–6736. Web site: www.bbonline.com/mi/lakeshore/.* The B&B has three rooms with private beach on Lake Michigan. Cottages are also available for families. $$

Yogi Bear Jellystone Park. *10990 U.S. 31 North, Grand Haven 49417; (616) 842–9395. Web site: www.ghjellystone.com.* Seven miles south of Grand Haven, this park has 240 sites, outdoor pool, and a beach. $

For More Information

Grand Haven/Spring Lake Area Visitors Bureau, *1 South Harbor Drive, Grand Haven 49417; (616) 842–4910 or* *(800) 303–4096. Web site: www. grandhavenchamber.org.*

West Michigan–North

T he northern part of west Michigan takes in some of the state's most inviting places to visit, from former industrial towns on the verge of finding new life as tourist destinations to small towns that are growing by leaps and bounds, to others that nearly close in winter.

Muskegon

Welcome to Muskegon, the Lumber Queen City, at the intersection of I–96 and U.S. Highway 31. In the nineteenth century Muskegon's now-razed mills and surrounding forests of white pine provided the lumber to rebuild Chicago after its 1871 fire and to construct homes in much of the West. Some of that heritage remains in historic homes-turned-museums.

The city knows how to throw a beach party, too, with nine public beaches along 26 miles of shoreline in the county, four beachfront state parks within a few miles of downtown, and more natural beauty than you can shake a sand dune at.

AIR FAIR (all ages)

Takes place at Muskegon County Airport, 101 Sinclair, just west of Seaway Drive (Business U.S. 31) over a weekend in mid-July; (800) OK–AIRSHOW. Take Grand Haven Road south to Ellis, then go west to the entrance. Tickets are about $14.00 for adults and $6.00 for ages five to twelve, which includes parking. Kids younger than five enter Free. *Spectators can also catch some of the show from neighboring Mona Lake or Lake Michigan as the planes land and take off. Web site: www.travelmuskegon.org*

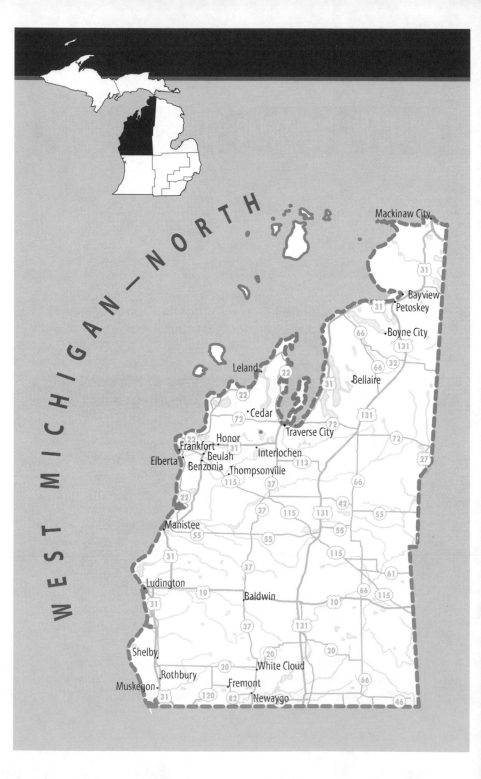

WEST MICHIGAN — NORTH

Mackinaw City

Bayview
Petoskey

Boyne City

Leland

Bellaire

Cedar

Traverse City

Honor
Frankfort
Elberta
Beulah
Benzonia
Interlochen
Thompsonville

Manistee

Ludington

Baldwin

Shelby

Rothbury
White Cloud
Muskegon
Fremont
Newaygo

In summer, top billing goes to this event, which for hundreds of thousands of aircraft enthusiasts is an air fair to remember. The show has become one of the state's biggest. Starting Friday, planes from across the country begin flying into the airport, where there's live music, food, and sunset flights.

Saturday and Sunday are highlighted by static displays of more than 120 of the largest, smallest, and fastest aircraft in the world along the flight line. Some pilots will let young children climb in and sit at the controls, or at least peer into the cockpit of an F–16. Famed World War II and Korean War craft will be there, too, and the first aerial shows kick off around 2:00 P.M. A perennial hit is "shockwaves," a truck powered by three jet engines for fire-breathing 300 mph runs down the runway.

Bill's Favorite Events in West Michigan—North

- **Winterfest** (January), downtown Mackinaw City, (231) 436–5664.
- **North American Snowmobile Festival** (February), Cadillac, (231) 755–0657 or (800) 225–2537. Web site: www.michiweb.com/cadillac.
- **Spring Fling, Crystal Mountain Ski Resort** (March), Thompsonville, (231) 378–2000.
- **Victorian Easter Parade** (April), downtown Manistee, (231) 723–3688.
- **Trillium Festival, Gillette Visitor Center, P. J. Hoffmaster State Park** (May), Muskegon, (231) 798–3573.
- **Mesick Mushroom Festival** (May), Mesick, (231) 885–1675.
- **Summer Arts and Crafts Fair** (June), Mackinaw City, (231) 436–5664.
- **National Forest Festival** (July), Manistee, (231) 723–2575.
- **National Coho Festival** (August), Honor, (231) 882–5801 or (231) 882–5802.
- **Fur Traders Rendezvous** (September), White Pine Village, Ludington, (231) 843–4808.
- **Hemingway Weekendfest** (October), downtown Petoskey, (231) 348–2755 or (800) 845–2828.
- **Festival of Trees** (November), Frauenthal Theater, Muskegon, (231) 739–3786.
- **Victorian Sleighbell Parade** (December), Manistee, (231) 723–2565.

USS *SILVERSIDES* AND MARITIME MUSEUM (all ages)

1346 Bluff at Pere Marquette Park, on the south side of the Muskegon Lake channel, (231) 755–1230. Open from April through October. Hours are 10:00 A.M. to 5:30 P.M. daily from June through August; 1:00 P.M. to 5:30 P.M. Monday through Friday and 10:00 A.M. to 5:30 P.M. on weekends in May and September, in April and October the museum is open only on weekends from 10:00 A.M. to 5:30 P.M. Admission is $4.75 for adults, $3.75 for youths ages twelve through eighteen, $2.75 for children ages five through eleven, and $3.25 for seniors ages sixty-two and older; kids ages four and under are **Free**. *Group rates available. Ask about the overnight encampment program. Web site: www.silversides.org.*

Along the Muskegon River outlet, board the *Silversides*, billed as the country's most famous surviving World War II submarine. It also played a role in a 1950s television show about an appendix operation done on board while at sea using only directions from a medical book. You'll climb below deck to see how its crew shared bunk space in shifts and how they lived on patrol, and learn how it ranked third highest among all World War II subs in ships sunk. The exhibit also includes the Coast Guard cutter *McLane*.

MUSKEGON FURY (all ages)

The Fury play in Walker Arena downtown along the waterfront area; (231) 726–2400. Season runs from October through April. Tickets cost between $7.00 and $8.50 for adults, $5.00 for children eighteen and younger; children younger than two get in **Free**.

The city's entry in the United Hockey League plays thirty-seven home games.

P. J. HOFFMASTER STATE PARK (all ages)

Just south of Muskegon; (231) 798–3711. To reach Hoffmaster State Park, exit U.S. 31 at Pontaluna Road and drive west 2 miles. A $4.00 daily or $20.00 annual vehicle permit is required to enter. Camping is $15.00 nightly.

One of the state's most beautiful parks, with 333 shaded campsites amid the rolling dunes of Lake Michigan. The park encircles 2½ miles of lake shoreline and 10 miles of hiking trails through dunes and the forests that have taken hold behind them. Picnicking and swimming are available.

MUSKEGON WINTER SPORTS COMPLEX (ages 8 and up)

Inside Muskegon State Park; (616) 744–9629. The track is open to the public on Friday night, Saturday, and Sunday. Cost of the orientation session is $17. All-day track passes are $20 for the lower and $30 for the upper track for adults and $15 for the lower and $20 for the upper run for children ages twelve and younger. Web site: www.msports. org/luge.htm.

In cold weather, hold your own family Winter Olympics and ride a luge at the complex. Here's a place for the kids to live up to their "No Fear" hats and slip down an ice-covered, banked track on a sled barely a yard long, faster than Dad or Mom. The beginners' run starts a ways down the track, and when you've got some experi-

Away for the Weekend Pick a beach, any beach, in summer. There are so many in this region to choose from. My favorites include Ludington's miles of secluded dunes, along with its great city park beach. Other top spots to enjoy summer include Muskegon and Grand Haven. There are lots of inexpensive places to stay in each area. Check a few miles inland, where prices are more moderate, and all you have to do is drive a few minutes to find the shore.

Trying skiing this winter? Head for Crystal Mountain, near Thompsonville, with one of the state's best children's programs. Farther north, Shanty Creek Resort's children's learn-to-ski program also rates highly.

ence, you can work your way up to the top for the full trip down one of only two luge runs in the nation. After instruction that includes a video, sliders can hit around 25 mph on the lower track and up to 45 mph on the upper. There's also a skating rink and lighted cross-country ski trails.

DUCK LAKE STATE PARK (all ages)

About 15 miles north of Muskegon; (616) 744–3480. From Muskegon State Park, take Scenic Drive, itself a great tourist attraction as it slips past expensive lakefront homes and scenic views and passes Duck Lake. The day-use park is open daylight to dusk. A state vehicle permit is required for entry, $4.00 daily or $20.00 annually.

The park is fairly undeveloped, but there's a wonderful public beach on Lake Michigan at the mouth of Duck Lake and another on Duck Lake. There are designated swimming areas on Lake Michigan and Duck Lake but no lifeguards.

MICHIGAN'S ADVENTURE AMUSEMENT PARK AND WILD WATER ADVENTURE (all ages)

On U.S. 31, 4750 Whitehall Road at Russell Road, Muskegon 49445, 8 miles north of town; (616) 766–3377. Open daily from Memorial Day through Labor

Day. Admission is $20 per person; children ages two and younger get in **Free**, *and the price gets you in to both Michigan's Adventure and Wild Water Adventure. Web site: www.miadventure.com.*

Summer fun awaits you at the state's largest amusement park. Stare down from the 90-foot crest of the first hill on the Wolverine Wildcat, a wooden roller coaster, one of five in the park. The newest is Shivering Timbers, the third largest wooden coaster in the country and more than a mile long. Or, try tamer rides, too, among the thirty available, seven of which are just for youngsters. Kid's rides include Zach's Zoomer, a pint-size coaster named after the owner's son.

Wild Water Adventure is adjacent to Michigan's Adventure. If getting wet sounds like fun, visit the state's largest water park, with a wave pool, the state's longest water slide, and the meandering Lazy River inner tube ride. Two play areas and a tree house are just for kids.

PORT CITY *PRINCESS* (all ages)

Sailing from the waterfront at Hartshorn Marina, 1133 West Western Avenue, Muskegon 49441; (231) 728–8387 or (800) 853–6311. From Business U.S. 31 (Seaway Drive), follow the signs and take it downtown to Shoreline Drive then head left to Western Avenue, the first light. Turn west onto Western to the marina entrance. Ninety-minute sight-seeing cruises leave at 3:30 P.M. daily from Memorial Day through Labor Day and are $9.00 per adult and $7.00 for children ten and younger. Infants get in **Free**. *There also are lunch and dinner cruises at higher prices. Reservations are required for all cruises.*

The *Princess* takes passengers into Muskegon Lake, through the channel, and, if weather permits, briefly into Lake Michigan. On the way, you'll see the lake's shoreline and the Milwaukee Clipper, an old steamship now being refurbished into a museum and the Silversides (see listing).

Where to Eat

Doo Drop Inn. *2410 Henry Street; (231) 755–3791. From Business U.S. 31, head west on Sherman Boulevard. Then go north on Henry.* Owned by the same family for more than sixty years. Casual family fare for lunch and dinner. Try the perch with some onion rings. Children's menu. $$

Frosty Oasis. *2181 West Sherman, Muskegon 49441, west of Business U.S. 31; (231) 755–2903.* Great ice cream dishes. $

The Hearthstone. *3350 Glade, Muskegon 49444; (231) 733–1056. At the corner of Seaway (Business U.S. 31) and Norton.* Great soups and sandwiches and pasta for lunch and dinner. Children's menu. $$

Tony's Club. *785 West Broadway, Muskegon, 49441; (231) 739–7196. From Business U.S. 31, head west on Broadway.* Casual American meals. Children's menu. $$$

Where to Stay

Best Western Park Plaza Hotel. *2967 Henry Street, Muskegon 49441, west of Business U.S. 31, south of downtown; (616) 733–2651.* This hotel has 108 rooms, indoor pool, and restaurant. $$

Blue Country B&B. *1415 Holton Road, Muskegon 49445; (231) 744–2555 or (888) 569–2050. Web site: www. bbonline.com/mi/bluecountry/* This four-room B&B caters to families, with special theme children's breakfast, a toy room, and more amenities. Children can stay in own room. $

Comfort Inn. *1675 East Sherman Boulevard, Muskegon 49444, at the U.S. 31 Sherman exit; (231) 739–9092.* The inn has 117 rooms, 𝓕𝓻𝓮𝓮 continental break-

fast, indoor and outdoor pools, exercise area and sauna, and restaurant. $$

Holiday Inn–Muskegon Harbor. *939 Third Street, Muskegon 49441, downtown; (231) 722–0100. From Business U.S. 31, turn west on Third.* The hotel is just 2 blocks from Muskegon Lake. It has 200 rooms, indoor and outdoor pools, exercise area, sauna and whirlpool, and restaurant. $$

Seaway Motel. *631 West Norton Avenue, Muskegon 49441, at Business U.S. 31, south of downtown; (231) 733–1220.* This economical motel has twenty-nine modest rooms and an outdoor pool. Restaurant nearby. Kids stay 𝓕𝓻𝓮𝓮. Small pets okay. $

For More Information

Muskegon County Convention & Visitors Bureau, *610 West Western Avenue, Muskegon 49440; (616)* *722–3751 or (800) 250–WAVE. Web site: www.muskegon.org.*

Rothbury

Settled in 1865, Rothbury is a quiet suburb of the Muskegon/Whitehall area. The town is heavily wooded.

 DOUBLE JJ RESORT (all ages)
5900 South Water Road, Rothbury 49452; (231) 894–4444 or (800) 368–2535. To get to Double JJ, take the Rothbury exit (exit 136, Winston Road) off U.S. 31 and go east about a ¼ mile; then travel north on Water Road about 1

mile and watch for the signs. A week's stay starts at $593 per adult, $588 per kid ages seven through seventeen, and $467 per child ages four through six. Ages three and younger stay **Free***. Rates include meals, riding, and entertainment. There are weekend and three-day rates, too. Web site: www.doublejj.com.*

Hold on, pardner. You mean there's a real dude ranch in Michigan? Yup. In fact, the Double JJ is one of three in the state. Hit the trail here on daily rides headed by the staff of Western wranglers, who'll teach you the intricacies of "trottin'" and lopin'" (trotting and cantering, for you city slickers).

A highlight of the week is the rodeo, where new cowpokes can test their skills. Previously, Double JJ was for grown-ups only, but now there is a camp where parents drop their cowkids off and forget about them for the day—the Back 40 Kids Resort. Each generation has fun independently and learns ranch skills without the other. Parents and kids can meet up at the end of each day, if they wish, or they can stay at their own separate resort with around-the-clock supervision, sleeping in wagons, tepees, and bunkhouses in a replica of a western town. There is also a swimmin' hole with waterslide, a park, a petting farm, and, of course, a riding center.

In addition to all that, there's nightly music in the dance hall for the adults (kids have entertainment, too), pools and hot tubs, fishing in a private lake, and the Thoroughbred, an eighteen-hole Arthur Hills–designed championship golf course rated by *Golf Digest* as thirty-third in the nation's "Places to Play." Parents can stay in original cabins or new condos near the golf course. It's a surprising find that the whole family can enjoy.

Fremont

Fremont is about an hour north of Grand Rapids and northwest of Muskegon and is reached off U.S. 131 by turning west at Michigan 82 and following it into the city.

Fremont is the town that put Gerber baby food in the mouths of hundreds of millions of Americans. The company began when Mrs. Gerber told her hubby that she was tired of making her own baby food. Couldn't he try making some at his canning plant? The rest is pabulum history. The plant is reportedly the world's largest baby-food maker.

NATIONAL BABY FOOD FESTIVAL (all ages)

Located in downtown Fremont; (231) 924–2270 or (800) 592–2229. Most events are **Free***.*

Most of us leave it to the babies to gum down the millions of containers of strained fruits, vegetables, and meat that roll out the door at the Gerber Products Company, founded in 1928. Now it's your family's turn. During this unique festival, held annually here the third weekend in July, don your bib and dig in during the baby food–eating contest! You might even win some cash if you can down five jars of the stuff before your neighbor does.

Other events in the weeklong fest include a car show, entertainment in the city park, a midway, and a downtown parade held Saturday at 10:00 A.M.

Where to Eat

Pack's Family Restaurant. *1042 West Main Street, Fremont 49412; (231) 924–5770. Open 6:00 A.M. to 8:00 P.M.* Monday through Saturday. Serves breakfast all day, plus lunch and dinner. Children's menu. $$

Where to Stay

Harrington Inn. *117 West Main, Freemont 49412; (231) 924–3083 or (800) 233–5653.* The inn has thirty-eight rooms, outdoor pool, and exercise area. Children ages eleven and younger stay **Free** with parents. Continental breakfast is included in the room rate. $$

For More Information

Fremont Chamber of Commerce, *33 West Main Street, Fremont 49412; (231) 924–2270. Web site: www.fremont.chamcom.org.*

Newaygo

Located on the river valley banks above the Muskegon River, Newaygo is famed for salmon and steelhead fishing in the river below in fall and spring, for morel mushroom hunting in the surrounding woods in May, and other outdoor fun the rest of the year. The Newaygo Logging Fest takes place downtown each year on Labor Day weekend to celebrate the area's logging history. It features an arts-and-crafts fair, sidewalk sales, chicken dinners, and a lumberjack competition, along with a custom car show.

CROTON DAM FLOAT TRIPS (all ages)

5355 Croton Drive; (231) 652–6037. Three miles north of Michigan 82. From Newaygo, head east on Croton Drive, on the river's north side. Stop anytime.
    Canoeing is offered here below Hardy Dam's downstream partner, Croton Dam. There also are campsites here.

Where to Eat

Cory's Family Restaurant. *On Michigan 37, Newaygo 49337, just south of town; (231) 652–7222.* Serves breakfast, lunch, and dinner along with take-out. $$

Where to Stay

Besides local motels, mostly along Michigan 37, there are plenty of campgrounds available.

Newaygo State Park. *2793 Beech, Newaygo 49337; (231) 745–2888 (summer), (231) 845–4452, or (800) 44–PARKS (for reservations).* The park offers ninety-nine sites on the east shore of Hardy Dam Pond, all rustic. Most of the park is undeveloped, and there is no swimming on the lake, but the park has a boat launch.

Little Switzerland Resort and Campground. *254 Pickeral Lake Drive, Newaygo 49337; (231) 652–7939.* From Michigan 37, head to the signal light at 82nd, and turn west. The next street is Old Michigan 37. Turn right and go about 1½ miles and turn in on Pickeral Lake Drive. The resort has eighty campsites and seven housekeeping cottages open from May through October. Named after the area's old nickname because of its rolling hills and river valleys. $$

For More Information

Newaygo County Tourist Council, *46845 South Evergreen, Newaygo 49337; (231) 652–9298. Web sites:* *www.riverview.net or www.newaygo-online.com.*

White Cloud

If you don't come here to see or fish for salmon and steelhead in the nearby Muskegon River, in the deep-cut valley below Newaygo, 14 miles south along Michigan 37, then you ought to come to say you've roomed at a shack.

THE SHACK COUNTRY INN

2263 West Fourteenth, White Cloud 49349; (231) 924–6683. From the stop-light in downtown White Cloud, head 5½ miles west and then watch for the signs; the lodge is ¼ mile off the main road. The Shack is 8 miles northeast of Fremont. Rates start at $50 per room (single or double occupancy) for weekday stays. Open year-round.

It doesn't have the most inviting name, but this bed and breakfast is far from what its moniker and even its weird location—in the heart of downtown "Jugville," as its ads say—connote. Families who stay here for a night or a long weekend are bathed in rustic luxury, from the beautiful forty-five log-cabin rooms, thirty with hot tubs and eighteen with fire-places inside, to the inexpensive rates, which include full breakfast, din-ner, and even a 9:00 P.M. banana split. Sunday brunch is available. Kids like the beach on Robinson Lake, too. The lodge, rebuilt to original detail after a fire in 1945 and added to over the years, is one of the north's surprising secrets.

Where to Eat

See The Shack Country Inn and the Newaygo listing.

Where to Stay

If you're not up for The Shack, here's another option:

Sandy Beach Campground. *6926 Thirtieth Street, White Cloud 49349, on Hardy Dam Pond; (231) 689–7383. From Michigan 37, go east on Thirteeth Street. The campground has 150 sites with swimming beach open from mid-May through mid-September. Run by the Newaygo County Parks Commission. $*

Baldwin

Located along Michigan 37, this small town is busiest in summer, when canoeists and others come to enjoy the surrounding lakes and rivers of Lake County, and during fall hunting season.

SHRINE OF THE PINES (all ages)

The shrine is 2 miles south of Baldwin, off Michigan 37, Baldwin 49304; (231) 745–7892. Open from 10:00 A.M. to 6:00 P.M. daily from May 15 through October 15. Admission costs $3.50 for adults and teens, $2.75 for seniors, and $1.00 for children ages six through twelve. Ages five and under Free.

The legacy of Raymond W. Oberholzer, carved over the decades of his life in the woods south of this small community, is demonstrated in the impressive collection at this shrine, dedicated to the virgin white-pine forest that once blanketed the state. Over a period of thirty years, Oberholzer, a hunting and fishing guide, gathered tree stumps, limbs, roots, and trunks. Then, using such simple tools as broken glass, brushes, and deer hide, he handchiseled and rubbed smooth the wood to create natural works of art in the form of beds, chairs, and even chandeliers and candlesticks.

The centerpiece of the display here is a huge table carved from a single stump, complete with drawers. There's also a short nature trail through the woods.

Pere Marquette River Activities Step outside the log cabin, or stop at the public access along Michigan 37, and you're along the fabled "PM," where in spring the river's gravel becomes a nursery for steelhead trout and native brown trout. In fall, salmon take over. Anglers come for all three. Part of the river is for fly-fishing only. Canoe liveries are nearby for those who want to tackle the twists and turns of the stream, which can be paddled by beginners.

Where to Eat and Stay

See entries for Ludington, Newaygo, and White Cloud or call the Lake County Chamber of Commerce at (231) 745–4331.

For More Information

Lake County Chamber of Commerce, *911 Michigan Avenue, Baldwin 49304; (231) 745–4331.*

Shelby, Hart, and Mears

Named for a War of 1812 general who recaptured Detroit from the British, Shelby was settled in 1866. It's in the middle of west Michigan farm country. Hart, settled in 1856, was named after a local pioneer and is the seat of Oceana County. Mears is named for Charles Mears, a nineteenth century pioneer settler of the area.

SHELBY MAN-MADE GEMSTONES (all ages)

1330 Industrial Drive, Shelby 49455; (231) 861–2165. Showroom is open from 9:00 A.M. to 5:30 P.M. Monday through Friday and from noon to 4:00 P.M. Saturday. Theater admission is Free*, and the room is fully accessible to the physically disabled. The store is minutes off U.S. 31 from either the Hart or Shelby exits; just follow the signs east.*

You don't have to spend a lot for a "diamond," a "ruby," a "sapphire," or some other gem at the showroom in this tiny town near the Lake Michigan shoreline. The company is the world's largest maker of synthetic and simulated gems. It got its start producing industrial rubies to make lasers and then branched out to create crystals for science and other uses.

The synthetic rubies and sapphires are actually reconstituted smaller gems that are fused to form larger ones. They're identical to the ones dug out of the ground but are produced at a fraction of the cost. In the fifty-seat theater, you'll learn about the manufacturing process.

MAC WOODS' DUNE RIDES (all ages)

629 North Eighteenth Avenue, Mears 49436; (231) 873–2817. Nine miles west of U.S. 31 at the Hart or Shelby exits—depending on whether you're driving north or south. Rides run daily from 9:30 A.M. to dusk between Memorial Day and Labor Day. From mid-May through the day before Memorial Day and for fall tours from Labor Day through early October, the hours are 10:00 A.M. to 5:00 P.M. daily. Cost is $12.00 for adults, and $8.00 for children ages eleven and younger. Web site: www.oceana.net/dunerides.

Almost seventy years ago, on the Silver Lake dunes here, Malcom "Mac" Woods invented the sport of dune buggying when he fitted a Model A Ford with oversize tires and a big engine to travel the sands between Silver Lake and Lake Michigan. The craze he originated carries on across the country—and so does his Michigan attraction.

The forty-minute "dune scooter" rides in modified convertible trucks take visitors on an 8-mile route through one of the Midwest's largest dune complexes. En route, drivers provide a running narrative on the history of the dunes, and at one point zip along the hard sand beach to make sure everyone aboard gets "cooled off" by a wave or two.

SILVER LAKE STATE PARK (all ages)

Exit U.S. 31 at Shelby Road and drive west 6 miles, then go north on Scenic Drive, and follow the signs; (231) 873–3083 for information or (800) 447–2757 for reservations. Entry is by vehicle permit, $4.00 daily or $20.00 annually. Camping is $15.00 daily.

Near the dune rides, this park is one of Michigan's most popular. Besides camping at one of nearly 250 sites and swimming on Lake Michigan or Silver Lake, you can run your own registered dune buggy within the designated 600-acre off-road-vehicle area on the dunes. The big Silver Lake dune is inching eastward with each wind gust.

Where to Eat

Hart House of Flavors. *811 South State Street, Shelby 49420; (231) 873–2244. From U.S. 31 at the Hart exit, go east 1½ miles to the blinker and turn north about a ½ mile. Open Monday through Thursday 11:00 A.M. to 8:00 P.M., Friday through Sunday until 10:00 P.M.* Burgers, salads, and great ice cream treats. $

Silver Lake Whippydip. *591 Eighteenth Avenue, Shelby 49420, next to Mac Woods Dune Rides, 9 miles west of U.S. 31 at the Hart or Shelby exits; (231) 873–4715. Open Sunday through Thursday 11:00 A.M. to 11:00 P.M., Friday and Saturday Memorial Day to Labor Day until midnight, and weekends in May and September 11:00 A.M. to 11:00 P.M.* Known for its turtle sundaes and pizza. $

Where to Stay

Gateway Motel. *3781 North Oceana Drive, Hart 49420. Take the Hart exit off U.S. 31 and go east about 1½ miles to Oceana and turn left; (231) 873–2125.* *Web site: www.oceana.net.* Nineteen units with picnic and play areas and cable TV. Ten minutes from Silver Lake State Park. $–$$

Yogi Bear's Jellystone Park Camp Resort. At 8329 Hazel Avenue, Hart 49420. From U.S. 31, go west from the Hart exit and follow the signs to Silver Lake for about 6 miles; (231) 873–4502. There are 200 campsites, heated outdoor pool, playground, organized games, and arts and crafts. $

For More Information

Hart–Silver Lake Chamber of Commerce, 100 State, Hart 49420; (231) 873–2247.

Oceana County Tourism Bureau, 100 State Street, P.O. Box 168, Hart 49420; (231) 873–3982 or (800) 874–3982. Web site: www.oceana.net.

Bill's Top Family Adventures in West Michigan–North

- **Michigan's Adventure Amusement Park, Muskegon.** Ride Michigan's only wooden roller coaster.
- **Mac Woods's Dune Rides, Silver Lake Dunes, Shelby.** Ride the ride that started the dune-buggy craze.
- **SS *Badger*, Ludington.** Sail away on a day trip to Wisconsin in the state's last remaining overnight car ferry. Rides can be during the day, or book passage on a night trip.
- **Sleeping Bear Sand Dunes National Lakeshore, Empire.** Walk up the dune, then see if you can keep from running down.
- **Mackinaw City.** Historic parks, great views, and more at this gateway to the Upper Peninsula and Mackinac Island.

Ludington

It's hard to find a more picturesque Lake Michigan town. Located west of U.S. 31 and at the Michigan terminus (the highway continues in Wisconsin) of U.S. 10, Ludington is a favorite for summer vacationers and for salmon and steelhead anglers. It's also the home port of the Great Lakes's last overnight passenger ferry. The Car Ferry Festival takes place citywide in mid-May to celebrate the start of the ferry's cross-lake seasonal service each year. A parade and more are part of the fun.

SS *BADGER* (all ages)

700 South William, Ludington 49431, at the end of U.S. 10 in Michigan; (800) 841–4243 or (888) Ferry–4–U. The ferry runs from mid-May through early October; departures vary by date. The round-trip fare is $63 per person ($58 for seniors) and $94 per vehicle; children ages five through fifteen pay $31 each, and anyone age four or younger rides Free. *Ask about special rates and discounts. Pets are okay in the owner's vehicle or in a portable kennel provided by the owner. Web site: www.ssbadger.com.*

If you can't afford that Caribbean cruise for the family, here's a Great Lakes alternative. Climb aboard the only cross–Great Lakes car ferry still operating, and you'll have a relaxing four-hour cruise between Ludington and Manitowoc, Wisconsin. The 410-foot *Badger* accommodates more than 100 vehicles and 600 passengers. It was built in 1952 and was recently renovated to create more passenger-friendly comfort features, such as onboard cafeteria service, live entertainment, a family movie lounge, bingo, and special children's activi-

Sportfishing in Ludington

At the harbor you can book a charter for salmon and steelhead fishing on the big lake, or launch your own at the mouth, near the Coast Guard station. Small boats can fish in Pere Marquette Lake when it's too rough to go onto the big lake. Best salmon action is from August onward, but there's good steelhead fishing most of the summer offshore. A 19-foot boat or larger with radio and fish-finding equipment is recommended for Lake Michigan, as storms can blow out of Wisconsin in a hurry.

ties. There are special two-hour shoreline cruises also scheduled in mid-May, on July 4, and on September 4 in Ludington for $29 per person.

Badger Boutique. 700 South William, Ludington 49431, at the SS *Badger* dock; (616) 845–3955. If you don't want to go cruising, here's where you can buy Badger clothing, kids' souvenirs, and even smoked fish, in an old renovated fish market.

WHITE PINE VILLAGE (all ages)

1687 South Lakeshore Drive, Ludington 49431; (231) 843–4808. Three miles south of Ludington, west of old U.S. 31 (Pere Marquette Highway). Head west on Iris, Hesslund, or Chauvez Roads and north on South Lakeshore Drive. The attraction is open at various hours from early May through mid-October, so it's best to call ahead. Admission is $5.00 for adults, $4.00 for ages six to eighteen, $4.50 *for seniors, and $15.00 for the entire family. Web site: www.lumanet.org/ whitepine/village.htm.*

On a wooded hill south of town, White Pine Village is a reconstructed 1800s town of twenty buildings on a bluff overlooking Lake Michigan. Events centered around the buildings are scheduled throughout the summer.

LUDINGTON CITY BEACH (all ages)

Along North Lakeshore Drive, Ludington 49431, downtown at the lakefront; (231) 845–0324. Open during daylight hours Memorial Day through Labor Day. The city beach is Free.

Fun in Ludington includes a beautiful city beach. You'll not only find great swimming, but beachfront minigolf and shuffleboard.

Where to Eat

Gibbs Country House Restaurant. *3951 West U.S. 10, Ludington 49431, about 2 miles west of U.S. 31; (231) 845–0311. Web site: www. gibbsrestaurant.com.* Good family menu and marvelous sticky buns. Very good salad and dessert bar. Take-home frozen baked goods, too. Open for lunch and dinner, and for breakfast July through August. Children's menu. $$

House of Flavors. *Downtown on the north side of U.S. 10, Ludington 49431; (231) 845–5785.* Great made-on-the-premises ice-cream treats plus grilled items. $

Scotty's. *5910 East Ludington Avenue (U.S.10), Ludington 49431, about 2 miles west of U.S. 31; (231) 843–4033.* Good American menu for lunch and dinner, such as steak and seafood. $$$

P.M. Steamers. *502 West Loomis, Ludington 49431; (231) 843–9555. Just south of Ludington Avenue, along the waterfront.* My favorite for dinner because of the harbor view and entrees such as prime rib and walleye. $$$

Where to Stay

Four Seasons Lodging and Breakfast. *717 East Ludington Avenue, Ludington 49431, downtown; (231) 843–3448 or (800) 968–0180.* The motel has thirty-one rooms. Restaurants nearby. $$

Land's Inn. *4079 West U.S. 10, Ludington 49431, just west of U.S. 31; (231) 845–7311 or (800) 707–7475.* Here you'll find 116 rooms, indoor pool, spa, and restaurant. The hotel also hosts Points North Theatre for dinner theater. $$

Ludington State Park. *At the end of Michigan 116, Ludington 49431, which runs from Ludington about 8 miles through the dunes; (231) 843–8671 or (616) 843–2423. A $4.00 daily or $20.00 annual state park vehicle permit is required for entry. Camping is $15.00 nightly.* The park has 344 campsites and three mini-cabins that each sleep four, with electric heat. There are beaches on both Lake Michigan and Hamlin Lake. One of the popular things do to at the Lake Michigan beach is to surf the water coming out of Hamlin Lake at the mouth. There also are 18 miles of hiking trails through the dunes and woods, as well as a unique canoe trail.

Nova Motel. *472 South Pere Marquette Road (Old U.S. 31) Ludington 49431; (231) 843–3454. From U.S. 10, turn south on Pere Marquette about ½ mile.* The motel has thirty-two rooms and outdoor pool. $$

Snyders Shoreline Inn. *903 West Ludington Avenue, Ludington 49431, on the lakefront; (231) 845–1261.* The inn has forty-four rooms, outdoor pool, and beach access, with breakfast room. Other dining is nearby. $$

Twin Points Resort. *2684 Piney Ridge Road, Ludington 49431; (231) 843–9434. Follow U.S. 10 into town and turn north toward the sand dunes of Ludington State Park, onto Michigan 116. Go about 4 miles to Piney Ridge Road, turn east, and watch for the sign.* Renting a lakeside cottage is one of the most inexpensive ways for a family to vacation, and one of the best places in the area to do so is owned by Jim and Barb Husted. There are ten log cottages, with one to three bedrooms each, perched atop wooded bluffs above Hamlin Lake, where there's a large beach and plenty of shallows for children. *Note:* Before you book a cottage anywhere, look. Check out each early in the season to be sure you'll enjoy the stay and that the accommodations are what you'd expect.

For More Information

Ludington Convention and Visitors Bureau, *5827 U.S. 10, Ludington 49431; (800) 542–4600 or (231) 845–0324. Web site: www.ludingtoncvb.com.*

Manistee

A city that prides itself on its beautiful Victorian-era downtown (listed on the National Register of Historic Places), Manistee, located along U.S. Highway 31 and nicknamed the Victorian Port City, is surely one of the most charming towns in the nation. Blocks of its quaint buildings are lit by antique-style street lamps. The Manistee Trolleys take visitors on a tour of town and leave from several points downtown from mid-June through Labor Day. Call (231) 723-6525 for schedules.

Street fests take place in Manistee throughout the year. The National Forest Festival takes place over the Fourth of July downtown. Parades, dances, a midway, antique boat and custom car shows, a boat parade, and fireworks over Lake Michigan are among the features of this festival. Call (231) 723-2575 or (800) 288-2286. Web sites: www.manistee.com/~edo/ or www.multimag.com/city/mi/manistee.

The Victorian Port City Festival takes place the weekend after Labor Day downtown. Among its highlights are an antique- and classic-car show, Native American arts and dance performances, a big fishing tournament on Lake Michigan, and an arts-and-crafts fair. Call (231) 723-3541 for more information.

Manistee is also one of the lake's prime salmon- and trout-fishing charter ports, with fishing available throughout the summer. Contact the Manistee Chamber of Commerce on how to get aboard one like Capt. Joe Wolff's *Ginger Brandy,* by calling (616) 398-3474.

LAKE MICHIGAN RECREATION AREA (all ages)

West of U.S. 31, south of the Manistee city limits, 10 miles south of the junction with Michigan 55; (231) 723–2211. Usually open daily during daylight hours from April 1 through October 1. Free. Camping is $10 per night.

There are ninety-nine campsites at this gem of a recreation area, supervised by the Manistee National Forest. It has 3½ miles of gravel biking and hiking trails, a great beach on Lake Michigan, and a picnic area with playground, all adjoining the Nordhouse Dunes Wilderness Area to the south. The campground is extremely popular on weekends, and each site can take up to eight people and two vehicles. $

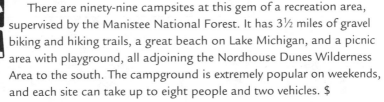

C abins for Rent Cottage vacations are one of my favorite family ways to have fun. A comfy pine cottage looking over a lakefront, with a rowboat that's usually available, and outboard rentals, too. Swimming, fishing, and plenty of relaxin'.

Mind you, the usual cabin is not a fancy condo. There may be plenty of makeshift items, nonmatching dinnerware, and the like, but that's all part of the fun. Cottages are a dying breed with the increasing "condoization" of the north. If you can find a good one, stick with it. It deserves your business, and you deserve the good time you'll have.

Where to Eat

Captain's Corner. *267 Arthur Street, Manistee 49660, a mile north on U.S. 31;* (616) 723–3474. Serves lunch and dinner. Children's menu. $$

Gregory's. *200 Arthur Street (U.S. 31), Manistee 49660, about a mile from downtown;* (231) 723–4661. Open for breakfast, lunch, and dinner, at the Best Western Manistee. $$

Kilwin's of Manistee. *386 River Street, Manistee 49660, downtown, on the south side of the Manistee River;* (231) 723–3933. Handmade chocolates, ice cream, other goodies, and coffees. $

River Street Station. *350 River Street, Manistee 49660, downtown;* (231) 723–8411. *On the river.* Great Reuben sandwiches and burgers and other entrees for lunch and dinner, with entertainment on most weekends. $$

Where to Stay

There are at least eight bed and breakfasts operating in the Manistee County area, including five in Manistee. For descriptions and locations, call the Manistee Area Convention & Visitors Bureau (see For More Information). Other accommodations include the following:

Best Western Manistee. *200 Arthur Street (U.S. 31), about a mile north of downtown on U.S. 31;* (231) 723–9949 or (888) 296–0835. The motel has sixty-five rooms, indoor pool, exercise area, and restaurant. $$

Days Inn. *1462 Manistee, about 1⅓ miles south of town on U.S. 31;* (231) 723–8385. The inn has ninety rooms, indoor pool, and continental breakfast. Restaurants nearby. $$

Orchard Beach State Park. *The park is 2 miles north of Manistee on Michigan 110;* (231) 723–7422. *A $4.00 daily or $20.00 annual motor vehicle permit is required for entry.* Camping, which costs $12.00 extra, is offered at 174 campsites on dunes looking over the lake, with a great Lake Michigan beach. $

For More Information

Manistee Area Convention & Visitors Bureau, *180 Harrison Street, Manistee 49660;* (231) 723–7975 or (800) 288–2286. *Web site: www. manistee.com/~edo/.*

Thompsonville

Settled in the late 1800s and named for a local lumberman, the small town of Thompsonville now sees hundreds heading for the resort just north of town along Michigan 115.

CRYSTAL MOUNTAIN SKI AREA (all ages)

Just north of Thompsonville along Michigan 115, Thompsonville 49683; (231) 378–2000 or (800) YOUR–MTN. The resort is open year-round, for golf in summer and skiing generally from early December through late March. Plan on spending around $36 daily for lift tickets and rentals for adults, about $20 for children. Web site: www.crystalmtn.com.

Crystal caters to families, with baby-sitting and a great children's learn-to-ski program available. It has both indoor and outdoor pools and thirty-four ski runs. It also has 184 slopeside rooms available, along with an on-site restaurant. $$

Where to Eat and Stay

Besides the resort, which has its own restaurant, see Cadillac and Frankfort listings.

Benzonia, Frankfort, Elberta, Honor, and Beulah

A fantastic beach, great accommodations, and super salmon fishing make this cluster of small towns along U.S. 31 a vacation winner.

SPORTFISHING (all ages)

At Elberta, across Betsie Lake from Frankfort; (231) 882–FISH. Cost is about $70 per person, with a minimum of four, or $530 for a full nine-hour day.

If you know how to fish steelhead, you're a "scum." Floyd Ikens and other charter-boat operators take anglers into the lake starting in June to search for the lake-run rainbow trout under what anglers have termed the "scum line"—tiny rivers of bugs and other debris that signal different water temperatures where steelhead themselves like to fish. Chinook salmon fishing action runs June through August.

PLATTE RIVER STATE FISH HATCHERY (all ages)

East of Honor along U.S. 31; (231) 325–4611. Open for Free *self-guided tours daily 8:00 A.M. to 4:00 P.M. year-round.*

In fall, families can watch as thousands of salmon darken the river bottom at the hatchery.

Sleeping Bear Dunes National Lakeshore

Roll or run down a giant sand dune or trek across it and learn how it got there. It's all waiting at the state's first national lakeshore, north of Frankfort. Named by Native Americans who said one of the hulking formations was actually a slumbering mama bear, the dunes are among the largest freshwater sand piles in existence, rising to nearly 500 feet. At the visitor center, find out how they were formed; then head for the dune slide, where you can make the climb to the top and have fun coming back down.

Before you go, tour the 7-mile Pierce-Stocking Scenic Drive, with overlooks on Lake Michigan. You can also visit a restored station of the U.S. Lifesaving Service, forerunner of the Coast Guard, at the edge of the lake. For more information call the headquarters (9922 Front Street, Empire 49630) at (231) 326–5134. Web site: www.nps.gov/slbe/.

Where to Eat

Cherry Hut. *Along northbound U.S. 31, Beulah; (231) 882–4431.* Open daily Memorial Day weekend through October. Great regional foods focusing on cherries, including great cherry pie. $$

Where to Stay

Betsie River Campsite. *1923 River Road, Frankfort 49635, at Michigan 115; (231) 352–9535.* There are one hundred campsites along the lower Betsie River, with playground and recreation room.

Hotel Frankfort. *231 Main, Frankfort 49635, downtown; (231) 352–4303. Web site: www.brooksideinn.com.* This lovely hotel offers eighteen rooms in a Victorian setting, with restaurant. $$$

For More Information

Frankfort/Elberta Area Chamber of Commerce, *P.O. Box 566, Frankfort 49635; (231) 352–7251. Web site: www.benzie.com.*

Benzie County Chamber of Commerce, *P.O. Box 505, Beulah 49617; (231) 882–5801. Web site: www. benzie.org.*

Interlochen

Named for two lakes it sits between, Interlochen was settled around 1900 and soon became known as an artists retreat.

 ### INTERLOCHEN SUMMER ARTS FESTIVAL (all ages)

On Michigan 137, Interlochen 49643, south of the U.S. 31 intersection; (231) 276–6230 for ticket information or (231) 276–7200 for general information. Summer concert series usually runs from mid-June to late August; fees range from around $3.00 to $50.00. Web site: www.interlochen.org.

Every summer since 1928, talented young persons from across the nation have converged on this unique wood-shrouded campus to learn from the best teachers that music, theater, and written and visual arts have to offer. The National Music Camp was established by an arts teacher who also founded the full-time arts academy here in 1962.

Performers like pianist Van Cliburn, who once studied here, come back to teach students and play. The Interlochen Summer Arts Festival features nearly 500 concerts with student and faculty performers and up to thirty-five professional concerts each year. There are five concert venues, and visitors can also sit in on classes, rehearsals, and impromptu performances on the grounds of the 1,200-acre campus.

ℱ𝓇𝑒𝑒 guided tours of the campus are available in summer at 10:00 A.M. and 2:30 P.M. Tuesday through Saturday, 4:00 P.M. Sunday, and other times by appointment.

 ### FUN COUNTRY WATER PARK (all ages)

Intersection of U.S. 31 and Michigan 137, Interlochen 49643, at the entrance to the Interlochen area; (231) 276–6360. Open 11:00 A.M. to 11:00 P.M. daily Memorial Day through Labor Day. The water slides close at 6:30 P.M. An all-day pass is $12.00 for ages four and older and $6.00 for children three and younger; it entitles you to unlimited water slides, amusement rides, one go-cart ride, and one minigolf round.

269

Splashy fun awaits. There are two 330-foot-long water slides, along with water fun for the smallest youngsters, including bumper boats. There's also a small carousel.

Where to Eat

Besides the Stone Student Center (see Where to Stay), see listings under Traverse City and Frankfort.

Where to Stay

Interlochen State Park. *A mile south of U.S. 31 on Michigan 137, Interlochen 49643; (231) 276–9511 or (800) 447–2757 for reservations. A $4.00 daily or $20.00 annual motor vehicle permit is required for entry. Camping is $14.00 nightly. Web site: www.dnr.state.mi.us/www/parks.* The park has 490 sites on both Green and Duck Lakes, near Interlochen's performing arts center. The first campground to open in Michigan's state parks, it offers a beach on the lake, bathhouse, and boat rentals.

As you might imagine, the park is very popular in summer during the concert series at Interlochen, so reserve well in advance.

Stone Student Center. *On the Interlochen campus, overlooking Green Lake, Interlochen 49643; (231) 276–7570 or (231) 276–7200.* There are a limited number of rooms and cottages with kitchens available. Inexpensive campus meals also are available. $$

For More Information

Interlochen Area Chamber of Commerce, *(231) 276–7141 or (231) 276–6230.*

Cedar

Founded in 1885 and named for its closeness to a cedar forest, this little crossroads town is reached from Michigan 72 by taking County Roads 651 and 616 north. Follow the signs to Sugar Loaf from Michigan 72, and you'll get there, too.

SUGAR LOAF RESORT (all ages)

*4500 Sugar Loaf Mountain Road, Cedar 49021, off Michigan 72; (231)
228–5461 or (800) 952–6390. From Empire, head east and follow the signs.
From Traverse City, go west on Michigan 72 and follow the signs. Open year-
round. Plan on spending around $40 for lift tickets and ski rentals for adults, $25
for children. Sugar Loaf has an excellent children's ski school for toddlers on up and
baby-sitting. Lodging: $$*

Some of the dunes are now covered by trees, and you can ski on
them. There are twenty-four runs with six chairlifts, rental equipment,
lessons, lodging, and a restaurant. There also is golf in summer and
both indoor and outdoor pools.

Where to Eat and Stay

Try Sugar Loaf or see listings under
Traverse City and Leland.

Leland

This small town along scenic Michigan 22 has developed a good reputation as
a place to browse its small shops, many of which have been transformed from
former fishing wharves below the town dam. There are lots of good restaurants
as well. Visit the Leland Web site at www.leelanau.com.

FISHTOWN (all ages)

In Leland, below the dam.

Shop for smoked fish at Carlson's, visit a quaint shop, or book a
fishing charter from one of the craft moored at the docks in the pic-
turesque former fishing village.

NORTH AND SOUTH MANITOU ISLANDS (all ages)

*The ferry leaves the Fishtown wharf at 10:00 A.M. and 4:00 P.M. The trip across
takes about ninety minutes. Tickets cost $20 for adults, $13 for kids twelve and
younger. For island transportation, tips, days of operation and other information,
call (231) 256–9061.*

The most remote part of the Sleeping Bear Dunes National
Lakeshore, these islands are reached by ferry from Leland, the fishing

271

village turned tourist town. According to a Native American legend, the islands are the cubs of the mother bear that became Sleeping Bear Dune, and she eternally waits for them to come ashore. The islands feature primitive hiking and campgrounds, and South Manitou has a restored 1839 U.S. Coast Guard lighthouse as well as one modern shipwreck. Don't forget your mosquito repellent; they can be terrors at times. Tours of South Manitou Island are available ($7.00 for adults, $4.00 for children three to twelve; two and younger **Free**), and there are rustic campgrounds on South Manitou Island. Camping on North Manitou is primitive.

Where to Eat

The Cove. *111 River, Leland 49654, just west of Main (Michigan 22); (231) 256–9834.* It'll be hard to find a more romantic spot for lunch and dinner, with the waterfall from the Leland River splashing merrily. Children's menu. $$$

Where to Stay

Homestead Resort and Ski Area. *Along Michigan 22, Leland 49654, north of town; (231) 334–5000.* More than 115 rooms and condos on the beach and in the wooded dunes overlooking Lake Michigan. The Homestead's historic inn was also being renovated at press time and will feature seventeen rooms. $$$

For other places to eat and stay nearby, see entries for Cedar and Traverse City or look up www.leelanau.com on the Internet.

For More Information

Traverse City Convention and Visitors Bureau, *101 West Grandview Parkway (U.S. 31/Michigan 37), Traverse City 49684; (231) 947–1120 or (800) TRAVERS. Web sites: www.tcvisitor.com or www.tcchamber.org.*

Traverse City

Named for the *traverse,* or portage that voyagers made between the bays, the region retains its reputation as the nation's largest tart cherry–growing district. While many of the orchards have been plowed under for expensive homes and condos, there are still plenty around, and April and May are great times to visit and watch for the annual cherry blossom opening. This rapidly growing city has become the spot to vacation for many Michigan families. With great shopping downtown and plenty of waterfront accommodations on East and West Grand Traverse Bays, it's no wonder. Traverse City is at the intersection of Michigan Highway 72 and U.S. Highway 31.

AMON ORCHARDS (all ages)

It's 2 miles north of the northern Traverse City limit on U.S. 31 in Acme; (231) 938–9160. Open daily from June through December. There are orchard tours in July. On October weekends, Amon Orchards holds its Family Fun Fest. Web site: www.amonorchards.com.

Despite creeping urban sprawl, the environs are still America's tart-cherry capital. This orchard, just north of the city, offers visits to its tree lots both to handpick the fruit and to see how it's done commercially. Besides cherries, which usually are ready in July, the adjacent eighty-acre orchard has you-pick apricots, peaches, nectarines, and other fruits. There's also a market offering nearly everything cherry, from salad dressing to ice cream toppings, and a petting farm for the kids.

NATIONAL CHERRY FESTIVAL (all ages)

Takes place annually starting around July 4, with its focus on downtown. For information call (231) 947–4230. Web site: www.cherryfestival.org.

The cherry harvest usually coincides with the festival. There's a carnival downtown, activities on the waterfront, and fresh-baked cherry pies sold everywhere, both in town and from farm roadside stands approaching the city. Big parades are part of the festival, the biggest of which is the Cherry Royale. Usually there is an air show scheduled along with concerts, arts and crafts, and more.

OLD MISSION PENINSULA LIGHTHOUSE (all ages)

Along Michigan 37, Old Mission 49684, which bisects the Old Mission peninsula separating the east and west arms of Grand Traverse Bay.

Your kids can stand halfway between the equator and the North Pole outside of this nineteenth-century lighthouse. It's a highlight of a 37-mile drive on Michigan 37 north. There's also a great beach with a very gradual dropoff.

CLINCH PARK (all ages)

Across from downtown Traverse City along U.S. 31 at Cass, Traverse City 49684; (231) 922–4904. Free *parking is across the street. The* Free *park is reached via an underground pedestrian walkway from the parking lot.*

There's a large beach with lifeguards on duty. The beach is one of several parks along both arms of the bay.

CLINCH PARK ZOO (all ages)

On Grandview Parkway, Traverse City 49684, next to the beach downtown; (231) 922–4904. Open from 9:30 A.M. to 5:30 P.M. daily from Memorial Day through Labor Day, 9:30 A.M. to 4:30 P.M. daily from mid-April through Labor Day, and from the day after Labor Day, through October 31. Admission is $2.00 for adults, $1.50 for kids ages five through thirteen. Kids four and younger are admitted Free.

This small zoo features wildlife native to Michigan, such as black bears and elk, and a small steam train that you and the kids can ride from Memorial Day through Labor Day. Stroller access. Picnic area near the beach.

PIRATE'S COVE (ages 2 and up)

1710 U.S. 31 North, Traverse 49686; (231) 938–9599. Open 11:00 A.M. to 11:00 P.M. daily, weather permitting, from Memorial Day through Labor Day, except the minigolf courses, which stay open usually until the first snow. Web site: www.piratescove.net.

Give the kids a time-out here and let them play on the two water slides, go-carts, and for the smallest youngsters, battery-operated four-wheeler replicas. You must be 42 inches tall to go on the water slides. Nearly all the rides use tokens, purchased at the gate at five for $5.00, up to twenty-five for $18.00.

TALL SHIPS MALABAR AND MANITOU (all ages)

On Grand Traverse Bay's west arm at 13390 South West Bay Shore Drive, Traverse City 49684. For cruise schedules call (231) 941–2000 or (800) 678–0383. Web site: www.tallshipsailing.com.

Try a cruise on this 105-foot ship, one of the Great Lakes's largest sailing crafts. In summer the 114-foot *Manitou* and *Westwind* ply the bay during the day, and the *Malabar* acts as a floating bed and breakfast and makes evening sunset trips, too.

VASA PATHWAY (all ages)

Reach the pathway at Acme Township Park, Traverse City 49686; (231) 947–1120. From U.S. 31, take Bunker Hill Road east to Bartlett. **Free**. Web site: www.vasa.org.

Used in winter for the giant Vasa cross-country ski race that brings in racers from across the country, the trail is used by mountain bikers and hikers in summer. There are three loops ranging from 5 to 27 kilometers through the woods.

SAND LAKES QUIET AREA (all ages)

East of Traverse City; (231) 922–5280. Take Michigan 72 east to Broomhead Road and turn south. The area is open year-round, all the time. **Free**. Parking is available at the entrance to the area.

All motorized vehicles are banned in this heavily wooded preserve. There are nearly 10 miles of trails with fishing and camping available, but mostly for hikers who pack in. It's a wonderfully quiet place to visit and just enjoy what the area must have looked like to early settlers. Parking is available. Trails wind through the woods, so bring a child backpack since strollers are not of much use here.

Where to Eat

Boone's Long Lake Inn. 7208 Secor Road, Traverse City 49684; (231) 946–3991. About 5½ miles southwest of the city. Take U.S. 31 south, then head 4 miles southwest on Silver Lake Road and 1½ miles west on Secor. Open Monday through Saturday 4:00 to 11:00 P.M. and Sunday noon to 10:00 P.M. Vegetarians, beware. For the money, it's one of the best for steak lovers, including eighteen-ounce New York strips. Children's menu. $$$

Gordie Howe's Tavern and Eatery. 851 South Garfield Road, Traverse City 49686; (231) 929–4693. From U.S. 31, turn south onto Garfield, along the west arm

of the bay. Have lunch or dinner in the restaurant owned by one of professional hockey's greatest players, surrounded by National Hockey League memorabilia. $$

La Senorita. 1245 South Garfield Road, Traverse City 49685; (231) 947–8820. About a mile south of the junction of Michigan 37 and 72 at the Old Mission Peninsula turnoff. Open Monday through Thursday 11:00 A.M. to 11:00 P.M., Friday and Saturday until midnight, and Sunday noon to 10:00 P.M. Very good Mexican food for lunch and dinner. $$

Where to Stay

Choose from scores of places to stay that ring both the east and west arms of Grand Traverse Bay. The majority are along U.S. Highway 31, which skirts the bottoms of both arms. Besides those mentioned, there are about a dozen bed and breakfasts operating in the area as well.

Days Inn and Suites Traverse City. *420 Munson Avenue, Traverse City 49686; (231) 941–0208 or (800) 982–3297. Two miles east of downtown on U.S. 31.* This economical chain property offers 183 rooms, some whirlpool rooms, indoor pool, and adjacent restaurant. $$

Driftwood Resort. *1861 U.S. 31 north, Traverse City 49686; (231) 938–6100.* The resort has thirty-nine rooms, indoor pool, and recreation area. You can also swim in the bay. Restaurants nearby. $$

Grand Beach Resort Hotel. *1683 U.S. 31, Traverse City 49886, about 4½ miles east of downtown; (616) 938–4455.* The hotel has ninety-five rooms on Grand Traverse Bay, with swimming in the bay or an indoor pool. Exercise room and continental breakfast included in the room rate. $$$

Grand Traverse Resort and Spa. *100 Grand Traverse Village Boulevard, Acme 49610; (231) 938–2100 or (800) 748–0303. From Traverse City, head north on U.S. 31, just past the intersection with Michigan 72.* This grand resort has 669 rooms, suites, and condos surrounding two golf courses, including the Jack Nicklaus–designed Bear. $$$

Park Place Hotel. *300 East State Street, Traverse City 49684; (231) 946–5000.*

There are 140 restored rooms in the city proper's tallest building. Rooftop dining overlooking the bay, indoor pool, exercise area, and packages. $$

Pineview Resort. *2275 Pinehurst Trail, Mayfield 49684; (231) 947–6742. Just south of U.S. 31, 6 miles southeast of Traverse City.* Weekly rates range from $525 to $610. One of a vanishing breed of cottage resorts in the condoland of west Michigan, it has twelve two- to three-bedroom units on Arbutus Lake, some with fireplaces. Small pets okay. $$

Timber Ridge Campground. *4050 Hammond Road, Traverse City 49686, 7½ miles southeast of the city; (231) 947–2770. Head east about 4¼ miles on U.S. 31, then south 2 miles on Four Mile Road and east 2 miles on Hammond.* Here you'll find 221 sites in a well-run, quiet location, with pool and wading pool, minigolf, and children's programs. $

Traverse City State Park. *1132 U.S. 31, Traverse City 49686, on the eastern edge of downtown; (231) 922–5270 or (800) 447–2757. A $4.00 daily or $20.00 annual state motor vehicle permit is required for entry. Camping is extra.* The park has 343 sites opposite Grand Traverse Bay. A pedestrian bridge over U.S. 31 connects the campground with 700 feet of sandy beach. Located near the highway and tourist attractions, it's not the quietest park, but it's convenient to all things happening in the area. $

Waterfront Inn. *2061 U.S. 31 North, Traverse City 49686; (231) 939–1100.* The inn has 128 rooms on Traverse Bay's east arm, with beach, indoor pool, and restaurant. $$$

For More Information

Traverse City Convention and Visitors Bureau, *101 West Grandview Parkway, Traverse City 49684; (231)* *947–1120 or (800) 872–8377. Web site: www.tcvisitor.com or www.traversecity.com.*

Bellaire

The Antrim County seat was founded in 1879 and was so named for its pleasant air. The name still applies. There are several large lakes within a few minutes' drive of the city.

SHANTY CREEK RESORT (all ages)

Shanty Creek Road, Bellaire 49615; (800) 678–4111. The resort is off Michigan 88, just south of Bellaire and 12 miles west of Mancelona. From I–75, take Michigan 72 west to U.S. 131 north, which leads to M–88 west. The resort is open year-round. It has an excellent children's ski school, and baby-sitting is available. Plan on a daily fee of at least $40 for lift ticket and ski rentals for adults, $35 for children ages seven and older. Web site: www.shantycreek.com

The resort actually is comprised of two bases, Summit Village and the New Schuss Mountain. Schuss's ski runs have undergone a large expansion upward and also added twelve runs sculpted in the trees that make the resort more in contention with its bigger northern neighbors. Construction also has begun on a new multistory, slopeside hotel. Currently there are forty-one runs, with equipment rentals and instruction. Free shuttles connect the resort bases. Summer brings golfers to the complex's course, including its Arnold Palmer–designed Legend.

Where to Eat and Stay

Shanty Creek Resort. *See the aforementioned listing for directions and address;* *(231) 533–8621.* Both Schuss and Summit Village have excellent lodging with condos also available. They also have good restaurants, with Summit's buffet dinners and Sunday brunch recommended highly. $$

Boyne City, Boyne Falls, and Walloon Lake

Settled in 1865, the Boynes were named after Ireland's Boyne River. Walloon Lake was settled about seven years later. The area now is known as a vacation destination.

NATIONAL MOREL MUSHROOM FESTIVAL (all ages)

Takes place the weekend after Mother's Day in downtown Boyne City; (231) 582–6222.

It happens each spring. Just as the wild white trilliums sprout delicately to cover the forest in greenery once again, morel mania takes over during the festival. Pickers from across the country converge here to head for the rolling hardwood hills around Boyne, an ideal habitat for morels. It takes a little effort at first, but once you find one, their trademark caps with furrows and pockets are easy to spot. Since there are false morels that some people are allergic to, attend the festival to learn what you're looking for. Guided hunts and contests take place each day.

BOYNE MOUNTAIN (all ages)

Just south of Boyne Falls off U.S. 131, Boyne Falls 49713; (231) 549–2441 or (800) 462–6963. Call for price information. Web site: www.boyne.com

Boyne Falls is the site of what many regard as the Lower Peninsula's premier ski area, Boyne Mountain, with at-slope lodging, fifty runs including twelve trails built in 1996, rentals, instruction, dining, outdoor pool, and more. In summer Boyne Mountain also features championship golf courses. Condos or slopeside rooms are available in winter and summer. Boyne has an excellent children's learn-to-ski program and a baby-sitting service.

Where to Eat

There are restaurants at Boyne Mountain and others in town.

Where to Stay

Brown Trout Motel. *2510 Nelson, Boyne Falls 49713, along U.S. 131, south of Michigan 75; (231) 549–2791. The* motel has fourteen rooms and an indoor pool. $$

For More Information

**Petoskey, Harbor Springs, and
Boyne Country Visitors Bureau,** *401
East Mitchell Street, Petoskey 49770; (231)*

*348–2755 or (800) 845–2828.
Web site: www.westwin1.com.*

Petoskey

Located on the shores of Little Traverse Bay, Petoskey features modern accommodations and unique shopping. Petoskey's Historic Gaslight District downtown is worth a look. The Petoskey harborfront is a pleasant place to bring the family, and the state park's rolling dunes and clear water are great places to relax.

KILWIN'S CANDY KITCHENS (all ages)

355 North Division Road, Petoskey 49770; (231) 347–2645 or (800) 255–0759. From Mitchell Street, the main downtown thoroughfare, go east about a block, then north on Division. **Free** *tours lasting about twenty minutes are offered from June through August (times vary; call first). Web site: www.kilwins. com.*

What more delicious thought can there be to a child than a candy factory tour? In Petoskey, a great vacation city, they can watch and sniff as the chocolates are formed, then buy some in the shop.

Michigan 119 Scenic Drive The drive starts north of

downtown Petoskey. From U.S. 31, head north on Michigan 119. You'll soon discover why state residents have many times voted it to be Michigan's most scenic highway. The highway has breathtaking overlooks on bluffs high above blue Lake Michigan. The roadway is nicknamed the "Tunnel of Trees" because of the thick foliage. It can be twisty in spots, so follow the low speed limit and enjoy.

Where to Eat

Villa Ristorante Italiano. *887 Spring
Street (U.S. 131, just south of U.S. 31),
Petoskey 49740; (231) 347–1440. Open*

4:30 to 11:00 P.M. nightly. Children's menu. Save money and order a pizza. $$

Where to Stay

Best Western of Harbor Springs.
8514 Michigan 119, Harbor Springs
49740, north of the U.S. 31 and Michigan
119 intersection; (231) 347–9050. The
property has forty-six rooms, indoor
pool, and breakfast room. $$

Petoskey State Park. Along Michigan
119, Petoskey 49770, north of downtown, 4

miles north of the U.S. 31 junction; (231)
347–2311 or (800) 447–2757. A $4.00
daily or $20.00 motor vehicle entry fee is
required. Camping is $15.00 nightly. The
park has ninety campsites nestled in
the dunes along Lake Michigan's Little
Traverse Bay. A great beach, nature
trails, and programs. $

For More Information

**Petoskey/Harbor Springs/Boyne
Country Visitors Bureau,** 401 East
Mitchell Street, Petoskey 49770; (800)

845–2828 or (231) 348–2755. Web site:
www.boynecountry.com.

Bayview

North on U.S. 31 from downtown Petoskey is this area of magnificent 1870s
Victorian summer homes and marvelous bed and breakfasts and inns that
originally were part of a religious settlement connected with the Methodist
Church. Turn north on Michigan 119 for a scenic drive you'll never forget.

 BOYNE HIGHLANDS AND NUBS NOB (all ages)
(231) 526–3000 or (800) 462–6963 for Boyne Highlands, at (231) 526–
2131 or (800) 754–6827 for Nubs Nob. From Bayview, head north on U.S. 31,
then turn north on Michigan 119 to Pleasantview Road, head north and follow the
signs. Web site: www.boyne.com.
    These two downhill ski areas are across the street from each other.
Nubs Nob opened twelve new runs in the 1997–98 ski season, bringing
its total to thirty-eight. It has rentals and instruction, but it has no
slopeside lodging. Boyne Highlands is a genteel ski area that caters to
families. Slopeside rooms surround a large, heated outdoor pool that's
warm even when the air's fifteen degrees below zero in winter. It also
offers rentals, instruction, children's programs, and baby-sitting. Nubs
has children's programs but no baby-sitting.

Where to Eat

La Senorita. *At the junction of U.S. 31 and Michigan 119, Bayview; (231) 347–7750.* Good Mexican food. $$

Stafford's Bay View Inn. *2011 Woodland Avenue (U.S. 31), Bayview; (231) 347–2771.* Serves breakfast, lunch, and dinner plus Sunday brunch in cozy dining room. $$$

Where to Stay

Apple Tree Inn. *915 Spring (U.S. 131), Petoskey 49770, just south of town; (231) 348–2900.* The inn has forty rooms, indoor pool, play area, continental breakfast, and dining nearby. $$

Baywinds Inn. *909 Spring (U.S. 131), Petoskey 49770, a mile south of town; (231) 347–4193.* The inn has forty-eight rooms, indoor pool, and exercise area. Restaurant nearby. $$

Best Western Inn. *1300 Spring (U.S. 131), Petoskey 49770, 1⅓ mile south of town; (231) 347–3925.* The inn has eighty-five rooms and indoor pool. Restaurant nearby. $$

Econo Lodge. *1858 U.S. 131 south, Petoskey 49770, 2 miles south of the U.S. 31/131 intersection; (231) 348–3324.* This property has sixty rooms and indoor pool. $$

Stafford's Bayview Inn. *2011 Woodland Avenue (U.S. 31), Bayview 49770, down the hill from downtown Petoskey; (231) 347–2771. Web site: www.staffords. com.* Here you'll find eight rooms in a historic 1886 inn in the heart of the Bayview historic home district. $$$

Mackinaw City

Ask even a local here why the island is spelled *Mackinac* but the city is *Mackinaw,* and he or she probably won't know (they're both pronounced "Mackinaw"). The answer is lost with the 300-odd years since the first European settlers arrived here, first the French, then the British (probably the reason for the spelling differences). Three beautiful state parks and a lot of other fun await in this town, which comes alive in summer and hibernates in winter. Three ferry lines serve the island: *Arnold Transit,* (800) 542–8528; *Star,* (800) 638–9892; and *Shepler's,* (800) 828–6157. They leave regularly from docks in downtown Mackinaw City.

COLONIAL MICHILIMACKINAC STATE HISTORIC PARK (all ages)

Under the southern ramp of the Mackinac Bridge in Mackinaw City; (231) 436–5563. Admission is $7.50 for adults, $4.50 for kids ages six through eleven, or $22.00 for the whole family. Children five and younger are admitted Free. *You can also purchase a pass for entrance into three area historic parks for $16.00 for adults, $9.00 for ages six through eleven, or $44.00 for the family. Web site: www.mackinac.com/historicparks.*

This park stands on the location of the fort used by the French, then the British, until a larger, more defensible fort (or so everyone thought) on Mackinac Island was completed. In summer, interpretive programs with costumed docents in character tell about life at the fort in the seventeenth century. There are demonstrations of musket and cannon firing, cooking, and blacksmithing.

SEASHELL CITY (all ages)

At I–75 exit 326 (Levering Road) in Cheboygan; (231) 627–2066. Hours are 9:00 A.M. to 6:00 P.M. daily from May 1 through Labor Day and 9:00 A.M. to 5:00 P.M. daily from the day after Labor Day. Web site: www.seashellcity.mi.com.

This place is a must for any tourist-attraction aficionado. Just a few miles south of Mackinaw City along I–75 is Seashell City, where, besides what's billed as a "Giant Man-Eating Clam" (it actually is just a big shell and never ate anybody), you'll discover thousands of shells from across the world. It is a gas and also sells gas.

MACKINAC BRIDGE

You'll know it when you see it from I–75; (231) 643–7600. One-way bridge fare for passenger cars is $1.50.

This big structure leads north to Michigan's Upper Peninsula. Before the bridge was built, ferries crammed the lakefront there, taking cars and trucks across the straits. On busy weekends, traffic jams stretched for miles as vacationers waited for passage. The bridge celebrated its fortieth anniversary in 1997. From cable anchorage to cable anchorage, it's the Western Hemisphere's longest suspension bridge, measuring 5 miles. The only time you can walk it is during the annual Labor Day Bridge Walk. More than 80,000 people on foot are led across each year by Michigan's governor. There are Free parks on both south and north ends of the bridge for picnicking.

Where to Stay

Anchor Inn. *138 Old U.S. 31, Mackinaw City 49701; (231) 436–5553 or (888) 262–4679. Just north of exit 337 from I–75.* The inn has thirty-two rooms, outdoor pool, and playground. $

Best Western Dockside Waterfront Inn. *505 South Huron Avenue, Mackinaw City 49701; (231) 436–5001. The inn is 3 blocks south of Central, the town's main east-west road, along U.S. 23.* It has eighty-eight rooms with indoor pool. Beach and restaurants nearby. $$

Best Western of Mackinaw City. *112 Old U.S. 31, Mackinaw City 49701; (231) 436–5544 or (800) 647–8286. From I–75, exit at either exit 338 or 337 and go into town.* The property has seventy-three rooms with indoor pool. Continental breakfast included in room rates. Restaurants nearby. $$

Chief Motel. *10470 U.S. 23, Mackinaw City 49701, a mile south of town; (231) 436–7981.* This little motel has sixteen rooms, outdoor pool, picnic area, and beach access. $

Days Inn. *825 South Huron (U.S. 23), South Huron 49701; (231) 436–5557 or (800) 329–7466.* The inn has eighty-four rooms, indoor pool, restaurant, putting green, and shuffleboard. Located next to one of the ferry lines to the island. $$

Mackinaw Mill Creek Camping. *On U.S. 23, Mackinaw City 49701, 3 miles south of the city; (231) 436–5584.* Privately owned, with 600 sites, pool, playground, and minigolf. $

Wilderness State Park. *About 12 miles west of Mackinaw City via County Road 81 and Wilderness Park Drive, Mackinaw City 49701; (231) 436–5381, or (800) 447–2757.* A $4.00 daily or $20.00 annual motor vehicle permit is required for entry. Choose from 210 campsites or, in the heart of the park, six trailside cabins (and three group-style bunkhouses) reached by short hikes. They don't have electricity and are equipped with a woodstove for cooking and warmth, a hand pump for water, and a pit toilet. Cabins rent for $30.00 per night, plus a $4.00 reservation fee, and reservations are a must. A campsite costs $15.00 nightly.

For More Information

Mackinaw Area Tourist Bureau, *708 South Huron Avenue, Mackinaw City 49701; (231) 436–5574. Web site: www.mackinawcity.com.*

Upper Peninsula—East

ichigan's Upper Peninsula, the UP for short, can be divided into two distinct regions. The eastern part is where farms mix with forest, cities, and other attractions that make this section of the state unique. The western region is more rugged and wild. Bear, deer, moose, and many say even cougar roam.

Mackinac Island

Mackinaw City, the Mackinac Bridge's southern anchor, is one of the two spots to catch the high-speed ferry services that run to this unique vacation island. The other is St. Ignace, on the north end of the bridge. Those whom the islanders call "fudgies" (because most leave with its most popular export, fudge) are part of the hundreds of thousands who visit here annually. Historic spots around the island include War of 1812 battlefield sites, fur trading posts, and churches.

Tourists in search of cool breezes invade this island each summer day to walk its streets, ride its bike trails, and enjoy the jewel of a lake that surrounds it. Nearly the entire island is a state park. The pace slows on the island, and except for the clothes, it could be one hundred years ago, as the only modes of transportation here are horses, bicycles, and feet.

To get to Mackinac Island, leave from either the Mackinaw City side or the St. Ignace side of the bridge. Don't worry about missing the boat, unless it's late at night and you're due for an overnight stay. Ferries leave continuously from three docks and take about sixteen minutes to get across. Parking is generally **Free**. Call *Arnold Line* at (906) 643–3351, *Shepler's* at (800) 828–6157, or *Star* at (800) 638–9892.

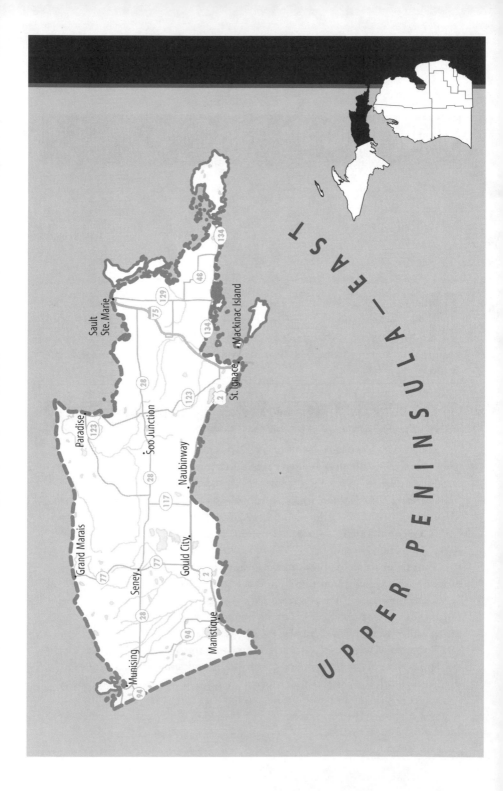

UPPER PENINSULA—EAST

Sault
Ste. Marie

Mackinac Island

St. Ignace

Paradise

Soo Junction

Naubinway

Grand Marais

Seney

Gould City

Munising

Manistique

Bicycle Rentals on Mackinac Island The number of bikes
for rent on the island are legion, and they need to be. Biking tours of
the island are fun, leisurely ways to enjoy the sights. Just make sure that
when you get back on, it's the one you've rented, as many look alike.
Bikes go for around $3.50 per hour, and there are rental booths down-
town.

SKULL CAVE (all ages)
*On the Garrison Road pathway and bicycle trail, actually the only state highway
where autos aren't allowed, Michigan 185.*

The cave, which resembles a skull from the outside, served as a
Native American burial chamber and also was the hiding place of local
settlers during the Native American revolt in 1763.

HORSE-DRAWN CARRIAGE TOURS (all ages)
*(906) 847–3573. Cost is $12.00 per person ages twelve and older, $6.00 for kids
ages four through eleven; ages three and younger ride* **Free**. *Tours run from 8:30
A.M. to 5:00 P.M. daily from mid-June through Labor Day and 8:30 A.M. to 4:00
P.M. daily from mid-May to mid-June and after Labor Day to mid-October. You can
usually find a seat when you land, but you can also call ahead for information.*

Tours leave daily from the ferry dock and several other points downtown and are great ways to become acquainted with the island. Between
jokes and the clip-clop (and other noises) coming from the horses, the
driver will tell you a lot about both the history of the island, before it
became a vacation spot, as well as the present. Tours take in Arch Rock
and Skull Cave and historical stops, along with a drive-by of the Governor's mansion, where he stays when he's on the island, and the grand
dame of summer hotels, the Grand Hotel.

You can also rent drive-it-yourself carriages, but the narrated tour is
the best way for newcomers to see it.

FORT MACKINAC STATE PARK (all ages)
*The fortress on a bluff above downtown Mackinac Island is part of the state park;
(906) 847–3328. Admission is $6.75 for adults, $4.00 for kids ages six through
twelve, or there is a $20.00 family rate. A combination ticket for Fort Mackinac
and the mainland's Colonial Michilimackinac and Historic Mill Creek is $13.00
for adults, $7.50 for kids ages six through twelve, or $38.00 for a family. Parks are
open daily from 9:00 A.M. to 6:00 P.M. from June 15 to Labor Day, with reduced
hours in spring and fall.*

Peer inside the quarters at Fort Mackinac State Park, which dates from 1780, when the British moved here from the mainland. They lost the fort after the Revolutionary War, regained it after invading the island during the War of 1812, and lost it for good afterwards.

In summer the fort is "patrolled" by actors who portray uniformed soldiers. They demonstrate cannon firing and musket practice and tell what life was like on station in the wilderness of the 1790s.

GRAND HOTEL (all ages)
(906) 847–3331 or (800) 334–7263.

Gleaming white on a hill looking toward the Lower Peninsula, the Grand is nearly the only structure one can easily identify from the mainland. Elegant it is, and summery, with its predominant colors of green, white, and yellow. There are 324 high-ceilinged rooms and the famous outdoor pool Esther Williams swam in. The 660-foot-long porch has plenty of wicker chairs and rockers to pass the day on. A few years ago, the hotel became so popular for drop-ins that it began charging nonguests just to come in, but the fee can be charged off to lunch, which is open to all comers. Dinner and breakfast are for guests only, and there's a coat-and-tie dress code after 6:00 P.M.

Attack of the 10,000 Fudgies

They're the attraction that coined the word *fudgie,* and they're located throughout downtown. One reason they're so popular? As employees cool and form the confection on marble tables strategically located in the front windows, shops also blow the sugar-sweet-laced exhaust air directly onto the streets, tempting your neurons to come inside for a sample. No fools, they. Warning: There's no known antidote. You'll find everything from peanut butter to pistachio, and chocolate walnut, too. My favorite brand? JoAnne's. Make the rounds and choose which you like best. Free samples are usually waiting inside.

Package stays are the best, most inexpensive ways to enjoy Grand Hotel, usually including two meals and two nights. Just ask your travel agent. Booking not using a package can be expensive. Rooms feature simple elegance, and some are themed, including a few that honor Hollywood greats who've made films here, complete with framed autographs. Early season, usually the weeks after opening in early May, and late season in October offer the best prices, which often feature theme weekends, from decorating to murder mysteries. Carriages meet all incoming ferries and transport you and your luggage to the hotel. There is no tipping.

If you're a guest, one of the best parts about a stay here is morning and being awakened by the sound of horse hoof-falls on the pavement outside. Cribs are available.

Where to Eat

Tourists do not live by fudge alone. There are plenty of places to grab a burger or other meal on the island. Most are downtown.

Mustang Lounge. *On 8 Astor Street, Mackinac Island 49757, off Main; (906) 874–9916.* The hangout for locals, which serves lunches and dinners that include burgers, hot dogs, and chicken. $$

Pink Pony. *1 Main Street, Mackinac Island 49757, in the Chippewa Hotel, downtown; (906) 847–3343.* Burgers and other items available, children's menu. $$

Where to Stay

Besides Grand Hotel, which is *the* place to stay, accommodations range from hotels to cozy bed and breakfasts, and most offer package stays that greatly trim the per-night charge. Inquire at each about them.

Island House. *1 Lakeshore Drive, Mackinac Island 49757, about 3 blocks east of the ferry dock; (906) 847–3347.* Here you'll find ninety-four rooms in an 1852-era hotel with pool and dining. Children's programs in summer. $$$

Lakeview Hotel. *1 Huron Street, Mackinac Island 49757, downtown; (906) 847–3384.* This restored 1862 hotel offers eighty-five rooms, pools, and restaurant. $$$

For More Information

Mackinac Island Chamber of Commerce, *P.O. Box 451, Mackinac Island 49757; (906) 847–6418 or (906) 847–3783.*

Bill's Top Family Adventures in Upper Peninsula–East

- **Mackinac Island.** You can't beat a bike ride with a half pound of fudge and the kids as your companions. Why the fudge? Silly question . . .

- **Soo Locks and Valley Camp, Sault Ste. Marie.** Grown-ups and kids alike will gawk at the huge freighters inches from the sides of the locks, at the trip through on the tour boats, and the enormity of the water flowing through the area each second. Boarding one of those freighters to see how they work and to get an idea of how huge they actually are is educational and great fun.

- **Tahquamenon Falls, Tahquamenon Falls State Park.** The twin falls are a scenic wonder.

- **Great Lakes Shipwreck Museum.** Learn about just how treacherous the lakes can be and why even seagoing vessels fear their storms.

- **Pictured Rocks National Lakeshore, Munising.** Another of Nature's wonders in the UP.

St. Ignace

St. Ignace was founded by Father Jacques Marquette in the 1600s. Besides being the other town to catch the ferry to Mackinac Island, St. Ignace hosts lots of special events. The Straits Area Antique Auto Show literally takes over town during the last full weekend of June each year. Avoid the hassle of finding a parking spot by heading for the **Free** parking lot just west of the bridge and taking a shuttle for $1.00. For further details call (800) 338–6660. Another waterfront car show is in mid-September.

CASTLE ROCK (all ages)

Off I–75 at exit 348 north of downtown; (906) 643–8268. Admission is just 25 cents per person. Open 9:00 A.M. to 9:00 P.M. from May 1 to October 15.

Head for one of two tourist attractions that have been here for decades. An ancient lookout used by Native Americans is one of the most inexpensive attractions you'll ever visit. It features a nearly 200-foot-tall limestone formation to climb, as well as a souvenir shop and campground.

MYSTERY SPOT (all ages)

Along U.S. 2, St. Ignace 49781, 5 miles west of the bridge; (906) 643–8322. Open 8:00 A.M. to 9:00 P.M. daily from early May through Labor Day and from 9:00 A.M. to 7:00 P.M. daily after Labor Day until late October. Admission is $4.00 for adults, $3.50 for kids ages five through eleven; children ages four and younger get in **Free**.

The spot is one of the region's first tourist draws that still brings in the curious (some would say gullible). Inside, see where the laws of physics are supposedly turned upside down by clever use of gravity and optical illusions. The kids will get a lesson in science and in the line made famous by P. T. Barnum. It's a fun diversion.

Where to Eat

Clyde's Drive-in. *Along west U.S. 2, St. Ignace 49781, west of downtown; (906) 643–8303.* Known for its three-quarter-pound burgers. $

The Galley. *241 North State Street, St. Ignace 49781, downtown; (906) 643–7960.* Features Great Lakes perch, whitefish, and a special Upper Peninsula delicacy, tasty sautéed whitefish livers, as well as chicken and burgers. $$

State Street Bar & Grill. *250 South State Street, St. Ignace 49781, downtown; (906) 643–9511.* Menu features pizza, burgers, and whitefish. $$

U.S. 2 Scenic Drive

Starting at the intersection with I-75, this two-lane highway has been called one of the nation's most beautiful regardless of the season, but especially in summer and fall. Follow it along bluffs for scenic overviews of the Lake Michigan shore and freighters a few miles off the coast. The highway then opens into miles of sandy beachfront where you can pull the car off the road and take a swim. Highway 2 is a scenic wonder for its entire length.

Where to Stay

This is motel central, if there ever was one. More than forty of them are spread along I-75, U.S. Highway 2, and downtown Business I-75, or State Street. There also are bed and breakfasts and nearby cottage resorts. During the height of the tourist season, plan on paying top dollar in town for a room with amenities such as a pool or beach. Prices start dropping as you travel west along U.S. Highway 2.

Best Western Georgian House Lakefront Inn. *1131 North State Street (Business I–75), St. Ignace 49781; (906) 643–8411. Take the downtown St. Ignace exit and follow State through town.* The inn has eighty-five rooms and indoor pool. Restaurant nearby. $$

Castle Rock Mackinac Trail Campark. *Four miles north of St. Ignace off I–75 at exit 348; (906) 643–9222 or (800) 333–8754.* Here you'll find eighty campsites on Lake Huron beach with playground, Laundromat. $

Clearwater Resort Hotel & Condos. *In nearby Brevort, about 20 miles west of the bridge along U.S. 2, Brevort 49760; (906) 292–5506 or (800) 638–6371.* I still classify this as the St. Ignace area because it is so accessible, the beachfront location unique, and the price is reasonable for what's offered. There are nineteen rooms below the bluff and on the Lake Michigan waterfront. A restaurant serves breakfast, lunch, and dinner. There's also swimming, 2,000 feet of private beach, and racquetball courts. $$

Comfort Inn. *927 North State Street (Business I–75), St. Ignace 49781; (906) 643–7733.* The inn has one hundred rooms, with indoor pool, exercise area, and beachfront. $$

Gustafson's Resort. *In Brevort, west of St. Ignace on the north side of U.S. 2; (906) 292–5541.* The resort has twenty-one motel rooms and cottages, too, with a restaurant that features great *pasties* (meat-filled pastries). Open May 15 to October 15. $$

Holiday Inn Express. *965 North State Street; St. Ignace 49781; (906) 643–0200.* This economical chain property offers eighty-five rooms and indoor pool. $$

K-Royale Motor Inn. *1037 North State Street (Business I–75), St. Ignace 49781; (906) 643–7737 or (800) 882–7122.* The inn has ninety-five rooms on Lake Huron beachfront, with **Free** continental breakfast, playground, and picnic area. Restaurants nearby. $

Lake Michigan Forest Campground. *On the lake, 16 miles west of town on U.S. 2, St. Ignace 49781; (906) 643–7900.* The campground has thirty-six rustic sites operated by the National Forest Service; on the beach. $

Pass de Pasties No visit to the UP is complete without a taste of that peninsular delicacy, the pasty. The original UP fast food, pasties are handheld meat pies filled with meat, rutabaga, carrots, potatoes, onions, and spices. Miners used to take pasties with them into the pits because they were easily eaten and stayed warm. You'll see pasty signs all over the UP, including the outskirts of Marquette and surrounding cities. Have fun holding your own taste contest to see which purveyor is best. If you get hooked, many will ship frozen pasties to your home.

For More Information

St. Ignace Tourist Association, *560 West State Street, St. Ignace 49781; (906)* *643–6950 or (800) 338–6660. Web site: http://visit-usa.com.mackinac.*

Naubinway

Naubinway is located along U.S. 2, about 40 miles west of St. Ignace. Settled in 1879, the town's name, in local Native American language, means "place of echoes." No, I haven't heard any. It's past was in lumbering, and present business focuses on tourism. There is a beach at the rest stop on U.S. 2.

 GARLYN FARM AND ZOOLOGICAL PARK (all ages)
Six miles east of Naubinway on U.S. 2, Naubinway 49762; (906) 477–1085. Open from 11:00 A.M. to 7:00 P.M. from April through December 24. Admission is $4.75 for adults, $3.75 for youth ages three through sixteen and **Free** *for ages two and younger. Family rate is $15.00. Stroller accessible. Web site: www.angelfire.com/biz/garlynfarm.*

The peninsula's largest collection of live animals in a parklike setting. More than two dozen species—including reindeer, wolves, sitka deer, llamas, ostrich, pheasants, and more—can be seen and fed. There's also a gift shop with wildlife-related items.

Sault Sainte Marie

Commonly called "The Soo," this city was founded by Father Jacques Marquette. Michigan's oldest city, it is now one of the state's most popular destinations for its natural and historical attractions. The waterway through town that looks like a river is actually a canal. It feeds the world's longest power plant and doubles as a fisheries research station for Lake Superior State University in town. The main tourist attractions are located along Portage Street.

SOO LOCKS INFORMATION CENTER AND LOCKS PARK HISTORIC WALKWAY (all ages)
Downtown along Portage Street, Sault Sainte Marie 49783; (906) 632–2394. The center is open daily 7:00 A.M. to 11:00 P.M., and the park is open daily 6:00 A.M. to midnight. **Free**. *Stroller access everywhere except the second-story observation platform.*

See the locks up close from the riverside. Step up alongside the concrete ditches and watch as ships inch their way inside, then are either raised or lowered without pumps to the level of Lakes Superior or Huron. The visitor center explains how it's done.

SOO LOCKS BOAT TOURS (all ages)

515 and 1157 East Portage Avenue, Sault Sainte Marie 49783; (906) 632–6301 or (800) 432–6301. Ships depart daily from mid-May through October starting at 9:00 A.M. Cost is $16.00 for adults, $13.00 for youths ages thirteen through eighteen; $7.00 for kids ages five through twelve, and **Free** *for children ages four and younger. Call ahead for times of the last trip. Web site: www.soolocks.com.*

For a real family treat, take a tour to see the giant Soo Locks up close and personal. Two-hour trips leave from two locations along the swift St. Marys River and travel up to and through the locks.

Captains narrate as you travel, explaining the history of how the raging St. Marys Rapids, dropping Lake Superior waters 22 feet into Lake Huron, forced ships to portage around the rapids on rails, and how the locks evolved from a wooden structure in 1855 to the longest in the world, handling 1,000-foot-long Great Lakes freighters. You'll drift by giant Canadian steel mills and past the Canadian shoreline before returning. Dinner cruises also are available at extra cost.

Away for the Weekend

Make your eastern UP headquarters for vacationing either in St. Ignace or The Soo. There are plenty of accommodation choices, and attractions from Mackinac Island and the Soo Locks, along with neighboring Canada, are close by. Tahquamenon Falls and Whitefish Point also are short drives away, as is Seney and the trout of the Fox River, where Ernest Hemingway fished and wrote about it in the Nick Adams stories. He tried to hide his fishing spot, however, or liked the name when he named his story's river the Big Two Hearted, after the stream to the north. For accommodations, families can't beat cottages for economical stays, as long as you check them out first.

SOO LOCKS TOUR TRAIN (all ages)

315 West Portage, Sault Sainte Marie 49783; (906) 635–5241 or (800) 387–6200. Tours leave on the half hour from Memorial Day through early October. Fare is $5.25 for adults, $3.50 for kids ages six through sixteen. Twin Soo

Tours are $9.75 for adults, $6.00 for children ages six through seventeen; five and younger ride 𝐅𝐫𝐞𝐞.

Take a tram ride past the city's historic buildings and other sites during a one-hour trip on this "train," actually shaded trailers pulled by a jeep. The two-hour version also will take you across the International Bridge for a short trip into Canada for shopping or sight-seeing.

Where to Eat

Abner's. *2865 Business I−75, Sault Sainte Marie 49783, off exit 392; (906) 632−4221. Turn toward town. Look for the restaurant on the right.* Good selection of American-style food in a rustic setting, including ample dinner buffets and a breakfast buffet in summer. $$

The Antlers. *804 East Portage Street, Sault Sainte Marie 49783, east of Business I−75; (906) 632−3571.* In a nondescript building is one of the most unusual eateries you'll ever encounter, right down to the snake curling up a tree built into one end of the bar. Canoes hang from the rafters, along with animal heads and other items bartered for meals by locals or found at estate sales. Pick out steaks from a cooler, or enjoy other items. It's a fun spot. $$

Freighters. *240 West Portage Street, Sault Sainte Marie 49783, inside the Ojibway Hotel; (906) 632−4100.* Here you'll find what is probably the best dining view of the locks, except for the tourboat dinner cruises. Enjoy breakfast, lunch, or dinner as the ships go by outside the panoramic windows. $$$

La Senorita. *4478 Business I−75, Sault Sainte Marie 49783, off exit 392; (906) 632−1114.* Good Mexican food, with some American dishes. $$

Studebaker's. *3583 Business I−75, Sault Sainte Marie 49783, off exit 392; (906) 632−4662. On the westbound side of the road.* Cute 1950s theme restaurant with lunch and dinner. Breakfast buffet on weekends. $$

Where to Stay

Best Western Sault Ste. Marie. *4281 Business I−75, Sault Sainte Marie 49783, off exit 392; (906) 632−2170.* The motel offers 111 rooms and indoor pool. Restaurant nearby. $$

Hampton Inn. *3295 Business I−75, Sault Sainte Marie 49783, just east off exit 392; (906) 635−3000.* The inn has eighty-two rooms and indoor pool. Restaurants nearby. $$

Ojibway Hotel. *240 West Portage Street; Sault Sainte Marie 49783, (906) 632−4100. Take Business I−75 into town to Portage Street and turn west.* This restored 1928 hotel is on the north side of the street. It has seventy-one modern rooms, indoor pool, and exercise room. $$$

Sunset Motel. *Outside the city on Mackinaw Trail, Sault Sainte Marie 49783; (906) 632–3906. From I–75, take exit 386 and head east to Michigan 28 and County Road H–63. The motel has fifteen rooms. Restaurant nearby.* $

For More Information

Sault Sainte Marie Convention and Visitors Bureau, *2581 I–75 Business Spur, Sault Sainte Marie 49783; (906)* *632–3301 or (800) 647–2858. Web site: www.saultstemarie.com.*

Soo Junction

Located along Michigan 28, west of Sault Sainte Marie. Soo Junction was settled in the 1890s and named for its location at the junction of two rail lines. The focus now is on bringing tourists to see the Tahquamenon Falls. Even though the town is a few miles south, the tiny town calls itself the home of the falls.

TOONERVILLE TROLLEY AND RIVERBOAT RIDE TO TAHQUAMENON FALLS (all ages)

Rides leave from Soo Junction, just north of Michigan 28 (watch for the sign); (906) 876–2311. Fare is $20.00 for adults and $10.00 for kids ages six through fifteen. The train-trip-only excursion runs Tuesday through Saturday in July and August and is $10.00 for adults, $5.00 for ages six through fifteen, four and younger ride Free. *Cruise times vary, so call ahead. Open mid-June through early October. Web site: www.uptravel.com/uptravel/attractions.*

See the falls that inspired Longfellow's epic poem "Hiawatha," either by car or all-day adventures that combine trains and riverboat rides that have been running more than seventy years. Near this map-dot town is an excursion lovingly nicknamed "the trolley." The six-and-a-half-hour trip combines a 5½-mile, thirty-five-minute railroad trip aboard the narrow-gauge train hauling up to 250 persons, followed by a 21-mile river cruise accompanied by narration and lots of wildlife from beaver to deer. After the boat docks, it's a short hike to the upper falls, where 50,000 gallons of tea-colored water spews over the lip each second. At 100 feet high, it's Michigan's largest falls and the second largest east of the Mississippi. It's one of nearly 150 waterfalls in the Upper Peninsula. If you're in a hurry, the trolley also offers the train ride only, a one-and-three-quarter-hour trip.

TAHQUAMENON FALLS STATE PARK (all ages)

On Michigan 123, Paradise 49768. From the Soo Junction area, head east on Michigan 28, then north on Michigan 123 about 22 miles to Paradise. The state park is 5 miles west of Paradise; (906) 492–3415 for information or (800) 447–2757 for reservations. The falls are open daily, year-round. Camping is $14.00 nightly. Entry is by $4.00 daily or $20.00 annual vehicle permit. Web site: www.elnr.state.mi.us/www/parks.

You can drive to see both the Upper and the cataract-like Lower Falls at this park, where camping is available at 180 sites near the falls and another 130 sites in its river mouth unit along Lake Superior. This park offers picnicking and hiking trails. Parking is available a short walk from both falls.

Where to Eat

Tahquamenon Falls Brewery and Pub. *Michigan 123, Paradise 49768, on private property within the boundaries of the state park; (906) 492–3300.* Lunch and dinner, along with house-brewed beer and root beer, are served in this log lodge near the river. $$

Timber Charlie's Food 'n Spirits. *110 Newberry, Newberry 49868, on the west side of Michigan 123; (906) 293–3363.* Local eatery serving lunch and dinner in a rustic setting. $$

Where to Stay

Comfort Inn Tahquamenon Falls. *At the intersection of Michigan 28 and 123, Newberry 49868; (906) 293–3218.* This basic motel has fifty-four rooms. Restaurant nearby. $$

Days Inn. *Along Michigan 28, Newberry 59868, east of Michigan 123; (906) 293–4000.* An economical chain motel offering forty-two rooms and indoor pool. Restaurant nearby. $$

Paradise

Some may not think of it as paradise in February, but after all, it was named for its site along Lake Superior, which is inviting to summer vacationers and winter snowmobilers.

GREAT LAKES SHIPWRECK MUSEUM (all ages)

110 Whitefish Point, Paradise 49768, just north of town; (906) 635–1742. Open from 10:00 A.M. to 6:00 P.M. daily from May 15 through October 15. Admission is $7.00 for adults, $6.00 for seniors, and $4.00 for kids ages twelve and younger. Family passes are $20.00. Web site: www.shipwreckmuseum.com.

A lighthouse at Whitefish Point, 20 miles north of Tahquamenon Falls, is now the museum, a haunting tribute to the more than 5,000 ships that ventured onto what explorers called the Great Northern Seas, never to make port.

Accompanied by the eerie words of Canadian singer-songwriter Gordon Lightfoot's ballad "The Wreck of the Edmund Fitzgerald," you'll see exhibits on many of the ships claimed by the lake's storms and other mishaps. From the wreck of the sailing schooner *Invincible* in 1816, and the great storm of 1913 to the loss of the *Fitzgerald* with twenty-nine hands aboard only a few miles west in the 1970s, your family will get a feel of what fury the lakes can hold and how even saltwater sailors fear them in bad weather. The working lighthouse is the oldest on Lake Superior, guiding ships around the point since 1849. The present structure has been there since 1861.

Where to Eat and Stay

See listings under Sault Sainte Marie or St. Ignace.

Gould City

Gould City was settled in 1886 and was named after a local lumberman. There's not much there now, except the following attraction:

MICHIHISTRIGAN (all ages)

On U.S. 2, Gould City 49838, 15 miles west of Naubinway; (800) 924–8873. The campground, cabins, and two restaurants are open year-round (there's also snowmobile trail access); the course is open from late May to late September. The cost of a minigolf round is $4.00 per person.

Want to teach your kids some Michigan history while having fun? It's not that difficult. Head to a unique miniature golf course 65 miles west of the Mackinac Bridge along U.S. Highway 2.

Owner Fred Burton began building a cartoon-themed minigolf course, but he changed his theme when he spilled some clay onto some ice in winter, and the more he added to it, the more it looked like a part of the Lower Peninsula.

The theme stuck, and so did the weird name, coined by Burton and his brainstorming wife. Using aerial photos of the state, he built a scale model of more than thirty acres. While you play, learn the history behind the towns after which each of the eighteen holes are named. At the nineteenth hole, fish for (or feed by hand) the stocked rainbow trout in the "Great Lakes" around the course, and then have dinner in the restaurant.

There's also a campground, and Burton's latest project is a nine-hole, full-size golf course.

Seney

In the 1800s, this tiny map-dot of a town was one of the most notorious lumber camps in the nation. Later, it figured in the Nick Adams short stories of novelist Ernest Hemingway, who vacationed and explored this area. It's also the eastern end of the "Seney stretch," a 20-plus-mile length of Michigan 28 that's straight as an arrow and features no services between Seney and Shingleton, to the west.

SENEY HISTORICAL MUSEUM (all ages)

In town. Open daily in summer. Call (906) 499–3322, and you'll reach the town supervisor, who can provide more information, including directions and hours.

The small museum explores Seney's colorful and often raucous past, when local characters reportedly bit the heads off snakes for fun, turned city folk just off the train upside down to shake out loose change, or, it was rumored, shanghaied the unsuspecting to work in lumber camps in the surrounding forests.

SENEY NATIONAL WILDLIFE REFUGE (all ages)

Just south of town along Michigan 77, Seney 49883; (906) 586–9851. The refuge is open during daylight hours only. The visitor center is open daily from 9:00 A.M. to 5:00 P.M. mid-May through mid-October. **Free**.

This refuge contains nearly 96,000 acres of wetland and woods. From a visitor center off Michigan 77, take a scenic drive through part of the refuge and get a chance to spot bald eagles, deer, Canada geese, and other wildlife.

Where to Eat

Golden Grill. *Downtown along Michigan 28, Seney 49883; (906) 499–3323.*

Fresh-made pasties (meat pies) and other dishes from breakfast onward. $

Where to Stay

Fox River Motel. *On the corner of Michigan 28, Seney 49883, at Michigan 77; (906) 499–3332 or (906) 499–3337.*

This local motel offers thirteen rooms. Restaurant nearby. $

Munising and Grand Marais

Munising is along Michigan 28. Grand Marais is along the Superior shore as well and is reached via Michigan 77 from Seney. It's considered the eastern gate to the Pictured Rocks, since County Road H–58 begins here.

PICTURED ROCKS CRUISES (all ages)

Cruises cost $22.00 for adults and $7.00 for kids ages six through twelve; children ages five and younger ride **Free**. *Departure times vary by month, so call ahead at (906) 387–2033. Boats run daily from the city dock in Munising from Memorial Day weekend through October 10. Web site: www.picturedrocks.com.*

In Munising are two waterborne attractions you shouldn't miss. This is one of them. See the lakeshore formations up close aboard the tour boats, leaving daily from Munising's downtown harbor, weather permitting. The 37-mile trips last nearly three hours and take you almost within touching distance of the rocks.

It's Always Christmas Here

In the town just over the hill, west from Munising on Michigan 28, it's Christmas every day. The town got the name "Christmas" from an old toy factory that no longer exists. Stop to have your picture taken in front of the giant Santa.

GRAND ISLAND SHIPWRECK TOURS (all ages)

1204 Commercial Street, Munising 49862; (906) 387–4477. Watch for the signs along Michigan 28, west of downtown. Cost is $20.00 for adults, $8.50 for *kids ages six through twelve; children ages five and younger ride* **Free**. *Tours leave at 10:00 A.M. and 5:00 P.M. in June and September and at 10:00 A.M. and 1:00 and 5:00 P.M. in July and August. Web site: www.shipwrecktours.com.*

A few blocks west of the Pictured Rocks Cruises departure point is the other don't-miss attraction, the Grand Island Shipwreck Tours. Step aboard Michigan's only glass-bottomed boat for a view of three of the 5,000 shipwrecks at the bottom of the Great Lakes. The 42-foot boat also takes up to one hundred passengers on two-and-a-half-hour narrated tours while sailing past Grand Island National Recreation Area. Wrecks you'll see include an intact 1860s-era, 160-foot-long cargo schooner.

Pictured Rocks National Lakeshore (all ages) Shaped by
wind and water over eons, the spectacular cliffs can be seen on both land and water. Administered by the National Park Service, the lakeshore encompasses 70,000 acres of wilderness along 42 miles of Lake Superior. Glacier-carved rocks and waves and wind have created rock formations that resemble battleship prows and castles, in multicolored hues from minerals seeping from the soil and rock. County Road 58 through the lakeshore from Grand Marais to Munising is open from May until the first large snowfall. It's about 25 paved miles and 30 miles of gravel that at times can be pretty rough, so inquire about its condition, especially at the eastern end.

Drivers can stop at platforms at spots like Grand Sable Dunes and the Miners Castle to look down onto the lake 200 feet below. Three rustic campgrounds plus backpack camps for backcountry hikers are available here. A visitor center is in Munising at Michigan 28 and County Road H–58, Munising 49862. For information call (906) 387–3700. Web site: www.nps.gov/piro.

MUNISING FALLS (all ages)
On Sand Point Road, Munising 49862, about 3 miles east of town. Open anytime. Access is via a paved path. **Free**.

One of six waterfalls within the city limits, the Munising Fall's water here drops over the lip of a huge natural amphitheater.

Where to Eat

Dogpatch. *820 East Superior, Munising 49862, downtown a block east of Michigan 28; (906) 387–9948.* Good family din- ing for breakfast, lunch, and dinner in a rustic setting. Serves items from pancakes to steak. $$$

Where to Stay

Best Western. *On Michigan 28, Wetmore 49895, east of downtown Munising about 3 miles; (906) 387–4864. Web site: www.munising.org/l_bestwestern.htm.* This chain motel has eighty rooms, indoor pool, and a restaurant that serves breakfast through dinner. $$

Camel Riders Restaurant and Resort. *On Forest Highway (FH) 13, Wetmore 49895, south of Munising; (906) 573–2319. Take Michigan 94 south to FH 13, head south to County Road 440, and* then turn east. Located on this area's version of the chain of lakes. Cabins with boats provided for stays by the day or, if available, overnight. Towels aren't provided, so bring your own. The adjacent restaurant is open for breakfast, lunch, and dinner. $$

Terrace Motel. *420 Prospect, Munising 49862, east of Michigan 28; (906) 387–2735.* The motel has eighteen rooms and a sauna. Restaurant nearby. Pets okay. $

For More Information

Alger County Chamber of Commerce, *422 East Munising Avenue,* *Munising 49862; (906) 387–2138. Web site: www.munising.org.*

Manistique

A new route for U.S. Highway 2 bypasses downtown Manistique to go closer to the Lake Michigan shoreline. There are walkways along the beach, but be sure to drive into town on Business U.S. 2.

SIPHON BRIDGE (all ages)
In town along Business U.S. 2, across the Manistique River. Free.
The river is actually higher than the bridge. A marker at the bridge explains how it's done.

PALMS BOOK STATE PARK, BIG SPRING (all ages)

Turn north from U.S. 2 onto Michigan 149 and follow it and the signs about 10 miles; (906) 341–2355. Admission is by state vehicle entry permit, which costs $4.00 daily and $20.00 annually.

It was called *Kitch-iti-kipi,* or "Mirror of Heaven," by Native Americans, and it's easy to see why when you stare into this pool of crystal-clear spring water. Board the rope-tethered raft with a center viewing area and let the kids pull your family across the 200-foot-wide spring. About halfway across, look down. Some 60 feet below you, huge trout are being tickled by the 16,000 gallons of water that flow out of the boiling bottom each minute, at a constant temperature of forty-five degrees. It empties into a river that feeds nearby Indian Lake. Sorry, no fishing's allowed, and there's no camping here. However, there are hiking trails and a gift shop.

Bill's Favorite Events in Upper Peninsula–East

- **Sled Dog Endurance and Fun Winterfest** (January), St. Ignace, (906) 643-8717

- **I-500 Snowmobile Race** (February), Sault Sainte Marie, (800) 647-2858

- **Tahquamenon Falls Nordic Invitational Ski Race** (March), Newberry, (906) 293-5562

- **Spring Show** (April), Sault Sainte Marie, (906) 632-3301

- **Memorial Day Celebration** (May), Mackinac Island, (906) 847-3783

- **Straits Antique Auto Show** (June), St. Ignace, (906) 643-8717

- **Art Fair** (July), Manistique Marina, (906) 341-5010

- **Antique Wooden Boat Show** (August), Hessel, (906) 484-3935 or (888) 364-7526

- **Mackinac Bridge Walk** (September), St. Ignace, (906) 643-7600

- **Autumn Apple Days** (October), St. Ignace, (906) 643-8717

- **Christmas Parade of Lights** (November), Sault Sainte Marie, (906) 632-3301

- **Red Cross Tour of Homes** (December), Sault Sainte Marie, (906) 632-8111

303

Where to Eat

The Nifty 50s. *Three miles east of town along U.S. 2, Manistique 49854, in Fairview Square; (906) 341–6464.* Malts, ice cream, and more in summer. $

Sunny Shores Restaurant. *Along U.S. 2, Manistique 49854; (906) 342–5582.* Open from mid-April through midwinter, this restaurant offers inexpensive meals for breakfast, lunch, and dinner. $

Where to Stay

Best Western Breakers Motel. *Two miles east of town on U.S. 2, Manistique 49854; (906) 341–2410.* The motel has forty rooms, indoor and outdoor pool, and beach access. Restaurant nearby. $$

Cottages and Resorts. There are quite a few to choose from, especially along Indian Lake's shoreline. Compare before you reserve so you won't be disappointed. Don't expect ritzy accommodations at many, but there are also quite a few comfortable, inexpensive places. A list is available from the local chamber of commerce.

Econolodge. *Along U.S. 2, Manistique 49854, 1½ miles east of town; (906) 341–6014.* This property has thirty-one rooms. Restaurant nearby. Small pets okay at extra charge. $$

For More Information

Manistique Area Tourist Council, *(906) 341–5853 or (800) 342–4282. Web site: www.uptravel.com/uptravel/counties/schoolcraft/schoolcraft.htm.*

Schoolcraft County Chamber of Commerce, *1000 West Lakeshore Drive (U.S. 2), Manistique 49854; (906) 341–5010. Web site: www.manistique.com.*

Upper Peninsula—West

Y ou want wilderness? It's got wilderness. You want big cities? It's got the biggest in the region. The western Upper Peninsula is a mix of the historic and the present-day, from ghost towns where copper and iron ore once ruled to modern cities where iron ore still plays a big part in the economy. Tourism is also important here, especially in winter and summer. This region is what many people think of when they talk about the Upper Peninsula, or the UP for short. For general UP information, call the Upper Peninsula Tourism and Recreation Association in downtown Iron Mountain at (906) 774–5480 or (800) 562–7134. Web site: www.uptravel.com.

Marquette

Marquette was fortunate enough to prosper from the right combination of time and the growth of America. When surveyors Douglas Houghton and, later, William Burt reported crazy readings coming from iron-ore outcroppings on the surface in Negaunee, the rush was on. Combined with the copper country in the far western UP, it caused a land rush that rivaled California's gold rush in the mid-1840s.

They still mine iron ore here, but emphasis is on the rich vein of tourism that the area attracts, too. You'll be surprised at the town's beauty. Downtown and only a few miles outside, moose, bear, and, some say, even mountain lion roam.

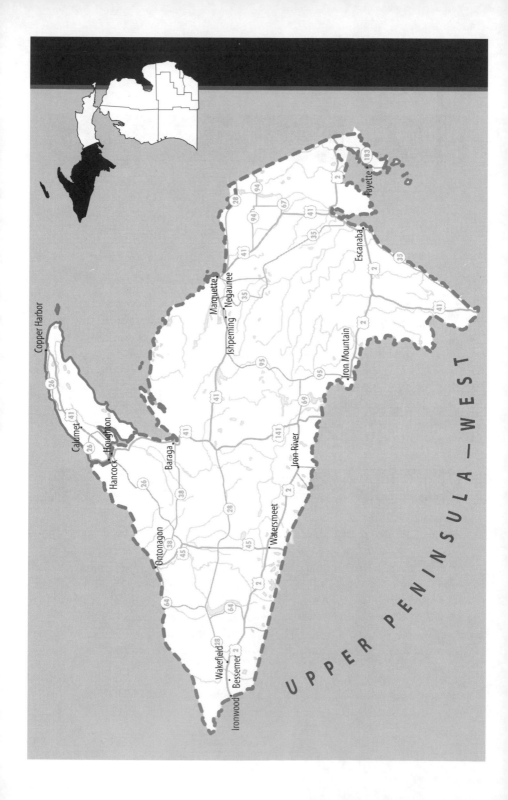

Copper Harbor

Calumet
Houghton
Hancock
Baraga
Ontonagon
Wakefield
Bessemer
Ironwood
Watersmeet
Iron River
Iron Mountain
Ishpeming
Negaunee
Marquette
Escanaba
Payette

UPPER PENINSULA — WEST

PRESQUE ISLE PARK (all ages)

At the north end of the city in the area called the Upper Harbor, at the end of Lakeshore Boulevard, Marquette 49855; (906) 228–0460. Open daily from 7:00 A.M. to 11:00 P.M. Admission is **Free**.

Presque Isle Park is a jewel, designed by Frederick Law Olmsted, the same landscape architect who created New York's Central Park and Detroit's Belle Isle. A small road leads around the 328-acre facility perched on a rock outcropping jutting into Lake Superior. At the entrance, you might see a Great Lakes ore freighter tied up to Marquette's huge ore dock, where high-grade iron ore pellets thunder into ship holds from bins. Overlooks in the park are countless. Picnic facilities and an outdoor pool are located here as well. The pool and a waterslide are open daily from noon to 8:00 P.M. They are **Free**.

GREAT NORTHERN ADVENTURES (ages 12 and up)

(906) 225–TOUR. Trips operate year-round. Some general prices are: $75 per person for a day of kayaking; $175 per person for a day of dogsledding; and $315 per person for a two-night trip to the ice caves (includes all food, lodging, and guide services). Call for more specific price information, or write Great Northern Adventures, P.O. Box 361, Marquette 49855. Web site: www.greatnorthernadventures. com.

Now if your family's idea of enjoying winter is cuddling under a blanket with the TV remote or a good book, Rah Trost wants to show you something different, with a bit of Jack London thrown in. Trost takes groups from neophytes to experts on what may be some of the most unusual adventure trips you'll ever experience. In winter, it may be an overnight journey by dogsled into Michigan's woods. Trost will teach you how to handle a dog team even on the one-night tour. Like the characters in one of London's novels, you'll mush into the woods, help set up camp, and, with no light other than your headlamp and the fire, and despite your probable best efforts to the contrary, you'll learn to enjoy it.

Other winter trips include treks to the area's famous but little-visited ice caves of Rock River Canyon Wilderness Area. Just so you aren't roughing it too much, many of the overnight trips use inns or motels as base lodging, or even inn-to-inn adventures. In summer, Trost leads you into the woods on backpacking and mountain biking/kayak trips.

MARQUETTE COUNTRY TOURS (all ages)

809 West College Avenue, Marquette 49855; (906) 226–6167. Prices vary depending on type of trip, so call for specific information.

Besides canoeing and hiking trips, operators also take visitors on less-rugged four-wheel-drive trips to waterfalls, to old mines, and on historic tours, as well as on sight-seeing treks after the elusive Upper Peninsula moose. Trips may be custom-designed according to your family's needs and desires.

 UPPER PENINSULA CHILDREN'S MUSEUM (ages 3–11)

123 West Baraga Avenue, Marquette 49855; (906) 226–3911. From Michigan 28/U.S. 41, go north on Front Street to Baraga Avenue and turn west. Admission is $4.50 for adults and $3.00 for seniors and children ages two through seventeen. Open Monday through Thursday and Saturday 10:00 A.M. to 6:00 P.M., Friday 10:00 A.M. to 8:00 P.M., and Sunday noon to 5:00 P.M. Web site: www.up.net/~ron/upcm.

One of the city's newest family-friendly attractions is the Upper Peninsula Children's Museum. Located downtown, most of the exhibits were suggested by local youngsters and illustrate concepts such as the importance of groundwater. Kids love it.

 MARQUETTE MOUNTAIN SKI AREA (ages 7 and up)

Just south of town on County Road 553, Marquette 49855; (906) 225–1155. From U.S. 41/Michigan 28, turn west on Furnace near the Pizza Hut. Follow it to Division and go south until it ends. Then take 553 south to the ski area.

One of the state's higher ski areas, this one has eight runs, instruction for adults and children, and rental equipment.

"Waterfalling" There may be more, but there are at least a dozen waterfalls within Marquette County, some of the hundreds across the peninsula. Typical is Warner Falls, which can be viewed from the highway as it plunges 20 feet. To reach it, take Michigan 28 west about 5 miles, and then turn south onto Michigan 35. Drive 9 miles, and then continue about ½ mile beyond the town of Palmer. The falls are on the right side of the road. Find more listed on a **Free** map from the local visitors bureau (see For More Information at the end of the Marquette section).

Where to Eat

Jean Kay's Pasties & Subs. *1639 Presque Isle Avenue, Marquette 49855; (906) 228–5310 or (800) 727–2922. Leave U.S. 41/Michigan 28 and continue north on Front Street to Washington Street. Turn west to Fourth Street and go north. It jogs to become Presque Isle.* Authentic UP pasties, an enclosed meat pie that was a favorite of UP miners and now is something everybody's at least got to taste. They're made vegetarian style, too. $

Marquette Harbor Brewery and Historic Vierling Saloon. *Corner of Front and Main Streets, Marquette 49855, downtown; (906) 228–3533.* The Vierling may have left its shady saloon days behind, but it still keeps the name of this downtown landmark. It's now a brewpub with a family atmosphere and a children's menu to prove it. Open for lunch and dinner. $$

Northwoods Supper Club. *In the woods, but easy to find, 3½ miles west of downtown on U.S. 41/Michigan 28, at 260 Northwoods Road, Marquette 49855. Turn south at the sign; (906) 228–4343.* Another landmark restaurant here, open since 1934 and still using the original log building that's been expanded a few times. Serves lunch, dinner, and Sunday brunch. Children's menu available. $$$

Sweetwater Cafe. *517 North Third Street, Marquette 49855; (906) 226–7009. North and west of downtown, bordering the campus of Northern Michigan University.* Innovative meals for lunch and dinner in a university-style setting. $$

Thill's Fish House. *At the end of East Main Street, Marquette 49855, 1 block east of Front Street; (906) 226–9851.* Fresh-caught and smoked fish are a specialty. $

Where to Stay

Days Inn. *2403 U.S. 41 west, Marquette 49855, about 5 miles west of downtown; (906) 225–1393.* This economical motel has sixty-five rooms, indoor pool, suana, and **Free** continental breakfast. Restaurants nearby. $$

Landmark Inn. *230 North Front Street downtown, Marquette 49855; (906) 228–2580 or (888) LANDMARK.* A classic downtown hotel with sixty-two overnight rooms, most decorated with items that look back on Marquette's history, some even tongue-in-cheek. The Abbott and Costello Room was named, for instance, after the appearance that the comedy pair made here during World War II. Another is decorated like a UP hunting cabin. There's a health spa, and a restaurant that serves breakfast, lunch, and dinner. $

For More Information

Marquette Country Convention and Visitors Bureau, *2552 U.S. 41 West, Suite 30, Marquette 49855; (906) 228–* 7749 or (800) 544–4321. Web site: www.marquettecountry.org.

Negaunee

This is the city that began it all for the state's iron industry, when the area's first iron mine opened here in 1846.

MICHIGAN IRON INDUSTRY MUSEUM (all ages)

73 Forge Road, Negaunee 49866; (906) 475–7857. From U.S. 41, take Michigan 35 south to County Road 492. Go west to Forge Road and turn north to the museum. Hours are 9:30 A.M. to 4:30 P.M. from May through October. Admission is **Free**. *Wheelchair access also is available. Web site: www.sos.state.mi.us/ history/museum/museiron/index.html.*

This unique museum chronicles the life both above and below the earth of the immigrant miners who came to the UP's Marquette Iron Range and two other mining sites. Using a special time-line motif, exhibits tell the range's past from prehistory to the present. Mining cars and other equipment are also on display. Hands-on exhibits for the kids include a model of the Soo Locks and a working model of an ore freighter and loading dock. Visitors walk to the museum on paths through part of a typical UP forest to give them a sense of what the country was like when it was new.

Where to Eat and Stay

See Marquette listing.

Ishpeming

Mine headframes still tower over the city that was the center of the area's mining industry, where the ground still bleeds red after a rain from the iron it contains. Nearly all of the town lies south of U.S. 41/Michigan 28. The historic downtown area is along Division Street. Take Lakeshore Drive south from U.S. 41/Michigan 28.

TILDEN OPEN PIT MINE TOURS (ages 10 and up)

Tours run from mid-June to mid-August and leave from the Ishpeming Chamber of Commerce at 12:30 P.M.; (906) 486–4841. Due to safety concerns, the tour is open only to adults and to children ages ten and older accompanied by adults. No open-toed shoes, dresses, or skirts allowed. Cost is $6.00 per person. Reservations are a must.

After you've seen the iron museum, you can see where iron ore is still being mined, down and dirty, still driving the western UP's economy. Now families can take daily tours of the giant. One of two such operations in the UP, this mine offers two-hour tours that take you from an overlook of the 500-foot-deep pit to the giant refining mill, where ore is crushed and formed in the world's largest kilns into marble-size taconite pellets ready for rail transport to Marquette's freighter docks.

Bill's Favorite Events in Upper Peninsula—West

- **Michigan Tech Winter Carnival** (January), Houghton, (906) 487-2818

- **Winter Fun Fest** (February), Ishpeming, (906) 486-4841

- **Camper, R.V. and Travel Show** (March), Superior Dome, Marquette, (906) 227-1032

- **Kiwanis Sports and Recreation Show** (April), Escanaba, (800) 437-7496

- **Arts and Crafts Show** (May), Marquette, (906) 226-8864

- **Annual Riverfest** (June), Ontonagon, (906) 884-4735

- **Art on the Rocks Show and Sale and Outback Art Show and Sale** (July), Marquette, (906) 225-1952

- **Keweenaw Bay Indian Community Pow-Wow** (July), Ojibwa Campground near Baraga, (906) 353-6623

- **Upper Peninsula Rodeo** (July), Iron County Fairgrounds in Iron River, (906) 265-5605

- **UP Vintage Tin Antique Car Show** (July), Ludington Park in Escanaba, (906) 786-2192 or (800) 437-7496

- **Waterfront Art Festival** (August), Ludington Park in Escanaba, (906) 786-2192 or (800) 437-7496

- **Porkiefest** (September), Porcupine Mountains State Park, Ontonagon/Silver City, (906) 885-5885

- **Leif Erickson Fall Festival** (October), Norway, (906) 563-7172

- **Christmas Tree Galleria** (November), Caspian, (800) 225-3620

- **Old Fashioned Christmas Fair** (December), Wakefield, (906) 224-8151

DA YOOPERS TOURIST TRAP (all ages)

490 U.S. 41/Michigan 28, Ishpeming 49849; (906) 485–5595. West of town; watch for the signs. Open 9:00 A.M. to 9:00 P.M. Monday through Friday from Memorial Day until December; shorter hours thereafter.

You've got to see this store to believe it. Da Yoopers, a singing group who poke fun at UP life, right down to "da accent," opened a shop to sell souvenirs, oddities, and other folderol, hence the unabashed name. The group's irreverent music has become so popular around the state, Da Yoopers tour each year.

Outside, someone's built a "replica" UP deer camp, and there are other items unique to the peninsula, including a giant mosquito and nowhere-else-but-the-UP contraptions like a snowmobile on motorcycle wheels to ride in summer. It's a fun place to visit, and a tape or CD of Da Yoopers to play in the car will help put you in a "Yoo P frame-a-mind, you betcha."

Where to Eat

See Marquette listing.

Where to Stay

Best Western Country Inn. *850 U.S. 41 west, Ishpeming 49849, north of town; (906) 485–6345.* This chain property offers sixty rooms, indoor pool, and restaurant. $$

Van Riper State Park. *Seventeen miles west of Ishpeming on Michigan 41; (906) 339–4461 for information or (800) 447–2757 for reservations. Entry is by $4.00 daily or $20.00 annual vehicle permit. Camping is extra.* There are 189 sites, with a boat launch and swimming on Lake Michigamme. Fishing has taken somewhat of a downturn on the lake, but it's in a beautiful park in the midst of moose country. A plaque erected by the Michigan Outdoor Writers Association tells visitors of the moose lift that used helicopters to transplant Canadian animals to the woods here to reintroduce the species to this part of the UP. Hiking trails take strollers past old mine sites. $

For More Information

Ishpeming-Negaunee Chamber of Commerce, *661 Palms Avenue, Ishpeming 49849; (906) 486–4841. Web site: www.ishneg.bresnanlink.net.*

Escanaba

Besides its historical importance as a Great Lakes port and center for iron-ore shipment, Escanaba also is a favorite for anglers. Big and Little Bays de Noc are popular for walleye salmon, and it's one of the few areas of the state known for "coaster" brook trout, larger than their stream cousins because they live in the open lake. The county has the most freshwater shoreline of any in the nation. Lots of things in town and the area are named "Ludington," including the city's main street, after Nelson Ludington, an early lumberman.

UPPER PENINSULA STATE FAIR (all ages)

Takes place in mid-August each year at the fairgrounds at the eastern outskirts of Escanaba along U.S. 2; (906) 786–4011. Admission is $3.00 for adults, $1.00 for kids ages five through eleven, and Free *for kids younger than five. Grandstand shows are extra. Parking is $1.00. Web site: www.upstatefair.com.*

Michigan is so large, we need two state fairs to cover the bounty that the summer brings. This one comes first, and then the Michigan State Fair, in Detroit, takes place the week before and including Labor Day weekend. Tilt-A-Whirl and tractor-pull fans can get their fill here among the daily entertainment, and plenty of offbeat, family-fun attractions make this state fair an exciting event for the entire family, from pig racing to baking and homemaker-of-the-year contests. With respect for the peninsula's heritage, Native American Day is celebrated with traditional tribal dances and other activities. At the grandstand, watch for big-name country and rock stars, as well as motorcycle racing.

Where to Eat

Delona Restaurant. *Located 4½ miles north of Escanaba along U.S. 2/41, Escanaba 49829; (906) 786–6400.* A local favorite for breakfast, lunch, and dinner in a log cabin atmosphere. $$

Dobber's Pasties. *827 North Lincoln (U.S. 2/41), Escanaba 49829, just north of the intersection with Ludington Avenue in Escanaba; (906) 786–0222 or (800) 786–4443. Web site: www.dobberspasties. com.* Lots of pasty gourmets contend that these are the Upper Peninsula's

best. I've had both meat and veggie varieties, and they're great. They also ship. $

Hereford & Hops Restaurant & Brewpub. *624 Ludington, Escanaba 49829, inside the Delta Hotel downtown; (906) 789–1945.* Four varieties of home-brewed beer, plus home-brewed root beer for the kids. Eat there or carry out. Food ranges from burgers to chicken and fish. $$

Where to Stay

Bay View Motel. *7110 U.S. 2/41, Gladstone 49837, about 4½ miles north of Escanaba; (906) 786–2843 or (800) 547–1291.* The motel has twenty-four rooms, indoor pool, sauna, and playground. Restaurant nearby. $

Best Western Pioneer Inn. *2635 Ludington Avenue, Escanaba 49829, about 1*

mile west of town on U.S. 2/41. (906) 786–0602. The inn has seventy-three rooms, indoor pool, and restaurant. $$

Fishery Pointe Beach Cottages. *E5041 M–35, Escanaba 49829, 5 miles south of town; (906) 786–1852.* Nine cottages on Lake Michigan, beach, and sauna. Usually rents weekly. $$

For More Information

Delta County Chamber of Commerce, *230 Ludington Street, Escanaba 49829; (906) 786–2192 or (888)*

335–8264. Web sites: www.DeltaMI.org or www.deltafun.com.

Fayette

You don't have to travel to the West to see a real ghost town—just go to Fayette, now a state park. Located along Lake Michigan's Bay De Noc, the former iron-smelting town once was home to more than 500 employees of the Jackson Mine Company and their families from 1867 to 1891. Raw ore was brought to the town, where it was refined into blocks of iron called "pigs" in its charcoal-fired furnaces. The pig iron was later shipped down the lake to Chicago, Detroit, and Cleveland for steelmaking. Once the trees for charcoal-making disappeared, and larger ships were built to carry raw ore south, the town slowly died out.

 FAYETTE STATE HISTORIC PARK (all ages)
To reach the park, turn south off U.S. 2 onto Michigan 183 and follow the signs about 17 miles to the town of Garden; (906) 644–2603 for information or (800) 447–2757 for reservations. The historic site is open daily 8:00 A.M. to 8:00 P.M. from May 15 through October 15. Entry is by state park vehicle permit, $4.00 daily or $20.00 annually. Camping is extra. Web site: www.state.mi.us/www/parks.
About 10 miles from Escanaba, one of the peninsula's largest cities, this historic site will take you back more than one hundred years. Pilings that once supported docks that Great Lakes schooners called home still dot the shoreline of the bay.

In the visitor center, a scale model of the city at its heyday will orient you to what's outside. Along with reconstructed kilns and furnaces are twenty restored original buildings. There are sixty-one campsites as well, plus miles of easy hiking and cross-country ski trails at another part of the park.

Where to Eat and Stay

See Escanaba listing.

Baraga and L'Anse

STURGEON RIVER GORGE PARK (all ages)
Along the west side of U.S. 41, 17 miles south of Baraga. Open all year daylight to dusk. Free.

See the Sturgeon River surge through sheer rock cliffs at the river and falls. A path takes walkers on a short hike through the woods from the parking area along the river as the noise from the falls gets closer. Rapids culminate in the falls, where the river, colored like tea from the tannic acid it's carrying, enters the rock gorge. Keep track of small children near the river. There is no stroller access, so bring your child backpack.

Where to Eat

Carla's. *On Route 1, Baraga 49908; (906) 353–6256. Six miles north of Baraga on U.S. 41, inside Carla's Lake Shore Motel.* Fresh fish and steaks for dinner. Children's menu. $$

The Hilltop. *On U.S. 41, L'Anse 49946, 1 mile south of town; (906) 524–7858.* Cinnamon buns bigger than your fist await on the north side going into L'Anse, looking over the scenic Keweenaw Bay. Buns are $1.95 each. The restaurant also serves breakfast, lunch, and dinner. $

Where to Stay

Baraga State Park. *A mile south of town on U.S. 41, Baraga 49908; (906) 353–6558 for information or (800)* *447–2757 for reservations. Web site: dnr.state.mi.us/www.parks. Along Keweenaw Bay near Baraga. A $4.00 daily or $20.00*

315

annual fee sticker is required for entry. Camping is $11.00 nightly. The park offers 119 sites and a minicabin that sleeps four. As one might guess, road noise can keep light sleepers awake, as U.S. 41 travels right by the park along the bay. You can swim in Lake Superior, if you dare, from a beach. The lake temperature rarely rises above fifty degrees in late summer. There's also a short hiking trail. $

Best Western Baraga Lakeside Inn. *900 U.S. 41, Baraga 49908; (906) 353–7123.* The inn has thirty-six rooms, indoor pool, and restaurant. $$

Carla's Lake Shore Motel. *On U.S. 41, Baraga 49908, 6 miles north of town; (906) 353–6256.* This basic motel has ten rooms. Pets okay at extra charge. $

Ojibwa Campground. *Two miles north of Baraga; watch for the sign and turn west; (906) 353–6623.* This tribal-run campground has fifty sites. Beach nearby. $

Houghton

Located along U.S. Highway 41 in the middle of the Keweenaw Peninsula, Houghton and several nearby cities—Hancock to the south and Lake Linden, Laurium, and Calumet to the north—are at the heart of hundreds of years of Upper Peninsula history revolving around the decades when copper was the main export here. When Horace Greeley coined the famous phrase "Go West, young man" in the mid-1800s, he wasn't talking about California. He was referring to the massive copper strikes in the UP. In all, the Keweenaw Peninsula produced more than eight-and-a-half billion—yup, *billion*—pounds of copper. The sites in this area will tell you the story. Houghton also is home to Michigan Technological University, or Michigan Tech for short.

MICHIGAN TECH WINTER CARNIVAL (all ages)

Held in late January to early February on the campus of Michigan Tech. For information and directions, call (906) 487–2818.

The Keweenaw gets a lot of winter, sometimes running from November well into May, and holds one of the oldest celebrations of all that snow, dating from 1922. It brightens up the campus and is run by students. The four-day event's highlight is the construction of huge snow and ice sculptures to conform with the particular year's chosen theme. The structures extend along U.S. 41 for more than 1½ miles. Be prepared for cold, as temperatures can reach a balmy twenty degrees below zero. Dorms provide convenient warming shelters.

Where to Eat

Suomi Home Bakery & Restaurant.
*54 Huron Street, Houghton 49931, down-
town, "under the covered street"; (906)
482–3220.* Serves breakfast all day

along with other meals, including
Finnish dishes, great pasties, and other
items. $

Where to Stay

If you want inexpensive lodging, this is
the region. You'll still find plenty of
local motels with few amenities where
three persons can still get change back
from $50.

Best Western Franklin Square Inn.
*820 Shelden Avenue (U.S. 41), Houghton
49331; (906) 487–1700.* The inn has

102 rooms, restaurant, and indoor
pool. Pets okay. $$

Vacationland Motel. *About 3 miles
southeast of Houghton on U.S. 41, Houghton
49931; (906) 482–5351.* This basic
motel has twenty-four rooms and out-
door pool. $

For More Information

Keweenaw Tourism Council, *1197
Calumet Avenue, Calumet 49931; (906)*

*482–2388 or (800) 338–7982. Web site:
www.keweenaw.org.*

Keweenaw National Historical Park At the core of three
towns in the Keweenaw Peninsula is this national park, actually a
public-private mix of attractions ranging up and down the peninsula,
including the Quincy Mine Hoist in Hancock and the Coppertown USA
Museum in Calumet. For general information on the park, call (906)
337–5768 or write Keweenaw National Historical Park, P.O. Box 471,
Calumet 49931. Web site: www.nps.gov/kewe/.

Hancock

This former mining town is just south of Houghton along U.S. Highway 41. From
Hancock north, the highway is considered one of the state's most scenic, travel-
ing past lakes and through groves of hardwoods that nearly blot out the sun. The
drive is spectacular any time of year but is especially so in summer and fall.

QUINCY MINE HOIST (all ages)

Part of the Keweenaw Peninsula National Park, the Quincy Mine is atop the hill on the Hancock side of the Keweenaw shipping canal, along U.S. 41, Hancock 49931; (906) 482–5569 or (906) 482–3101. Admission is $3.00 for adults and children for the surface tours; combined surface and underground tours cost $12.50 for adults, $7.00 for children ages six to twelve, and free *for children five and younger. Open 10:00 A.M. to 5:00 P.M. daily from May through October. Web site: www.nps.gov/kewe/.*

The machinery comprises the world's largest ore hoist, on display at the old Quincy mine. The famed shaft operated from 1848 to the 1960s, producing 300 million pounds of copper. When the last load of ore was hauled up, its shafts had reached nearly 2 miles under the city and Lake Superior. Visit the hoist room, where you'll see the hoist and photos of what it was like working deep in the mine, where temperatures were in the nineties. The shaft house is the area's most recognizable structure, standing 150 feet tall.

As part of the park displays, you can also step into a portion of the mine worked in the 1960s and then used by Michigan Tech for classes. You'll travel 2,000 feet into the hill to view original workings from the Civil War era, and into the huge *stopes,* or mined-out underground rooms. A gift shop features historical photos, books, and paintings.

Where to Eat

See Houghton listing.

Where to Stay

Best Western Copper Crown Motel. *235 Hancock Avenue (U.S. 41), Hancock 49930; (906) 482–6111.* The motel has forty-seven rooms, indoor pool, and saunas. Restaurants nearby. $

F. J. McLain State Park. *North of Hancock 10 miles along Michigan 203, Hancock 49930; (906) 482–0278 for information* or (800) 447–2757 for reservations. Web site: www.dnr.state.mi.us/www/parks. There is a $4.00 daily or $20.00 annual vehicle entry fee. Camping is $14.00 nightly. The park has 103 campsites along the bluffs on the Lake Superior shoreline, with a beach and swimming. Also hiking paths. $

Calumet

Founded in the 1860s, for decades the town was, along with nearby Houghton Hancock, the center of copper mining on the Keweenaw Peninsula. Area Web site: www.uptravel.com/uptravel/attractions/44.htm.

COPPERTOWN USA MUSEUM (all ages)

On Red Jacket Road, Calumet 49913, 2 blocks west of U.S. 41; (906) 337–4354. Open from 10:00 A.M. to 5:00 P.M. Monday through Saturday from mid-June to mid-October and also from 1:00 to 4:00 P.M. Sunday in July and August. Admission is $3.00 for adults, $1.00 for children twelve and older, and Free *for children younger than twelve. Web site: www.uppermichigan.com/coppertown/main.html.*

This museum is at the core of the Keweenaw Peninsula National Park. It acts as a visitor center for the entire Keweenaw Peninsula. Family members can follow the evolution of the mines, beginning when Native Americans extracted pure copper with stone hammers and continuing with the "copper rush" that brought thousands of immigrants to the area, and walk into a mine replica.

Copper Harbor

Take a drive north on U.S. Highway 41 from Houghton, and you'll know why the tip of the Keweenaw Peninsula is, in summer, one of the UP's most popular tourist destinations. Most vacationers save the area for late July and August, since biting black flies and cold weather can be a problem here in early summer. In late summer, you'll find beautiful scenery and lots to do. Area Web site: www.copperharbor.org.

FORT WILKINS STATE PARK (all ages)

About a mile east of Copper Harbor on U.S. 41, Copper Harbor 49918; (906) 289–4215 for information, (800) 447–2757 for reservations. Open in summer. Historic buildings are open from mid-May to mid-October. There's also a modern 165-site campground. Admission is by park vehicle permit, which costs $4.00 daily or $20.00 annually. Camping is extra. Web site: www.dnr.state.mi.us/www/parks.

Built in 1844 to protect rugged copper miners more from themselves than from local tribes, the fort lies along fish-rich Lake Fanny Hooe at the tip of the Keweenaw. It's purported to be the last remaining all-wooden fort east of the Mississippi. Amazingly, it was abandoned two years after it was built, then regarrisoned in 1867 and decommissioned in 1870.

Eighteen buildings, twelve of them original, survive. From mid-May to mid-October, living-history workers, with help from video presentations and other exhibits, portray life in the mid-1800s in this then-remote part of the nation.

COPPER HARBOR LIGHTHOUSE BOAT TOURS (all ages)

Tours run from Copper Harbor Marina, Copper Harbor 49918, between 10:00 A.M. and 5:00 P.M., and the cost is $11.00 for adults and $6.00 for kids ages twelve and younger. Hours vary, and tours are weather-dependent, so call ahead: (906) 289–4966.

Attached to Fort Wilkins State Park is the Copper Harbor lighthouse, and the only way to see it is by this tour. The boat leaves the public marina ¼ mile west of downtown. On seventy-five to ninety-minute narrated tours, you'll learn the history of the town and visit the light, built in 1866. Take a walk down a short trail to the first copper mine shaft—or at least the first attempt at the mine shaft—in the Keweenaw Peninsula, dating from 1844.

Eagle River On your way to Copper Harbor, you'll pass Eagle River. This town is the Keweenaw County seat and site of the state's oldest courthouse and monument to Douglass Houghton, who started it all. It sits like a New England fishing village on the shore of Lake Superior. If you or your kids are into Free souvenir collecting, stop along one of the Superior stone beaches here and search for agates and greenstones.

KEWEENAW BEAR TRACK TOURS (all ages)

On the very beginning of U.S. 41, along First Street, Copper Harbor 49918; (906) 289–4813. Half-day trips cost $20 for adults and $10 for kids twelve and younger; full-day trips cost $40 for adults and $20 for kids twelve and younger. Trips by appointment are also available (call a few weeks in advance). Open year-round. Web site: www.portup.com/keweenaw/list/t/t18.htm.

Laurel, Jim, and Hannah Rooks offer a variety of trips that'll interest you. Families can get off the road and step into some of the peninsula's wildest country on daily guided tours and hikes. Buy crafts of the north woods in The Laughing Loon gift shop.

Isle Royale National Park

Michigan's only national park lies some 50-plus miles off Copper Harbor in Lake Superior. The *Isle Royale Queen* leaves from Copper Harbor from mid-May to September 30 on four-and-a-half-hour trips. The larger *Ranger III* leaves from Houghton on six-and-a-half-hour journeys from early June to mid-September, and float plane service runs from mid-May to late September. For lodge information call (906) 337–4993 or, in preseason, (502) 773–2191. For information on the park itself, call (906) 482–0984. Web sites: www.isle.royale.national-park.com or www.nps.gov/isro/.

The nation's only island national sanctuary is accessible only by boat or seaplane. But don't think you have to rough it when you visit. True, most people come with a pack to explore the island's hundreds of miles of hiking trails and backcountry campgrounds, but Rock Harbor Lodge offers excellent accommodations for those without backpacks. Lodge rooms with meals included or modern housekeeping cabins where you cook (bring your groceries with you; the island's store has limited provisions) are perfect for driving travelers.

Rent a canoe, charter a lake-trout fishing trip, go after panfish and pike on the island's many lakes, or take a sight-seeing trip aboard the boat *Sandy* to see secluded lighthouses and a re-created Great Lakes fishing camp. You can also just take day hikes on the well-marked but secluded trails. Wildlife you might meet includes 1,400 or so—the number varies annually, depending on the severity of the winter—hulking moose (they're more afraid of you than you may think, even if you startle one, but steer clear of cow moose with calves), foxes, eagles, and about fourteen shy wolves.

DEVIL'S WASHTUB (all ages)

West of Copper Harbor along the lake on Michigan 26. Free.

This is a great spot along Lake Superior to stop for a picnic or a rest. It's a hollow of rock at the water's edge, which, if the lake's waves are right, becomes a swirling tub of water.

*B*rockway Mountain Drive

West of Copper Harbor, point your car up. Up, that is, on this scenic highway. One visit, and your family will know what an eagle must feel like contemplating its domain. Via the winding road with plenty of turnoffs, travel to the top, 700 feet above the town. If you're lucky, watch as passing freighters cruise shimmering Lake Superior. It's the highest above-sea-level drive in the country between the Rockies and the Alleghenies. You'll be looking at nearly fifty types of trees and 700 species of wildflowers. The hardwood and conifer mix of trees along the drive makes this a spectacular spot for fall color. On the way down west, and along Michigan 26 back to Copper Harbor, you'll pass waterfalls and roadside parks along the Superior shoreline that are perfect places for picnics or for kids with energy to burn.

Where to Eat

Driftwood Ice Cream Parlor and Eatery. *South of Copper Harbor in Eagle Harbor on Michigan 26; (906) 389–4800.* Open daily from Father's Day through Labor Day. Soups, sandwiches, and pies, including great ice cream treats. $

Pines Restaurant. *On U.S. 41, Copper Harbor 49918; (906) 289–4222 or* 289–4229. Good, inexpensive, family-style food. Save room for one of "Red's" huge cinnamon rolls. $

Tamarack Inn. *At U.S. 41 and Michigan 26, Copper Harbor 49918; (906) 289–4522.* Children's menu and local dishes, including fresh whitefish. $$

Where to Stay

Astor House Motel and Minnetonka Resort. *At U.S. 41 and Michigan 26, Copper Harbor 49950; (906) 289–4449.* The property has twenty-five rooms. Restaurant nearby. $

Eagle River Inn. *100 Front Street, Eagle River 49950, south of Copper Harbor in Eagle River, 2 blocks off Michigan 26, overlooking Lake Superior; (906) 337–0666 or (800) 352–9228.* The inn has twelve rooms, whirlpool, beach, and restaurant. $

Keweenaw Mountain Lodge. *On U.S. 41, Copper Harbor 49918, at the hill above Copper Harbor; (906) 289–4403.* Accommodations in the area include this Depression-era lodge. It has well-kept log cabins sprinkled around a golf course, and there's also a restaurant. $

Pines Resort. *On U.S. 41, Copper Harbor 49518; (906) 289–4222 or* 289–4229. The resort has fifteen motel and cabin units. Restaurant on premises. $

Shoreline Resort. *South of Copper Harbor along Michigan 26, Eagle Harbor 49950; (906) 289–4441.* The resort has just eight rooms, each with a view of Lake Superior. Restaurant on premises serves breakfast, lunch, and dinner. $

Ontonagon

Ontonagon is located along Michigan 38 in Ontonagon County, on Lake Superior. If you're not a Michigander, bet you never thought Michigan had mountains until you read this book. You'll find them here in another of Michigan's finest parks.

PORCUPINE MOUNTAINS WILDERNESS STATE PARK (all ages)
At the end of Michigan 107, Ontonagon 49953, west of town; (906) 885–5275 for information or (800) 447–2757 for reservations. Camping is available. Bring plenty of repellent for biting black flies in early summer. Admission is with vehicle permit, $4.00 daily or $20.00 annually. Camping is $14.00 nightly. Open daily all year. Web site: www.dnr.state.mi.us/www/parks.

Take a gander off the edge of the rock escarpment and down at Lake of the Clouds. You'll be looking over just part of the 60,000-acre park, Michigan's largest. There's hiking, including an easy walk down to the lakeshore of Lake of the Clouds or a bit farther to Mirror Lake, beyond the next ridge. A visitor center features a slide show and more information to help orient you.

There are two campgrounds for auto campers, one near the escarpment on Union Bay, which features a great beach, and another, primitive site at the west end of the park at Presque Isle, reached by a highway off Michigan 28. There's also camping along the nearly 90 miles of hiking trails through the park.

Want a unique experience? Rent one of the park's sixteen primitive cabins and treat the family to a rugged overnight stay indoors. Cabins have bunks, a wood-burning cooking and heating stove, and basic table and cooking utensils. Those on lakes also come with boats. Toilets are outdoors. You bring bedding and towels, food, lighting, and other utensils. You'll also be drawing your own water. A cookstove is recommended in summer to use outside. The cabins are very popular, so reserve in advance. And remember, the park has many black bears. Most of them are shy, but some have turned into Yogis, looking for your food. Take care with your food and cooking utensils, as well as toiletries, especially when using a cabin or camping in the backcountry, or you may have an unwelcome visitor knocking at your door, not to mention a park ranger with a citation book.

MEAD LAKE MINE SITE (all ages)
Along Michigan 107. **Free.**
The former mine features a horizontal shaft you explore for about 75 feet, if you're careful to pick your way through the dripping water. After that, the mine is home to about 14,000 hibernating bats in fall. In summer, they fly out at dusk to dine on those pesky UP mosquitoes and black flies, thank goodness. If you're not afraid of them, head there at dusk to see the flights. There's a historical marker at the site, along with a picnic area on a pond formed from the mine seepage.

Where to Eat

Paul's Restaurant. *Inside Best Western Porcupine Mountain Lodge in Silver City, about 16 miles west of Ontonagon; (906) 885–5311.* Serves breakfast, lunch, and dinner from 7:00 A.M. to 9:00 P.M. A full menu and nightly specials are available. $$

Syl's Country Kitchen. *713 River Street, Ontonagon 49953, downtown; (906) 884–2522.* Serves breakfast (anytime), lunch, and dinner. Enjoy specialties such as pasties, desserts, and the biggest pancakes around. $

Where to Stay

Best Western Porcupine Mountain Lodge. *In tiny Silver City, about 16 miles west of Ontonagon, at the entrance to the Porkies; (906) 885–5311.* The lodge has seventy-one rooms on Lake Superior with pool and restaurant. Small pets okay at extra charge. $$

Inn Towne Motel. *314 Chippewa, Ontonagon 49953, in downtown at Michigan 64 and U.S. 45; (906) 884–2100.* This basic motel has nineteen rooms. Restaurant nearby. $

Rainbow Motel & Chalets. *In Silver City, about 16 miles west of Ontonagon, on Michigan 64, east of Michigan 107 near the entrance to the Porkies; (906) 885–5348.* The property has sixteen rooms and two chalets, mountain-bike rentals, whirlpool, and beach access. Restaurant on premises. $

River Pines RV Park & Campgrounds. *600 River Road, Ontonagon 49953, ½ mile south from Michigan 64 on the Ontonagon River; (906) 884–4600 or (800) 424–1520.* The park has thirty sites with marina and Lake Superior access, playground. Pets okay. $

Scott's Superior Inn & Cabins. *277 Lakeshore Road (Michigan 64), Ontonagon 49953, about 1½ miles west of Ontonagon; (906) 884–4866.* The facility has fourteen rooms along Lake Superior with whirlpool, beach, and nearby restaurants. Pets okay at extra charge. $

Sunshine Motel and Cabins. *1442 Michigan 64, Ontonagon 49953, 3 miles west of Ontonagon; (906) 884–2187.* This property offers fifteen motel rooms and five cabins with beach access.

Union River Campground. *In Silver City, about 16 miles west of Ontonagon, on Michigan 107, near the entrance to the Porkies; (906) 885–5324.* Open roughly from early June to early October, depending on the weather. Here you'll find sixty sites along Lake Superior. Pets okay.

For More Information

Ontonagon Chamber of Commerce, *P.O. Box 266, Ontonagon 49953; (906) 884–4735.*

Porcupine Mountains Chamber of Commerce, *P.O. Box 493, White Pine 49971; (906) 885–5399.*

Ironwood, Bessemer, and Wakefield

The state's westernmost group of cities—farther west, incidentally, than St. Louis, Missouri—only a few miles from one another along Michigan 28 and U.S. Highway 2, claim a particular soft spot among waterfall lovers because of the highway of the Black River. It's also known among skiers for the three ski areas within a few miles of each other, including one that's the state's highest.

BLACK RIVER NATIONAL SCENIC BYWAY (all ages)
Take County Road 513 from U.S. 2/Michigan 28. Watch for the unique "Indianhead" signs that mark scenic locations here in Gogebic County. For more information call (906) 667–0261. **Free.**

Of Michigan's dozen or so Black Rivers, this one is by far the most beautiful. The highway weaves by trails through the woods to the five waterfalls up to 40 feet high that this restless river tumbles over in a stretch only 11 miles long. Names like Conglomerate, dropping over a rock ledge; Sandstone, named for the red rock riverbed; and Gorge, which roars into a chasm 22 feet below, are given to the cascades that range from close by the road to a distance along a trail from which you can faintly hear the water.

Two of the falls are handicapped accessible, with paved sidewalks. The drive ends at a Lake Superior shoreline park, with a kid-friendly swinging bridge over the now-gentle river.

Along the Black River Scenic Byway, about 10 miles northwest of Ironwood, you'll also pass Copper Peak Ski Flying Hill, the only ski flying hill in the Americas and the largest artificial slide in the world. There are tours to the top in summer and events that feature skiers from around the world in late January.

PINES & MINES MOUNTAIN BIKE TRAIL SYSTEM (ages 4 and up)

In the forests around Ironwood and in neighboring northern Wisconsin; (800) 522–5657.

The trail system offers more than 200 miles of marked and mapped routes in Iron County, Wisconsin. In Michigan, pathways such as the Pomeroy/Henry Lake Mountain Bike Complex features 100 miles of routes, mainly on gravel roads, from beginner routes to moderate pedals of 7 to 16 miles. An accompanying system, the Ehlco Tract, is more remote, taking bikers deep into the area's forests.

INDIANHEAD MOUNTAIN SKI AREA (all ages)

500 Indianhead Road, Wakefield 49938, just outside downtown; (906) 229–5181 or (800) 346–3426. Open twenty-four hours a day from mid-November to mid-April. Lift tickets cost $36.00 for adults, $28.00 for children thirteen to seventeen, and $22.00 for kids twelve and younger. One child age six and younger per paid adult skis **Free***. Rentals are available (call for price information). Web site: wwwindianheadmtn.com.*

Many skiers say this might be the state's best ski resort, with twenty-two runs, five chairlifts, rentals, instruction, and on-slope lodging. Baby-sitting is available.

Where to Eat

Big Boy. *111 East Cloverdale Drive (Michigan 28), Ironwood 49938. Open daily 7:00 A.M. to 10:00 P.M.* Offers a variety of family fare from salads to the trademark triple-decker burger.

Where to Stay

Besides these and other Michigan accommodations, there are more in neighboring Wisconsin. You'll find most along U.S. 2 from Wakefield west. During ski season, many motels also offer discount lift tickets to individual ski areas they're closest to.

Armata Motel. *124 West Cloverland, Ironwood 49938, on U.S. 2; (906) 932–4421.* The motel has twelve rooms. Restaurant nearby. Pets okay at extra charge. $

Black River Campground. *Near Bessemer at the end of the Black River Scenic Byway; (906) 932–7250 for information, and (800) 280–2267 for reservations.* The campground has forty sites in a beautiful setting along Lake Superior. Flush toilets. $

Black River Lodge. *N12390 Black River Road, Ironwood 49938; (906) 932–3857 or (800) 666–9916.* Web site: www.crestviewmotel.com. The lodge has twenty-four rooms, condos, and suites on the Black River Scenic Byway, along the river. Indoor pool, cross-country ski and hiking trails, and restaurant. $$

Big Powderhorn, Indianhead Mountain, and Blackjack. Each of these ski areas offer restaurants and accommodations from ski chalets to motels. With nearby Whitecap in Wisconsin and Porcupine Mountains ski area near Ontonagon, the resorts make up the Big Snow Country group. Call each individually, or the group at (906) 932–4850.

Crestview Cozy Inn. *424 Cloverland (U.S. 2), Ironwood 49938; (906) 932–4845.* The inn has twelve inexpensive but well-kept rooms and sauna. Restaurant nearby. Pets okay at extra charge. $

Davey's Motel. *Along U.S. 2, Ironwood 49938; (906) 932–2020. Web site: www.westernup.com/daveys.* The motel has twenty-three rooms, sauna, and hot tub. Restaurants nearby. $

Eddy Park Campground. *On Sunday Lake in Wakefield; (906) 229–5131.* The campground has ninety-four sites on the lake, beach, swimming, and fishing. $

Ottawa National Forest Campgrounds. There are rustic campgrounds scattered in the forest throughout the area, most on lakes or rivers. In early summer, be aware that some campgrounds may be bothered by biting insects, including black flies and "no-see-ums," pepper-grain-size chompers. Make sure tents have windows with "no-see-um" netting, or you'll be harried at night. By early July, most biting bug populations are reduced. Contact the Forest Supervisor's office for locations at (906) 932-1330 and for reservations at (800) 280-2267. $

Powdermill Creek. *11330 Powderhorn Road, Bessemer 49911, near the base of Big Powderhorn, at 1½ miles north of U.S. 2 near Bessemer; (906) 932–0800.* The inn has fifty rooms, indoor pool, restaurant, whirlpool, and playground. $$

Regal Country Inn. *On U.S. 2, Wakefield 49968, east of downtown; (906) 229–5122. Web site: www.westernup.com/regalinn.* The inn has eighteen themed rooms from historical, furnished with local antiques, to country and Victorian. Adjacent ice cream parlor. $$

For More Information

Western U.P. Convention & Visitor Bureau, *P.O. Box 706, Ironwood 49938;* *(906) 932–4850 or (800) 272–7000. Web site: www.westernup.com.*

Iron River, Caspian, and Stambaugh

State fisheries biologists call the waters around these towns some of the best brook-trout fishing in Michigan, including the Iron River, which flows at the bottom of the hill, just east of the downtown that shares its name. Iron mining was big in the area, but now the mines are closed.

 ## IRON COUNTY MUSEUM (all ages)

In the former mining town of Caspian, off Michigan 189 about 2 miles south of U.S. 2 in Iron River; (906) 265–2617. Open from mid-May through October from 9:00 A.M. to 5:00 P.M. Monday through Saturday, 1:00 to 5:00 P.M. Sunday June through August, 10:00 A.M. to 4:00 P.M. in September and 8:30 A.M. to 3:00 P.M. in May. Admission is $5.00 for adults, $2.50 for youths ages seventeen and younger. Web site: www.ironcountymuseum.com.

This museum is built around the old mine site in Caspian, the headframe of the old Caspian Mine, which at its peak was the area's largest iron ore producer. It's the oldest steel headframe in the Midwest. The museum also features twenty locally historic buildings, from settler's cabins to a school. The Lee LeBlanc Wildlife Art Gallery displays work by the nationally known artist. The Carrie Jacobs-Bond Home was the home of the composer of those late-nineteenth-century hits that you can still occasionally hear today, "I Love You Truly," and "Perfect Day."

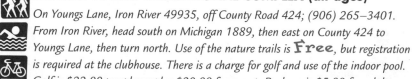   ## GEORGE YOUNG RECREATIONAL COMPLEX (all ages)

On Youngs Lane, Iron River 49935, off County Road 424; (906) 265–3401. From Iron River, head south on Michigan 1889, then east on County 424 to Youngs Lane, then turn north. Use of the nature trails is **Free**, *but registration is required at the clubhouse. There is a charge for golf and use of the indoor pool. Golf is $22.00 per player plus $20.00 for a cart. Pool use is $5.00 for adults, $3.00 for children twelve and younger. Hours are 10:00 A.M. to 9:00 P.M. daily. Web site: www.georgeyoung.com.*

Set deep in the woods on the western side of Chicagon Lake and near so many skeletons of the area's heyday of heavy mining operations is this gem of a recreational complex you have to see to believe. The land and complex were donated to the city and area by George Young, a local boy who made it big in the Chicago brick-making business. He wanted to give something back to his community, so he did: a 3,300-acre recreational center that is unique. Each year, according to the will, improvement must be made to make it even more attractive.

A beautiful eighteen-hole public golf course, where both golfers and wildlife from deer to bear play, is the centerpiece. Each hole is based on the late George Young's favorite holes from championship courses across the nation.

The clubhouse also doubles as a community center, with indoor swimming pool, whirlpool, and sauna. There are nature trails for hiking, biking, and cross-country skiing, including a 1½-mile Wolf Track Nature Trail with signs that tell you what you're looking at. Even if you don't golf, it's worth driving into the complex.

Keep That Camera Handy!

The area around Iron River is wild country indeed, containing one of the state's largest deer populations, and it pays to have your camera at the ready. On a recent fishing trip there to try for walleye in catch-and-release Winslow Lake with champion anglers Mark Martin and Gary Roach, I was traveling between my accommodations near Chicaugon Lake and downtown Iron River when I noticed something black along the roadside that looked like a Labrador retriever at first. But when I pulled up, I saw about a one hundred-pound black bear sniffing the weeds on that June afternoon. Just as I was rolling down the window to snap a picture, however, he high-tailed it into the woods. As I said, have your camera ready. You never know what you may come across.

Where to Eat

Losey's Landing. *On County Road 424, Gaastra 49927, at the southern end of Chicaugon Lake, across from the Chicaugon Lake Inn; (906) 265–3343.* Good dinners from fish to steak. $$

Mr. T's Family Restaurant. *On U.S. 2, Iron River 49935; (906) 265–4741.* Open for breakfast, lunch, and dinner daily. $$

Where to Stay

There are plenty of resort cottages on area lakes as well as motels. Call (906) 265-5605 for more.

Brule Motel. *4025 West U.S. 2, Iron River 49935, a mile west of town; (906) 265–6116.* This basic motel has ten modest rooms. $

Chicaugon Lake Inn. *1700 County Road 424, Gaastra 49927, at the southern end of Chicaugon Lake; (906) 265–9244. Web site: www.iron.org/biz/chicaugon/chi-caugon.html.* The nearest post office is in tiny Alpha, population 229, southeast of Iron River and east of Caspian. Seemingly in the middle of nowhere, this is a quiet and well-kept new motel with twenty-four rooms, some with whirlpools. Restaurant across the street and others nearby. Within a block of the public boat launch for Chicaugon Lake, with fishing for walleye and other species. The inn is a popular spot for snowmobilers and skiers in winter. $$

Hillberg's Cabins. *On the north end of Chicaugon Lake, 2 miles south of U.S. 2, Iron River 49935; (906) 265–2982.* Four cabins on seventy acres of forested lakeshore with beach, playground equipment, and fishing for walleye and lake trout in the lake. $

Iron River Motel. *3073 East U.S. 2, Iron River 49935; (906) 265–4212.* This small motel has ten rooms close to the Paint River. Pets okay. $

Lac O'Seasons Resort. *1176 Stanley Lake Drive, Iron River 49935, on Stanley Lake; (906) 265–4881. Web site: www.webstruction.com/lost/. From Iron River, head south on M–189 about ½ mile to Hiawatha Road. Turn west and follow the signs.* The resort has two- and three-bedroom cottages, indoor pool, canoes, and boats. $$

Trav-Lure's Motel & Art Gallery. *About 1½ miles west of Iron River on U.S. 2, Iron River 49935; (906) 265–5181.* The motel has nineteen rooms and outdoor pool. Restaurants nearby. $

Iron Mountain

Also founded on the city's backbone of ore, mines operated here continuously from the 1800s through the 1930s.

IRON MOUNTAIN IRON MINE (all ages)

The mine is actually in Vulcan, along U.S. 2 about 9 miles east of Iron Mountain. It's open 9:00 A.M. to 5:00 P.M. daily Memorial Day to mid-October. Last tour leaves at 4:25 P.M. Admission is $5.50 for adults, $4.50 for ages six through twelve. Call (906) 563–8077.

Don a raincoat (to protect yourself from the dripping water) and a hard hat to go hundreds of feet below ground through 2,600 feet of tunnels for a glimpse of the inside of the mine that operated until 1945. As a guide explains, you'll go by the same train that used to ferry miners into this underground world.

MENOMINEE RANGE HISTORICAL MUSEUM (all ages)

300 East Ludington, Iron Mountain 49801, a block east of U.S. 2; (906)
774–4276. Open from 10:00 A.M. to 4:00 P.M. Monday through Saturday and
noon to 4:00 P.M. Sunday in summer. Admission to the museum alone is $4.00 for
adults, $3.50 for seniors, and $2.00 for youths ages ten through eighteen.

Inside a former Carnegie library, the museum features more than one
hundred exhibits on life in the iron range at the turn of the twentieth
century, including displays of the area's Native American heritage.

MILLIE MINE BAT CAVE (all ages)

On Park, just off East A; (906) 774–5480. Best viewing times are late April and
September. **Free.** *Open any time.*

This former mine is 350 feet deep, and with a constant forty-degree
temperature, it is perfect for bats. In fact, it's the second-largest known
colony of hibernating bats in North America. The bats move out in April
and settle in for winter come September, so those are the only viewing
times when you're bound to see clouds of the creatures. Informational
plaques are situated near benches, where you can sit and watch the
flights.

Where to Eat

Dobber's Pasties. *1400 South Stephen-*
son (U.S. 2), Iron Mountain 49801; (906)
774–9323. Traditional Cornish and
veggie pasties, too. $

Romagnoli's. *In downtown along U.S. 2,*
Iron Mountain 49801; (906) 774–7300.

Not only did Finns and other Scandina-
vians come to the UP's mines, but the
Italians did, too, and some opened
restaurants. This is one of the best, for
lunch and dinner. $$

Where to Stay

Best Western Executive Inn. *1518*
South Stephenson Avenue, Iron Mountain
49801, near U.S. 2 and 141; (906)
774–2040. The inn offers fifty-seven
rooms and indoor pool. Restaurant
nearby. Pets okay at extra charge. $$

Days Inn. *W8176 South U.S. 2, Iron*
Mountain 49801, about 2 miles east of
town; (906) 774–2181. This economical
motel has forty-four rooms, indoor
pool, and continental breakfast.
Restaurant nearby. Pets okay at extra
charge. $

Lake Antoine County Park. *N3393 Quinnesec Lake Antoine Road, Iron Mountain 49801; (906) 774–8875.* The park has eighty campsites and a beach. $

For More Information

Upper Peninsula Travel and Recreation Association. *P.O. Box 400, Iron Mountain 49801; (906) 774–5480. Web sites: www.uptravel.com or www. ironmountain.org (for Iron Mountain).*

P

Paint Creek Mill and Restaurant, Rochester, 80
Paint Creek Trail, Lake Orion, 83
Palms Book State Park, Big Spring, Manistique, 303
Paradise, 297–98
The Parlor at the All-Star Dairy, Jackson, 120
Parshallville, 89–90
Parshallville Cider Mill, 89
Pasties, 292
Peanut Shop, Lansing, 130
Penny Whistle Place, Flint, 140
People Mover and Trolley, Detroit, 55–56
Perchville USA festival, East Tawas, 181–82
Pere Marquette Rail Trail, Midland, 169–70
Pere Marquette River activities, 258
Petoskey, 279–80
Phyllis Haehnle Memorial Sanctuary, Jackson, 119
Pictured Rock Cruises, Munising, 300
Pictured Rocks National Lakeshore, Munising, 301
Pinconning, 179
Pine Knob Music Theater, Clarkston, 91–92
Pines & Mines Mountain Bike Trail System, Ironwood, 326
Pines Theater, Houghton Lake, 187
Pirate's Cove, Traverse City, 274
P.J. Hoffmaster State Park, Muskegon, 250
Planet Walk, Lansing, 127
Planetarium, Bloomfield Hills, 77
Platte River State Fish Hatchery, Honor, 268
Plymouth, 61–63
Plymouth International Ice Sculpture Spectacular, 62, 64
Plymouth Orchards and Cider Mill, 62

Porcupine Mountains State Park, Ontonagon/Silver City, 323–24
Porkiefest, Porcupine Mountains State Park, Ontonagon, 311
Port Austin, 160–61
Port City *Princess,* Muskegon, 252
Port Huron, 102–5
Port Huron Museum of Arts and History, 102–3
Potter Park Zoo, Lansing, 128
Prehistoric Forest, Irish Hills, 107–9
Presque Isle Lighthouse Museum, Rogers City, 203–4
Presque Isle Park, Marquette, 305
Prime Outlets at Birch Run, 143–44
Proud Lake Recreation Area, 73
Public Museum of Grand Rapids and Van Andel Center, 235
Purple Rose Theater, Chelsea, 8–9

Q

Quincy Mine Hoist, Hancock, 318

R

Red Arrow Hobbies, Stevensville, 215
Red Flannel Festival, Cedar Springs, 243
Redford Theater, Detroit, 53–54
Renaissance Center, Detroit, 54–55
River Crab restaurant, St. Clair, 101
River Raisin Battlefield Visitor Center, Monroe, 4
Riverbends Park, Shelby Twp., 95–96
Rivertown district, Detroit, 51
Robert T. Longway Planetarium, Flint, 138
Rochester, 79–81
Rochester Hills, 81–82
Rockford, 239–40
Rogers City, 203–4
Romeo, 83–85
Rothbury, 253–54
Royal Oak, 73–76
Ruby Tree Farm and Cider Mill, Port Huron, 104